THE STATE OF THE WORLD'S CHILDREN 2008

WITHDRAWN

Acknowledgements

This report was made possible with the advice and contributions of many people, both inside and outside of UNICEF. Important contributions were received from the following UNICEF field offices: Afghanistan, Angola, Argentina, Bangladesh, Benin, Bolivia, Bosnia and Herzegovina, Brazil, Cambodia, Cameroon, Chile, China, Colombia, Congo, Côte d'Ivoire, Dominican Republic, Ecuador, Egypt, Eritrea, the Gambia, Ghana, Haiti, India, Islamic Republic of Iran, Jamaica, Jordan, Kazakhstan, Kenya, Mongolia, Morocco, Mozambique, Nicaragua, Niger, Nigeria, Pakistan, Papua New Guinea, Peru, Saint Lucia, Senegal, Somalia, South Africa, Sudan, Suriname, Tajikistan, United Republic of Tanzania, Timor-Leste, Turkmenistan, Uganda, Uruguay, Bolivarian Republic of Venezuela, Yemen, Zambia and Zimbabwe. Input was also received from UNICEF regional offices and the Innocenti Research Centre.

Special thanks to President Ellen Johnson-Sirleaf, Tedros Adhanom, Paul Farmer, Paul Freeman, Melinda French Gates, Jim Yong Kim, Elizabeth N. Mataka, and Henry Perry.

RESEARCH AND POLICY GUIDANCE
Programme Division; Division of Policy and Planning

STATISTICAL TABLES
Strategic Information Section, Division of Policy and Planning

DESIGN AND PRE-PRESS PRODUCTION
Prographics, Inc.

PRINTING
Hatteras Press, Inc.

Produced, translated and distributed by Editorial, Design and Publications Section, Division of Communication

United Nations Children's Fund
3 United Nations Plaza

New York, NY 10017, USA

Email: pubdoc@unicef.org
Website: www.unicef.org

Cover photo: © UNICEF/HQ07-0108/Thierry Delvigne Jean

Foreword

In 2006, for the first time in recent history, the total number of annual deaths among children under the age of five fell below 10 million, to 9.7 million. This represents a 60 per cent drop in the rate of child mortality since 1960.

However, there is no room for complacency. The loss of 9.7 million young lives each year is unacceptable, especially when many of these deaths are preventable. And despite progress, the world is not yet on track to achieve the Millennium Development Goal target of a two-thirds reduction in the rate of child mortality by 2015.

Data compiled by the Inter-agency Group for Child Mortality Estimation reveals that progress has been made in countries in every region of the world. Since 1990, China's under-five mortality rate has declined from 45 deaths for every 1,000 live births to 24 per 1,000, a reduction of 47 per cent. India's under-five mortality rate has declined by 34 per cent. The rates in six countries – Bangladesh, Bhutan, Bolivia, Eritrea, the Lao People's Democratic Republic and Nepal – were reduced by 50 per cent or more since 1990, although under-five mortality rates in these countries remain high. And Ethiopia achieved a nearly 40 per cent reduction since 1990.

Of the 62 countries making no progress or insufficient progress towards the Millennium Development Goal on child survival, nearly 75 per cent are in Africa. In some countries in southern Africa, the prevalence of HIV and AIDS has reversed previously recorded declines in child mortality. Achieving the goal in these countries will require a concerted effort.

Widespread adoption of basic health interventions, including early and exclusive breastfeeding, immunization, vitamin A supplementation and the use of insecticide-treated mosquito nets to prevent malaria, are essential to scaling up progress, in sub-Saharan Africa and elsewhere.

More needs to be done to increase access to treatment and means of prevention, to address the devastating

© UNICEF/HQ07-1608/Georgina Cranston

impact of pneumonia, diarrhoea, malaria, severe acute malnutrition and HIV.

We know that lives can be saved when children have access to community-based health services, backed by a strong referral system.

The focus must be on delivering key interventions at the community level, as part of integrated efforts to support the establishment of stronger national health systems. And particular attention must be paid to the special needs of women, of mothers and of newborn children.

The World Health Organization, the World Bank and UNICEF, at the invitation of the African Union, have jointly developed a framework, examined in detail in this year's *The State of the World's Children* report, to help African countries achieve the MDG for child survival.

One source of hope is the new momentum on global health. Public and private interest is high, and innovative partnerships are being established and strengthened, as we collectively seek to capitalize on this momentum.

Partnerships hold great promise for accelerating progress towards the achievement of the Millennium Development Goals. UNICEF is working closely with UN system partners and with governments, regional and non-governmental organizations, foundations and the private sector to coordinate activities and to pool expertise and knowledge.

Our challenge now is to act with a collective sense of urgency to scale up that which has proven successful.

Ann M. Veneman
Executive Director
United Nations Children's Fund

CONTENTS

1 Child survival: Where we stand

2 Lessons learned from evolving health-care systems and practices

SUMMARY Child mortality is a sensitive indicator of a country's development and telling evidence of its priorities and values. Investing in the health of children and their mothers is not only a human rights imperative, it is a sound economic decision and one of the surest ways for a country to set its course towards a better future.

Impressive progress has been made in improving the survival rates and health of children, even in some of the poorest countries, since 1990. Nonetheless, achieving Millennium Development Goal 4 (MDG 4), which aims to reduce the global under-five mortality rate by two thirds between 1990 and 2015, will require additional effort. Attaining the goal is still possible, but the challenge is formidable.

Reaching the target means reducing the number of child deaths from 9.7 million in 2006 to around 4 million by 2015. Accomplishing this will require accelerated action on multiple fronts: reducing poverty and hunger (MDG 1), improving maternal health (MDG 5), combating HIV and AIDS, malaria and other major diseases (MDG 6), increasing the usage of improved water and sanitation (MDG 7) and providing affordable essential drugs on a sustainable basis (MDG 8). It will also require a re-examination of strategies to reach the poorest, most marginalized communities.

Every child has the right to live a healthy life. *A group of children at a community child centre, Malawi.*

The remarkable advances in reducing child deaths achieved by many developing countries in recent decades provide reason for optimism. The causes of and solutions to child deaths are well known. Simple, reliable and affordable interventions with the potential to save the lives of millions of children are readily available. The challenge is to ensure that these remedies – provided through a continuum of maternal, newborn and child health care – reach the millions of children and families who, so far, have been passed by.

1

Child survival: Where we stand

The current situation

What is a life worth? Most of us would sacrifice a great deal to save a single child. Yet somehow on a global scale, our priorities have become blurred. Every day, on average more than 26,000 children under the age of five die around the world, mostly from preventable causes. Nearly all of them live in the developing world or, more precisely, in 60 developing countries. More than one third of these children die during the first month of life, usually at home and without access to essential health services and basic commodities that might save their lives. Some children succumb to respiratory or diarrhoeal infections that are no longer threats in industrialized countries or to early childhood diseases that are easily prevented through vaccines, such as measles. In up to half of under-five deaths an underlying cause is undernutrition, which deprives a young child's body and mind of the nutrients needed for growth and development. Unsafe water, poor sanitation and inadequate hygiene also contribute to child mortality and morbidity.

In 2006, the most recent year for which firm estimates are available, close to 9.7 million children died

before their fifth birthday. Although the numbers have changed, the problem is no less poignant today than it was 25 years ago when the 'child survival revolution' was launched by the United Nations Children's Fund (UNICEF). The current focus of the development community in relation to child survival is Millennium Development Goal 4 (MDG 4), which aims to reduce the global rate of under-five mortality by two thirds between 1990 and 2015. Since child deaths in 1990 numbered around 13 million in absolute terms, meeting MDG 4 implies that during the next seven years the number of child deaths must be cut in half – to fewer than 13,000 child deaths per day, or fewer than 5 million per year.[1]

The enormity of the challenge should not be underestimated. The world will have to reduce the number of child deaths between 2008 and 2015 at a far faster rate than it has managed since 1990 (see Figure 1.6, page 7). Moreover, the bulk of the efforts must be focused on the most difficult situations and circumstances: in the poorest countries, among the most impoverished, isolated, uneducated and marginalized districts and com-

munities, within nations ravaged by AIDS, conflict, weak governance and chronic underinvestment in public health systems and physical infrastructure.

Business as usual will be grossly insufficient to meet the health-related Millennium Development Goals for children. This is abundantly clear in sub-Saharan Africa, the region furthest behind on almost all of the health-related MDGs, but also in several countries in South Asia and in other countries across the developing world. If current trends continue, 4.3 million child deaths will occur in 2015 that could have been averted had MDG 4 been met (see Figure 1.1, page 2).

To underscore the need to position children's issues at the heart of the international agenda, *The State of the World's Children 2008* returns to a theme that marked the launch of the series in the early 1980s. Then, as now, UNICEF and its partners aspired to reduce the number of child deaths by about half by a target date. Then, as now, it proposed simple, effective, low-cost, practical solutions and strategies to reduce child mortality and improve child health. Now, as then, it is inviting partners from all walks of life – from religious leaders to Goodwill Ambassadors, from mayors to Heads of State, from sports personalities to parliamentarians, from professional associations to trade unions – to join the child survival and development movement.

Far from ploughing a lone furrow as it often did in the 1980s, UNICEF today is championing child survival as part of a large community of concern. The partnerships that have developed during the past two decades are proving vital in tackling problems that demand more complex systemic and sociocultural changes than the early architects of the child survival revolution realized. *The State of the World's Children 2008* outlines the results born from these partnerships, as well as from the experiences and approaches to child survival and health of recent decades.

Figure 1.1

The benefits of meeting Millennium Development Goal 4 – and the cost of failing to reach the goal

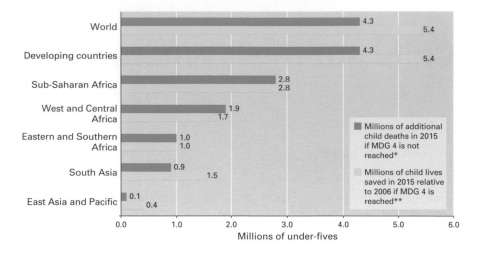

* Number of additional deaths among children under age five that will occur in the year 2015 if current annual rates of reduction in the under-five mortality rate persist.

** Number of deaths among children under five that will be averted in the year 2015 alone, compared with the number of deaths in 2006, by reaching the MDG 4 target of a two-thirds reduction in the under-five mortality rate observed in 1990.

Source: UNICEF estimates based on data in Statistical Tables 1 and 10, pp. 114 and 150 of this report.

The under-five mortality rate: The indispensable gauge of child health

The under-five mortality rate, often known by its acronym U5MR or simply as the child mortality rate, indicates the probability of dying between birth and exactly five years of age, expressed per 1,000 live births, if subject to current mortality rates. It has several advantages as a barometer of child well-being in general and child health in particular.

First, it measures an 'outcome' of the development process rather than an 'input', such as per capita calorie availability or the number of doctors per 1,000 population – all of which are means to an end.

Second, the U5MR is known to be the result of a wide variety of inputs: the nutritional status and the health knowledge of mothers; the level of immunization and oral rehydration therapy; the availability of maternal and child health services (including prenatal care); income and food availability in the family; the availability of safe drinking water and basic sanitation; and

the overall safety of the child's environment, among other factors.

Third, the U5MR is less susceptible to the fallacy of the average than, for example, per capita gross national income (GNI per capita). This is because the natural scale does not allow the children of the rich to be 1,000 times as likely to survive, even if the human-made scale does permit them to have 1,000 times as much income. In other words, it is much more difficult for a wealthy minority to affect a nation's U5MR, and it therefore presents a more accurate, if far from perfect, picture of the health status of the majority of children (and of society as a whole).

See References, page 104.

The report begins by examining the state of child survival and primary health care for children, with a strong emphasis on trends in child mortality. It then appraises the lessons from failures and successes in child survival over the past century. The centrepiece of the report looks at several of the most promising approaches – community partnerships, the continuum of care framework and health-system strengthening for outcomes – to reach those mothers, newborns and children who are currently excluded from essential interventions. By highlighting examples from countries and districts where these have been successful, as well as exploring the main challenges to their expansion, this report offers practical ways to jump-start progress.

Why child survival matters

Investing in the health of young children makes sense for a number of reasons beyond the pain and suffering caused by even one child's death. Depriving infants and young children of basic health care and denying them the nutrients needed for growth and development sets them up to fail in life. But when children are well nourished and cared for and provided with a safe and stimulating environment, they are more likely to survive, to have less disease and fewer illnesses, and to fully develop thinking, language, emotional and social skills. When they enter school, they are more likely to succeed. And later in life, they have a greater chance of becoming creative and productive members of society.

Investing in children is also wise from an economic perspective. According to the World Bank, immunization and vitamin A supplementation are two of the most cost-effective public health interventions available today.

Improving vitamin A status can strengthen a child's resistance to disease and decrease the likelihood of childhood mortality.[2] For only a small sum, a child can be protected from vitamin A deficiency and a number of deadly diseases, including diphtheria, pertussis, tetanus, polio, measles, childhood tuberculosis, hepatitis B and Hib (*Haemophilus influenzae* type b), which is a major cause of pneumonia and meningitis.[3] Providing cotrimoxazole, a low-cost antibiotic, to HIV-positive children dramatically reduces mortality from opportunistic infections.

Improvements in child health and survival can also foster more balanced population dynamics. When parents are convinced that their children will survive, they are more likely to have fewer children and provide better care to those they do have – and countries can invest more in each child.[4]

Underlying and structural causes of maternal and child mortality

Maternal, newborn and under-five deaths and undernutrition have a number of common structural and underlying causes, including:

- Poorly resourced, unresponsive and culturally inappropriate health and nutrition services.

- Food insecurity.

- Inadequate feeding practices.

- Lack of hygiene and access to safe water or adequate sanitation.

- Female illiteracy.

- Early pregnancy.

- Discrimination and exclusion of mothers and children from access to essential health and nutrition services and commodities due to poverty and geographic or political marginalization.

These factors result in millions of unnecessary deaths each year. Their wide-ranging nature and interrelatedness require them to be addressed at different levels – community, household, service provider, government and international – in an integrated manner to maximize effectiveness and reach.

The solutions to these impediments are well known, particularly those relating to the direct causes of maternal, neonatal and child deaths. The necessary interventions involve the provision of packages of essential primary-health-care services for children across a *continuum of care* that spans pregnancy, childbirth and after delivery, leading to care for children in the crucial early years of life (*see Panel, page 17, for a full definition of the continuum of care*).

See References, page 104.

Until the mid to late 1990s, estimates of the number of child deaths occurring during the neonatal period (the first month of life) were drawn from rough historical data rather than from specific surveys. More rigorous estimates for newborn deaths emerged in 1995 and 2000, as data from reliable household surveys became available. Analysis of these data made it evident that previous estimates had seriously understated the scale of the problem. Although the global neonatal mortality rate has decreased slightly since 1980, neonatal deaths have become proportionally much more significant because the reduction of neonatal mortality has been slower than that of under-five mortality: Between 1980 and 2000, deaths in the first month of life declined by a quarter, while deaths between one month and five years declined by a third.

The latest evidence is that 4 million babies die each year in their first month of life, and up to half of these die in their first 24 hours – a child is about 500 times more likely to die in the first day of life than at one month of age. Neonatal mortality accounts for almost 40 per cent of all under-five deaths and for nearly 60 per cent of infant (under-one) deaths. The largest absolute number of newborn deaths occurs in South Asia – India contributes a quarter of the world total – but the highest national rates of neonatal mortality occur in sub-Saharan Africa. A common factor in these deaths is the health of the mother – each year more than 500,000 women die in childbirth or from complications during pregnancy, and babies whose mothers have died during childbirth have a much greater chance of dying in their first year than those whose mothers remain alive.

Even these figures understate the vast scale of the problems that affect child health during the neonatal period. For example, more than a million children who survive birth asphyxia each year go on to suffer such problems as cerebral palsy, learning difficulties and other disabilities. For every newborn baby who dies, another 20 suffer birth injury, complications arising from preterm birth or other neonatal conditions.

Significant improvements in the early neonatal period will depend on essential interventions for mothers and babies before, during and immediately after birth. According to the latest estimates for 2000–2006, at present in the developing world, one quarter of pregnant women do not receive even a single visit from skilled health personnel (doctor, nurse, midwife); only 59 per cent of births take place with the assistance of a skilled attendant; and just over half take place in a health facility.

Averting neonatal deaths is pivotal to reducing child mortality. *The Lancet* Neonatal Survival Series, published in 2005, estimated that 3 million of the 4 million deaths could be prevented each year if high coverage (90 per cent) is achieved for a package of proven, cost-effective interventions that are delivered through outreach, families and communities, and facility-based clinical care across a continuum of neonatal care (antenatal, intrapartum and postpartum). While increasing skilled care is essential, the Neonatal Survival Series underlines the importance of interim solutions that can save almost 40 per cent of newborn lives in community settings. Expanding programmes that prevent mother-to-child transmission of HIV is also crucial.

Actions required to save newborns include setting evidence-based, results-oriented plans at the national level with specific strategies to reach the poorest, greater funding, agreed targets for neonatal mortality reduction, and promotion of greater harmonization and accountability on the part of stakeholders at the international level.

Figure 1.2

Global rates of neonatal mortality, 2000

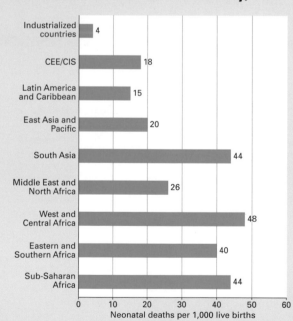

Neonatal deaths per 1,000 live births

- Industrialized countries: 4
- CEE/CIS: 18
- Latin America and Caribbean: 15
- East Asia and Pacific: 20
- South Asia: 44
- Middle East and North Africa: 26
- West and Central Africa: 48
- Eastern and Southern Africa: 40
- Sub-Saharan Africa: 44

Source: World Health Organization, using vital registration systems and household surveys. Country and regional data for neonatal mortality rates in 2000 can be found in Statistical Table 1, p. 114 of this report.

Figure 1.3

High-impact, simple interventions to save newborn lives within the continuum of maternal and child health care

Service delivery continuum		Pregnancy	Birth	Neonatal period	Infancy
Facility-based clinical care		Skilled obstetric and immediate newborn care, including resuscitation Emergency obstetric care to manage complications, such as obstructed labour, breech, haemorrhage, pre-eclampsia and preterm labour Antibiotics for preterm rupture of membranes* Corticosteroids for preterm labour*		Emergency newborn care for illness, especially sepsis management, resuscitation of newborns and care of very low birthweight babies	
Outreach services	Folic acid	Four-visit antenatal package including tetanus immunization, detection and management of syphilis, other infections, pre-eclampsia and pregnancy complications Malaria intermittent presumptive therapy** Detection and treatment of bacteriuria*		Postnatal care to support health practices Early detection and referral of complications	
Family and community		Birth preparedness and promotion of demand for care and readiness for emergencies Counselling and preparation for newborn care	Clean delivery Hygienic cord/skin care, thermal care, promotion of early and exclusive breastfeeding	Health home care, including breastfeeding promotion, hygienic cord/skin care, thermal care, promoting demand for care Extra care for low birthweight babies Community case management for pneumonia	

Maternal, newborn and child continuum

* Additional interventions for settings with stronger health systems and lower mortality.

** Situational interventions necessary in certain settings, such as areas of high malaria prevalence.

Note: This figure includes 16 interventions with proven efficacy in reducing neonatal mortality. Other important interventions are delivered during this time period but are not shown here because their primary effect is not on neonatal deaths (e.g., prevention of mother-to-child transmission of HIV). For some of the interventions listed, the service delivery mode may vary between settings.

Source: *The Lancet* Series Team, '*The Lancet* Series on Neonatal Health Executive Summary', *The Lancet*, 3 March 2005, p. 3.

See References, page 104.

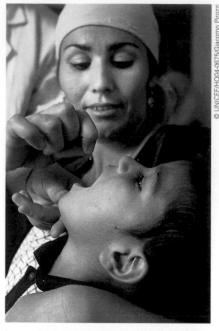

Immunization and micronutrient supplementation provide cost-effective and life-saving protection against disease and illness. *A boy receives a dose of vitamin A, Tajikistan.*

The numbers

Far fewer children are dying today than in 1960, the earliest year for which the annual number of child deaths is currently available. In fact, over the past 46 years, the annual number of child deaths has halved, from roughly 20 million in 1960 to under 10 million in 2006. Recent years have seen important and, in some cases, remarkable advances in child survival. Despite considerable impediments, most notably the onslaught of AIDS in Eastern and Southern Africa and internecine conflict in many high-mortality countries, the global child mortality rate has been steadily reduced since 1990. In 2006, it was estimated at 72 deaths per 1,000 live births, 23 per cent lower than the 1990 level.

In a number of regions, the rate of reduction in child mortality since 1990 has been striking. Child mortality rates have been roughly halved in East Asia and the Pacific, Central and Eastern Europe and the Commonwealth of Independent States (CEE/CIS), and Latin America and the Caribbean – bringing the under-five mortality rate for each of these regions below 30 per 1,000 live births in 2006. Although much more progress would be needed to match the low average rate of industrialized countries (6 per 1,000 live births in 2006), only about 1 in every 36 children born in these three regions now dies before the age of five.

Other regions are following behind. The Middle East and North Africa region has seen steady progress in

---

Figure 1.4

The global child mortality rate declined by almost one quarter between 1990 and 2006

Under-five deaths per 1,000 live births

Region	1990	2006
Sub-Saharan Africa	187	160
Eastern and Southern Africa	165	131
West and Central Africa	208	186
Middle East and North Africa	79	46
South Asia	123	83
East Asia and Pacific	55	29
Latin America and Caribbean	55	27
CEE/CIS	53	27
Industrialized	10	6
Developing countries/territories	103	79
Least developed countries	180	142
World	93	72

Figure 1.5

Fewer than 10 million children under five died in 2006

- CEE/CIS, 100,000
- Latin America and Caribbean, 300,000
- Industrialized countries, 100,000
- Middle East and North Africa, 400,000
- Sub-Saharan Africa, 4.8 million
- South Asia, 3.1 million
- East Asia and Pacific, 900,000

Source: UNICEF, World Health Organization, United Nations Population Division and United Nations Statistics Division. Country and regional data can be found in Statistical Tables 1 and 10, pages 114 and 150 of this report.

reducing rates but still had an under-five mortality rate of 46 per 1,000 live births in 2006 – equivalent to 1 in every 22 children dying before age five. South Asia is also making headway, although among the regions it has the second highest number of deaths among children under five, accounting for 32 per cent of the global total. In 1990, 1 in every 8 South Asian children died before age five; by 2006, the ratio had decreased to 1 in 12.

Sub-Saharan Africa remains the most troubling geographic area. In addition to having by far the highest rate of child mortality – on average, 1 in every 6 children dies before age five – the region as a whole has shown the least progress since 1990, managing to reduce the burden of

child mortality by only 14 per cent between 1990 and 2006. A number of countries in the region are still registering increases in under-five mortality rates. In 2006, 49 per cent of all deaths of children under age five occurred in sub-Saharan Africa, despite the fact that only 22 per cent of the world's children are born there.

Child survival and the Millennium Development Goals
Half of the world's regions are making insufficient progress towards MDG 4

Although overall gains in child survival have been impressive, they have not been nearly sufficient in several regions to achieve MDG 4. Four regions are on track to meet the goal,

but progress in reducing child mortality in the Middle East and North Africa, South Asia and sub-Saharan Africa (both Eastern and Southern Africa and the West and Central subregions) is currently insufficient.

On a country-by-country basis, the prospects are mixed. Globally, of the 191 countries with adequate data for the 1990–2006 comparison in child mortality, UNICEF estimates that 129 are on track – having reduced the under-five mortality rate to below 40 per 1,000 live births or achieved an average annual reduction rate of 3.9 per cent or more since 1990 – or they have already met the 2015 goal for reducing child mortality. Around 18 per cent, or 35 countries, are making progress but at a rate that

---

Figure 1.6

Global progress in reducing child mortality is insufficient to reach MDG 4*

Average annual rate of reduction (AARR) in the under-five mortality rate (U5MR) observed for 1990–2006 and required during 2007–2015 in order to reach MDG 4

	U5MR No. of deaths per 1,000 live births		AARR		
	1990	2006	Observed % 1990–2006	Required % 2007–2015	Progress towards the MDG target
Sub-Saharan Africa	187	160	1.0	10.5	Insufficient progress
Eastern and Southern Africa	165	131	1.4	9.6	Insufficient progress
West and Central Africa	208	186	0.7	11.0	No progress
Middle East and North Africa	79	46	3.4	6.2	Insufficient progress
South Asia	123	83	2.5	7.8	Insufficient progress
East Asia and Pacific	55	29	4.0	5.1	On track
Latin America and Caribbean	55	27	4.4	4.3	On track
CEE/CIS	53	27	4.2	4.7	On track
Industrialized countries/territories	10	6	3.2	6.6	On track
Developing countries/territorries	103	79	1.7	9.3	Insufficient progress
World	**93**	**72**	**1.6**	**9.4**	Insufficient progress

*Progress towards MDG 4, with countries classified according to the following thresholds:

On track – U5MR is less than 40, or U5MR is 40 or more and the average annual rate of reduction (AARR) in under-five mortality rate observed from 1990 to 2006 is 4.0 per cent or more.

Insufficient progress – U5MR is 40 or more and AARR observed for the 1990–2006 period is between 1.0 per cent and 3.9 per cent.

No progress – U5MR is 40 or more and AARR observed for 1990–2006 is less than 1.0 per cent.

Source: UNICEF estimates based on the work of the Interagency Child Mortality Estimation Group.

Figure 1.7

Almost one third of the 50 least developed countries have managed to reduce their under-five mortality rates by 40 per cent or more since 1990

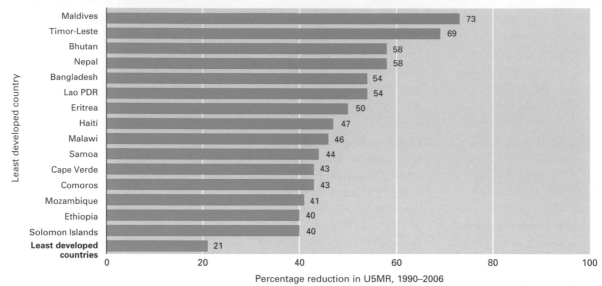

Percentage reduction in U5MR, 1990–2006

Source: UNICEF, World Health Organization, United Nations Population Division and United Nations Statistics Divisions. Country and regional data can be found in Statistical Tables 1 and 10, pages 114 and 150 of this report.

The main proximate causes of child deaths

The countries and regions in which children under five are dying in large numbers are well known, and the main proximate causes of premature deaths and ill health are also well established.

Almost 40 per cent of all under-five deaths occur during the neonatal period, the first month of life, from a variety of complications (*see Panel, page 4*). Of these neonatal deaths, around 26 per cent – accounting for 10 per cent of all under-five deaths – are caused by severe infections. A significant proportion of these infections is caused by pneumonia and sepsis (a serious blood-borne bacterial infection that is also treated with antibiotics). Around 2 million children under five die from pneumonia each year – around 1 in 5 deaths globally. In addition, up to 1 million more infants die from severe infections including pneumonia, during the neonatal period. Despite progress since the 1980s, diarrhoeal diseases account for 17 per cent of under-five deaths. Malaria, measles and AIDS, taken together, are responsible for 15 per cent of child deaths.

Many conditions and diseases interact to increase child mortality beyond their individual impacts, with undernutrition contributing up to 50 per cent of child deaths. Unsafe water, poor hygiene practices and inadequate sanitation are not

Figure 1.8

Global distribution of cause-specific mortality among children under five

Undernutrition is implicated in up to 50 per cent of all deaths of children under five.

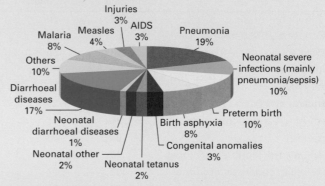

Source: World Health Organization and UNICEF.

only the causes of the continued high incidence of diarrhoeal diseases, they are a significant contributing factor in under-five mortality caused by pneumonia, neonatal disorders and undernutrition.
See References, page 104.

is insufficient to meet MDG 4 in full and on time.

Of most concern are the 27 countries that have registered scant progress since 1990 or have an under-five mortality rate that is stagnant or higher than it was in 1990. Of the 46 countries in sub-Saharan Africa, only Cape Verde, Eritrea and Seychelles are on track to meet MDG 4, and nearly half the countries have registered either no change or an increase in child mortality rates since 1990. The region as a whole only managed to reduce child mortality at an average annual rate of 1 per cent from 1990–2006, and double-digit reductions will be needed during each of the remaining years if it is to meet MDG 4.[5]

Individual countries face different challenges in child survival, without doubt some greater than others. But the notable achievements suggest that geography is no barrier to saving children's lives. Perhaps most important, these gains are evident in some of the world's poorest countries and across the developing regions, as illustrated in Figure 1.7. These gains suggest that remarkable progress is possible, despite such obstacles as geographic location or socio-economic disadvantage, when evidence, sound strategies, sufficient resources, political will and an orientation towards results are consciously harnessed to improve children's lives.

Furthermore, dramatic improvements in child mortality and health can be rapidly attained. Since 1990, more than 60 countries have managed to reduce their under-five mortality rate by 50 per cent.

Figure 1.9

Health and the Millennium Development Goals

Goal	Health Targets	Health Indicators
GOAL 1 Eradicate extreme poverty and hunger	**Target 2** Halve, between 1990 and 2015, the proportion of people who suffer from hunger	Prevalence of underweight children under five Proportion of population below minimum level of dietary energy consumption
GOAL 4 Reduce child mortality	**Target 5** Reduce by two thirds, between 1990 and 2015, the under-five mortality rate	Under-five mortality rate Infant mortality rate Proportion of one-year-olds immunized against measles
GOAL 5 Improve maternal health	**Target 6** Reduce by three quarters, between 1990 and 2015, the maternal mortality ratio	Maternal mortality ratio Proportion of births attended by skilled health personnel
GOAL 6 Combat HIV and AIDS, malaria and other diseases	**Target 7** Halt and begin to reverse, by 2015, the spread of HIV and AIDS	HIV prevalence among pregnant women aged 15–24 Condom use rate of the contraceptive prevalence rate Ratio of school attendance of orphans to school attendance of non-orphans aged 10–14
	Target 8 Halt and begin to reverse, by 2015, the incidence of malaria and other major diseases	Prevalence and death rates associated with malaria Proportion of population in malaria-risk areas using effective malaria prevention and treatment measures Prevalence and death rates associated with tuberculosis Proportion of tuberculosis cases detected and cured under Directly Observed Treatment Short-Course (DOTS)
GOAL 7 Ensure environmental sustainability	**Target 10** Halve, by 2015, the proportion of people without sustainable access to safe drinking water and basic sanitation	Proportion of population using an improved water source, urban and rural
	Target 10 By 2020, achieve a significant improvement in the lives of at least 100 million slum dwellers	Proportion of population using improved sanitation, urban and rural
GOAL 8 Develop a global partnership for development	**Target 17** In cooperation with pharmaceutical companies, provide access to affordable essential drugs in developing countries	Proportion of population with access to affordable essential drugs on a sustainable basis

Source: Adapted from World Health Organization, *Health and the Millennium Development Goals*, WHO, Geneva, 2005, p. 11.

Pneumonia: The forgotten killer of children

Pneumonia kills more children than any other disease – more than AIDS, malaria and measles combined. It is a major cause of child deaths in every region. Children with pneumonia may exhibit a wide range of symptoms, depending on age and cause of the infection. Common symptoms include rapid or difficult breathing, cough, fever, chills, headaches, loss of appetite and wheezing. In young infants, severe cases of pneumonia can cause convulsions, hypothermia, lethargy and feeding problems.

In childhood, pneumonia and malaria have major overlaps in terms of symptoms, the requirements for their effective management and the feasibility of providing care in the community. In effect, especially in very young children, it may be impossible to tell whether a high fever, coughing and fast breathing is evidence of either pneumonia or malaria, and in such cases children often receive treatment for both. Once a child develops pneumonia, a caregiver must recognize the symptoms and seek appropriate care immediately.

Healthy children have natural defences that protect their lungs from the pathogens that cause pneumonia. Undernourished children, particularly those who are not exclusively breastfed or have inadequate zinc intake, or those with compromised immune systems, run a higher risk of developing pneumonia. Children suffering from other illnesses, such as measles, or those living with HIV, are more likely to develop pneumonia. Environmental factors, such as living in crowded homes and being exposed to parental smoking or indoor air pollution, may also play a role in increasing children's susceptibility to pneumonia and its consequences.

Prevention is as important as cure in reducing child deaths from pneumonia. The key preventive measures for children are adequate nutrition (including exclusive breastfeeding, vitamin A supplementation and zinc intake), reduced indoor air pollution and increased immunization rates with vaccines that help prevent children from developing infections that directly cause pneumonia, such as *Haemophilus influenzae* type b (Hib), and with those immunizations that prevent infections that can lead to pneumonia as a complication (e.g., measles and pertussis). Vaccines to protect against *Streptococcus pneumoniae* – the most common cause of severe pneumonia among children in the developing world – will be increasingly becoming available for infants and young children.

Since a large proportion of severe pneumonia cases in children of the developing world are bacterial in origin – mostly *Streptococcus pneumoniae* or *Haemophilus influenzae* – they can be effectively treated using inexpensive antibiotics at home, provided that families and caregivers follow the advice they receive and treat the child correctly, including returning for help as necessary. If these conditions are in place, evidence from across the developing world suggests that community-based management of pneumonia can be very effective. A meta-analysis of results from nine studies in seven countries, including the United Republic of Tanzania, that investigated the impact of community-based case management of pneumonia revealed substantial reductions not only in pneumonia mortality but in child mortality more generally. Trials resulted in a reduction of child mortality of 26 per cent and a 37 per cent reduction in mortality from pneumonia.

See References, page 104.

Figure 1.10

More than half of children under five with suspected pneumonia are taken to an appropriate health provider

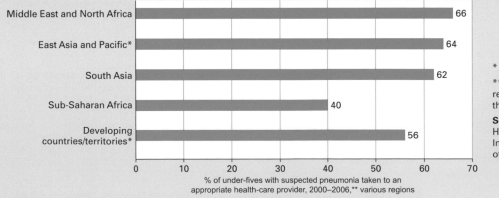

* Excludes China.

** Data refer to the most recent year available during the period specified.

Source: Demographic and Health Surveys, Multiple Indicator Cluster Surveys and other national surveys.

% of under-fives with suspected pneumonia taken to an appropriate health-care provider, 2000–2006,** various regions

Progress towards the other health-related MDGs is mixed

Although advancements on all eight Millennium Development Goals are important to the survival and well-being of children, MDGs 1, 5, 6, 7 and 8, as well as MDG 4, have targets that directly affect children's health. Progress in the areas targeted by these goals could have a dramatic effect on the lives and prospects of children.

Enhancing nutritional status (MDG 1)

Undernutrition is the main underlying factor for up to half of all deaths of children under five. Improving nutrition and achieving MDG 1, which aims to reduce poverty and hunger, would help avert child deaths from diarrhoea, pneumonia, malaria, HIV and measles, and it would reduce neonatal mortality. In other words, improving maternal and child nutrition is a prerequisite for achieving MDG 4.

The standard indicators used to measure MDG 1, however, do not reveal the full extent of undernutrition among children in the developing world. One of the indicators focuses on hunger, as measured by the proportion of children under five who are underweight. But that captures only one dimension of nutrition. A child may die from a weakened immune system when vitamin A is lacking, for example, without being apparently hungry or underweight.

Adequate nutrition needs to begin during a mother's pregnancy and continue when a child is born. Immediate and exclusive breastfeeding is the best source of nutrition for a child, providing physical warmth and strengthen-

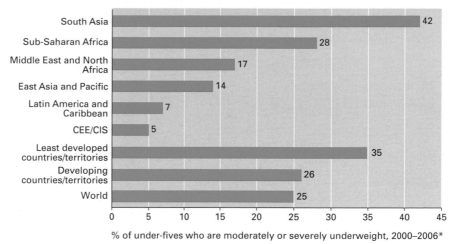

Figure 1.11

South Asia has the highest level of undernutrition among the regions

% of under-fives who are moderately or severely underweight, 2000–2006*

South Asia	42
Sub-Saharan Africa	28
Middle East and North Africa	17
East Asia and Pacific	14
Latin America and Caribbean	7
CEE/CIS	5
Least developed countries/territories	35
Developing countries/territories	26
World	25

*Data refer to the most recent year available during the period specified.

Source: Demographic and Health Surveys, Multiple Indicator Cluster Surveys, World Health Organization and UNICEF. Country and regional data can be found in Statistical Table 2, p. 118 of this report.

ing immune systems. Micronutrients such as iron, vitamin A and iodine can also have a profound impact on a child's development and a mother's health. In cases of severe acute undernutrition, specific therapeutic foods are advised. Although these remedies are low-cost and highly effective, millions of children and mothers still do not have access to or are not adopting them. More than 30 per cent of households in the developing world do not consume iodized salt. More than 60 per cent of infants were not exclusively breastfed during the first six months of life, and 28 per cent lacked full coverage (two doses) of vitamin A supplementation in 2005.

Improving maternal health (MDG 5)

To reduce child mortality, improving the health of pregnant women and new mothers is critical. More than half a million women die each year due to pregnancy related causes, and many more suffer debilitating long-term effects, such as fistula, that could be easily avoided through adequate maternal care. Furthermore, improving maternal health is vitally important for a child's prospects of survival. Evidence shows that a motherless child is more likely to die before reaching age two than infants whose mothers survive.[6]

Improving the health and nutrition of mothers-to-be and providing quality reproductive health services are pivotal to addressing many underlying causes of child mortality. Poor nutrition in women can result in preterm births and babies with low weight at birth. Visits to, or from, a trained health-care provider during pregnancy can help avert early deliveries and neonatal tetanus, which is almost always fatal. A skilled

Figure 1.12

The probability of maternal mortality is far higher in the developing world than in industrialized countries

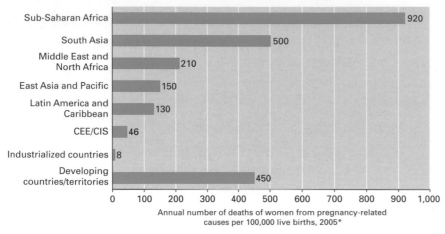

Annual number of deaths of women from pregnancy-related causes per 100,000 live births, 2005*

* These estimates reflect periodic adjustments made by UNICEF, WHO, UNFPA and the World Bank to national data to account for the well documented problems of under-reporting and misclassification of maternal deaths and to develop estimates for countries with no data. Consequently, they may differ markedly from reported national estimates.

Figure 1.13

Low levels of maternal care contribute to high rates of maternal death in South Asia and sub-Saharan Africa

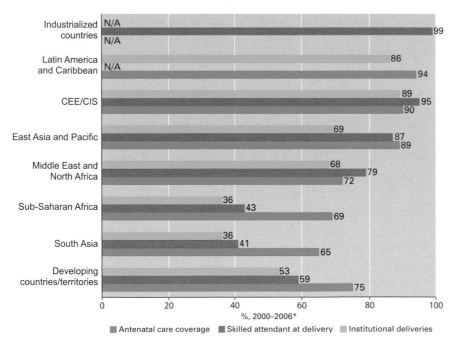

%, 2000–2006*

■ Antenatal care coverage ■ Skilled attendant at delivery ■ Institutional deliveries

* Data refer to the most recent year available in the period specified.
Antenatal care coverage – Percentage of women 15–49 years old attended at least once during pregnancy by skilled health personnel (doctors, nurses or midwives).
Skilled attendant at delivery – Percentage of births attended by skilled health personnel (doctors, nurses or midwives).
Institutional deliveries – Percentage of women 15–49 years old who gave birth in the two years preceding the survey and delivered in a health facility.

Source: Table 8, Women, p.142 of this report.

attendant present at delivery, backed by emergency obstetric care, decreases the risk of a woman dying in childbirth and can help prevent and treat infections and complications. Postnatal care has a central role in encouraging new mothers to breastfeed, in the resuscitation of newborns, if necessary, and in averting hypothermia and pneumonia.

Despite the importance of maternal health, the available data reflect woefully inadequate access to care. Across the countries and territories, 1 in 4 pregnant women receives no antenatal care, and more than 40 per cent give birth without the assistance of a skilled attendant.

Combating AIDS, malaria and other major diseases (MDG 6)

Millennium Development Goal 6 focuses on reducing the enormous burdens caused by HIV and AIDS, malaria and other major diseases. While few of the indicators focus on children specifically, the direct and indirect impact of major diseases on children can be profound. Half of the infants who are infected with HIV will die before age two,[7] and more than 15 million children under age 18 have lost one or both parents to AIDS or related causes. Malaria accounts for 8 per cent of deaths in children under five and measles for another 4 per cent.

HIV and AIDS

Worldwide, 2.3 million children under age 15 are living with HIV, and 530,000 children were newly infected with the virus in 2006 – mostly through mother-to-child transmission. Girls are at particular risk of contracting HIV, both because of their physiology and because of social and cultural power imbalances in their relationships with men and boys. Preventing new infections is the first line of defence against AIDS. It is also the best way to protect the next generation.

Once a pregnant woman is infected with HIV, there is a 35 per cent chance that without intervention she will pass the virus on to her newborn during pregnancy, birth or breastfeeding.[8] Antiretroviral drug therapy can greatly reduce the chances that transmission will occur and is essential to stemming the rise in child mortality rates in countries where AIDS has reached epidemic levels. With the appropriate drugs and proper care, infants who are HIV-positive can remain healthy indefinitely, though their long-term prospects for survival are unknown.[9] Yet despite the obvious benefits of drug therapy and its relatively low cost, only 11 per cent of pregnant women in low- and middle-income countries who were HIV-positive were receiving services to prevent transmission of the virus to their newborns in 2005. Preliminary estimates for 2006, which were not yet released when this report went to press, indicate that coverage rates rose to 20 per cent in 2006.[10] The vast majority of these women live in sub-Saharan Africa.

Malaria

Malaria causes more than a million deaths each year, up to 80 per cent of them in children under five.[11] Pregnant women and their unborn children are particularly vulnerable to the disease, which is a prime cause of low birthweight in newborns, anaemia and infant deaths.

Malaria sickens and kills many children every year. *A mother sleeps with her infant under an insecticide-treated mosquito net, Côte d'Ivoire.*

Figure 1.14

Sub-Saharan Africa accounts for almost 90 per cent of paediatric HIV infections

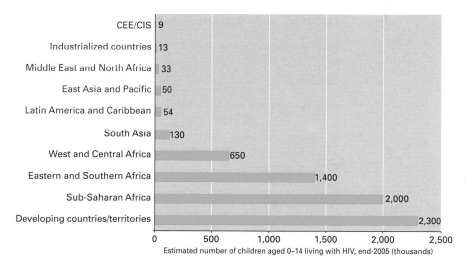

CEE/CIS	9
Industrialized countries	13
Middle East and North Africa	33
East Asia and Pacific	50
Latin America and Caribbean	54
South Asia	130
West and Central Africa	650
Eastern and Southern Africa	1,400
Sub-Saharan Africa	2,000
Developing countries/territories	2,300

Estimated number of children aged 0–14 living with HIV, end-2005 (thousands)

Source: UNAIDS, *Report on the Global AIDS Epidemic*, 2006.

Figure 1.15

Around 80 per cent of the developing world has access to improved water sources

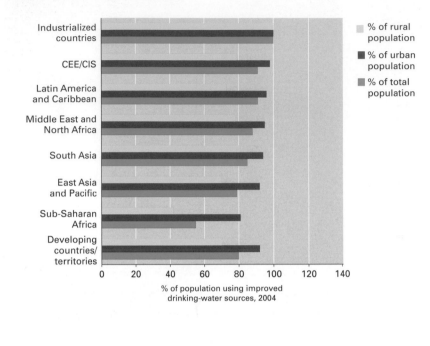

% of population using improved
drinking-water sources, 2004

Figure 1.16

Only half of the population in the developing world has access to adequate sanitation

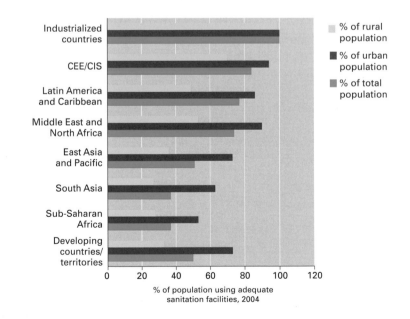

% of population using adequate
sanitation facilities, 2004

Source: UNICEF, WHO, Multiple Indicator Cluster Surveys, and Demographic and Health Surveys.

In sub-Saharan Africa alone, more than 2,000 children under-five a day die from malaria.[12] For those who survive, episodes of fever and anaemia can inhibit a child's mental and physical development.

Preventing and treating malaria requires several basic interventions, including sleeping under an insecticide treated mosquito net (ITN) and providing antimalarial drugs for pregnant women and children with evident signs of the disease. ITN coverage is growing rapidly, albeit from a low base, in part due to a tenfold rise in international funding for malaria control. Trend data for sub-Saharan Africa show a rise in use of ITNs across all countries, and in 16 of 20 countries where such data is available coverage rates have at least tripled since 2000. Notwithstanding these recent gains, overall levels are still low, and most countries are falling short of global malaria goals.

Just over one third of children with fever in sub-Saharan Africa use antimalarial drugs. Furthermore, resistance to established antimalarial drugs is increasing. A potential breakthrough in treatment is artemisinin-based combination therapy, or ACT. A safe, effective and fast-acting treatment for strains of malaria that are multi-drug resistant, ACT also helps prevent recurrence of the disease.[13]

Increasing use of safe water and basic sanitation (MDG 7)

According to the most recent data, the world as a whole is on track to meet the MDG target for safe water, with only 23 developing countries lagging behind. Progress towards improved sanitation, however, has been insufficient, with 41 countries unlikely to meet the goal.[14]

In developing countries, 1 in 5 people do not use safe water, and roughly half are without adequate sanitation. The repercussions are often deadly. The number of children under five worldwide dying from diarrhoea is estimated at almost 2 million per year; in many countries the proportion of child deaths due primarily to diarrhoea is around 20 per cent.[15] An estimated 88 per cent of diarrhoeal deaths are attributed to poor hygiene practices, unsafe drinking-water supplies and inadequate access to sanitation.[16]

Accelerating progress on the health-related MDGs

The key interventions needed to address the major causes of child deaths are well established and accepted. In fact, research reveals that only about 1 per cent of deaths among children under five have unknown causes and that two thirds of them are entirely preventable.[17]

The most basic, yet important, services and practices identified include: skilled attendants at delivery and newborn care; care of low birth-weight infants; hygiene promotion; prevention of mother-to-child transmission of HIV and paediatric treatment of AIDS; adequate nutrition, particularly in the form of early and exclusive breastfeeding during the first six months of life; complementary feeding combined with continued breastfeeding for at least two more years; micronutrient

Access to adequate sanitation helps to combat diarrhoea, a prevalent killer of children worldwide. *Practising good hygiene at school, Philippines.*

© UNICEF/HQ06-1450/Ninfa Bito

supplementation to boost immune systems; immunization to protect children against the six major vaccine-preventable diseases; oral rehydration therapy and zinc to combat diarrhoeal disease; antibiotics to fight pneumonia; and insecticide-treated mosquito nets and effective medicines to prevent and treat malaria.[18]

Although much has been achieved so far, implementing these seemingly simple solutions has proved far more arduous than experts predicted at the start of the child survival revolution, and the results have been more elusive. Increasingly, the development community is coalescing around several priorities, organized according to the following categories, which could

provide the impetus needed to achieve the health-related MDGs:

• Focusing on 60 countries where the burden of child mortality is highest.

• Providing a continuum of care for mothers, newborns and children by packaging interventions for delivery at key points in the life cycle.

• Strengthening community partnerships and health systems.

As the subsequent section shows, action on the first priority is well under way. Progress has been made on the second priority, but much more needs to be done. On the third priority, despite many pilot projects

Figure 1.17

The 60 priority countries for child survival targeted by Countdown to 2015

Source: Countdown to 2015, *Tracking Progress in Child Survival: The 2005 report,* UNICEF Health Section, New York, 2006, p. 37.

and proven programmes, further scaling up is urgently required.

Priority 1: Focusing on countries where the burden of child mortality is highest

In 2003, concerned that progress on child survival was behind schedule, a group of technical experts working on diverse aspects of child health came together for a workshop on child survival in Bellagio, Italy, sponsored by the Rockefeller Foundation. Later that year, the Bellagio Child Survival Group published a series of articles on maternal, newborn and child survival and health in the British medical journal

The Lancet. Called The Child Survival series, the articles helped to spur awareness and called for immediate action to translate knowledge into practice. The group's work is now being continued by a new coalition of scientists, policymakers, activists and health-programme managers participating in the Countdown to 2015: Tracking Progress in Maternal, Newborn and Child Mortality. The Countdown initiative is sponsoring a series of conferences that began in December 2005 and will take place approximately every two years until 2015 (the next one will be held in April 2008 in Cape Town, South Africa).[19]

The Countdown gathers data on the progress countries are making as they broaden coverage of interventions that have proved effective in reducing the deaths of children under five. Early on it was recognized that although every region of the world needed to accelerate progress, countries with the greatest number or the highest rates of under-five deaths should be prioritized. To this end, Countdown to 2015 partners, including UNICEF, have identified 60 priority countries for child survival initiatives, based on two criteria: countries with more than 50,000 deaths of children under five and countries with an annual under-five mortality rate

The continuum of maternal, newborn and child health care across time and place

The continuum of maternal, newborn and child health care emphasizes the interrelationship between undernutrition and the deaths of mothers, newborns and children. The continuum consists of a focus on two dimensions in the provision of packages of essential primary-health-care services:

• **Time:** The need to ensure essential services for mothers and children during pregnancy, childbirth, the postpartum period, infancy and early childhood (*see Figure 1.18*). The focus on this element was engendered by the recognition that the birth period – before, during and after – is the time when mortality and morbidity risks are highest for both mother and child.

• **Place:** Linking the delivery of essential services in a dynamic primary-health-care system that integrates home, community, outreach and facility-based care (*see Figure 1.19*). The impetus for this focus is the recognition that gaps in care are often most prevalent at the locations – the household and community – where care is most required.

The continuum of care concept has emerged in recognition of the fact that maternal, newborn and child deaths share a number of similar and interrelated structural causes with undernutrition. These causes include such factors as: food insecurity, female illiteracy, early pregnancy and poor birth outcomes, including low birthweights; inadequate feeding practices, lack of hygiene and access to safe water or adequate sanitation; exclusion from access to health and nutrition services as a result of poverty, geographic or political marginalization; and poorly resourced, unresponsive and culturally inappropriate health and nutrition services.

The continuum of care also reflects lessons learned from evidence and experience in maternal, newborn and child health during recent decades. In the past, safe motherhood and child survival programmes often operated separately, leaving disconnections in care that affected both mothers and newborns. It is now recognized that delivering specific interventions at pivotal points in the continuum has multiple benefits. Linking interventions in packages can also increase their efficiency and cost-effectiveness. Integrating services can encourage their uptake and provide opportunities to enhance coverage. The primary focus is on providing universal coverage of essential interventions throughout the life cycle in an integrated primary-health-care system.

Figure 1.18

Connecting caregiving across the continuum for maternal, newborn and child health

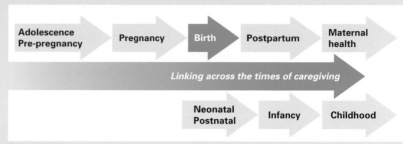

Source: Partnership for Maternal, Newborn & Child Health, <www.who.int/pmnch/about/continuum_of_care/en/index.html>, accessed 30 September 2007.

The projected impact of achieving a high rate of coverage with a continuum of health care could be profound. In sub-Saharan Africa, achieving a continuum of care that covered 90 per cent of mothers and newborns could avert two thirds of newborn deaths, saving 800,000 lives each year.

The paradigm is increasingly being adopted in international public health policies and programmes, and forms the foundation of the work of the Partnership for Maternal, Newborn & Child Health (*see Chapter 2, page 43, for details of the Partnership*).

See References, page 104.

Figure 1.19

Connecting caregiving between households and health facilities to reduce maternal, newborn and child deaths

Source: Partnership for Maternal, Newborn & Child Health, <www.who.int/pmnch/about/continuum_of_care/en/index.html>, accessed 30 September 2007.

of at least 90 per 1,000 live births. In 2005, these 60 countries accounted for 93 per cent of all deaths of children under five worldwide. Of these, only seven – Bangladesh, Brazil, Egypt, Indonesia, Mexico, Nepal and the Philippines – are considered to be on track to meet MDG 4. In contrast, 19 of the priority countries will need to achieve annual reductions of 10 per cent or more per year to achieve the 2015 target.[20]

Priority 2: Providing a continuum of care by packaging interventions and delivering them at key points in the life cycle

Astonishing results have been achieved by some child health programmes that target specific diseases and conditions. These 'vertical' interventions, as they are known, are usually one-time events or disease-specific in nature, such as immunization campaigns covering one

disease. Lessons from the past, explored in greater detail in Chapter 2, show that such programmes are ill-suited to providing the more comprehensive and sustained care that mothers, newborns and children need. More recent experience suggests that even greater progress is possible if these life-saving interventions were combined into 'packages' of care and administered at key points in the life cycle.

Child health in complex emergencies

Meeting the health needs of children, women and families presents considerable challenges in peacetime. These challenges are compounded many times during emergencies, natural or human-made. Yet delivery of health services to populations in general and to children in particular is especially critical in these contexts. In effect, a significant proportion of the children who are not currently being reached through existing interventions live in countries where the delivery of health services has been severely disrupted. Between 1989 and 2000, 110 recorded conflicts took place; 103 of them were civil wars, many of them protracted, accompanied by institutional collapse and violence directed against civilians. At present, more than 40 countries, 90 per cent of them low-income nations, are dealing with armed conflict. UNICEF's *Humanitarian Action Report 2006* highlighted 29 emergency situations affecting children and women.

A complex emergency is defined broadly as a situation of armed conflict, population displacement and/or food insecurity with associated increases in mortality and malnutrition. Most of the major causes of child mortality in complex emergencies are the same as the top killers of children in general. They include measles, malaria, diarrhoeal diseases, acute respiratory infections and malnutrition. These are often compounded by outbreaks of other communicable diseases, such as meningitis, and nutritional deficiencies that can contribute substantially to child morbidity and mortality. The highest mortality rates in refugee populations, for example, tend to occur among children under five.

Child mortality rates are usually highest during the acute early phase of a complex emergency. By contrast, in post-

emergency settings, where children have remained in stable refugee camps for prolonged periods, child mortality might be lower in the refugee population than among neighbouring resident children. Obstacles to the provision of health care to children in complex emergencies include limited access, cultural barriers, insecurity, limitations in resources such as drugs and supplies, and a lack of communication among the various organizations providing relief.

Community leadership and engagement is especially critical in these contexts. Contrary to the assumption that communities in situations of crisis are fragile and tend to fragment under the stress of war, famine or mass dislocation, research increasingly suggests that some form of community mobilization is almost always possible and that important elements of community remain intact and even gain in importance under conditions of stress. Evidence from Ethiopia, Malawi and Southern Sudan focusing on the challenges of treating severe malnutrition in complex emergencies suggests that the success of an intervention depends critically on involving key community figures (such as traditional leaders, teachers and community health workers), as well as community organizations, volunteer networks and women's organizations. In addition, involving traditional heath practitioners can be equally important, because in many cases they are the first to be consulted in health-seeking behaviour and can therefore play a critical role in identifying severely malnourished children at an early stage.

See References, page 105.

Packaging and integrating proven, cost-effective interventions – for example, immunization and vitamin A supplementation – is efficacious. It also ensures more comprehensive care for the children served. Recently, a package of 16 proven interventions was identified that could avert up to 72 per cent of all newborn deaths. These include tetanus toxoid immunization, skilled attendants at birth, access to obstetric care, immediate and exclusive breastfeeding, drying and keeping newborns warm, access to resuscitation, if needed, special care of low-birthweight infants and treatment of infection.[21]

The timing of these packaged interventions can be crucial. More than half of all maternal and newborn deaths occur at birth and during the first few days of life, but this is also the period when health coverage is lowest. An effective continuum of care (*see Panel, page 17*) connects essential maternal, newborn and child health packages through pregnancy, childbirth, postnatal and newborn periods, and into childhood and adolescence. The advantage is that each stage builds on the success of the previous stage. For example, providing integrated services to adolescent girls means fewer unintended or poorly timed pregnancies. Visits to a health-care practitioner can prevent problems during pregnancy and make it more likely that mothers will get the appropriate care at birth. Skilled care before, during and immediately after birth reduces the risk of death or disability for both the mother and the baby. Continued care for children supports their right to health.

An effective continuum of care also addresses the gaps in care, whether in the home, community, health centre or hospital. Babies with birth asphyxia, sepsis or complications from a preterm birth can die within hours or even minutes if appropriate care is not provided. Because more than 60 million women in the developing world deliver at home,[22] it is critical that a skilled attendant be present at birth with strong backup by a local health clinic or other first-level facility and the hospital, should complications arise. Quality of care at all of these levels is crucial.

Priority 3: Strengthening health systems and community partnerships

Delivering comprehensive health care for children requires preventive measures, as well as treatment of illness. Prevention typically requires behaviour changes that start in the household and can gain support through the community. Improvements in nutrition, for example, are often the result of better infant feeding practices by mothers or other caregivers, whether through breastfeeding or, later, by providing a diversified diet through kitchen or community gardens. Such practices must be learned by an individual and reinforced by the community. Wells, pumps and toilets are important to good hygiene. But their effectiveness depends on a community primed to maintain them and to use them. Children must learn to wash their hands and practise good hygiene, habits that are cultivated in the home, in school and among neighbours and friends.

As an integral part of the larger health system, community partnerships in primary health care can serve a dual function: actively engaging community members as health workers and mobilizing the community in support of improved health practices. They can also stimulate demand for quality health services from governments. Community involvement fosters community ownership. It can also add vitality to a bureaucracy-laden health system and is essential in reaching those who are the most isolated or excluded. As the following chapters in this report will show, many countries, including some of the poorest in the world, have implemented successful community-based health programmes. The challenge now will be to learn from their experiences, take the programmes to scale and reach the millions of children whom the health system, so far, has passed by.

Creating a supportive environment for child survival strategies

Prospects for child survival are shaped by the institutional and environmental context in which children and their families live. It comes as no surprise, for example, that infant and child mortality rates are highest in the poorest countries, among the most impoverished, isolated, uneducated and marginalized districts and communities, and in countries ravaged by civil strife, weak governance and chronic underinvestment in public health systems and physical infrastructure. Of the 11 countries where 20 per cent or more of children die before age five – Afghanistan, Angola, Burkina Faso, Chad, the Democratic Republic of the Congo, Equatorial Guinea, Guinea-

Empowering women to advance maternal, newborn and child health

Empowering women, especially at the community level, is essential both to lowering the number of deaths among children under five and to reaching Millennium Development Goal 5, which aims to reduce maternal mortality by three quarters by 2015. Yet the low status of women in many societies and their limited decision-making power within the household often present serious challenges to achieving significant progress in either area. Analysis of the data from recent Demographic and Health Surveys in 30 countries, for example, suggests that in many households, especially in South Asia and sub-Saharan Africa, women have little influence in health-related decisions in households, whether concerning their own health or that of their children. In Burkina Faso, Mali and Nigeria, almost 75 per cent of women respondents reported that husbands alone make decisions about women's health care. In the two countries surveyed in South Asia, Bangladesh and Nepal, this ratio was around 50 per cent.

This exclusion compromises the health and well-being of all family members, particularly women and children, and is often linked to high maternal and child mortality rates – all five countries mentioned above are among the 60 selected as priority countries for child survival by the Countdown to 2015 (*see Figure 1.17, page 16, for further details*). The situation is often most severe in rural areas or in urban slums, where women are largely illiterate and suffer from socio-cultural barriers to accessing health services, such as restrictions on leaving their homes or on interacting with strangers, and frequently do not have access to a health centre or a health clinic.

For example, in Afghanistan, women are prohibited from receiving health care at hospitals staffed exclusively by male health personnel, while cultural norms restrict women from working and receiving advanced medical training.

A number of community health worker programmes that train primarily women have successfully circumvented gender-based barriers to utilization of health services. In Bangladesh, the community health workers trained by BRAC are married, middle-aged women, and their 'doorstep' health services allow women to circumvent purdah restrictions that prevent them from leaving their homes to access health facilities on their own. In Pakistan, where in 1999 only about half the women of childbearing age were immunized against tetanus, a campaign initiated by the Ministry of Health succeeded in raising that proportion to 80 per cent of a target group of 5 million women by relying on home visits by the Lady Health Workers, who were more acceptable to women than male vaccinators.

Furthermore, interventions that have enhanced women's empowerment and leadership at the community level have been equally important in improving the health status of women and children. In Ghana, the prevalence of Guinea worm disease, which is spread by water and can incapacitate an infected person for months, required a comprehensive eradication campaign. Women volunteers, who were more familiar with the improved water sources than men, conducted door-to-door surveillance, distributed filters, identified potentially contaminated water supplies and provided community education. As a result, incidence of the disease fell by 36 per cent between 2002 and 2003. Similarly, in Puerto Rico, a programme to prevent dengue fever, carried out by WHO and the US Centers for Disease Control and Prevention, relied on community-nominated women to act as promoters. The women made house-to-house visits, interviewing heads of households and inspecting the premises for vector breeding sites. They also engaged in community-awareness activities, including the creation of a dengue prevention exhibit at the local supermarket. Through this strategy, 20 per cent of households joined the campaign.

See References, page 105.

Bissau, Liberia, Mali, Niger and Sierra Leone[23] – more than half have suffered a major armed conflict since 1989. Similarly, fragile states, characterized by weak institutions with high levels of corruption, political instability and a shaky rule of law, are often incapable of providing basic services to their citizens.

Institutional and environmental factors can sometimes be the dominant factor in child survival. In countries where AIDS has reached epidemic levels, for example, combating the syndrome is the main challenge for child survival. The scale and nature of the epidemic is such that all other interventions will prove ineffective unless AIDS is addressed. Countries that suffer from food insecurity or are prone to droughts are also at risk of having poorer child survival outcomes. The inability to diversify diets leads to chronic malnutrition for children, increasing their vulnerability to ill health and, ultimately, death.

Giving women a voice in making health-related decisions translates into better care for their children. *Discussing health care at a meeting, India.*

The challenge of reaching children in countries with such intractable problems is daunting. Nevertheless, if the political will is there, there are steps these countries can take to create a supportive environment for child survival and development.

Create laws to protect children from violence, and see that they are enforced

Data from countries in the Organisation for Economic Co-operation and Development (OECD) indicate that among children under 18, infants less than a year old face the second-highest risk of dying by homi-cide. The risk of death is about three times greater for children under one than for those aged one to four, and the younger the child, the more likely that death will be caused by a close family member. Where deaths are not recorded or investigated, the extent of fatal violence to children is not accurately known and may become obscured by the generally high rates of under-five mortality. It is assumed that violence in one form or another – including neglect – may often play a part in infant and young child deaths that are not recorded as homi-cides or perhaps not recorded at all. It is widely agreed that violence against children by family members results in deaths far more often than official records suggest.[24]

Forced marriage is another form of violence inflicted on children – and often socially condoned – with implications for child survival. When girls give birth before their bodies are fully developed, there is a much higher risk of death for both mother and child. Pregnancy-related deaths are the leading cause of mortality for girls 15–19 years old worldwide, whether they are mar-ried or not.[25] Those younger than 15 are five times more likely to die in childbirth than women in their twenties.[26] Their children are also less likely to survive. If a mother is under 18, her baby's chances of dying during the first year of life are 60 per cent higher than those of a baby born to a mother older than 19.[27]

In addition to laws that prohibit child marriage and other forms of violence against children, a policy of zero tolerance should be adopted by countries seeking to create an environment in which children can survive and thrive. Another essential form of protection is birth registration of all children. This legal acknowledgement of the child's existence is often required to access essential services, such as vaccinations and vitamin A supplementation. It also establishes family ties where inheritance is an issue.[28]

Educate and empower women

The latest estimates indicate that, on average, almost 1 out of every 4 adults (defined here as those age 15 and over) is illiterate. Almost two thirds are women, according to the most recent data from the UNESCO Institute for Statistics.[29] Research shows that less-educated caregivers generally have poorer access to information on basic health care than their better-educated peers.[30] This, in turn, can lead to ill-informed decisions about when and how to seek care for sick children.[31] In contrast, evidence from Bangladesh shows that a child born to a mother with primary education

Birth registration: An important step towards accessing essential services

The right to a name and a nationality is well established by the Convention on the Rights of the Child, which explicitly calls in article 7 for the registration of a child immediately after birth. Yet every year the births of around 51 million children go unregistered. These children are almost always from poor, marginalized or displaced families or from countries where systems of registration are not functional, and the consequences for their health and well-being are often severe and long-lasting.

Figure 1.20

Levels of birth registration* are low in South Asia and sub-Saharan Africa

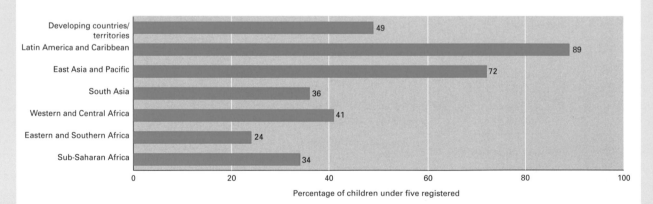

Percentage of children under five registered

* Birth registration refers to the percentage of children under five who were registered at the moment of the survey. The numerator of this indicator includes children whose birth certificate was seen by the interviewer or whose mother or caretaker says the birth has been registered. Multiple Indicator Cluster Survey data refer to children alive at the time of the survey.

Source: Multiple Indicator Cluster Surveys, Demographic and Health Surveys, other national surveys and vital registration systems. Country and regional data can be found in Statistical Table 9, page 146 of this report.

is about 20 per cent more likely to survive compared to a child born to a mother with no education; the odds increase to 80 per cent when the mother has obtained a secondary education.[32]

Empowering women socially and economically can establish another path towards improving child survival. In many countries, women are deprived of basic decision-making responsibilities, even concerning their own health or that of their children.

It is also well known that when women are in charge of household finances, they tend to spend a larger portion of the household budget on food and other necessities for children. For these reasons, giving women the means to become more economically self-reliant will likely have positive spin-offs for children.

Promote social equity

Because they are poor and disenfranchised, millions of women and children have been excluded from

progress in recent decades. The disparities in child survival prospects between poor and better-off children are stark, not only among countries but within them. For example, in every country where data are available, children living in the poorest 20 per cent of households are far more likely to die before their fifth birthday than children living in the richest quintile of the population; in some countries the risk is up to five times higher.[33] Policy interventions to eliminate these inequalities – that is,

Although sub-Saharan Africa has the highest proportion (66 per cent) of children not registered at birth, South Asia, with a corresponding ratio of 64 per cent, has the highest number. The challenges are particularly daunting in some countries, such as Afghanistan, Bangladesh, the United Republic of Tanzania and Zambia, where birth registration rates are very low due to the absence of effective and functioning birth registration systems. In Bangladesh and Zambia, UNICEF estimates that only 10 per cent of births are registered, while in the United Republic of Tanzania the registration rate is just 8 per cent.

Birth registration and access to health care in particular are closely linked, especially for children under five. For instance, data from several African countries suggest a close correlation between the presence of a skilled attendant at birth and child registration. In Benin, for example, 74 per cent of children who were delivered by a skilled attendant were registered, as compared to 28 per cent of those who were not. Furthermore, the data also suggest that birth registration levels are associated with the number of vaccinations received and with the provision of vitamin A supplementation, as well as with the level of medical care available. For example, in Chad, 38 per cent of children receiving vitamin A supplementation have been registered, compared to 15 per cent of those not receiving supplementation. Conversely, in the absence of birth registration, in many countries children are denied access to vital interventions or programmes.

The challenges encountered by parents in registering the birth of their children often signal and overlap with broader

patterns of social exclusion and lack of access to social services. Thus, particularly in remote areas, parents often do not see the benefits of their own citizenship, let alone the benefits that birth registration would confer on their children. Furthermore, even when parents do plan to register a birth, the high cost of registration and long distances to registration centres often act as powerful deterrents. High cost in particular was revealed by a recent UNICEF analysis to be the primary reason for the lack of birth registration in no fewer than 20 developing countries, resulting in large registration disparities between rich and poor children. In the United Republic of Tanzania, where overall birth registration is very low, there is a strong disparity between rich and poor, with only 2 per cent of the poorest fifth of children being registered compared to 25 per cent of the richest fifth.

Achieving universal birth registration requires governments, parents and communities to work together to make birth registration a priority, and an integrated approach – such as combining national immunization campaigns with birth registration campaigns – often provides the best strategy. Where such cooperation has been achieved, it has led to remarkable results even in the most trying circumstances. In Afghanistan, in 2003, a nationwide campaign to register all children under the age of one was combined with the country's National Polio Immunization Days. The campaign was expanded in 2004 and had reached 2 million children under five by mid-October of that year.

See References, page 105.

Child survival in post-conflict situations: Liberia's challenges and triumphs

by Ellen Johnson-Sirleaf, President of Liberia

According to the Women's Commission for Refugee Women and Children, based in New York, a society's treatment of children is a reflection of its worth. In the case of post-conflict Liberia, the country's fate is inextricably tied to the fate of its most vulnerable population. The survival of children in Liberia is a fundamental underpinning of our development agenda because it shapes how we progress as a nation.

The impact of conflict on the survival of Liberia's children is stark: At 235 deaths per 1,000 live births, Liberia's under-five mortality rate is the fifth highest in the world; its infant mortality is the third highest and maternal mortality the twenty-first highest. Maternal mortality trends are an important benchmark for achieving Millennium Development Goal 4 and other health-related MDG targets for children because maternal health bolsters child survival – and without a sound policy on women's development and empowerment, children in any post-conflict situation will ultimately be neglected reminders of a nation's failures.

It is disconcerting that, despite all the improvements in modern medicine, children under five in Liberia still perish because of malaria (18 per cent of total deaths), diarrhoea and vaccine-preventable diseases, such as measles, neonatal tetanus, diphtheria, whooping cough and acute respiratory infections. Underlying these conditions are chronic malnutrition and vitamin and mineral deficiencies, which are common in children under five. Fifty-one per cent of the population is food insecure. HIV infection in pregnant women is estimated at 5.7 per cent in 2007 compared to 4 per cent in 2004 – another example of the impact of 15 years of conflict and the structural problems in the economy that disadvantage women and girls.

Access to basic health care is improving, but coverage and distribution remain inadequate, especially in the rural areas. The task of achieving universal access is enormous, owing to such devastating effects of armed conflict as the destruction of health infrastructure, low availability of trained health workers and low public sector resources for health. The Government of Liberia is making strenuous efforts to significantly reduce child morbidity and mortality by 2011. A national health policy and plan of action leading to universal access have been developed and are being implemented, while a national strategy and plan to accelerate child survival has been developed. A strategy and plan of action to serve as the 'road map' to reducing maternal mortality are under way. Peace has allowed immunization for young children and pregnant women to increase significantly.

The challenges remain, however.

Safe water, essential for survival, had been available in the large population centres, including Monrovia, Liberia's capital, prior to the conflict, but most of the piped systems were destroyed. Currently, other than Monrovia, where the piped water system is being gradually rehabilitated, urban centres are without access to pipe-borne water. Children cannot survive, much less thrive, without safe, potable drinking water, which stands at a low 32 per cent currently in Liberia.

Health and education are the pillars of any sound child survival strategy. The two are opposite sides of the same coin and must be tackled simultaneously in Liberia to ensure MDG 4. Illiteracy is high in the population, estimated at 68 per cent (male 55 per cent and female 81 per cent); literacy and education, especially of girls, are closely associated with improved child survival rates. The 2006 Girls' Education Policy aims to provide education to all girls. In order to ensure child survival, girl children also need to be protected. The conflict left many young girls pregnant or already mothers. Special efforts are needed to protect adolescent girls from sexual exploitation and abuse, from pregnancy and AIDS, both to ensure they enjoy their own rights to survival and to guarantee the rights of their children.

There needs to be renewed momentum around the issue of child survival, and Liberia is leading that clarion call. We want to ensure that our children move beyond survival and into a phase of development that enables them to thrive and transform into productive citizens.

bringing child mortality rates in the poorest 80 per cent of the population up to par with those of the richest 20 per cent – would have a dramatic effect on the under-five mortality rate for a country as a whole.[34] Worldwide, about 40 per cent of under-five deaths could be prevented in this way.[35]

Children are also excluded from health services by discrimination, geographic isolation, low levels of parental education, AIDS at epidemic levels and complex emergencies, such as armed conflict and natural disasters. Many children are affected by these circumstances simultaneously, which further decreases the likelihood that life-saving interventions will reach them.

Successful approaches used to tackle these inequities include programmes that bring health interventions to those who are hardest to reach. Subsidizing health care for the poor and directing social marketing to those who have been excluded are other options. Perhaps most crucial is ensuring that equity is a priority in the design of child survival interventions and delivery strategies. Doing so will require a thorough knowledge of the situation through the collection of survey data, which can also be used for education and advocacy. Regular monitoring must be instituted along with mechanisms to ensure accountability, both at national and international levels.

Rising to the challenge of providing a continuum of care for mothers, newborns and children

These are the types of challenges that health-care providers face in reaching children currently excluded from essential services. The main challenge to child survival no longer lies in determining the proximate causes of or solutions to child mortality but in ensuring that the services and education required for these solutions reach the most marginalized countries and communities. As the rest of this report will show, many countries, including some of the poorest in the world, have made significant strides in reaching large numbers of children and families with essential services. Effective scale-up, however, requires that we learn from the lessons of recent decades – with a particular emphasis on strengthening integrated approaches to child health at the community level.

SUMMARY The marked decline in deaths among infants and children in many parts of the world during the past century is one of the greatest success stories in international public health. It has also had a profound positive effect on life expectancy. A closer look at these generally favourable trends, however, reveals that progress has been unevenly distributed. In some countries and regions, advances have sharply decelerated since the 1990s. In Southern Africa, infant and under-five mortality have increased as AIDS reduces life expectancy and increases mortality from opportunistic infections, tuberculosis, malaria and undernutrition. Maternal mortality, meanwhile, remains unacceptably high in Africa and South Asia, with scant advances registered over the past decades.

With the 2015 target date of the Millennium Development Goals (MDGs) drawing near, and with many countries making insufficient progress on all of the targets, critical questions arise, namely: How can momentum on maternal, newborn and child survival be recaptured and progress accelerated in the next eight years? What levels of maternal mortality reduction can be realistically achieved in this same time period? How should countries set priorities in maternal, newborn and child health?

An examination of different approaches to the delivery of essential services from the beginning of the 20th century to the present demonstrates that a range of effective interventions and policies holds the most potential for accelerated

More focus is needed on strategies to accelerate progress in the continuum of health care for mothers, newborns and children. *A clinic at a refugee camp, The former Yugoslav Republic of Macedonia.*

progress. These life-saving measures include applying proven, cost effective health, nutrition, water, sanitation and hygiene, and HIV and AIDS interventions across a wider range of settings in order to deliver quality health care to women and children. They also include reducing barriers to access and mobilizing additional financial and human resources. A focus on results requires strategies that build on the collective knowledge on maternal, newborn and child survival and health in order to identify the solutions that work best for each country and community.

2

Lessons learned from evolving health-care systems and practices

A results-oriented, evidence-based approach to formulating a continuum of quality primary health care for mothers, newborns and children necessitates reviewing the best information, data and analysis to arrive at the most useful lessons that can inform current and future actions. A requisite step involves a closer examination of the diverse approaches currently employed to deliver essential health services for children and mothers.

These range from initiatives targeted towards a single disease or condition, such as measles or undernutrition, to the ideal of providing a continuum of comprehensive primary health services that integrate hospital and clinical facilities, outpatient and outreach services, and household and community-based care.

Intense debate on the relative merits of each of the major interventions and policy changes, particularly on the benefits and constraints of the most comprehensive strategies compared with more selective ones, has taken place over the years, resulting in an extensive literature. The differ-

ences between any two of these strategies are far from sharp, since each one of them has emerged partly as a response to the limitations of the previous strategy. The subsequent historical review of the accomplishments and the remaining and emerging challenges of health-care systems and public health practices during the past century, even though brief, provides important perspectives on the current situation and helps guide the way forward.

The colonial period: 1900–1949

Until the dawn of the 20th century, deaths of infants and children were very common worldwide. High mortality and disability from such causes as diarrhoea, malaria, measles, pneumonia, smallpox, tuberculosis and various forms of undernutrition affected a large proportion of the world's population.

By 1900, the world population numbered around 1.65 billion. At that point, although some gains in life expectancy had already been observed in several places – such as England and the Scandinavian countries – the estimated global average life expectancy was only about 30 years.[1]

Early in the 20th century, efforts to control infectious diseases, such as hookworm, malaria and yellow fever, would set the basis of future disease control interventions. In the first half of the century, a few key malaria programmes were developed, linking research into the disease with control of it on the African continent. These preliminary efforts were fragmented, undertaken by colonial governments focusing on colonial territories and workforces. Despite their narrow focus, some of the initiatives – for example, malaria control from 1930–1950 in and around copper mines in what is present-day Zambia – were quite successful.

All the colonial health services had sharply segregated health facilities that gave priority to their expatriates and military. In anglophone Africa and India, research on exotic diseases led to tropical specialties and programmes. Few medical schools admitted local students, and then only as part of the 'golden handshake' that accompanied independence for many developing countries in the 1950s and 1960s.

Health services for the people were pioneered mostly by missions and mostly consisted of facility-based care. Training of local staff started with nursing schools. Because of the overwhelming workload, male and female nurses were soon running most peripheral services. District governments in some countries started clinics and small district hospitals, but in most countries mission hospitals provided 50–80 per cent of hospital beds. Public health focused on environmental protection, in particular on early efforts to provide safe water and improved sanitation facilities in urban areas.

Health services in francophone and other European colonies were uniquely different from those in anglophone countries, since the latter placed great emphasis on

the Grandes Endémies programme. In this, separate levels of a national network focused on a single disease, such as sleeping sickness, elephantiasis, leprosy and other high-prevalence conditions affecting the capacity to work. Mass care was provided by mobile units, often generously equipped with complete travelling facilities. The rationale was that relying on outreach to treat patients at mass gatherings was more effective in reaching larger numbers of people than investing in static facilities. Repetitive cycles of treatment focused on simple curative interventions rather than on prevention and control.

As in Africa, the early Chinese hospitals were mainly established by missions. A national public health

system began in the 1920s with efforts to control the rapidly spreading pneumonic plague in the province of Manchuria.

An important historical footnote is that the first published case study of successful community-based primary health care concerns a project of this period. The project took place in Ding Xian (formerly Ting Hsien), about 200 kilometres south of Beijing. In this province of about half a million people, health care was provided by health workers who were the forerunners of China's 'barefoot doctors'. For a quarter of a century and for more than a fifth of the world's population, China had one of the most equitable health systems ever

The Measles Initiative

The Measles Initiative shows how a well resourced, targeted and managed global vertical initiative can reach scale rapidly and produce dramatic results. The initiative is a partnership that groups UNICEF and WHO with other leading international agencies and prominent private organizations. Launched in 2001, the Measles Initiative adopted the goal set at the UN General Assembly Special Session on Children in May 2002 to reduce deaths due to measles among children between 1999 and 2005. It has been the main sponsor of the mass campaign to boost measles vaccination, which has resulted in vaccinating more than 217 million children between 2001 and 2005 – mostly in Africa.

The results have exceeded the UN target: Measles deaths fell by 60 per cent between 1999–2005. Africa contributed 72 per cent of the absolute reduction in deaths. Estimates concluded that immunization helped avert almost 7.5 million deaths from the disease.

The reduction in measles deaths reflects support and commitment by the Measles Initiative to boosting immunization coverage and by national governments to following the WHO/UNICEF comprehensive strategy for reducing measles mortality. The strategy consists of four key components:

• Provide at least one dose of measles vaccine, administered at nine months of age or shortly after, through routine vaccination coverage of at least 90 per cent of children in each district and nationally.

• Give all children a second opportunity for measles vaccination.

• Establish effective surveillance.

• Improve clinical management of complicated cases – including vitamin A supplementation.

Measles control activities are contributing to health-system development in several ways – for example, through promoting safe injection practices, developing enhanced cold chain capacity for vaccination storage and establishing the development of a global public health laboratory network. In addition, vaccination campaigns are often combined with such other essential interventions as vitamin A supplementation, deworming medicines and the distribution of insecticide-treated mosquito nets.

A new global goal was set at the World Health Assembly in May 2005 – to reduce measles deaths by 90 per cent by 2010,

designed. This experience provided important lessons for planning the 1978 International Conference on Primary Health Care that took place in Alma-Ata, Union of Soviet Socialist Republics (now Almaty, Kazakhstan).

Early in the century, such countries as Denmark, the Netherlands, Norway and Sweden managed to reduce maternal mortality very quickly. The way in which skilled attendance at birth was organized appears to have been the major factor contributing to these gains. In the case of these four countries, efforts focused on providing professional care close to where women lived, mainly by enhancing the skills of community midwives.[2]

Mass disease control campaigns: 1950–1977

By 1950, the population of the world exceeded 2.5 billion, and global average life expectancy had risen to 47 years.

The 1950s, 1960s and 1970s witnessed a number of disease control efforts, often termed 'mass campaigns' or 'disease-focused responses'. These efforts employed scientifically sound, epidemiologically proven interventions through free-standing programmes designed to combat a specific disease or condition. Often characterized by clearly defined goals, they included time-delineated targets for either the reduction or the eradication of the disease, using a specific technol-

ogy delivered by dedicated health workers.[3]

The most successful of these campaigns was the smallpox eradication initiative, which reported its last case of human-to-human transmission in 1977. Other mass campaigns have been successful in eradicating or substantially reducing such illnesses as Guinea worm disease, trachoma and yaws.

The success of the smallpox eradication campaign was a key element informing the design of possibly the most successful preventive public health programme in history – the Expanded Programme on Immunization (EPI), launched in 1974. EPI initially aimed to vaccinate children

Figure 2.1

Global burden of measles deaths*

Children under five account for 90 per cent of measles deaths

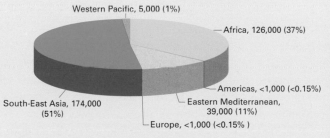

Western Pacific, 5,000 (1%)

Africa, 126,000 (37%)

Americas, <1,000 (<0.15%)

Eastern Mediterranean, 39,000 (11%)

Europe, <1,000 (<0.15%)

South-East Asia, 174,000 (51%)

* Regions refer to World Health Organization regions.

Source: World Health Organization estimates published in *The Lancet*, vol. 369, 20 January 2007, p. 194

compared to 2000 data. The target is challenging, and its attainment will require sustaining the progress made in those countries that performed well and making large inroads in countries with high numbers of measles deaths, such as India

and Pakistan. There is some way to go in the fight against measles – 345,000 people died of the disease in 2005, and 90 per cent of them were children under five. This highly contagious disease remains an important cause of under-five deaths, accounting for about 4 per cent of the global burden. It weakens children's immunity to other life-threatening diseases and conditions, including pneumonia, diarrhoea and acute encephalitis, and remains one of the leading causes of vaccine preventable deaths among children.

The success of efforts to reduce measles in 1999–2005 has shown what can be done if political will, financial commitment and sound strategies on the part of international partners and national governments are implemented to deliver proven, cost-effective treatments. Provided that this degree of commitment is sustained, there is every reason to believe that the new target can be met, helping advance progress towards Millennium Development Goal 4.

See References, page 106.

against six target diseases – diphtheria, tetanus, pertussis (whooping cough), polio, measles and tuberculosis – during their first year of life. When the programme began, less than 5 per cent of the world's children were immunized against these diseases. The most recent statistics show that global immunization rates, as measured by coverage of the diphtheria, tetanus and pertussis vaccines, now exceed 75 per cent.

Early in the history of mass campaigns, the various approaches used to deliver health services were often described as either 'vertical' (or 'categorical') or 'horizontal' approaches. These distinctions were measures, in essence, of two dimensions in programme structure:

- The degree to which programme management was integrated into general health-system management, especially at lower management levels (horizontal), as opposed to strictly separate management positions (vertical).

- The degree to which health workers had one function (vertical), as opposed to many functions (horizontal).[4]

The relative merits and constraints of vertical and horizontal approaches are well documented, and a comprehensive review of the debate is beyond the scope of this retrospective. In many ways the merits of one reflect the constraints of the other.

Primary health care: 1978–1989

The International Conference on Primary Health Care held in Alma-Ata in 1978 came about as a result of successful innovations in community health care developed after World War II in resource-poor settings. These included under-five clinics in Nigeria, community health workers in Indonesia, barefoot doctors in China, and the health systems of Cuba and Viet Nam.[5] The Alma-Ata conference and its accompanying declaration were milestones of major importance. The conference was, at the time, the largest conference ever held on a single theme in international health and development – 134 nations and representatives from 67 non-governmental organizations and the United Nations attended. By crystallizing innovative concepts that were to become conventional wisdom it paved the way to such major global commitments as Health for All by the Year 2000, agreed to at the Alma-Ata conference, the commitments made at the World Summit for Children in 1990 and, more recently, the Millennium Declaration and the Millennium Development Goals.

The primary-health-care approach that emerged from Alma-Ata encompasses the tenets of equity, community involvement, intersectoral collaboration, use of appropriate technology, affordability and health promotion. These have become guiding principles in the development of health systems that take into account broader population health issues, reflecting and reinforcing public health functions; that emphasize the integration of care across time and place; that link prevention, acute care and chronic care across all components of the system; that evaluate and strive to improve performance; and that return to the population health criteria as the basis for decision-making affecting how health-care services are organized, financed and delivered to individuals and communities.[6]

The Alma-Ata Declaration recommended that primary health care include, at a minimum, the following activities:

- Health education.

- Promotion of adequate supplies of food and proper nutrition.

- Safe water and basic sanitation.

- Maternal and child care.

- Immunization against the major childhood diseases.

- Appropriate treatment of common diseases and injuries.

- Prevention and control of locally endemic diseases.

- Provision of essential drugs.

The district health system concept, also known as 'catchment area focus' or the 'small area' or 'intermediate group' approach in Europe and other countries, was subsequently developed by the World Health Organization as a model for the implementation of primary health care.[7]

Despite the many benefits of primary health care, its implementation suffered from unfavourable economic climates – particularly in the 1980s –

that triggered a significant withdrawal by states from provision of such public services as health care, water distribution, waste disposal and food quality control. This situation led to the near collapse of peripheral health services in many developing countries, as well as to a decline in support for community health work.[8]

Selective primary care and the child survival revolution: 1980s

At the outset of the 1980s, child health continued to constitute a 'silent' emergency, as close to 15 million children were still dying annually before their fifth birthday. In the late 1970s, two scientists, Julia Walsh and Kenneth Warren, published 'Selective Primary Health Care: An interim strategy for disease control in developing countries' – a milestone paper that proposed an alternative strategy for rapidly reducing infant and child mortality at a reasonable cost.[9] After breaking down the relative role of each major cause of child mortality and listing the existing interventions proved to be effective in addressing them, they concluded that a small number of causes (diarrhoea, malaria, respiratory diseases and measles, among others) were responsible for the vast majority of under-five deaths and that these deaths could be easily prevented by immunization (only 15 per cent of the world's children were immunized at the time), oral rehydration therapy, breastfeeding and antimalarial drugs.[10] Their research came at a critical moment in the debate on the relative merits of horizontal versus vertical approaches and on whether the principles of comprehensive primary health

care could translate into effective programmes.

The result was a new strategy known as 'selective primary health care'.[11] Introduced a year after the Alma-Ata Declaration, this strategy was initially seen as a first step towards the implementation of comprehensive primary health care, but it quickly became a model in its own right. Integrating key elements of vertical approaches by targeting the diseases identified as the most important contributors to high infant and child mortality rates, it was intended to be more focused and more feasible than primary health care.[12]

The 'child survival revolution', spearheaded by UNICEF and launched in 1982, was based on this framework. It focused on four low-cost interventions collectively referred to as GOBI – growth monitoring for undernutrition, oral rehydration therapy to treat childhood diarrhoea, breastfeeding to ensure the health of young children and immunization against six deadly childhood diseases. GOBI was supported by major programmes led by WHO, including the Expanded Programme on Immunization and programmes to control diarrhoeal diseases and acute respiratory infections.

Subsequently, GOBI added three more components – food supplementation, family spacing and female education – and became GOBI FFF.[13] Global advocacy efforts concerning the importance of these basic interventions for child survival were successful in encouraging a large number of countries to create their own national systems to promote and deliver key interventions.[14] From the outset, selec-

Immunization has proved to protect children from major childhood diseases. *A child receives DPT3 vaccine, Côte d'Ivoire.*

tive primary health care received solid support from donors keen on channelling resources into 'child survival' programmes. These initiatives retained their community-oriented primary-health-care roots, but at the same time held the appeal of using relatively inexpensive medical technologies to reach specific objectives.

Selective primary care initiatives have proved relatively successful in recent decades. GOBI FFF and the World Health Organization's initiatives are credited with contributing to notable improvements in primary-health-care coverage, particularly immunization and oral rehydration therapy. These efforts undoubtedly contributed to the sharp fall in the global under-five mortality rate, from 115 per 1,000 live births in 1980 to 93 in 1990 – a reduction of 19 per cent over the course of the decade.

Focusing on integrated, sector-wide approaches and health systems: 1990s

Despite the gains of selective primary health care, by the late 1980s, health systems in many developing countries were under severe stress. Population growth, the debt crisis in many Latin American and sub-Saharan African countries, and political and economic transition in the former Soviet Union and Central and Eastern Europe were but three of the contributing factors.

In response, a number of countries embarked on efforts to reform deteriorating, under-resourced health systems, raise their effectiveness, efficiency and financial viability, and increase their equity.

The Bamako Initiative

One such approach used by many countries was the Bamako Initiative, which was launched in 1987 at the World Health Organization meeting of African health ministers in Bamako, Mali. This strategy focused on increasing access to primary health care and meeting basic community needs in sub-Saharan Africa by delivering an integrated minimum health-care package through health centres. A strong emphasis was placed on access to

drugs and regular contact between health-care providers and communities. (*See Panel, page 36, for further details on the Bamako Initiative.*)

Integration

The emphasis on integrating essential services that was a central feature of the Bamako Initiative was to become the driving force of approaches in the 1990s. Integrated approaches sought to combine the merits of selective primary care and primary health care. Like selective approaches, they placed a strong emphasis on providing a core group of cost-effective solutions in a timely way to address specific health challenges; like primary health care, they also focused attention on community participation, intersectoral

National immunization days and child health days

National immunization days (NIDs) originated as one-day mass polio vaccination campaigns across the developing world. NIDs, which still take place in many countries, are supplementary and do not replace routine immunization. Their original aim was to prevent the spread of polio by immunizing all children under the age of five, regardless of their previous polio vaccination history.

The concept of setting aside a day for mass interventions on child health is not new. Successful trials of days took place in the 1980s in such places as Burkina Faso, Colombia and Turkey. More recently, active civil wars have been halted to provide days of tranquility that allow children to be safely vaccinated in such countries as Angola, Sierra Leone and Somalia. Mass vaccinations allow for economies of scale, as skilled professionals can supervise a cadre of volunteers, especially for oral polio vaccine, which does not require a needle and syringe.

Child health days have expanded the scope of interventions beyond polio immunization to include vitamin A supplementation, and in the case of Zimbabwe, distribution of insecticide-treated mosquito nets and other immunizations. Other countries that conduct similar events include Nepal and Nigeria.

Nepal's national vitamin A programme is particularly noteworthy because it employs an existing network of female community health volunteers to deliver the supplements. The programme is found to be highly cost-effective, with a cost per death averted estimated at US$327–$397, while the cost per disability-adjusted life year (DALY) gained was approximately US$11–$12. The programme was steadily expanded, from the original 32 priority districts to cover all 75 districts, in annual increments of 8–10 districts over an eight-year period. Expansion was assisted by using national immunization days to advance coverage.

Integrating the delivery of a range of interventions in a single location and at a single point in time, child health days are efficient for both households and health service providers. Related concepts, such as child health weeks, are enhancing the opportunities to reach a large number of usually excluded children with essential interventions.

See References, page 106.

collaboration and integration in the general health-delivery system.

A long-standing example of the greater emphasis on integration during the 1990s is IMCI, the Integrated Management of Childhood Illness. Developed in 1992 by UNICEF and WHO, and employed in more than 100 countries since then, IMCI adopts a broad, cross-cutting approach to case management of childhood illness, acknowledging that there is usually more than one contributing cause.[15] Indeed, in many cases, sick children exhibit overlapping symptoms of disease, complicating efforts to arrive at a single diagnosis even in communities with adequate first-level examination facilities, let alone those with more challenging circumstances.

IMCI strategies have three primary components, each of which requires adaptation to the country context:

- *Improving health worker performance:* This involves training health workers to assess symptoms of diseases, correct mapping of illness to treatment, and provision of appropriate treatment to children and information to the caregivers. Through provision of locally adapted guidelines, health staff are taught case management skills for five major causes of childhood mortality: acute respiratory infections, especially pneumonia; diarrhoeal diseases; measles; malaria; and undernutrition.

- *Improving health systems:* This component seeks to strengthen health systems for effective management of childhood illnesses. Measures employed include supporting drug availability, enhancing supervision, strengthening referral and deepening health information systems. Planning guides are provided for managers at the district and national levels.

- *Improving community and family practices:* The final component is often referred to as Community Integrated Management of

---

Health sector financing: Sector-wide approaches and the Heavily Indebted Poor Countries Initiative

During the 1990s, concerns escalated about the potential predominance of vertical approaches, which tend to create and utilize managerial, operational and logistical structures separate from those of the national health system to address disease control. These concerns contributed to the development of a new mode of health financing: sector-wide approaches (SWAps). Under SWAps, the major funding contributions for the health sector support a single plan for sector policy, strategy and expenditure backed by government leadership. Common approaches to health service delivery are adopted across the sector, and government procedures increasingly control the disbursement and accounting of funds.

SWAps were created for several purposes: to address the limitations of project-based forms of donor assistance, ensure that overall health reform goals were met, reduce large transaction costs for countries and establish genuine partnerships between donors and countries in which both had rights and responsibilities. SWAps are a dynamic process rather than an end point, and they display considerable variation across countries. SWAps have led to greater dialogue and trust, a sharper focus on a select number of key sector priorities and closer links between policy and implementation. However, constraints include an overemphasis on details in planning and the development of procedures; limited civil society participation; weak performance management; and a slow shift from emphasizing donor coordination to considering service improvement and results.

At the end of the 1990s, in the context of the Heavily Indebted Poor Countries Initiative implemented by the International Monetary Fund and the World Bank, the focus on the health sector and financing reform in many low-income countries broadened to include Poverty Reduction Strategy Papers (PRSPs). Medium-term expenditure frameworks, the multi-annual public planning instruments associated with PRSPs, are used to plan future budget requirements for public services and to assess the resource implications of policy changes and new programmes.

See References, page 106.

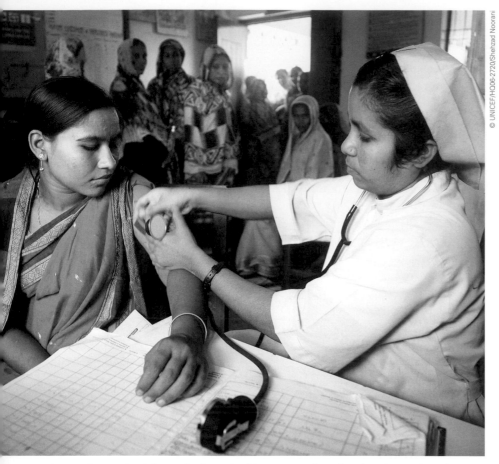

Approaches to the delivery of primary health care must be tailored to the needs and resources of each individual country and community. *A nurse measures the blood pressure of a pregnant woman, Bangladesh.*

Childhood Illness (C-IMCI). It is based on the basic household practices for families and communities outlined in the Panel in Chapter 3, page 47.[16]

The integration of case management seeks to protect children from, and offer treatment for, all major diseases, not just one or two. It also emphasizes adapting curative solutions to the capacity and functions of local health systems, along with promoting disease prevention by educating health workers and caregivers on the importance of essential services. The role of parents and other primary caregivers in detecting common symptoms of ill health, taking children to health facilities and implementing such preventive measures as appropriate feeding and hygiene practices is critical.

Integrated Management of Childhood Illness has been rigorously evaluated since its inception in the mid-1990s. Several agencies – including WHO, UNICEF, the United Kingdom's Department for International Development (DFID) and the United States Agency for International Development (USAID) – conducted multicountry evalua-

tions in the early 2000s. In 2004 and 2005, UNICEF also reviewed the community and family component (C-IMCI).[17] Although initial results were disappointing, mainly because of incomplete implementation of the three core IMCI components, later results have demonstrated some notable successes. According to studies, IMCI case management has enhanced the quality of health care delivered in first-level facilities, motivated health workers and managers, and improved health worker performance. And it has been implemented at costs equivalent to or lower than those of existing services.[18]

Positive results for IMCI have been noted in several countries in sub-Saharan Africa. A study conducted in rural districts of the United Republic of Tanzania, for example, found that those districts implementing a health-system-strengthening initiative and IMCI demonstrated a 13 per cent greater reduction in child mortality than control districts.[19]

Survey results in Malawi, South Africa, the United Republic of Tanzania and Uganda indicated that wide-scale implementation of the C-IMCI strategy can result in significant improvement in some of the key family practices, such as steps to improve nutrition and early survival, disease prevention, home care or care-seeking for sick children, and provision of a supportive environment for child growth and development.[20]

Successes such as these have led health policy experts to recommend the development of national policies based on country priorities, with

Integrated Management of Neonatal and Childhood Illnesses in India

During the 1990s, India experienced marked reduction in the under-five mortality and infant mortality rates. These trends were not been matched by declines in the rate of neonatal deaths. By 2000, neonatal deaths were around two thirds of all infant deaths in the country, and around 45 per cent of under-five deaths. Close to half of neonatal deaths occur in the first week of life. Many of these deaths could be averted if parents recognized warning signs, undertook appropriate feeding practices or had access to skilled health workers and facility-based care.

In 2000, the Government of India adapted the Integrated Management of Childhood Illness (IMCI) strategy to focus greater attention on neonatal care. The resulting approach, Integrated Management of Neonatal and Childhood Illnesses (IMNCI), modifies IMCI with specific actions taken to promote neonatal health and survival. Like IMCI, IMNCI supports three pillars for the effective delivery of essential services to neonates, infants and young children: strengthening health-system infrastructure, enhancing the skills of

health workers and promoting community participation – all with additional emphasis on neonatal health and survival.

In practice, IMNCI consists of three home visits in the first 10 days after birth to promote best practices for the young child; a special provision at the village level for follow-up of infants with low birthweights; reinforcement of messages through meetings of women's groups and establishing a linkage between the village and the home; and assessment of the child at local health facilities based on referral.

IMNCI is incorporated as part of the government's Reproductive and Child Health II programme, an integrated approach to women's health that aims to provide a continuum of care from birth until adulthood. The additional cost of adding the newborn component, mostly the home visits, is just US$0.10 per child.

See References, page 106.

clearly defined roles for IMCI and other child health interventions, and the need to critically analyse and address the system constraints.[21]

Stimulated by a series of studies on maternal, newborn and child survival published by *The Lancet*, integrated models of health care have been developed within the context of the maternal, newborn and child health continuum of care (*see Chapter 1, page 17 for further details on the continuum of care and the partnership*). In effect, the continuum of care concept expands IMCI to include integrated management of neonatal illness.[22] Successful preliminary experience with the new approach, called the Integrated Management of Neonatal and Childhood Illnesses (IMNCI) has been pioneered and fully implemented in India (*see Panel above*).

Figure 2.2

Selective primary health care and trends in immunization rates since 1980

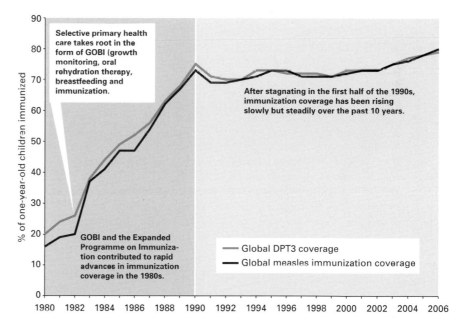

Source: Data provided by Strategic Information Section, United Nations Children's Fund.

The Bamako Initiative

The Bamako Initiative, sponsored by UNICEF and WHO and adopted by African ministers of health in 1987, was based on the realization that, despite accepting in principle the core tenets of comprehensive primary health care, by the late 1980s many countries – especially in sub-Saharan Africa – were burdened by a lack of resources and practical implementation strategies. In particular, many health facilities lacked the resources and supplies to function effectively. As a result, health workers were sometimes merely prescribing drugs to be bought from private outlets, often unlicensed and unsupervised, while many patients had lost confidence in the inefficient and under-resourced public health facilities. All of these developments threatened to reverse the gains of the 1980s. The core challenges were to promote additional donor investment, stop and reverse the decline of government expenditure on social spending in general and health in particular, and attract the money spent in the private and informal sectors back into the public system.

The Bamako Initiative aimed to increase access to primary health care by raising the effectiveness, efficiency, financial viability and equity of health services. Bamako health centres implemented an integrated minimum-health-care package in order to meet basic community health needs, focusing on access to drugs and regular contact between health-care providers and communities. Based on the concept that communities should participate directly in the management and funding of essential drug supplies, village committees engaged in all aspects of health-facility management, with positive results for child health in West Africa in particular.

The purpose of community financing was to capture a fraction of the funds households were already spending in the informal sector and combine them with government and donor funding to revitalize health services and improve their quality. The most effective interventions were priced below private sector charges and cross-subsidized through higher markup and higher co-payments on lower priority interventions. Immunization and oral rehydration therapy were supplied free of charge. Local criteria for exempting the poor were established by the communities.

Although countries followed different paths in implementing the Bamako Initiative, in practice they had a common core objective: providing a basic package of integrated services through revitalized health centres that employ user fees and community co-management of funds. A number of common support structures were organized around this core agenda, including the supply of essential drugs, training and supervision, and monitoring.

'Going to scale' was a critical step in the implementation process. The pace of expansion varied depending on the availability of internal and external resources, local capacity, the need to work at the speed of community needs and pressure from governments and donors. Most of the sub-Saharan countries that adopted the Bamako Initiative employed some form of phased scaling up, and several countries – most notably Benin, Mali and Rwanda – achieved significant results.

In essence, implementing the Bamako Initiative was a political process that involved changing the prevailing patterns of authority and power. Community participation in the management and control of resources at the health-facility level was the main mechanism for ensuring accountability of public health services to users. Health committees representing communities were able to hold monitoring sessions during which coverage targets, inputs and expenditures were set, reviewed, analysed and compared. It is estimated that the initiative improved the access, availability, affordability and use of health services in large parts of Africa, raised and sustained immunization coverage, and increased the use of services among children and women in the poorest fifth of the populace.

The Bamako Initiative was not without its limitations. The application of user fees to poor households and the principles of cost recovery drew strong criticism, and though many African countries adopted the approach, only in a handful were initiatives scaled up. Even in those countries where Bamako has been deemed a success, poor people viewed price as a barrier in the early 2000s, and a large share did not use essential health services despite exemptions and subsidies. The challenge that Benin, Guinea and Mali still face, along with other African nations that adopted the Bamako Initiative, is to protect the poorest and ensure that costs do not prevent access to essential primary health-care services for poor and marginalized communities.

See References, page 106.

The Millennium Development Goals and results-based approaches: 2000 and beyond

By 2000, global life expectancy had increased from 47 years in the early 1950s to around 65 years. However, many countries had failed to share in the health gains that contributed to this increase in longevity, and the AIDS pandemic threatened to reverse the gains in high-prevalence areas. This prompted the inclusion of three health-related goals in the eight Millennium Development Goals that were adopted by 189 countries in 2000, with the target deadline of 2015 (*See Figure 1.9, page 9, for the full list of the health-related MDGs and their associated indicators.*)

As Chapter 1 explained, progress towards the health-related MDGs has been less rapid than the architects of the MDGs had hoped. There are serious concerns that without a concerted, sustained drive to expand access to essential interventions to the millions of mothers and children who are currently missing out, the goals, particularly in sub-Saharan Africa, will be missed by a wide margin.

In recent years, a number of high-level meetings have taken place to identify opportunities for achieving the MDGs, explore best practices, make commitments to measurable results at the country level and support the pertinent institutional adjustments required at country, regional or global levels. A key concern of these meetings is progress in sub-Saharan Africa, the region with the highest rates of maternal, newborn and child mortality and the one making the least progress towards the health-related Millennium Development

Figure 2.3

IMCI case management in the outpatient health facility, first-level referral facility and at home for the sick child from age two months up to five years

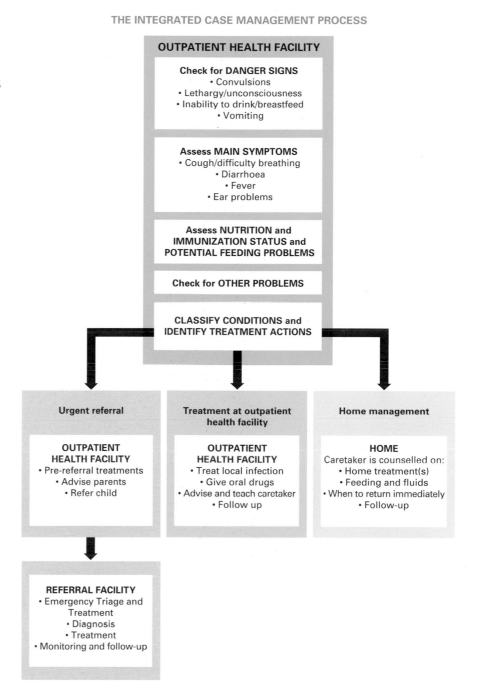

THE INTEGRATED CASE MANAGEMENT PROCESS

OUTPATIENT HEALTH FACILITY

Check for DANGER SIGNS
• Convulsions
• Lethargy/unconsciousness
• Inability to drink/breastfeed
• Vomiting

Assess MAIN SYMPTOMS
• Cough/difficulty breathing
• Diarrhoea
• Fever
• Ear problems

Assess NUTRITION and IMMUNIZATION STATUS and POTENTIAL FEEDING PROBLEMS

Check for OTHER PROBLEMS

CLASSIFY CONDITIONS and IDENTIFY TREATMENT ACTIONS

Urgent referral

OUTPATIENT HEALTH FACILITY
• Pre-referral treatments
• Advise parents
• Refer child

Treatment at outpatient health facility

OUTPATIENT HEALTH FACILITY
• Treat local infection
• Give oral drugs
• Advise and teach caretaker
• Follow up

Home management

HOME
Caretaker is counselled on:
• Home treatment(s)
• Feeding and fluids
• When to return immediately
• Follow-up

REFERRAL FACILITY
• Emergency Triage and Treatment
• Diagnosis
• Treatment
• Monitoring and follow-up

Source: World Health Organization and United Nation Children's Fund, *Model Chapter for Textbooks: Integrated Management of Childhood Illness.* WHO and UNICEF, Geneva and New York, 2001, p. 6.

Goals. At the current pace, most of the 46 countries in sub-Saharan Africa – along with Sudan – will fail to meet most of the MDGs. Current projections indicate that sub-Saharan Africa's poverty rate as measured by the proportion of people living on less than a dollar a day will reach almost 40 per cent in 2015.[23] In some countries, under-five mortality rates have stagnated or even reversed, and paediatric AIDS deaths continue to increase.

Despite this rather bleak outlook, there is hope from the experience of other countries, whose targetted approaches have brought about significant declines in under-five mortal-ity rates.[24] In recent years, several comprehensive reviews of evidence-based child survival interventions have reaffirmed that existing low-cost interventions can avert up to two thirds of under-five mortality and over half of neonatal mortality.[25] In addition, 88 up to 98 per cent of maternal deaths are preventable.[26]

Diagonal approaches: The Mexican way

According to one of its leading proponents, Jaime Sepulveda of Mexico's National Institute of Health, the diagonal approach is a "proactive, supply-driven provision of a set of highly cost-effective interventions on a large scale bridging health clinics and homes."

Vertical interventions are often the starting point of diagonal approaches, with the caveat that the number of these interventions be expanded over time with support from existing facilities and field workers. The diagonal approach stresses the importance of integration and coordination between vertical interventions, community-based initiatives and health facilities or extension services. It addresses a number of key issues by applying specific intervention priorities, including drug supply, facility planning, financing, human resources development, quality assurance and rational prescription.

In the 25 years from 1980–2005, Mexico implemented a number of successful vertical programmes that were subsequently scaled up. These programmes targeted diarrhoeal diseases (the distribution of oral rehydration salts and the Clean Water programme); vaccine preventable diseases (national vaccination days, measles vaccination campaigns, the Universal Vaccination Programme, national health weeks); vitamin A supplementation and anthelmintic therapy (national health weeks).

PROGRESA – a conditional cash transfer programme designed to engage the country's poorest families – provided financial incentives for improved health and nutrition practices, and for keeping children in school. Benefits are contingent on regular attendance at health clinics that supply essential health and nutrition services. Food supplements are distributed to all children aged 6–23 months and underweight children aged 2–4 years in targeted households. The programme has been associated with a strong positive impact on children's nutritional status.

A more comprehensive package covering the continuum of maternal, neonatal and child health has been introduced since 2001, when the Ministry of Health launched *Arranque Parejo en la Vida* (Equal Start in Life). This initiative promotes social and community participation, strengthens and expands antenatal and neonatal care, and provides folic acid supplementation for women, among other factors. It has reached a high level of coverage. Through Seguro Popular, a public health insurance initiative, maternal and child health became entitlements.

In part, the diagonal approach has emerged as a result of research into Mexico's health system and its development during the past 25 years. Unlike other approaches, its genesis appears to have emerged as a practical response to the growing complexity of disease profiles and the pressure faced by the country to develop health interventions and systems that provide quality services, are affordable, and reach the poorest and most marginalized populations.

Its implementation has led to Mexico being one of only seven countries on track to reach the Millennium Development Goals among the 60 nations selected in 2005 for priority attention by the Child Survival Countdown to 2015. The diagonal approach is now formalized and being championed by Mexico's former Minister of Health, Julio Frenk, who considers that the framework should be integrated into a broader health policy. It aims to bridge the dichotomies between horizontal and vertical approaches, intersectoral and sectoral policies, and national and international efforts by offering a 'third way' through which effective interventions become the drivers for health-system development.

See References, page 106.

Figure 2.4

Conceptual framework for achieving health-related Millennium Development Goals

Target health, nutrition and population outcomes: Millennium Development Goals	Actions at the micro level: Households and communities	Actions at the meso level: Health system and other sectors	Actions at the macro level: Policies and financing
Achieve the health-related Millennium Development Goals 1. *Eradicate hunger* 4. *Reduce under-five mortality* 5. *Improve maternal health* 6. *Combat HIV and AIDS, malaria and other diseases* 7. *Ensure environmental sustainability*	**Family/ community-level care** **Population-oriented (outreach)services** **Individual (clinical) care**	**Monitoring and information systems** **Training and supervision** **Social mobilization** **Equitable financing mechanisms** **Procurement and supplies** **Infrastructure and logistics**	**MDG focused and evidence based** National policies, strategies and plans Poverty Reduction Strategy Papers (PRSPs) Sector-wide approaches (SWAps) Budget support Medium-term expenditure framework (MTEF)
Protect household income **MDG1:** *Eradicate extreme poverty*			

Towards a unified framework for ensuring health outcomes for mothers, newborns and children

In recent years, governments and development partners have renewed their commitment to achieving the health-related MDGs and ensuring that their renewed resolve would translate effectively into joint or coordinated regional strategies. At the same time, experts in maternal, newborn and child health are increasingly coalescing around a set of strategic principles based on the lessons of the past century. These principles are threefold, namely:

A renewed recognition of the principles of primary health care, which emphasize the primacy of family and community partnership in the survival, growth and development of children.[27] This has triggered a renewed interest in another principle of primary health care, namely the need for community partnerships to support families in improving their care practices for children and to hold health systems accountable for providing quality affordable services. (Chapter 3 examines community partnerships in support of maternal, newborn and child health and family-care practices.)

The 'health systems development for outcomes' approach to health-service delivery combines the strengths of selective/vertical and comprehensive/ horizontal approaches. This new approach is being adopted as the framework for scaling up cost-effective intervention packages and integrating them into a continuum of care for mothers, newborns and children. It emphasizes the expansion of evidence-based, high-impact health, nutrition, HIV and AIDS, and water, sanitation and hygiene interventions and practices, and underlines the importance of removing system-wide bottlenecks to health-care provision and usage. If

Accelerated Child Survival and Development in West Africa

A more recent example of an integrated approach to primary health care is the Accelerated Child Survival and Development (ACSD) initiative, which was launched by national governments in cooperation with UNICEF in West and Central Africa and aims to reduce infant (under-one), under-five and maternal mortality rates. The programme originated when the Canadian International Development Agency (CIDA) asked UNICEF to develop an innovative project that would reduce child mortality. It was initiated in 2002 in four countries, covering 16 districts and 3 million people. Since then, ACSD has grown rapidly and by 2004 was targeting more than 16 million people in selected districts in 11 countries of West and Central Africa that have high rates of under-five mortality. ACSD concentrates on three service-delivery strategies to augment coverage for women and children:

- *Community-based promotion* of a package of family health and nutrition practices, employing mostly volunteers.

- *Outreach and campaigns* to provide essential services and products, such as immunization, vitamin A, anthelmintic treatment and selected prenatal services.

- *Facility-based delivery* of an integrated minimum-care package consisting of all the selected priority interventions.

These priority interventions are also organized around three areas that build on the strengths of existing programmes and approaches:

- *Antenatal Care plus (ANC+)*, which provides intermittent preventive treatment of malaria during pregnancy, iron and folic acid supplementation, tetanus vaccine and prevention of mother-to-child transmission of HIV.

- *Expanded Programme on Immunization plus (EPI+)*, which includes immunization, vitamin A supplementation and deworming.

- *Integrated Management of Childhood Illness plus (IMCI+)*, which covers promotion of insecticide-treated mosquito nets, oral rehydration therapy, antimalarial drugs, exclusive breastfeeding and complementary feeding.

The 'three by three' delivery and intervention framework is supported by cross-cutting strategies to address behavioural, institutional and environmental constraints. These strategies include:

- Advocacy, social mobilization and communication for behavioural change.

- A results-based approach to service delivery at the community level.

- District-based monitoring and micro-planning.

- Integrated training.

- Improved supply systems.

Accelerated Child Survival and Development adopts an integrative framework, building on existing interventions with international and local partners. The programme strongly emphasizes bringing the framework into the mainstream of national policies and programmes, such as health sector-wide approaches, poverty reduction strategies and associated medium-term expenditure frameworks, basket funding and budget support. It also emphasizes building capacity at regional, district and community levels.

ACSD has a strong community-based component and is considered a 'behaviour-centred' programme because the majority of interventions – such as utilizing insecticide-treated nets in communities where malaria is endemic, improving care of sick children and newborns, and encouraging breastfeeding and complementary feeding – promote behaviour change. ACSD also includes active outreach and mobile strategies that are essential to reaching the most remote areas.

Based on preliminary data presented by district health teams in Ghana, this integrated approach, which includes immunization, infant and young child feeding, integrated management of childhood illness, and antenatal care, is already having a positive impact on routine immunization coverage. Subsidized insecticide-treated mosquito nets are being distributed in conjunction with immunization-plus activities.

See References, page 106.

jointly scaled up and widely applied, these interventions are expected to have a dual and synergistic impact not only on child survival but also on children's growth and development.

This approach defies the long-standing dichotomy between vertical approaches to achieve outcomes and integrated approaches to strengthen systems, arguing that both aims can be realized by adapting health systems to achieve results. It also recognizes that optimal child survival, growth and development are more likely to be achieved and sustained if preventive measures are available to future mothers (i.e., adolescent girls and young women) before their children are born and if they benefit from a continuum of care that is part of an evolving integrated approach to reproductive, maternal, newborn and child health. (Chapter 4 elaborates on how to take these strategies to scale.)

Enhance ways of working at the national and international levels, with a strong focus on coordination, harmonization and results. A new way of working for the global community is needed to support countries in going to scale with diagonal approaches to primary health care. Harmonization of the multitude of health-related global initiatives and partnerships, and of donor support to health-related MDGs, is pivotal to a unified paradigm. Other requisites include:

- Stronger support to developing countries in national planning, policy and budgeting frameworks for the health-related MDGs.

- Aligning donors to support countries' own priorities and plans and

Young children need adequate nutrition to have a healthy start in life. *Eating a meal together, Honduras.*

© UNICEF/HQ05-2059/Donna DeCesare

provide predictable long-term funding for health-related MDGs.

- Strengthening health systems and other sectors for MDG outcomes.

- Improving the effectiveness and efficiency of multilateral support in a context of UN harmonization by stimulating a global collective sense of urgency for reaching the health-related MDGs.

- Changing institutional ways of doing business so as to achieve the MDGs; developing a more systematic and robust approach to knowledge management and learning.

- Seizing the opportunity presented by the renewed interest in health outcomes.

- Recognizing that the role played by civil society and the private

sector will be critical for success. (Chapter 5 discusses this new way of working.)

Figure 2.4 demonstrates the complementarity of these new strategic principles to achieve the health-related Millennium Development Goals. It makes clear that though the MDGs will be primarily determined at the household and community level, their attainment requires that families and communities receive support from health systems and other sectors. Policies and financing at both global and national levels are needed to enable health systems and other sectors to support families and communities and ensure accountability for results.[28]

Building on the lessons learned

As this brief review has shown, the public health community is continually learning and evolving. There is

HIV and AIDS in Africa and its impact on women and children

Elizabeth N. Mataka, United Nations Special Envoy of the Secretary-General for HIV/AIDS in Africa

It is disheartening to observe that nearly half of all adults living with HIV around the word are women. In sub-Saharan Africa alone, out of the 23 million adults aged 15–49 and infected with HIV, 13.1 million, or 57 per cent, are women. In Zambia for example, women and girls are highly vulnerable to HIV and AIDS, and women aged 15–24 are three times more likely to be infected than males in the same age group. The toll that HIV has taken on women, especially those in Africa, has been largely underestimated. Children have also not been spared from the effects of AIDS, and the impact is devastating. It is estimated that at the end of 2006 there were 2.3 million children less than 15 years old living with HIV.

Many children continue to lose parents as a result of AIDS, and this has led to an escalating number of orphans and vulnerable children, with predictions that by 2010 there will be around 15.7 million children orphaned by AIDS in sub-Saharan Africa alone. Children suffer long before their parents die, especially girls, who may be drawn out of school to look after sick parents, particularly their mothers. Children lose the opportunity for education and for the maximum development of their potential due to lack of support. When parents die, children may have to relocate – losing their friends, as well as the familiar surroundings and environment they are comfortable with. The real trauma suffered by these children remains unknown because child counselling services are not developed in Africa. I would guess that emphasis has been put on physical, visible needs to the neglect of the more complex and challenging psychological needs of children.

Children can no longer rely on the support of the traditional extended family system, which provided care and support for the aged, orphans and any vulnerable and disadvantaged family member. This coping mechanism has been overstretched by poverty and by the sheer numbers of children to be cared for, given the fact that AIDS affects the most productive family members in the prime of their productive and reproductive lives. As a result, children have sometimes gone into homes that are already overstretched and where they are really not welcome. Some become homeless and have to live on the streets of major capital cities in Africa.

All children need a roof over their heads, proper nutrition, parenting and support structures that will help in nurturing them and giving them a renewed hope for the future. Without the education and socialization that parents and guardians provide, children cannot acquire the skills and knowledge they need to become fully productive adult members of society. HIV and AIDS are leaving behind a generation of children being raised by grandparents, who in most cases also need support by virtue of their age.

The rates of infection among women and girls are a cause for deep concern, and when combined with the workload that women take on as well – in caring for AIDS patients, AIDS orphans and their own families – the situation becomes untenable, especially in southern Africa.

The socio-economic status disparity between men and women has a great impact in fuelling the spread of HIV, among women and girls in particular. Cultural norms and early marriages further increase the vulnerability of young girls to infection. Poor communication around sex issues limits their ability to negotiate safer practices and may force women to remain in risky relationships. And socio-economic problems may limit women's access to counselling and treatment. In this kind of set-up, women do not own property or have access to financial resources and are dependent on their husbands, fathers, brothers and sons for support. Without resources, women are susceptible to sexual violence, and the threat of this violence also limits women's ability to protect themselves from HIV and AIDS.

The crisis is far from being over. African governments must commit to strengthening initiatives that increase capacities of individuals, especially women and children, to protect themselves. Empowerment of women should no longer be dealt with under the general heading of 'Mainstreaming Gender in All Aspects of Development'. Empowerment of women, as well as support for orphans and vulnerable children, must move to the next level of well targeted, time-bound and well funded programmes with measurable results.

There is need for increased support of 'beyond awareness' initiatives that focus on skills development, community-based health promotion, positive living, gender equity and universal access to prevention, care and treatment.

The ramifications of the AIDS pandemic are multiple and impact negatively on every aspect of development. There is much to be done in Africa to ensure that the response is commensurate to the human and financial challenges that are posed by HIV and AIDS. There is a need for long-term sustained prevention, care and support programmes, and for consistent, predictable and sustained resource provision. There is also a need for the empowerment of women and for change in cultural practices that discriminate against women. Long-term sustainable responses are essential and can only be achieved if all relevant stakeholders work together.

Partnership for Maternal, Newborn & Child Health

The Partnership for Maternal, Newborn & Child Health (PMNCH), launched in September 2005, brings together 180 member maternal, newborn and child communities in an alliance to reduce mortality and morbidity. The PMNCH is the product of an alliance between the three leading partnerships on maternal, newborn and child health: the Partnership for Safe Motherhood and Newborn Health, hosted by WHO in Geneva; the Healthy Newborn Partnership, based at Save the Children USA; and the Child Survival Partnership, hosted by UNICEF in New York.

The partnership focuses on four key areas of work:

• **Advocacy**, its central mission, to raise the profile of maternal, newborn and child health on political agendas and press for more financial and other resources.

• Promotion and assessment of **effective, evidence-based interventions** for scaling up, with a focus on reducing inequity in access to health care.

• **Country support** to include maternal, newborn and child health care in national development and investment plans, strengthen health systems and improve equity in coverage.

• **Monitoring and evaluation** of coverage of priority interventions, progress towards MDGs 4 and 5, and equity in coverage, to hold stakeholders accountable.

PMNCH members are divided into six constituency groups: academic and research institutions, health-care professionals, UN agencies, non-governmental organizations, donors and foundations, and governments.

The partnership aims to place at least 50 per cent of the 60 countries identified by Child Survival Countdown to 2015 on track to achieve MDGs 4 and 5 by 2010. A defining principle of its work is to engender a continuum of care to address maternal, newborn and child care in an integrated manner, across both time (pregnancy, birth, newborn and young child periods) and location (home, community and health facilities).

See References, page 106.

---

a need to focus on proven strategies targeted towards relieving the major causes of child deaths, and to do so effectively, interventions must be provided within a continuum of care that engages communities and households, as well as outreach and facility-based care. Health systems must be strengthened and expanded to support new initiatives, including community partnerships, and they must be backed by strong national and international leadership and commitment. In addition, the many institutions involved in maternal and child survival, health and nutrition must work together effectively.

One overarching principle that has emerged from the review of six decades of approaches to child survival and health is that no single approach is applicable in all circumstances. The organization, delivery and intervention orientation of health-care services must be tailored to meet the constraints of human and financial resources, the socio-economic context, the existing capacity of the health system and, finally, the urgency of achieving results.

Chapter 3, which highlights the imperative of developing health systems to provide a continuum of quality care and focuses on the benefits of employing community partnerships in countries with weak health-system capacity, will show how the knowledge gleaned is being used. The results are often promising and sometimes impressive, but much more can be done – and there is a great deal more to be learned – about scaling up these approaches to reach the millions of mothers, newborns and children who currently live or die without access to quality health care.

SUMMARY Reaching the health-related Millennium Development Goals will necessitate strengthening health systems at all levels – facility-based services, formal public health programmes and community partnerships. A growing body of evidence shows that improved health practices in the community and household, combined with opportunities for health-system referrals, can have a powerful impact on reducing under-five mortality. As a result, integrated health systems and community-based primary health care are once again receiving greater attention and emphasis in national policies and international health partnerships and programmes.

Experience shows that successful community partnerships are based on several common factors: cohesive and inclusive community organization and participation; support and incentives for community health workers; adequate programme supervision and support; effective referral systems to facility-based care; cooperation and coordination with other programmes and sectors; secure financing; and integration with district and national programmes and policies.

National leadership and ownership of community partnerships are essential to ensure sustainability and foster expansion. Governments have a critical role in developing and implementing policies to lower barriers to primary health care, in improving the quality and efficiency of service providers and in increasing public accountability.

Community partnerships are essential to reducing maternal, newborn and under-five mortality. *A community development motivator, India.*

Developing effective, child-focused health policies and building strong institutions that link communities and health systems are crucial steps towards achieving the health-related Millennium Development Goals, because, in many countries, increases in health expenditure will need to be accompanied by substantial improvements in the policy environment to achieve significant progress. Donors, in turn, need to rally behind national polices and strategies for improved maternal and child survival, health and nutrition, and together with governments, they must invest sufficient human and financial resources to scale up and strengthen community partnerships.

Community partnerships in primary health care for mothers, newborns and children

The role and importance of community partnerships

When infants and children become sick, it is their families, especially parents and other primary caregivers, who form the first line of care. Household members, particularly mothers, undertake the primary diagnosis of illness, assess the severity and probable outcomes, select treatment and care options – including home treatment – and procure and administer drugs and other remedies. Families and caregivers make the decisions to seek formal health care for pregnant women or children who have fallen ill, and they decide whether to adopt diverse feeding and hygiene practices.

Empowering communities and households to participate in the health care and nutrition of mothers, newborns and children is a logical way of enhancing the provision of care, especially in countries and communities where basic primary health care and environmental services are lacking. The imperative of community participation in health care and nutrition for individuals and families was

established almost three decades ago, along with the movement that led to the concept of comprehensive primary health care embodied in the Declaration of Alma-Ata in 1978.[1] It has long been clear that without the participation of communities, the goal of "health care for all" will remain severely constrained, particularly in the most marginalized and impoverished areas.[2]

The known benefits of community partnerships form part of the learning experience required to improve health care over the longer term. Community participation is viewed as a mechanism to reduce and eventually eliminate profound disconnections between knowledge, policy and action that impede efforts to address both the supply and demand sides of care.[3]

The importance of participation in health care, hygiene practices, nutrition, and water and sanitation services goes beyond the direct benefits to community members as they engage in activities that can impact positively on their health. It forms the heart of a rights-based approach to human

progress. Participation is critical to enable people to achieve their full capabilities, exercise their rights to engage in public and community affairs, and foster equity, equality and empowerment – characteristics that are fundamental to sustainable human development and to the objectives of such compacts as the Universal Declaration of Human Rights, the Convention on the Rights of the Child, the Convention on the Elimination of All Forms of Discrimination against Women and the Millennium Declaration, among many others.

A multiplicity of community partnerships

There is no universal definition of community in the literature on public health, and it can be broadly or narrowly defined, depending on circumstances. Intuitively and in practice, however, 'community' often refers to a group of people residing in a specific geographic area who have common interests, heritage and shared assets. They may also experience similar deprivations of their rights to quality health care, adequate nutrition, and safe water and sanitation.[4]

© UNICEF/ HQ05-2186/Giacomo Pirozzi

Supporting pregnant women through community outreach enhances care for both mother and child. *HIV counselling for pregnant women at a local health centre, the Democratic Republic of the Congo.*

Based on this broad definition of community, *community partnerships* are approaches and strategies that seek to actively engage community members in their own health care and well-being, along with those of their children and other dependants.

Community partnerships in maternal, newborn and child health are rich in diversity. Some are small-scale, involving only a few thousand or even a few hundred people; other initiatives, such as the Brazilian community health workers network or the Lady Health Workers programme in Pakistan, encompass thousands of workers covering millions of children and women. Some programmes emphasize supply-side elements, such as service provision through community health workers, while others focus more on demand-side initiatives to mobilize social demand for accountability and results from governments. Some community health worker initiatives rely on voluntary participation, while oth-

ers include payment in kind, in part or in cash. Some community-based programmes are nationally supported and integrated into sector-wide policies and the broader health system, while others have yet to be fully or partially incorporated.[5]

The multiplicity of programmes and approaches to community participation in health care reflects, in part at least, the diversity of communities. Each one has its own social characteristics, organizational structure and links with other groups. To be effective, programmes and approaches directed towards communities must therefore adapt to the local needs and context and be owned by the community.

Adaptation of strategies for individual settings is a complex process because communities, like countries and regions, are often heterogeneous entities. Not only are there marked differences between communities in a particular country or district, there

are likely to be disparities within them as well. Members of communities may share common heritage and interests and experience similar deprivations, discrimination and disempowerment, but different members will have specific needs, concerns and expectations regarding health care. Communities are likely to comprise powerful individuals with the potential to help or hinder a health programme, depending on their viewpoint or interests.

Despite these variations, evidence and observation allow for the identification of common factors in community-based approaches to health care and nutrition. An overarching aim is that community-based programmes increase the potential of the local population to access health services and interventions. In addition, they are perceived as having the potential to accelerate advances in behaviour change, care practices and care seeking, and to empower communities and households to demand quality services.[6] Other common aspects of community-based approaches to health care and nutrition are illustrated in the panel on page 48.

Success factors in community partnerships

Several factors are commonly found in successful community-based approaches. Implementation in any setting depends on the local context. Identifying successful factors is not only a positive way of assessing

Basic practices for community-based health-care interventions

A number of agencies, including UNICEF and WHO, have agreed on 12 key household practices for neonates and infants that can help to promote child survival, health and nutrition in communities:

- *Exclusive breastfeeding:* Exclusive breastfeeding from birth to six months. (Mothers found to be HIV-positive require counselling about possible alternatives to breastfeeding.)

- *Complementary feeding:* Starting at about six months old, feeding children energy- and nutrient-rich complementary foods while continuing to breastfeed for at least two years could prevent more than 10 per cent of deaths from diarrhoea and acute respiratory infections, particularly pneumonia; and increase resistance to measles and other illnesses.

- *Micronutrient supplementation:* Improving the intake of vitamin A through diet or supplements in communities where it is deficient could reduce mortality among children aged 6 months to five years by 20 per cent.

- *Hygiene:* Better hygiene practices, particularly hand washing with soap (or ashes) and the safe disposal of excreta could reduce the incidence of diarrhoea by 35 per cent.

- *Immunization:* Vaccination against measles for children under age one could prevent most of the measles-related deaths each year. Caregivers should make sure children complete a full course of immunizations (bacille Calmette-Guérin; diphtheria, pertussis and tetanus vaccine; oral polio vaccine; and measles vaccine) before their first birthday.

- *Malaria prevention:* The use of insecticide-treated mosquito nets in households in malaria-endemic areas could lower malaria-related child deaths by as much as 23 per cent.

- *Psychosocial care and development:* Promote mental and social development by responding to a child's need for care and by talking, playing and providing a stimulating environment.

- *Feeding and fluids for sick children:* Continue to feed and offer more fluids, including breast milk, to children when they are sick.

- *Home treatment:* Give sick children appropriate home treatment for infections.

- *Care seeking:* Recognize when sick children need treatment outside the home, and seek care from appropriate providers.

- *Appropriate practices:* Follow the health worker's advice about treatment, follow-up and referral.

- *Antenatal care:* Every pregnant woman should have adequate antenatal care. This includes having at least four antenatal visits with an appropriate health-care provider and receiving the recommended doses of tetanus toxoid vaccination. The mother also deserves support from her family and community in seeking care at the time of delivery and during the postpartum and lactation period.

Further important practices that protect children include: providing appropriate care for those who are affected by HIV and AIDS, especially orphans and vulnerable children; protecting children from injury and accident, abuse and neglect; and involving fathers in the care of their children.

Many of these practices can be undertaken by community health workers or by community members themselves, given the appropriate support and distribution of products and services. The direct involvement of the community is perhaps most appropriate for those aspects of health care and nutrition that most closely affect members on a daily basis. These include infant and young child feeding, other caring practices, and water and sanitation.

See References, page 107.

---

programmes and 'learning by doing', it is far easier than trying to disaggregate the elements that did not work in a community-based programme from the contextual factors. Consequently, while the panel on page 48 lists several of the common challenges to community partnerships in primary health care, the chapter will concentrate mostly on identifying and explaining the common tenets of successful initiatives.

Success factors drawn from evidence and experience are identified as follows and summarized below. They include:

- Cohesive, inclusive community organization and participation.

- Support and incentives for community health workers.

- Adequate programme supervision and support.

- Effective referral systems to facility-based care.

- Cooperation and coordination with other programmes and sectors.

- Secure financing.

- Integration with district and national programmes and policies.

Each of these tenets is briefly summarized in the following pages.

Cohesive, inclusive community organization and participation

Cohesive, inclusive organization is a fundamental feature of successful community partnerships. Communities function under established norms and practices that are often deeply entrenched in social, religious or cultural heritage. Programmes that respect this heritage have been found to be among the most successful community-based approaches to health care and nutrition. In Asia, for example, the large-scale initiatives undertaken in Bangladesh (BRAC), India (Jamkhed and others), Pakistan (Lady Health Workers) and other countries have been led by local organizations – often women's groups. These groups have built on the established structures within communities that extend to other areas of development, including education and credit, as well as health.[7]

Common aspects and challenges of community partnerships in health and nutrition

Overarching aim

- Reduce maternal, newborn and child mortality and morbidity.

Objectives

- Improve access to basic preventive and curative services.

- Foster direct and more frequent contact between health workers and caregivers, mothers and children.

- Encourage sustainable behaviour change.

- Support caring practices.

- Stimulate social mobilization by the community to demand better services and accountability.

Central features

- Health care and nutrition activities take place outside formal health facilities.

- Community health workers, often volunteers or part-time workers, are frequently key participants in dispensing essential services and promoting better caring practices.

- Training, support and supervision for community health workers are common features of programmes.

- There is often a central point within the geographical vicinity for the delivery of services or home visits.

- A community organization supports the programme and contributes not only administration and implementation, but often design and evaluation as well.

- Other aspects of primary health care – especially water and sanitation, and agricultural interventions – are part of the programme.

Additional features common to some, but not all, community partnerships

- Referral to facility-based care.

- Support from outreach workers.

- Integration of the programmes into the wider health sector.

- Integration into national development programmes and policies.

- Measures to strengthen the supportive environment, e.g, gender equality initiatives.

Common constraints on community partnerships

- Lack of community health workers to deliver quality services.

- Inadequate coordination of diverse participants.

- Insufficient funding for community-based activities.

- Irregular supply of drugs and commodities.

- Poor support and supervision of community health workers.

- Entrenched traditional childcare practices.

- Low economic status of women.

See References, page 107.

Organization alone is not sufficient to bring lasting change. To be truly effective and universal in scope, community participation must be socially inclusive. Given that communities are often heterogeneous in composition and structure, establishing a socially inclusive community partnership may be challenging. Long-held patterns of exclusion and discrimination by gender, religion, ethnicity or disability can impede the reach of interventions. Divisions among community members may also be rooted in more recent events and circumstances, such as civil strife and the stigma attached to HIV and AIDS.[8]

Even when communities have respected, socially inclusive organizations, their participation in programmes is not automatic. Advocacy and communication are required to allow community organizations to state their preferences and needs for health care, nutrition, and water and sanitation services. Once a programme is launched and implemented, community members need to see that it is progressing towards their stated objectives, both individually and collectively. As programmes progress, their ongoing relevance should also be regularly assessed.[9]

Programmes that limit community participation to implementation run the risk of weak local ownership, with the result that participation will be tentative and tenuous.[10] Periodic meetings of community organizations involved with community programmes are an important component of participation. At these meetings, the results and evidence can be discussed as part of planning, monitoring and evaluation.

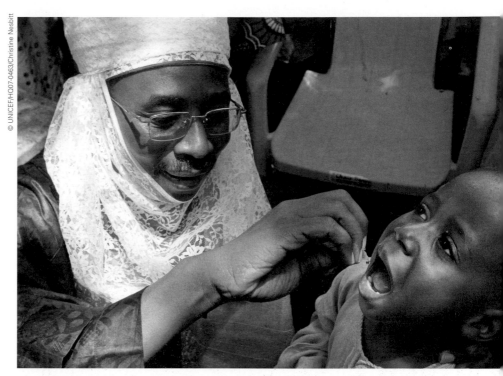

© UNICEF/HQ07-0463/Christine Nesbitt

Village leaders can be strong advocates for promoting essential health interventions within communities. *A district chief vaccinates his son against polio, Nigeria.*

Support and incentives for community health workers

Community health workers are established as an integral part of community-based programmes, serving as a bridge between professional health staff and the community, and helping communities identify and address their own health needs.

Community health workers are generally the main agents of community-based treatment, education and counselling, usually through household visits. They also attend local health facilities, obtain and dispense supplies of drugs and other essential products, participate in community meetings and fulfil their responsibilities in programme management. Other duties often include attending local district and regional meetings for training and feedback, and repre-

senting the community in dialogue with other communities and government health personnel.

Because they can reach vulnerable children who may otherwise lack access to basic health services, community health workers have been particularly effective in improving child survival outcomes at project level in countries as diverse as Ecuador, Ethiopia, Colombia and Nepal. Successful scale-up efforts across the developing world confirm the potential of community health workers to deliver equitable health services to children living in remote areas and to help fill the unmet demand for regular health services in countries with weak health systems.

Efforts to scale up community health worker programmes,

addressed in greater depth in Chapter 4, can face obstacles and bottlenecks. In fact, just being able to maintain adequate participant numbers and structure is often one of the greatest challenges. Existing programmes, regardless of their scale, grapple with poor training, inadequate supervision, lack of supplies and poor relationships with the communities they intend to serve. Attrition rates in community health worker programmes are often high. One review, for example, found attrition rates of 30 per cent over nine months in Senegal and 50 per cent over two years in Nigeria. Similar challenges have been identified in India, Sri Lanka and the United Republic of Tanzania.[11]

Attrition is related to multiple factors. Fulfilling the responsibilities of a community health worker takes time and financial resources, and may involve significant opportunity costs. Community health workers, particularly those who are volunteers or paid in kind or part, may have obligations to meet and require income to support their families. If the demands on their time and resources prove overwhelming, there is a risk they will not function effectively as health workers or will drop out of community partnerships.

The sustainability of community health worker programmes depends on creating a package of incentives that is sufficiently attractive to prevent attrition. These packages will vary among settings, reflecting the different functions community health workers undertake in different communities. But all need to focus on priorities that include compensating community health workers for lost economic opportunities; providing adequate supervision and peer support; offering personal growth and development opportunities; and creating a strong support system within the community.[12]

India: Reducing undernutrition through community partnerships

Challenge

Despite vast improvements in the country's economy, undernutrition continues to be a problem in India. In 1999, the National Family Health Survey found that 47 per cent of all children under age three were underweight – a higher average prevalence than in sub-Saharan Africa. Data from the most recent round of the survey, completed in 2006, show only a very small decline, with undernutrition levels remaining around 45 per cent for children under three; in several states, such as Madhya Pradesh and Bihar, undernutrition levels have increased since the previous survey. Reasons for this high prevalence include the inadequate knowledge of caregivers concerning correct infant and young child feeding, frequent infections worsened by bad hygiene, high population pressure, the low status of women and girls, and suboptimal delivery of social services.

To combat undernutrition in young children, the Government of India relies largely on the Integrated Child Development Scheme (ICDS). Begun in 1975, the scheme provides health and nutrition education for mothers of infants and young children, along with other services, such as supplementary nutrition, basic health and antenatal care, growth monitoring and promotion, preschool non-formal education, micronutrient supplementation and immunization. These services are delivered through a network of some 700,000 community anganwadi workers. The effectiveness of ICDS has been limited, however, by a variety of factors, ranging from the limited skill and knowledge of anganwadi workers to a lack of supervision, vacancies and flaws in programme policy, such as inadequate focus on very young children.

Strategy and approach

UNICEF is collaborating with the Government of India to increase the effectiveness of ICDS. The specific interventions supported include: strengthening the management and supervision system; improving the knowledge and skills of anganwadi workers and increasing the time and attention they give to infants; improving community involvement through joint village situation analysis, identifying village volunteers and providing them with basic training in infant care; and increasing the number of home visits made by anganwadi workers and volunteers in order to increase the caring behaviour of parents and improve the outreach of health services.

Results

The strategy described above was carried out in six states, in each of which at least 1,000 villages were covered, affecting more than a million people per state. After the interventions had been operational for about three years, impact assessments were conducted in several of the states, using representative household-based surveys to compare intervention villages with socially, economically and geographically similar control villages. In Rajasthan, for instance, it was found that early initiation of breastfeeding was higher and the prevalence of stunting significantly lower in intervention

The incentives required to retain and motivate community health workers are not necessarily monetary. The disappointing results of evaluations of post Alma-Ata large-scale training and deployment of community health workers underscore the fact that sound programme management and refresher training are more efficacious at sustaining workers' effectiveness than initial training. Active community participation and support is a vital element of successful and sustainable community health worker programmes throughout the world. In the Philippines, for example, health workers at the *barangay* level, the smallest political unit in the country, have become a significant driving force behind improved child survival. This success has been encouraged by the Barangay Health Workers' Benefits and Incentives Act of 1995, which includes such provisions as subsistence allowances, career enrichment and special training programmes, and preferential access to loans. Similarly, in Ceara, Brazil, a programme using a decentralized approach that allows community health workers to earn a substantial monthly income (twice the local average) has led to dramatic improvements in child health, including a 32 per cent reduction in child mortality.[13]

Adequate programme supervision and support

Supervision and support systems for community partnerships in primary health care can diminish the community health workers' sense of isolation and help sustain interest and motivation, reducing the risk of attrition. Skilled health workers based in, or closely linked to, health facilities generally undertake the supervisory function, which can add to their already heavy workloads. Supervisors themselves require training to acquire the appropriate skills for oversight of community-based programmes. Resource constraints – human, financial or organizational – can limit the breadth and

villages than in control villages (*see Figure 3.1*). In West Bengal, early initiation of breastfeeding (76 per cent in intervention villages versus 44 per cent in control villages), vitamin A supplementation (50 per cent versus 33 per cent) and immunization rates (89 per cent versus 71 per cent for measles) were higher in intervention villages than in control villages, and undernutrition rates were lower (27 per cent stunting versus 32 per cent). The cost of these 'add-on' interventions is modest: US$150–$200 per village per year, representing 9–10 per cent of the government's ongoing ICDS costs per village per year.

Lessons learned

Considering the continued high level of childhood undernutrition in India, it is important to demonstrate that low-cost changes can be made to the existing ICDS to significantly improve health care for infants and young children and that these changes can lead to nutritional improvements in a limited period of time. India has approximately 43 per cent underweight children under age five, so the success of low-cost solutions to undernutrition in the high-priority states of this country will have a global impact.

Remaining challenges

The governments of the states where these interventions are being implemented have decided to take them to larger scale using their own resources. UNICEF will continue to collaborate in order to assure that the quality of implementation remains adequate, as well as to address some behaviours that have been more difficult to change, such as the tendency of caregivers to delay the start of complementary feeding (much later than six months of age). Although the nutritional status of infants and children in the states involved has improved, it is clear there remains ample room for further improvement in the future.

See References, page 107.

Figure 3.1

Prevalence of stunting by age (months)

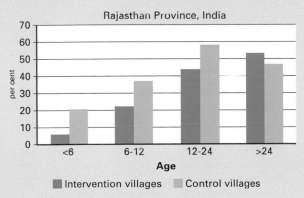

Rajasthan Province, India

■ Intervention villages ■ Control villages

Source: UNICEF India, *Annual Report 2006*, p. 47.

depth of training, leaving both supervisors and community health workers at a considerable disadvantage in implementing and managing programmes. Visits by supervisors to communities, in particular, are important for on-site training and learning by doing for both parties, but these visits are frequently compromised by constraints on financial resources or by poor transportation infrastructure.

Efficient administration of community programmes aids evaluation, and monitoring can help ensure that coverage is as universal as possible. Records of patients, treatments and outcomes should be kept up to date, and regular meetings should be held to build cooperative relationships between health workers and supervisors and to inform programme assessment and modification. Employing technology, such as computer-based databases, email and cellphones, can streamline the process of information gathering and dissemination while freeing time for workers and supervisors to visit communities and households and meet together.

Other types of support to programmes include logistics, supplies and equipment. Community health workers require sufficient tools, including training and products, to be able to do their job and maintain their standing in the community. The previously cited evaluations of large-scale community health worker programmes undertaken in the 1980s show that when these tools and products – especially drugs – are inappropriate or not resupplied regularly, the effectiveness of health workers is compromised. When communities are located far from supporting health facilities, evidence shows that programmes are more effective if there is a clear schedule of visits by supervisors and community

Preventing mother-to-child transmission of HIV: Impact of mothers2mothers programmes in eastern and southern Africa

The urgency of preventing mother-to-child transmission (PMTCT) of HIV is clear. An estimated 530,000 children were newly infected in 2006, mostly through mother-to-child transmission. Without treatment, half of the infants born with the virus will die before age two.

Significant reductions in mother-to-child transmission, however, can occur through implementation of basic but critical actions, such as identifying HIV-infected pregnant women by offering routine HIV testing, enrolling them in PMTCT programmes, ensuring that health systems are fully able to deliver effective antiretroviral regimens both for prophylaxis and for treatment, and supporting women in adhering to optimal and safe infant feeding.

Even when these services and interventions are available, many pregnant women do not access them because they do not receive the necessary information, they are afraid of attached stigma, or health-care workers are overextended. Lack of participation in programmes related to postpartum PMTCT is common in many countries, even if women have received PMTCT services during their pregnancy.

mothers2mothers (m2m) is an innovative, facility-based programme currently operating in 73 sites in South Africa and 15 sites in Lesotho. The programme adopts an approach using education and empowerment to prevent mother-to-child transmission of HIV, combat stigma within families and communities, and keep mothers alive through treatment adherence. Founded by Dr. Mitch Besser in 2001, m2m is based on the premise that mothers themselves are among the strongest mentors and supporters of expectant mothers.

The aim of m2m is to bring women in antenatal care together with peer counsellors and mentors to discuss health, HIV prevention and postpartum childcare. The programme trains and employs HIV-infected mothers who have already benefited by participating in PMTCT programmes as peer educators or 'mentor mothers', and is working with local health-care facilities and non-governmental organizations to implement a model that can be integrated with national PMTCT efforts in sub-Saharan Africa. Mentor mothers are peer educators for pregnant women. Their training allows them to counsel on HIV infection and antiretroviral treatment, promote behaviours to help prevent mother-to-child transmission, discuss the importance of appropriate follow-up for the mother and child after birth, and offer approaches for negotiating safer sexual practices and nutritional guidelines for women living with HIV.

The organization is expanding rapidly. It already has international partnerships in Botswana and Ethiopia and is in the process of rolling out new programmes in Kenya, Rwanda and Zambia.

health workers and preparations are in place for transportation to and from both locations.

Supervision should not be limited to the official health authorities, however, and community organizations have a role in oversight of health workers and programme outcomes. In principles widely accepted by practitioners, it is recommended that the community be involved in the initial selection of health workers, and that health workers accept community members' participation in identifying priorities and planning projects.[14]

Effective referral systems

Effective referral systems are an essential complement to successful community-based programmes to ensure a continuum of care (*see Chapter 4*). Hospitals provide services that cannot be safely replicated elsewhere, such as Caesarian sections and other emergency obstetric care. However, in the poorest countries with the highest maternal and child mortality rates, health-care resources are often limited and access to referral hospitals frequently low. In these situations, millions of children can be assisted

very rapidly by scaling up of proven, cost-effective interventions in primary health care, particularly those that are community-based.

At the same time, there is a need to invest in strengthening district health systems to provide basic referral care and to support expansion of essential primary-health-care services. Community health workers have proved to be effective in managing many serious childhood illnesses, such as diarrhoea, malaria, acute undernutrition and pneumonia; supervision and access to referral services strengthen the quality of this activity.

The importance of programmes like m2m cannot be overstated, given the growing escalation of treatment regimens and the stretched resources of many health facilities in settings of high HIV prevalence. New PMTCT guidelines from the World Health Organization are calling for introduction of more complex antiretroviral regimens in an effort to further reduce rates of transmission from mother to child. There is greater emphasis on increasing access of HIV-infected pregnant women to treatment for their own health, and a push to ensure that more children coming from PMTCT programmes receive early diagnostic testing. Programmes such as m2m, which involve committed, knowledgeable members of the community to promote the success of PMTCT initiatives, are increasingly vital in supporting health providers in the prevention and treatment of AIDS.

m2m strongly believes that mentor mothers should be appropriately recognized for their significant contributions. According to Dr. Besser, "Mentor mothers who have gone through PMTCT services themselves are recruited locally and paid a stipend for the work they do, making them professional members of the health-care team."

An independent evaluation of m2m was recently conducted by the Population Council's Horizons Programme. Several encouraging results associated with programme participation were noted, including the following:

- Postpartum women who had two or more contacts with m2m were significantly more likely to have disclosed their serostatus to someone than non-participants (97 per cent for participants against 85 per cent for non-participants; p-value <.01).

- Postpartum programme participants were significantly more likely to have received nevirapine to prevent mother-to-child transmission of HIV than non-participants (95 per cent for participants against 86 per cent for non-participants; p-value <.05).

- m2m programme participants were significantly more likely to report an exclusive method of feeding (either exclusive breastfeeding or infant formula but no breast milk) than non-participants.

- m2m participants were significantly more likely to undergo CD4 testing during their last pregnancy than non-participants (79 per cent vs. 57 per cent; p-value <.01). (CD4 cells are white blood cells that form a key part of the human immune system. They are also those most vulnerable to HIV infection. The lower the CD4 cell count, the weaker the immune system and the higher the risk of opportunistic infection.)

See References, page 107.

Leadership brings change for mothers and children in Ethiopia

by Tedros Adhanom, Minister of Health, Ethiopia

Ethiopia's experience with child survival shows that strong political leadership can bring about dramatic results. In 2004, Prime Minister Meles Zenawi challenged the Government and its partners to join him in charting a road map for universal health care, despite the enormous obstacles that stood in its path. While more than 80 per cent of child deaths are preventable, coverage and utilization of preventive services remained low, with less than 30 per cent of women receiving antenatal care and only 49 per cent of children receiving a full course of immunizations by their first birthday.

The Health Extension Program

The Government and its partners are tackling these challenges head-on through the Health Extension Program, a national strategy designed to promote community-based child and maternal health. Grounded in the philosophy that health is a product that can be produced by individuals, the Health Extension Program empowers communities to make informed decisions about their own health by equipping them with appropriate skills and knowledge.

To make this plan a success, the Government is deploying 30,000 female Health Extension Workers (HEWs) – a huge commitment of financial and human resources – to promote 16 basic interventions that address the major causes of child and maternal mortality. More than 17,000 HEWs have been employed to date, and an additional 7,000 are in training. Each *kebele* (the lowest administrative unit) is staffed by HEWs, who are locally recruited and trained by the Ministry of Health. The Government has also put in place an Enhanced Outreach Strategy, a transitional programme that delivers emergency and basic care to communities while they await the arrival of trained health workers.

At the same time, initiatives are under way to strengthen the infrastructure that supports referral-level hospitals. The Government is investing in a Health Management Information System designed to collect data at all levels, including the health post. In October 2006, the Government adopted a national Health Commodities Supply System to ensure that vaccines, essential drugs and other health commodities are readily available to public sector health facilities. These initiatives are vital to ensuring the sustainability of the progress made to date with vertical and community-based health initiatives.

Lessons learned

The Health Extension Program has taught a number of valuable lessons. The first is that scaling-up requires speed, volume, and quality. Robust planning processes have helped to ensure speed and volume. For instance, when the Government organized a national campaign for the distribution of insecticide-treated mosquito nets, donor partners, particularly the Carter Center, the Global Fund, UNICEF and the World Bank, coordinated their support for the national campaign, helping to achieve the target of 20 million nets within two years. Each household received two bed nets, which are used to protect primarily women and children against malaria.

The second lesson is that speed and volume do not necessarily ensure quality. Extra effort is needed to ensure that households know when and how to use health resources, including mosquito nets. The female HEWs are working to bridge communication gaps between the health sector and the communities it serves by winning the confidence of communities and talking directly to mothers.

The third, and perhaps most vital, lesson learned is the paramount importance of political leadership. Genuine political leadership requires active and meaningful engagement in every step of the process – from identifying the problem and setting targets, to mobilizing resources, and fostering community participation. Public discussion on health-care needs and priorities, and cooperation among all stakeholders, including donors, health-care providers, and communities, has helped foster broad ownership of the Health Extension Program.

Our partners, including UNICEF and other donors, support the national planning process, harmonizing their activities and support for Ethiopia's priorities. It is a tremendous achievement that all donor partners have signed a code of conduct and endorsed a single harmonization manual, which aims to create one plan, one budget and one final report. This is an ambitious objective that we are working together to achieve over the long term.

Ethiopia's road map to achieving MDG 4 still faces a number of hurdles, but the progress made to date demonstrates that our vision for universal access to affordable health care can be a reality.

Positive behavioural changes in the household and community lead to improvements in maternal, newborn and child health. *A community health worker demonstrates the use of water-treatment supplies, Indonesia.*

Community health workers have been less effective in identifying and managing complications during childbirth. Reducing maternal mortality therefore requires the scaling up of skilled attendance at birth with referral systems for emergency obstetric care.

District health systems also serve as a focal point for public health programme coordination, integrating direct care for patients with population-based campaigns and supervision and coordination of community-based care and other lower level health services. At higher referral levels (regional or national hospitals) this role is often broadened to include such functions as training and

research, and technical support and quality assurance for lower levels.

An essential component of an effective referral system is good communication between the community programme participants and facility-based staff. Reinforcing points made in the previous sections, referral hospitals should engage with community programmes, provide strong support for community health workers and spend a significant proportion of time providing advice through person-to-person contact or other modes of communication. Upgrading information and communications technology can facilitate dialogue and referral, even in low-income countries.[15]

Coordination and cooperation with other essential services and sectors

Just as referral systems are essential to support and coordinate activities at the community level, cooperation and communication between programmes at the district level and intersectoral collaboration are also important. Coordination with other health services can take many forms. The possible benefits are multiple, including the sharing of new ideas, training, resources and evaluation skills; and early warning, management and containment of disease outbreaks.[16]

In Cambodia, for example, non-governmental organizations share

Community health workers are the driving forces of community partnerships in primary health care. *A health worker weighs a child and monitors his growth in a rural community, Iraq.*

© UNICEF/MENA06218/Shehzad Noorani

resources through a national Child Survival NGO Group that meets regularly in Phnom Penh. Members of this group and representatives from the Ministry of Health visit each other's projects to examine and learn from advances and adaptations in approaches to maternal, newborn and child health care.[17] Through such groups, international organizations have been able to share best practices around the world. For example, the Care Group methods mentioned in the panel on Mozambique on page 59 are also being employed in Cambodia, Malawi and Rwanda.[18]

Within communities, linkages between groups can also be important for health programme sustainability. A series of large-scale household surveys in seven areas of Colombia, Ecuador, Nicaragua and Peru was carried out to assess the practical operational issues in the distribution and usage of insecticide-treated mosquito nets. The surveys revealed wide variation in usage of treated mosquito nets, from 25 per cent of households in the Nicaraguan areas to 90 per cent in the Peruvian Amazon. In four of the study areas, local women's clubs manufactured the nets, which were then sold by village health workers in the communities, who placed the earnings in a revolving fund.[19]

Intersectoral collaboration involves working with all sectors that influence household and community health outcomes. Not only does such cooperation provide an integrated and potentially more sustainable basis for advances in health outcomes, it can also empower communities by structuring a platform for their input on a broader range of issues that affect their health. Without collaborative action, sectors may work in isolation or at cross purposes, possibly overlooking synergies that will allow for multiplier effects.

An integrated approach to maternal, newborn and child health necessitates collaborative action between programmes and sectors addressing health, nutrition, hygiene, major diseases and food security, as well as initiatives to address the lack of transportation infrastructure and access to water and sanitation facilities.[20]

Another crucial reason for intersectoral collaboration is the high prevalence of co-morbidity in sick children. Although this is addressed in part through Community Integrated Management of Childhood Illness, actions to fight disease are strengthened by simultaneously improving environmental conditions. For instance, in the case of diarrhoeal disease – which remains a major cause of child mortality – the child may also suffer from undernutrition. Intersectoral collaboration between community health workers and those responsible for the improvement of water and sanitation facilities is therefore imperative. Measures to improve feeding practices – through, for example, greater attention to food hygiene – are often undermined by poor and contaminated water supplies and inadequate sanitation facilities.[21] Similarly, measures to strengthen referral systems would benefit from improved road infrastructure, facilitating transport to and from health facilities for patients, health workers and essential medical and food supplies.

Secure financing

Financing for community-based health programmes may come from a variety of sources, including community members themselves; municipal or district governments via local health facilities; private patrons or community organizations; and national governments or non-governmental organizations at higher administrative levels within the country or overseas.

Securing financing for community-based programmes is a complex and sometimes contentious process, and an in-depth review of the arguments is beyond the scope of this report. Much of the financing for child health in low-income countries, however, will continue to be provided by external donors. For a community-based programme to be successful, it must be sustainable over the longer term, with the concurrent assumption that it requires

a firm financing base once donor funding is withdrawn.

This is far from easy. Countries and districts with low health-system capacity and limited financial means may struggle to maintain even medium-sized programmes in the absence of donor funding. In addition, there are no simple answers to developing financial structures that are sound and self-sufficient. In particular, health workers at the community level require some type of financial incentives to feed their families and secure their continued participation and motivation in the programme. Similarly, skilled but often underpaid professionals may require financial compensation for work in deprived areas and with community programmes.

Considerations of sustainability and equity mean that the issue of cost-sharing in the form of user fees for health care and other essential services within the community should be addressed by communities themselves. When fees are charged, they should be set at levels that do not hamper attendance for important services. Such services as immunizations and emergency care should be free. It is desirable that any cost-sharing schemes charged for services within the community be retained and managed by the communities themselves and used for activities that directly benefit them, such as purchasing drugs or performance incentives for health workers. Community health committees, ideally comprising community members, health workers and local health-facility managers, should be the conduit for payment of community health workers. When the community decides to charge fees for

health services, a system should be set up so those who cannot afford to pay, as determined by the community, will receive all services at no cost.[22]

Integration of community programmes into district services and national policies

Community partnerships in health, nutrition, water and sanitation and AIDS abound across the developing world. Their potential is not in doubt, though there are clearly many elements involved in making them a success and, correspondingly, many threats to their sustainability and reach. Two key elements that can help sustain and support community-based initiatives are active support from provincial and central governments, and integration into government policies, plans and budgets.

Maternal and child survival, health and nutrition should feature prominently in national and decentralized plans and budgets, with clear goals and concrete benchmarks. Strategies for child survival must be formulated through consultative processes, involving representatives from the community, district and national levels, as well as the donor community. Understanding variations in the epidemiological profiles that exist within a country is an essential first step towards developing a targeted strategy. Equally important are detailed assessments of financial realities and existing levels of infrastructure at the community, district and national levels of health-care delivery. These aspects are vital to the successful execution of a national strategy for child and maternal health and must, therefore, be considered at the outset of any planning exercise.

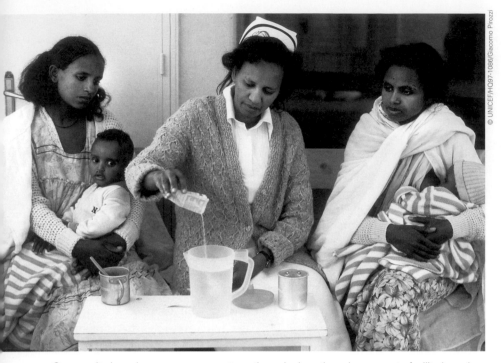

Community-based programmes are strengthened when there is access to facility-based care. *A health worker prepares a solution of oral rehydration salts, Eritrea.*

providers and in increasing public accountability. At the same time, health policies must be accountable to the communities and districts they serve. Governments and health systems must be closely attuned to the needs and interests of the population. Developing effective, child-focused health policies and building strong institutions between communities and health systems is critical; in most countries, increases in health expenditures will need to be accompanied by substantial improvements in the policy environment to achieve significant progress towards the health-related Millennium Development Goals.[25]

Finding the appropriate mix of solutions for enhanced health and nutrition outcomes

Each developing country has a unique mix of opportunities for, and constraints on, the development of its health system, owing to differing levels of economic progress, environmental and institutional circumstances, political situation and current health-system capacity. As a result, there is no universally applicable method of fostering improvement. Some may find that their greatest challenge lies not in scaling up community-based approaches to essential health-care packages nationwide, but in strengthening and expanding service delivery through facility-based programmes, decentralizing health services, and addressing non-communicable diseases and conditions, such as diabetes and obesity.[26]

For low-income countries, particularly those where large proportions

National strategies must give priority attention to the removal of obstacles to effective scaling up and implementation at different levels of the health systems (*see Chapter 4 for further details on measures to address bottlenecks in health-service delivery*). Well known bottlenecks include irregular immunization sessions, negative experiences with the health system, distance to health centres and lack of information. At the family and community level, effective coverage of primary-health-care services is often impeded by lack of basic affordable supplies, low demand and other fundamental challenges, such as mosquito nets not being treated with insecticide.[23]

Both the short-term, disease-specific initiatives – increasingly supported by new international donor partner-

ships – and longer-term, health-sector development programmes are likely to continue to coexist. Sufficient human and financial resources must be invested in both sets of initiatives to produce sustainable gains for child health. Donor-driven, disease-specific partnerships should consider adapting their approaches into multisectoral frameworks that align with national health priorities, with equitable benefits for the whole national health system.[24]

The ultimate responsibility for ensuring children's rights to health and nutrition lies with national governments in partnership with civil society. Governments have an important role in developing and implementing policies to lower the barriers to primary health care, in improving the quality and efficiency of service

Mozambique: Reducing under-five mortality through a community-based programme

Context and challenge: Mozambique is one of the world's poorest countries, with gross national income per capita of just US$340 in 2006 and an under-five mortality rate of 138 deaths per 1,000 live births. Life expectancy at birth is just 42 years, more than 40 per cent of children under five are suffering from moderate or severe stunting, and only one third of the population is using adequate sanitation facilities. Access to essential health-care services is limited, with 23 per cent of infants lacking a measles vaccine. Only 10 per cent of children sleep under a mosquito net (treated or untreated). And almost two thirds of the population live in rural areas, where only 1 in every 4 has access to an improved source of drinking water.

The challenge was to deliver an effective community-based child survival programme to rural communities with poor physical and environmental health infrastructure, and verify that the community programme contributed to mortality reduction.

Approach: The Chokwe Ministry of Health and World Relief partnership project in operation during 1999–2003 used the 'Care Group' approach to implement a child survival programme that aimed to address three elements of Community Integrated Management of Childhood Illness (C-IMCI):

• Improved partnerships between the health system and the community.

• Increased accessible care for community-based providers.

• Promotion of essential household practices for child health.

The Care Group approach trains community educators through group interaction. One volunteer Women's Health Educator provides peer-to-peer health education to 15 surrounding households, and 10 Women Health Educators form a Care Group that meets once a month with a paid supervisor. During monthly Care Group meetings, a health field staff member or a Women's Health Educator supervisor presents health messages about child survival and women's health. The Care Group members then practise training with each other, sharing the information presented. Before the next Care Group meeting, each volunteer is responsible for visiting the households under her jurisdiction to relay the messages she has just learned.

The child survival programme was designed to be comprehensive, integrating breastfeeding, complementary feed-

ing, use of oral rehydration therapy and insecticide-treated mosquito nets. The programme strengthened referral to local health facilities and case management of common illnesses at the facilities.

Partnerships with UNICEF and the International Committee of the Red Cross facilitated the provision of free insecticide-treated nets, vaccines and vitamin A supplements. Close cooperation with village health committees and local pastors provided support for the volunteers in carrying out health promotion and community mobilization for such as activities as distribution of insecticide-treated mosquito nets and conducting immunization campaigns.

Results: The project also implemented a community-based vital registration and health information system through the 2,300 community volunteers who collected data on births, deaths and childhood illnesses every month. These data were aggregated during the monthly meetings and the registers sent to health posts operated by community providers, or *socorristas*, who were trained by the district Ministry of Health. The collated information was sent back to local village health committees, health centres and the Ministry of Health.

Data from the community-based vital registration and health information system showed a 66 per cent reduction in infant mortality and a 62 per cent reduction in under-five mortality. To check the reliability of these findings, an independent mortality assessment was carried out by experienced researchers using a pregnancy history survey based on standard methodologies applied in the Demographic and Health Survey. This mortality survey found reductions of 49 per cent and 42 per cent in infant mortality and under-five mortality, respectively.

These results demonstrated the effectiveness of the Community IMCI and validated the fact that community health workers can collect reliable health data for monitoring mortality.

See References, page 107.

Community partnerships in water systems and school sanitation

Safe water systems in Afghanistan

The provision of safe water has been prioritized for many years in both emergency and ongoing development programmes throughout the world. Improving the quality of drinking water at the household level through point-of-use treatment and improved storage has been hailed by many as a simple and low-cost approach to preventing waterborne diseases. A development partnership has emerged between the Centers for Disease Control and Prevention, Population Services International, UNICEF, United States Agency for International Development (USAID) and WHO, as well as other institutions, to produce and distribute the products families need to achieve safe water in the household; together, these products are called safe water systems (SWS).

Safe water systems incorporate three elements:

• Point-of-use water treatment by consumers with a locally manufactured dilute sodium hypochlorite (bleach) solution.

• Safe storage of treated water in containers designed to prevent recontamination.

• Behaviour change with respect to improved water and food handling, sanitation and hygiene practices in the home and in the community.

Combining the skills and resources of various partners, SWS products are produced and distributed through public-private partnerships and market-based approaches, with community mobilization implemented by non-government organizations to encourage correct and consistent use and reach high-risk populations.

Safe water systems are being promoted and introduced in 23 countries worldwide, and have been shown to reduce the incidence of diarrhoeal disease by 25–84 per cent. They have been particularly effective in protecting the most vulnerable populations: infants, immunocompromised individuals and their families, and communities experiencing outbreaks of cholera.

In Afghanistan, a country with high maternal mortality and low ante- and postnatal attendance at health facilities, SWS have been introduced as part of the maternal health programmes. In order to attract greater attendance at health facilities, pregnant women and new mothers have been offered SWS and hygiene kits and taught how to use these simple technologies to protect themselves and their families.

Bangladesh: School sanitation and hygiene education

A water, sanitation and hygiene project in a remote village in Bangladesh, combined with a school sanitation and hygiene education (SSHE) component in the secondary school, demonstrate the importance of community participation and action and the positive impacts on the community. The village of Gava is located in south-western Bangladesh. NGO Forum decided to rethink its approach to water, sanitation and hygiene education at village level. One approach that seemed promising was to start with the village schools.

---

of mothers and children remain excluded from facility-based programmes, and whose health system capacity has been undermined by years of underinvestment and mismanagement, weak governance, mass migration of professional health workers, complex emergencies or the AIDS epidemic, determining the best strategy is neither straightforward nor without risks. In such countries, an important and perhaps overriding consideration is feasibility, under the guise of the following question: What is the most appropriate, cost-effective, timely and sustainable strategy for improving maternal, newborn and child survival and health and increasing coverage of essential services and commodities, given the current strength of a country's health, nutrition and environmental health systems?[27]

The feasibility paradigm aims to address the urgent needs of the poorest and most marginalized societies – where maternal, newborn and child mortality rates are highest – that are most lacking in basic preventive services, such as immunization and access to drugs and emergency care. In countries with relatively weak health, nutrition and water and sanitation systems and low health-system capacity, community-based approaches that rely less on health facilities and outreach services can help expand coverage of essential services, products and practices – particularly if basic preventive services such as immunizations are already in place.[28] It must be stressed, however, that in order to underpin sustainability, the expansion of

Young people of school age are open to new information and can be easily motivated, and the organization was keen to utilize this potential.

'WatSan' Committees were formed at the level of the school and for each class. The school headmaster was selected as the chairperson of the School WatSan Committee. The class committees consisted of teachers and students, both girls and boys, for each class of the school. A number of orientation sessions were organized for these committees, covering such issues as the promotion and use of safe water, better sanitation and hygiene practices, effective interpersonal communication between students and parents, and community mobilization. Motivational film shows were organized, and different behavioural change information, education and communication materials were distributed among the teachers and students for use in conducting group discussions in the community.

The students organized rallies and processions using different types of promotional posters and banners, chanting slogans on the importance of using safe water and hygienic latrines, and practising improved personal hygiene. This raised mass awareness throughout the village. Along with the committees, student brigades consisting of five boys and girls were formed in each class. These groups monitored the use of safe WatSan and hygiene practices at the household level. They also provided help with non-technical primary-health-care services, such as oral rehydration. The brigades also made plans to respond to natural disasters. Another

committee, the 'Teachers' and Parents' Forum', was created and held quarterly meetings to review progress.

A review of the project demonstrated that SSHE can contribute to the well-being and performance of students, for example, in helping to keep girls in school. Involving schools and students as community motivators is a powerful tool in improving WatSan and hygiene practices. In Gava village, before-and-after studies show greater knowledge of related diseases, an increase in the construction and use of hygienic latrines, higher usage of safe drinking water and increased hand washing by heads of households. The process of motivation started from the top and continued to the bottom.

NGO Forum is expanding from a few pilot villages to working in many more, each needing a programme approach. It is faced with two major issues. One is to refine the finances of such village projects so that maintenance becomes self-sustainable, and the other is to achieve the same impact in many villages with far fewer inputs. Nevertheless, there are great potential benefits from such programmes to the students and the communities they live in. Pilot projects such as this one in Gava demonstrate that the benefits are achievable.

See References, page 107.

community partnerships must be conducted in conjunction with efforts to overcome system-wide bottlenecks in facility-based maternal and child health and nutrition services, and address other behavioural, institutional and environmental constraints.

The next chapter focuses on scaling up community partnerships in health, nutrition and environmental health care. Although many of the arguments cited are perhaps most applicable to low-income countries and marginalized or impoverished communities,

much of the discourse is also relevant to countries and communities in less challenged circumstances.

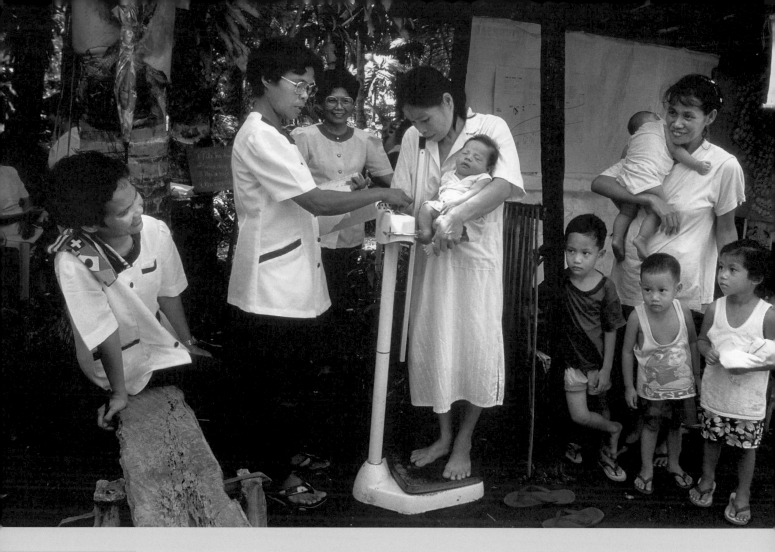

SUMMARY Accelerating progress in child survival will require applying the lessons learned from a century of health-sector development and taking effective approaches to strengthen community partnerships, the continuum of care and health systems.

This chapter brings together two strands – *action and partnerships* – into a framework for effective scale-up of a continuum of care for maternal, newborn and child health as the primary means to ensure health- system development for outcomes. It outlines five distinct yet related actions required in programmes, policies and partnerships in the coming decade.

Action I: Realign programmes from disease-specific interventions to evidence-based, high-impact, integrated packages to ensure a continuum of care.

Action II: Make maternal and child health a central tenet of integrated national planning processes for scaling up essential services.

Action III: Improve the quality and consistency of financing for strengthening health systems.

Action IV: Foster and sustain political commitment, national and international leadership and sustained financing to develop health systems.

Action V: Create conditions for greater harmonization of global health programmes and partnerships.

For governments, donors and international agencies and global health partnerships, effective scale-up will require a new way of working in primary health care among the key stakeholders. The central theme of this paradigm is *unity*. Initiatives and partnerships directed towards improving aspects of maternal and child health abound and continue to proliferate, but they will require greater coherence and harmonization to meet the health-related Millennium Development Goals for mothers and children.

Scaling up essential health-care interventions and approaches requires a comprehensive understanding of both the strategies that accelerate progress and the challenges that hinder it. *A health worker weighs a baby for growth monitoring, Philippines.*

Strengthening community partnerships, the continuum of care, and health systems

The review of community partnerships presented in Chapter 3 underlines their potential to accelerate improvements in maternal, newborn and child health. Evidence shows, for instance, that using a combination of community outreach programmes and family-community care strategies at 90 per cent coverage could reduce neonatal mortality by 18–37 per cent, even in the absence of improvements in facility-based care services.[1] What is needed, therefore, are innovative strategies for exploiting the full potential of community partnerships in primary health care on a large scale, ideally as part of an overall effort to strengthen national health systems.

The lessons learned from taking effective approaches to scale are being applied in an increasingly collaborative manner. The key international agencies working for maternal and child survival and health – UNICEF, United Nations Population Fund, World Health Organization and World Bank – are working with donors, governments and other leading international organizations, such as the African Union, around frameworks

and strategies to scale up access to primary health care.

'Going to scale': What will it take?

Scaling up existing interventions is critical to accelerating progress on the health-related Millennium Development Goals for children and women – particularly in sub-Saharan Africa and South Asia, which together accounted for more than 80 per cent of all child deaths in 2006.

There is consensus on expanding the provision of essential services and practices on a grand scale, but it is evident that this may be easier said than done. Scaling up involves a complex range of actions, many of which are interrelated, to both achieve breadth and ensure the long–term sustainability of the expansion.

At the programmatic and policy levels, it is not enough simply to expand the delivery of packages of low-cost, proven interventions: Behavioural, institutional and environmental impediments that can impede access must also be addressed as part of the

scaling-up process. Success requires an in-depth understanding of these obstacles, as well as of the strategies for circumventing them.

For governments, donors and international agencies and global health partnerships, effective scale-up will require a new way of working in primary health care among the key stakeholders. Initiatives and partnerships directed towards improving aspects of maternal and child health abound and continue to proliferate, but without greater coherence and harmonization, these disparate efforts risk falling short of achieving the health-related MDGs in the coming years.

This chapter brings together these two strands – *action and partnerships* – into a framework for effective scale-up of a continuum of care for maternal, newborn and child health. It outlines five distinct yet related actions that are required in programmes, policies and partnerships in the coming decade:

- **Action I:** Realign programmes from disease-specific interventions to evidence-based, high-impact, integrated packages to ensure a continuum of care across time and place.

- **Action II:** Ensure that maternal, newborn and child health are a central part of an improved and integrated national strategic planning process for scaling up services and strengthening health systems.

- **Action III:** Improve the quality and consistency of financing for strengthening health systems.

- **Action IV:** Foster and sustain the political commitment, national and international leadership and sustained financing for guaranteeing access to the continuum of care.[2]

- **Action V:** Create conditions for greater harmonization of global health programmes and partnerships.

I. Realigning programmes

From interventions to a continuum of care

To date, much of the work and support of the international health community for maternal, newborn and child health has focused on disease-specific approaches, which have a strong evidence base and track record in scaling up. When well resourced, targeted, managed, funded and implemented at scale, specific interventions have often contributed to reductions in disease incidence and child mortality.

These interventions are not without their limitations, however – not least because they have often failed to consider upstream constraints, such as governance, management and human resource limitations. In addition, the targeted focus of disease-specific approaches may

limit synergies that could strengthen the broader health system.

Scaling up to achieve a continuum of care across time and place is increasingly viewed as one of the most promising ways to accelerate progress towards the health-related MDGs. However, the evidence base on the effectiveness and feasibility of the continuum of care is much less developed than for disease-specific interventions, and there is a growing need to gather evidence on how the latter approach can function in practice. It will require new frameworks and processes, especially with regards to the organization of programmes. These will call for several changes, namely:

- Specifying the intervention packages.

- Identifying benchmarks and targets

- Integrating delivery strategies.

Figure 4.1

Conceptual framework for scaling up primary health care in developing countries

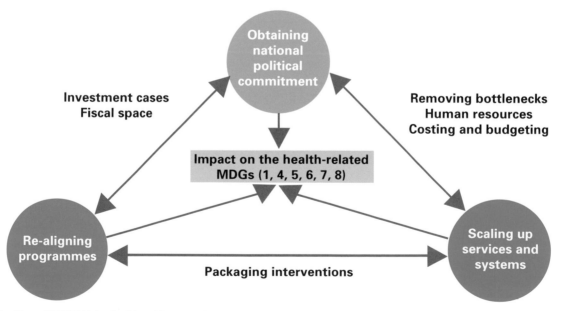

Investment cases
Fiscal space

Obtaining national political commitment

Removing bottlenecks
Human resources
Costing and budgeting

Impact on the health-related MDGs (1, 4, 5, 6, 7, 8)

Re-aligning programmes

Packaging interventions

Scaling up services and systems

Source: Derived from UNICEF, 'Joint Health and Nutrition Strategy for 2006-2015', UNICEF, New York, November 2005. p.10.

Scaling up the continuum of care will also require adapting programme management structures to reflect the integration of the various components of the intervention packages. This will necessitate enhancing institutional and individual capacities, overcoming resistance to change, and integrating and coordinating fragmented funding streams, particularly those coming from international donors and partnerships.[3]

Packaging interventions by service delivery mode

Packaging a range of evidence-based, cost-effective interventions has the potential to be among the most effective methods to accelerate improvements in maternal, newborn and child health. Scaling up requires that countries identify a continuum of care based on the following three service delivery modes:

- *Family-oriented, community-based services:* Provided on a regular basis by community health/nutrition promoters, with periodic oversight from skilled professionals.

- *Population-oriented scheduled services:* Provided by skilled or semi-skilled health staff, such as auxiliary nurses or birth attendants and other paramedical staff, through outreach or in facilities.

- *Individually oriented clinical services:* Interventions that require the attention of health workers with advanced skills, such as midwives, nurses or physicians, available on a permanent basis.[4]

The services delivered will depend on the country context and the capacity of its health system. The removal of bottlenecks can provide the scope for increased coverage.

Combining the delivery of interventions according to age-specific contacts with health and nutrition services can generate economies of scale in terms of both cost and time and enhance the number of services that are accessible to children and mothers. Packaging low-cost interventions, such as vaccines, antibiotics, insecticide-treated mosquito nets and vitamin A supplementation, and adding the promotion of improved feeding and hygiene practices, the packaged approach can markedly increase service coverage.[5]

Community partnerships are vital to the success of integrated packages. One effective intervention can often provide the entry point for successful integration of several measures into a child health package.

In Nepal, for example, the national vitamin A campaign trained community volunteers to build their capacities, creating a respected and credible cadre. By the time the volunteers were trained to assess and treat children for acute respiratory infections, they had already earned the trust of parents and developed the confidence necessary to perform this more complex task.

A similar experience is seen in Madagascar, where families are introduced to the importance of adopting several different improved health practices simultaneously, with immunization serving as the entry point for other services. An extensive community mobilization programme draws sustained attention to the essential actions required of families to promote children's health.[6]

Special attention to equity is needed when delivering packaged interventions to reach the poorest and most marginalized mothers and children. Although the packaged approach will indeed increase access to a greater range of services for many mothers and children at each point of delivery, it may also result in a growing gap in coverage between those with access to services and those who remain excluded.[7]

II. National strategic planning for scaling up services and strengthening health systems

Realigning primary health care from disease-specific interventions to a continuum of care and expanding the coverage of packaged interventions will require a sound policy base. This fact has been increasingly recognized in a series of high-level forums held since 2003 to assess ways of accelerating progress towards the health-related MDGs.[8] Over time, these gatherings have identified critical upstream constraints at the policy level that need to be urgently tackled to support effective scale-up. One of their main conclusions is that weak health systems and a lack of funding for health-system development risk limiting the impact of expanded efforts to fight specific diseases, as well as leaving mothers and children particularly vulnerable to a country's overall burden of disease.

Scaling up services and systems will require practical, effective strategies at the national level that take into account not only the potential for

Scaling up: Adequate nutrition for mothers, newborns and children

Undernutrition is the underlying factor in up to 50 per cent of under-five deaths, and there is evidence of links between a mother's nutritional status and the risk of maternal and child death. Among the developing countries and territories, more than one quarter of children under age five were moderately or severely underweight or stunted in 2000–2006, and 28 per cent of children aged 6–59 months were still not receiving vitamin A supplementation in 2005.

Food security, though necessary, is insufficient by itself to avert undernutrition, as evidenced by the many children who have been found to be underweight or stunted in food-secure or non-poor environments. Undernutrition results from an array of interrelated factors, including inappropriate feeding and care practices, inadequate sanitation, disease, poor access to health services, and weak knowledge of the benefits of exclusive breastfeeding, complementary feeding practices and the role of micronutrients. Diarrhoea, which often results from poor sanitation facilities and hygiene practices, is a contributing factor to undernutrition. Another contributing factor to undernutrition among infants and young children is the lack of supportive environments for many mothers, who may have limited time to care for themselves during pregnancy, or for their infants, due to household demands and insufficient access to health services.

Scaling up effective nutrition strategies across a continuum of care for mothers, newborns and children demands an integrated approach. It requires the sustained engagement of parents and communities, supported by local and national development of primary health care and environmental health services, particularly water and sanitation. When these prerequisites are in place, they can lead to remarkable results in a relatively short time. In Thailand, for example, moderate and severe undernutrition were reduced through such means by 75 per cent or more in a decade. And, in spite of considerable economic setbacks, many developing countries have made impressive progress in providing essential vitamins and minerals to their citizens. Nearly 70 per cent of households in developing countries consume iodized salt, about 450 million children now receive vitamin A capsules, and health strategies, particularly community partnerships, are employing new and innovative ways to promote and support breastfeeding.

Undernutrition in the developing regions is highest in South Asia, which has the highest rates of infants with low birthweights and of children under five who are moderately or severely underweight, wasted or stunted – and the lowest rates of vitamin A supplementation. Although sub-Saharan Africa has moderately better numbers for these indicators, it is the region with the lowest rates of exclusive breastfeeding for infants under six months, and severe acute undernutrition remains a pressing problem. The country examples below illustrate ways in which these issues are successfully being addressed in the region.

Benin: Teaching mothers about the importance of breastfeeding

In Benin, the 1996 Demographic and Health Survey (DHS) reported that only about 16 per cent of newborns in the Borgou Region were breastfed within the first hour, and in 1998 less than 1 in 5 infants under four months old, or 14 per cent, benefited from exclusive breastfeeding. To address this challenge, as well as some of the broader nutritional challenges associated the high rates of malnutrition and infant mortality, the Essential Nutrition Actions programme was introduced in 1997. In order to reinforce essential nutrition-related behaviours, the programme emphasized six measures in health facilities and communities:

- Exclusive breastfeeding for infants up to 6 months.

- Appropriate complementary feeding with continued breastfeeding from 6–24 months.

- Vitamin A supplementation for children.

- Iron and folic acid supplementation for pregnant women.

- Iodized salt supplementation.

- Support and counselling for undernourished and sick children.

Essential Nutrition Actions has effectively combined measures designed to strengthen the health system, such as training for health workers, with community mobilization and a large-scale communications campaign tailored to the specific conditions of the target populations.

Community leaders were actively involved in selecting community volunteers, known as *relais communautaires*, who provided the link between communities and health facilities and were trained in nutrition activities. Youth, traditional singers, community theatre groups, and women's and other community groups participated in workshops to develop messages and materials. Community theatre groups performed dramas in villages and neighbourhoods, while community radio stations broadcast spots, games and dramas developed in the workshops.

This vast community mobilization led to a genuine change in breastfeeding behaviour among mothers. In 2001, nearly 50 per cent of mothers with infants under four months old in these areas reported that their babies were exclusively breastfed. Furthermore, in 2002, selected communities in Borgou reported exclusive breastfeeding of infants under four months of 61 per cent, compared to 40 per cent in 1999.

Community-based management of severe acute undernutrition in Ethiopia, Malawi and Sudan

Severe acute undernutrition remains a major killer of children under five years of age. Until recently, treatment has been restricted to facility-based approaches, greatly limiting its coverage and impact, because in many poor countries children who are severely malnourished are never brought to a health facility. New evidence suggests, however, that large numbers of these children can be treated in their communities without being admitted to a health facility or a therapeutic feeding centre. The community-based approach involves timely detection of severe acute undernutrition in the community and provision of treatment for those without medical complications with ready-to-use therapeutic foods or other nutrient-dense foods at home. If properly combined with a facility-based approach for those undernourished children with medical complications and implemented on a large scale, community-based management of severe acute undernutrition could prevent the deaths of hundreds of thousands of children.

Recent evidence from Ethiopia, Malawi and Sudan illustrates the high impact and cost-effectiveness of community-based management of severe acute malnutrition. In contrast to treatment in health facilities – where in most developing countries fatality rates have remained largely unchanged for the past five decades – community-based therapeutic care has brought about a fundamental shift in the understanding of the disease and the implementation of treatment. To date, data from more than 20 programmes implemented in Ethiopia, Malawi, and North and South Sudan between 2000 and 2005 indicate these programmes achieved recovery rates of almost 80 per cent and reduced mortality rates to as little as 4 per cent. Coverage rates reached 73 per cent, while more than

three quarters of the severely undernourished children who presented were treated solely as outpatients. Furthermore, initial data indicate these programmes are affordable, with costs varying between US$12 and US$132 per year of life gained.

Community-based therapeutic care programmes use new, ready-to-use therapeutic foods that in many cases are made locally from local crops. Their implementation is based on three premises:

- Underlying all programmes is a strong emphasis on the importance of early care in the evolution of malnutrition and the need for patients to remain in a nutritional programme until recovery.

- Programmes start from the assumption that in order to present early and comply with treatment, families and communities must understand, accept and participate in the programmes.

- Programmes focus on the involvement of key stakeholders who can benefit from the feedback and attention successful programmes generate and thus have a stake in their long-term sustainability.

The results of community-based programmes to address severe acute undernutrition suggest that, even though they cannot eliminate the need for external assistance, scaled-up treatment can have a major public health impact, preventing hundreds of thousands of child deaths.

See References, page 108.

expansion of interventions but also the constraints and obstacles that might impede advances, outlining ways to overcome the latter. Key measures required in national strategic plans to scale up the packaged interventions outlined in the previous section include:

- Identify and remove health-system bottlenecks.

- Monitor progress and problems in coverage.

- Phase in intervention packages and health-system strengthening.

- Address the human resource crisis in health care.

- Develop health systems for outcomes.

- Strengthen health systems at the district level.

Identify and address health-system bottlenecks

Functional service delivery networks are necessary to provide a continuum of care, based on the three levels of service delivery outlined in the previous section: family and community; decentralized, close-to-client primary services; and facility-based referral care and specialized preventive services. An initial step involves gathering data and qualitative information on all existing service providers (public, private and informal) and organizations (including non-governmental organizations) that can be mobilized in support of the scaling-up effort.

One example of this process is provided by upper eastern Ghana, where

there are many non-governmental organizations supporting different health interventions. Collaboration between the Ghana Red Cross Mothers Clubs, the national health services and UNICEF under the Accelerated Child Survival and Development programme has succeeded in integrating the efforts of all these organizations and focusing their support on scaling up an evidence-based package of high-impact, low-cost interventions.[9]

Other important steps are to identify and analyse system-wide bottlenecks and constraints and to formulate strategies to remove or overcome them.[10] These may originate at the level of facilities, outreach or communities and households, or from the strategic and bureaucratic apparatus that sets policies, controls logistics and supplies, and drafts and implements regulations. Figure 4.2, page 69, illustrates the main potential bottlenecks to service delivery at each level of a country's health system, and the policy and governance context in which it operates. A new tool for analysing these constraints is Marginal Budgeting for Bottlenecks, outlined in the panel on page 70.

Many bottlenecks will demand a specific solution that involves addressing constraints at various levels of service delivery. For example, low demand for quality health services among community members or the limited capacity of health facilities and extension workers to deliver essential services may restrict the coverage of intervention packages, as may financial, social and physical barriers to access. Here, appropriately, the community partnerships elaborated in

Chapter 3 can play a unique and vital role in enhancing contact between dedicated health workers – including community health workers – and services, and households and communities that are currently lacking essential interventions. But facility-based care and outreach workers will be required both to support community health workers and to provide services for many health interventions that require more specialized assistance.[11]

Improving the performance and motivation of health workers and ensuring that facilities are adequately equipped and drugs are readily available are essential second-line requirements to support community partnerships in health and nutrition and to enhance the quality of service delivery. Part of the solution to improving service delivery undeniably involves increasing resources – human, financial and managerial – and providing training, but other incentives and better human resource management may also be needed.

Higher-level determinants of health-system performance – policy and strategic management, multi-sectoral public policies and environmental and contextual change – are among the most complex challenges for health-system development, for they form part of a political and institutional context that may not change readily or easily.[12] Nonetheless, sound leadership, advocacy, technical assistance and partnerships can help to prompt change.

Monitor progress and constraints in expanding coverage

Regular monitoring, feedback and adaptation of programmes on the basis of evaluation and evidence are widely recognized as integral components of a well functioning health system. Without these, rigorous assessment of programmes' effectiveness is not possible. Sound, evidence-based public health calls for a solid knowledge base on disease frequency and distribution, on the determinants and consequences of diseases and conditions, and on the safety, efficacy and effectiveness of interventions and their costs. Health surveys and research on the impact of approaches and strategies are imperative to collating essential evidence, learning key lessons and developing best practices.

Monitoring coverage is also vital to enabling rapid adjustments in policies and interventions to be made.

Measurements of the health-based MDGs depend considerably on such large-scale instruments as Demographic and Health Surveys (DHS) and Multiple Indicator Cluster Surveys (MICS). The MDG indicators provide core parameters by which progress towards the health-related goals can be measured. Many of these are provided as part of the minimum set of high-priority indicators for child survival that have been agreed upon by UNICEF and WHO in collaboration with partners in the context of the Countdown for Maternal, Newborn and Child Survival process.

MICS and DHS provide periodic data for determining effective coverage with the minimum package of essential interventions. To enhance surveillance, the interval between these surveys is

being reduced from five to three years. In addition, national, subnational and community-based monitoring processes are pivotal to analyse progress and problems in scaling up high-impact interventions.

Several developing countries are using innovative measures to monitor the impact of health programmes on populations and collate vital health information. One such country is Bolivia, where a census-based approach was used to identify the entire programme population through biannual visits to all homes. This census was then used to target selected high-impact interventions to those children at greatest risk of mortality. As a result of this approach, the mortality level of under-fives in areas where health programmes were

Figure 4.2

Ways of addressing bottlenecks in health-service delivery

ACTION	IMPACT
Select proven interventions.	Lower infant and maternal mortality.
Supervise training.	Improve quality of health-care provision (effective coverage).
Track defaulters and conduct home visits.	Improve the range and extent of health-care provision (adequate coverage).
Mobilize families and communities.	Enhance initial utilization of services (enhanced demand and affordability).
Implement health extension and micro-planned outreach.	Broaden geographic access to services.
Implement training and deployment of new staff by community promoters.	Increase availability of human resources in health-care provision.
Rationalize supply systems.	Bolster availability of drugs and other essential medical supplies.

Source: UNICEF, World Bank and World Health Organization, 'A Strategic Framework for Reaching the Millennium Development Goals in Africa through health system strengthening and implementing at scale of integrated packages of high-impact and low-cost health and nutrition interventions', draft prepared on request of the African Union by UNICEF, WHO and the World Bank, September 2006, p. 25.

'Marginal Budgeting for Bottlenecks'

'Marginal Budgeting for Bottlenecks' is a result-based planning and budgeting tool that utilizes knowledge about the impact of interventions on child and maternal mortality in a country, identifies implementation constraints and estimates the marginal costs of overcoming these constraints. This tool, which has been employed in the preparation of key strategic frameworks for maternal, newborn and child health in sub-Saharan Africa, was jointly developed by UNICEF, the World Bank and WHO. It is being used to assist in setting targets for proven high-impact interventions, and the estimation of their expected impact, cost per life saved and additional funding requirements, as well as a projection of the required fiscal space to finance these extra costs. (Fiscal space can be defined as the availability of budgetary room that allows a government to provide resources for a desired purpose, e.g., overcoming barriers to maternal, newborn and child health care without any prejudice to the sustainability of a government's financial position.)

Marginal Budgeting for Bottlenecks consists of five key steps:

- *An assessment of the key indicators, trends in and cause of maternal, newborn and child mortality and morbidity and access to essential services, and the selection and packaging of evidence-based, high-impact interventions* to address the proximate causes by service delivery mode, i.e., family/community-based care, schedulable population-oriented services and mobile strategies, or individually oriented clinical care at primary- and referral-level facilities.

- *Identification of system-wide supply and demand bottlenecks to adequate and effective coverage of essential primary-health-care services,* and obstacles to the application of high-impact intervention packages in each of the main service delivery modes. Adequate coverage includes such factors as the availability of essential drugs and supplies, access to health services and health workers, initial utilization of health-care services and continuity of usage of service. Subsequent examination of underlying causes of bottlenecks and the development of promising strategies to overcome them allows for the setting of 'frontiers' – coverage levels of intervention packages that are adequate, effective and achievable once bottlenecks are removed.

- *Estimation of the expected impact on survival rates for each of the interventions.* These estimations are based on recent, in-depth analysis of the evidence on the efficacy of high-impact interventions and packages in determining maternal and child survival and health outcomes. They are calculated in a residual way to avoid double counting survival rates.

- *Selection of the types, quantities and costs of additional inputs,* such as salaries, drugs and training, which are needed to implement the actions to overcome bottlenecks and to lift the effective coverage of intervention packages to their frontiers.

- *Analysis of budgetary implications, the identification of likely sources of funding and the comparison of the marginal costs and additional funding needs to the 'fiscal space'*

operating was one third to one half of the average under-five mortality rate in the control districts.[13]

Phase in intervention packages and strengthen health systems

It is increasingly recognized that actions to scale up packages of interventions may need to be phased, depending on such contingencies as budget availability, logistical constraints, technical capacity or socio-economic and cultural factors. While some interventions may be rapidly expanded, others will require a longer time frame. Scaling up minimum packages of essential interventions forms a key component of the new strategies, with the aim of achieving specific coverage targets. Intervention packages are being prepared to meet these agreed targets through the three core service delivery modes discussed previously, delivered in three phases.[14]

A phased approach to health service delivery will allow each country to define and implement an initial package of interventions that can then be expanded over time. Both the packaging and the delivery of the priority interventions will depend on the country's health-system capacity. The gradual removal of bottlenecks will facilitate the expansion of service delivery – including in situations of complex emergencies. Since the packaged approach is results-oriented, the implementation of priority interventions at scale can be planned and monitored in a phased manner.

The three phases recommended for expanding service delivery coverage

for health spending. (The fiscal space for health spending in each country is projected by the World Bank and the International Monetary Fund.)

Country examples of bottleneck analysis
Bottleneck analysis has been undertaken in around 25 developing countries and across the range of service delivery modes. Proxies used to assess the coverage determinants for each of the three modes of service delivery include the following parameters (the list is not exhaustive):

· *Family and community care:* Indicators include use of safe water and sanitation facilities, and of insecticide-treated mosquito nets; infant feeding and care for sick children and newborns.

· *Population-oriented schedulable services:* Indicators include levels of immunization and antenatal care.

· *Clinical care:* Indicators include skilled attendance at birth and emergency obstetric and neonatal care.

Results from countries where the tool has been used have revealed bottlenecks that were not immediately evident from the examination of levels or trend data.

As reported at recent workshops:

Honduras: A bottleneck analysis of water, sanitation and hygiene services revealed that despite ample access to improved drinking water, less than half of households consumed water that had been treated to make it safe. Strategies selected to address these bottlenecks include scaling up water treatment and providing information, education and communication initiatives to promote the exclusive use of safe drinking water.

Guinea: In 2000, 70 per cent of villages in the districts where the Accelerated Child Survival and Development (ACSD) programme was under way had a community health and nutrition promoter, 50 per cent of families owned a mosquito net, and 25 per cent of pregnant women slept under a net. However, effective coverage was found to be far lower than adequate coverage levels, since less than 5 per cent of individuals slept under a mosquito net that had been recently treated with insecticide. This bottleneck to protection against malaria was addressed through the free treatment of all existing mosquito nets with insecticide, combined with a heavily subsidized distribution of insecticide-treated mosquito nets that focused on pregnant women who were utilizing antenatal care and had completely immunized their children. By 2004, this integrated approach to removing bottlenecks had increased the effective coverage of insecticide-treated mosquito nets by 40 per cent, while also increasing the effective coverage of immunization (full course for children under five) and antenatal care (at least three visits) from 40 per cent in 2002 to 70 per cent two years later.

See References, page 108.

for countries with low health-system capacity are as follows:

Phase one: The initial phase focuses on reducing by half system-wide bottlenecks for family/community-based care and population-oriented outreach services, fostering demand for quality clinical services and providing a *minimum package* of high impact, low-cost interventions that can be implemented given the current policy, human resources and capacity conditions.

Operational strategies include the training and deployment of community health and nutrition promoters for improved family care practices. The minimum package of interventions typically includes the following components:

• Antimalaria interventions

• Nutrition

• Hygiene promotion

• Immunization complemented by measles mortality reduction campaigns

• Integrated Management of Neonatal and Childhood Illnesses

• Skilled delivery and newborn care and emergency obstetric care

• HIV and AIDS prevention and treatment

• Facility-based care

Phase two: The second phase comprises an *expanded package* that includes further neonatal and maternal interventions, improved water supplies and adequate sanitation through national policies and the mobilization of additional funding. This phase aims to sustain and strengthen all three service delivery modes by reducing supply and demand bottlenecks.

Phase three: The final phase involves the introduction and scaling up of innovative interventions, such as rotavirus and pneumococcal vaccines, and enhancing the supply and demand for this *maximum package*.[15]

Address the human resource crisis in health care across developing countries

In many countries, economic hardship and financial crises have destabilized and undermined health staff, creating a vicious circle of demotivation, low productivity and underinvestment in human resources.

Tackling the health worker crisis in developing countries will require a mix of measures across various time frames.

Short term: An immediate priority is to ensure that expanding national and global initiatives for maternal and child health do not result in further disruptions to the health system or further significant loss of personnel.

Short to medium term: The productivity and morale of existing health-care professionals need to be restored, including through such incentives as increased pay and improved supervision. The health workforce – including community health workers – also

needs to be expanded within the confines of the country's overall macroeconomic framework and poverty reduction strategies.

Longer term: Tackling the health worker crisis will also demand massive increases in education and training for health-care professionals. Without improved training for medical professionals and increased funding, the crisis may worsen, with devastating implications for maternal, newborn and child survival and health.

These measures will require strong national leadership, based on a broad consensus within society that prioritizes quality health care. Comprehensive plans to address the health worker crisis are required to move countries towards universal access to the continuum of care. Moreover, these plans must extend beyond the health sector to include such issues as civil service reform, decentralization and the macroeconomic environment.

The scale of this challenge should not be underestimated. Addressing the health worker crisis in sub-Saharan Africa alone will require an unprecedented surge in staffing levels in the coming decade. Of the almost 860,000 estimated additional workers needed to scale up health-care provision to the level required to meet the health-related MDGs in that region, more than half would be community health and nutrition promoters.

Efforts are under way to expand the number of community health workers in many developing countries, as well as to devise incentive packages

that will decrease attrition rates. Several countries, including India, Kenya, South Africa and Uganda are considering national programmes for community health workers, while Ethiopia is training 30,000 community-based female health extension workers to focus on maternal, newborn and child health, malaria, and HIV and AIDS.[16] Programmes for community health workers are also under way in countries as diverse as Afghanistan, Indonesia, Mozambique, Nepal and Pakistan.

Strengthening health worker programmes would initially focus on community health and nutrition providers to enhance service delivery in three areas:

• Improve family care practices through home visits.

• Distribute essential health and nutrition commodities for household use in communities with low access to facility-based care.

• Provide first-line care for sick children.

Performance-based incentives, such as payments based on successful behaviour changes in their communities, could be used to motivate workers, instead of fixed remuneration.

Evidence suggests that multiple incentive packages – often combining small monetary incentives or 'in kind' payments with a strong emphasis on community recognition and supervision, as well as personal growth and development opportunities – tend to have a significant effect on reducing

The effectiveness of health-care interventions is recognized through regular monitoring and assessment. *Children being screened for malnutrition prior to a distribution of high-protein biscuits, Iraq.*

attrition rates among community health workers. In Guatemala, for example, supervised community health workers had attrition rates two to three times lower than those who were unsupervised because their link with outside experts gave them a higher status.[17]

Upgrading the skills of existing health workers is an integral part of effective scale-up. Improved supervision and monitoring, in addition to results-based performance incentives and contracts, have the potential to motivate existing health workers, as well as being attractive features to prospective employees.

Developing health systems for outcomes

Efforts to improve harmonization of aid and to scale up activities, particularly in Africa, have increasingly focused on utilizing the health-related MDGs and other indicators as the benchmark for health-system strengthening outcomes. The emphasis on outcomes is intended to create a synergy between the outcomes and inputs. Health-system development is increasingly being framed as part of the process of achieving the goals, not distinct from them.

This linkage between systems and outcomes has been stressed in the strategic framework for reaching MDGs 4 and 5 through health-system strengthening, prepared jointly by UNICEF, WHO and the World Bank at the request of the African Union. The framework analyses system bottlenecks for 16 African countries and simulates the potential impact on the MDG of removing these bottlenecks country by country. Based on this framework, more than 10 countries in Africa are currently revising plans and budgetary mechanisms such as Poverty Reduction Strategy Papers, health-sector development plans, sector-wide approaches and medium-term expenditure frameworks to strengthen health systems with the aim of concrete health outcomes for mothers and children.

Scaling up: Safe water, adequate sanitation and improved hygiene practices

Clean water and safe toilets have the potential to transform children's lives. More than any other group, young children are vulnerable to the risks posed by contaminated water, poor sanitation and inadequate hygiene. Unsafe drinking water, inadequate availability of water for washing and cooking, and lack of access to sanitation together contribute to about 88 per cent of deaths from diarrhoeal diseases, or more than 1.5 million each year.

Better sanitation alone could reduce diarrhoea-related morbidity by more than a third; improved sanitation combined with better hygiene behaviours could reduce it by two thirds. Hand washing with soap or ashes would prevent 0.5 million to 1.4 million deaths per year. Improved household practices include consistent use of a toilet or latrine by each person in the household, safe disposal of young children's faeces, hand washing with soap or ash after defecation and before eating, and the installation of safe water sources in households and communities. Providing communities with the knowledge and resources to implement these basic household practices is a vital first step towards improving sanitation and hygiene.

Nicaragua and Peru: Promoting better hygiene to reduce diarrhoea

Like South Asia, Latin America and the Caribbean has experienced significant progress in the areas of water and sanitation, with 16 of the region's 33 countries on track to meet their MDG targets. Yet persistent disparities remain, especially between urban and rural areas.

In 2002, the joint Environmental Health Project-Pan American Health Organization 'Hygiene Behavior Change Project' initiated community-based strategies for the region suffering a combined total of 15,000 deaths and 75,000 hospitalizations due to rotavirus diarrhoea every year, despite enjoying a sound infrastructure of latrines and piped water. In Peru, reported cases of diarrhoea after implementation fell to 9 per cent, while in Nicaragua there were almost no reported cases of diarrhoea among children aged three and none in children aged four and five. Many of the hygiene practices promoted as part of the interventions in both countries, such as better hand washing and safe use and storage of water, showed statistically significant improvements from pre-intervention to midterm.

Mozambique: The child-to-child sanitation committees

Children can often serve as powerful advocates for change in their communities. In Mozambique, the child-to-child sanitation committees serve as a basis for child-centred hygiene education programmes in school and also aim to operate as an entry point to local communities for the adoption of hygiene practices at the household level through child-to-child and child-to-parent channels. A child-to-child sanitation committee consists of a group of 15 girls and boys trained in participatory hygiene education, including the dissemination of information on routes and barriers for water and sanitation-related disease transmission, appropriate hand washing with soap (or ashes), and proper use of latrines. The inclusion of girls in the committees is especially important because girls' school attendance is affected by inadequate water and sanitation facilities and by time spent travelling long distances to drinking-water sources. In combination with youth participatory strategies, these efforts helped increase the enrolment rates of girls 15–20 per cent nationwide since 2002–2003.

To get the other children's attention, the committees use focus group discussions, posters, expressive songs, theatre, dance, interviews, drawings and competitions. Following this approach, child-to-child sanitation committees have been established and are operational in 251 schools.

Southern Sudan: Community-based water and sanitation in complex environments

It is often assumed that community-based approaches are difficult if not impossible to implement in areas that have been affected by armed conflict, natural disasters or other complex emergencies. Yet evidence from South Sudan suggests that when they are successfully implemented, community-based approaches can play a crucial role in difficult environments. In South Sudan, a water and sanitation project involves local water teams who specialize in hand drilling. Each team has 10 members, usually selected from the local communities; of these, seven are usually drillers and three are responsible for handpump maintenance, including a team supervisor. Hand drilling provides a low-tech, low-cost approach of providing access to water. The rigs can be dismantled and transported between sites by the communities themselves. Their portability allows them to be transported even over difficult terrain and, critically, enables the drilling to continue during the wet season. Furthermore, the low cost and portability of the rigs is essential in insecure areas. By working together with communities, this project has successfully extended tube wells across large areas of northern Bahr el Ghazal.

Bangladesh and India: Community-led 'total sanitation'

Although investment in toilet construction is an important prerequisite of increasing sanitation coverage, evidence from South Asia suggests it is not always sufficient in order to achieve improved public health outcomes. Studies of state-wide sector assessments in India, for example, show that most people continue to defecate in the open not due to a lack of access to toilets but primarily because they see no reason to change their behaviour, as awareness of associated health risks is limited or ignored. In fact, usage of toilets is highest where households recognize the need for a toilet and therefore build one of their own.

In Rajshahi district, Bangladesh, a unique community mobilization approach was piloted in 2001 to achieve 100 per cent sanitation coverage. Community-led 'total sanitation' is based on the principle of triggering collective behaviour change. This approach helps communities understand the negative effects of poor sanitation and empowers them to collectively find solutions. In Rajshahi, this approach led the community to achieve a total ban on open defecation within the village. The ban was achieved without any external subsidy and was based entirely on community mobilization. Communities used their own resources, established action committees, developed innovative low-cost technologies and monitored progress.

The Rajshahi initiative represented a paradigm shift in promoting improved sanitation practices through a community-focused strategy, but scale-up in the area was limited to a village-by-village approach. The Rajshahi experience generated interest in India, however, leading to visits from policymakers, including representatives from the State Government of Maharashtra. Building on the Bangladeshi experience, the State Government of Maharashtra formulated a strategy to end open defecation in the state. The key features of this strategy were to bring local governments to the fore, provide fiscal support to the poor, and put in place strong monitoring and evaluation systems. The campaign included a strong emphasis on information, education and communication activities and exposure visits to the best-performing villages. As a result, between 2002 and 2006,

Maharashtra went from having not even one open defecation-free village to having more than 3,800, with more than 5 million households now living in an environment free of open defecation.

Maharashtra's success in turn led to a revision of national sanitation guidelines in India and to establishment of the *Nirmal Gram Puraskar*, or 'Clean Village Prize', introduced by the Government of India in 2004. The scheme offers cash rewards to local governments that achieve 100 per cent sanitation. The response has been tremendous: In February 2005, *38 gram panchayats* (the lowest tier of elected rural local government) received the prize; by February 2006, the number went up to 760 *gram panchayats* and 9 *block panchayats* (an intermediate tier of elected rural government).

Ghana: Bridging the urban-rural divide

Among the largest disparities in safe water and basic sanitation are those between urban and rural populations. Globally, access to improved drinking-water sources is 95 per cent in urban areas, compared with 73 per cent in rural areas. The urban-rural divide in drinking water is at its widest in sub-Saharan Africa, where 81 per cent of people in urban areas are served, compared with 41 per cent in rural areas.

In Ghana, coverage of rural water and sanitation was, until recently, behind the average for sub-Saharan Africa but is currently expanding at a rate of about 200,000 people, or more than 1 per cent of the population, a year. The change has been dramatic and reflects a sweeping reform programme introduced by the government in the early 1990s in order to address the inefficiencies of a top-down system that was unresponsive and failed to deliver, especially in rural areas. As a result of the reform process, responsibilities for water supplies were transferred to local governments and rural communities, and new political structures for water governance have been developed. Village structures are now part of the new system. To apply for capital grants, communities must form village water committees and draw up plans detailing how they will manage their systems, contribute the cash equivalent of 5 per cent of the capital costs and meet maintenance costs. This participatory approach has resulted in a dramatic increase in access to water, from 55 per cent in 1990 to 75 per cent in 2004, and access is currently accelerating.

See References, page 108.

These countries are also consolidating their bottlenecks, startegies, expected health outcomes and additional funding needs into 'investment cases' to leverage political and financial support for their national plans.

Strengthen health systems at the district level

Strengthening health systems remains a daunting and complex task, especially in many of countries that are making insufficient progress towards the health-related MDGs. The decentralization of health systems and an increasing focus on the district level can be seen as an effective vehicle for delivering primary health care to marginalized children and families at the community level.[18] But decentralization is not without risks: It can have unintended consequences, such as deepening existing inequalities in communities, based on factors such as poverty, gender, language and ethnicity.[19] Furthermore, even where decentralization efforts have been successful, experience suggests that transforming an administrative district into a functional health system takes time. In 2000, for example, only 13 of Niger's district hospitals were equipped to perform a Caesarean section. Only 17 of the 53 district hospitals in Burkina Faso had appropriate facilities 10 years after districts had been established; moreover, only 5 of those 17 hospitals had the three doctors required to ensure continuity of care throughout the year.[20]

Nevertheless, the experience of decentralization during the past decade suggests that, on balance, health districts remain a rational way for governments to roll out primary health care through networks of health cen-

The urgent need to address the health worker crisis in Africa

The lack of adequate human resources represents a major barrier to scaling up integrated approaches to maternal, newborn and child survival, health and nutrition at the community level. The current experience suggests that limited effectiveness, high staff turnover and inadequate supervision characterize most programmes in developing countries. The massive migration of health professionals, the impact of AIDS, which in some high-prevalence countries has decimated the workforce, as well as the presence of armed conflict, serve to undermine the national health workforce in many developing countries currently making slow or no progress in reducing child mortality. Within these contexts, community health workers can have an important role in improving community health in general and child health in particular. It should be emphasized, however, that community health workers are intended to complement, not substitute for, trained health professionals.

Health workers at the district and community levels
The number of health workers per 1,000 children, in particular nurses and doctors, is a significant determinant of variations in rates of infant, under-five and maternal mortality across countries. For example, research reveals that the prospects for achieving 80 per cent coverage of measles immunization and skilled attendants at birth are greatly enhanced where the health worker density exceeds 2.5 per 1,000 inhabitants. Yet many developing countries, particularly in sub-Saharan Africa, face overwhelming shortages of health personnel.

The migration of skilled health professionals is a cause of grave concern in many developing countries. A point of particular alarm is the massive migration of health professionals from poor countries to rich countries (the so-called 'brain drain'). But other forms of movements of health professionals within a country – from rural areas to zones of conurbation, from the public domain to the private sector, and from the health sector to other sectors – are also limiting the pool of skilled health professionals involved in primary health care in developing countries.

The reasons doctors and nurses leave the health sector altogether appear to be similar in places as diverse as the Pacific Islands and the European Union. They include low remuneration, inflexible hours with many extra duties, lack of continuing educational opportunities, difficult working conditions, demanding patients and shortages of supplies and equipment. Recent statistics indicate, for example, that half of medical school graduates from Ghana emigrate within 4.5 years of graduation, and 75 per cent leave within a decade. In South Africa, more than 300 specialist nurses leave every month – many never to return. The main destinations for migrant health workers are Europe and North America. This is particularly true for the United Kingdom, where one third of the health workforce originates from other countries. Research suggests that the density of health workers (doctors, nurses, midwives) is more than 10 times higher in Europe and North America than in sub-Saharan Africa. The negative impact of migration on the delivery of health services in developing countries is often severe, since this

tres, family practices or equivalent decentralized structures, backed by referral hospitals. Where districts have become stable and viable structures, they have demostrated notable results, even under situations of complex emergencies, as in the Democratic Republic of the Congo and Guinea. Similarly, Mali has broadened its health-centre networks and services for mothers and children.[21] In countries where decentralization has been accompanied by reforms of public administration, there has been significant progress within a few years. Examples include Mozambique, Rwanda and Uganda, all countries that experienced many years of conflict and economic collapse but have since made significant progress in reforming government institutions and performance, including their health systems.[22]

In recent decades, evidence on the performance of district health systems has grown. However, the evidence base is still relatively small, the study coverage is inconsistent, and the approaches advocated by practitioners do not enjoy the same level of consensus and visibility within the scientific community as those on essential interventions.

Work on the district approach to delivering the continuum of maternal, newborn and child health care requires a new impetus and more rigorous systematization. In particular, a key focus of research should be on the reorientation of national health systems to create the conditions in which district health and nutrition systems providing a continuum of care can thrive. Systematic analysis and case studies from countries that have tried this approach

movement of human capital affects the most highly trained professionals, in whom the government has invested heavily through training and professional development.

In addition to these general causes, the AIDS epidemic and armed conflict have also been powerful causes underlying the loss of health personnel in sub-Saharan Africa in particular.

In situations of conflict and post-conflict reconstruction, qualified health providers are vital to provide general and specialized services to vulnerable populations that may have been displaced and injured as a result of the strife. However, in many conflict-affected countries years and sometimes decades of conflict have led to an acute shortage of trained health-care personnel.

To address these shortages of skilled health personnel, at least in the short to medium term, national health systems must build incentives for practising health care at home. While this remains an ongoing challenge, a number of countries have been successful in recruiting and retaining heath workers, including in rural areas, where shortages are often most severe. Incentive packages to retain health workers or reverse migration are being devised to address the crisis. One such example is taking place in Mali, where the Ministry of Health encourages newly graduated doctors to serve in rural areas by offering them training, accommodation, equipment and transport if needed.

Training that is focused on local conditions can also help limit workforce attrition. Longstanding efforts to expand the numbers of health workers in rural areas suggest that training local workers – in local languages and in skills relevant to local conditions – facilitates retention. Such approaches to training often lead to credentials that do not have international recognition, which further limits migration. Success, however, is contingent on providing incentives and support at the local level.

There is a growing concern that affluent countries are benefiting from the brain drain at Africa's expense. As a result, there has been a growing movement calling for an end to the recruitment of health workers from Africa, or, if that proves unrealistic, as is likely to be the case, to conduct recruitment only in a way that is mutually beneficial. In the past five years, about a dozen international instruments have emerged from national authorities, professional associations and international bodies that have set norms for behaviour among the key stakeholders involved in the international recruitment of health workers, and similar concerns have been the focus of bilateral agreements.

See References, page 108.

The investment case for child survival and other health-related Millennium Development Goals in sub-Saharan Africa

The strategies outlined in 'A Strategic Framework for Reaching the Millennium Development Goals on Child Survival in Africa' – prepared for the African Union in July 2005 – are expected to create, in a relatively short time frame, the minimal conditions needed to increase effective coverage of primary health care in sub-Saharan Africa – including a minimum package of evidence-based, high-impact, low-cost services that can be delivered through family and community-based care and through population-oriented services and clinical care. The key interventions are expected to be antibiotics to combat pneumonia and neonatal infections; antimalarial combination drugs; infant feeding and hygiene promotion; insecticide-treated mosquito nets; oral rehydration therapy; skilled attendance at birth; and vitamin A supplementation, prevention and care of paediatric AIDS, and emergency obstetric and neonatal care. These strategies and interventions are expected to have a substantial impact on improving child nutrition, maternal mortality, women's status and poverty reduction through women's empowerment. (The three implementation phases are outlined on pages 71-72.)

In phase one, it is estimated that this strategy could reduce Africa's under-five mortality rate by more than 30 per cent and provide initial reductions of 15 per cent in maternal mortality at an incremental estimated annual cost of US$2–$3 per capita, or around US$1,000 per life saved.

In phase two, implementation at scale of an expanded package would lead to an estimated reduction in the region's under-five mortality rate in excess of 45 per cent and would diminish maternal mortality by 40 per cent and neonatal mortality by around 30 per cent. The incremental annual economic cost is estimated at around US$5 per capita, or less than US$1,500 per life saved.

In phase three, it is estimated that reaching the effective coverage frontiers with the maximum package of interven-

Figure 4.3

Estimated impact and cost of minimum, expanded and maximum packages for the Strategic Framework for Africa

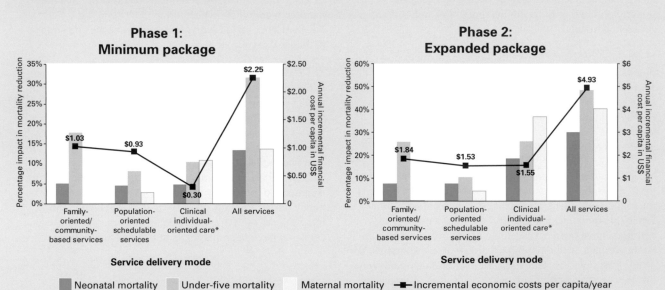

* Assumes that clinical individual-oriented care is available continuously.

tions would allow countries to meet or approach key targets for MDGs 1, 4, 5 and 6 by reducing the under-five mortality and maternal mortality rates by more than 60 per cent, cutting the neonatal mortality rate by 50 per cent and halving the incidence of malaria and undernutrition. The incremental annual economic cost to achieve phase three is estimated at US$12–$15 per capita, or around US$2,500 per life saved.

Assuming an incremental pace of implementation, the additional annual funding required for the proposed phased acceleration will increase between US$2 and US$3 per capita and per year to take the minimum package to scale in Phase one; it will increase by more than US$12–$15 per capita and per year to take the maximum package to scale by 2015 in Phase three. It is noteworthy that these additional costs have recently been estimated using different costing tools, each of which has generated similar projections, suggesting that the estimates are robust. The cost is for commodities, drugs and supplies. Insecticide-treated mosquito nets represent a very sizeable share of this cost, as do drugs. The cost is apportioned to human resources, health facilities and equipment, and for promotion, demand creation, monitoring and evaluation.

In the context of the Strategic Framework, the following co-financing scenario is proposed: In all three phases, almost half of the additional funding to scale up the minimum package would come from national budgets, including budget support, with 15 per cent coming from out-of-pocket expenditures, and one third from the Global Fund to Fight AIDS, Tuberculosis and Malaria (GFATM), UNICEF, the World Bank, WHO and other donors.

See References, page 108.

Figure 4.4

Funding sources 2007–2015

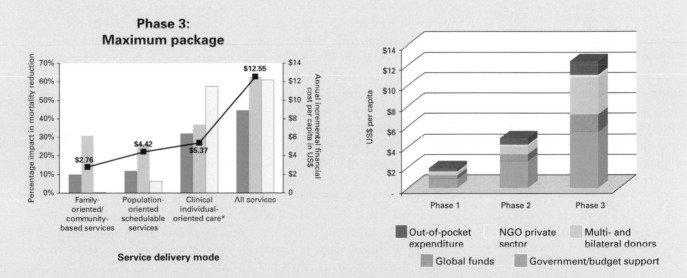

Phase 3: Maximum package

Service delivery mode

Sources Figures 4.3 and 4.4, pp. 78-79: Preliminary estimates based on the revised version of UNICEF, World Bank and World Health Organization, 'A Strategic Framework for Reaching the Millennium Development Goals in Africa through health systems strengthening and implementing at scale of integrated packages of high-impact and low-cost health and nutrition interventions', draft prepared on request of the African Union by UNICEF, WHO and the World Bank. Revised in October 2007.

The shortage of health workers in developing countries must be addressed in national plans to reverse its negative impact on the health of mothers, newborns and children. *A health worker examines a child at the regional centre for AIDS prevention and protection, Russian Federation.*

could yield important insights into the ways that current policy processes function and might be improved. Some significant problems – such as building institutional capacity and obtaining strategic intelligence for steering and monitoring resource flows and health-system performance – are already well recognized by practitioners.

It is clear that there is much work to be done in gathering evidence and knowledge on ways to build capacities for policy formation, regulation and steering that can inform gover-

nance of the health sector as a whole, as well as the organization of a continuum of maternal, newborn and child care at the district level.

III. Improving the quality and consistency of financing for strengthening health systems

Finding the money to finance health care is a significant obstacle to scaling up in low-income countries, where health-care sectors already face huge budget shortfalls. Policies determining government health-financing can have a profound effect on health outcomes for children and women, through subsidizing or taxing critical services affecting maternal, newborn and child survival, health and nutrition or by supporting equitable cost-sharing mechanisms.

Adequate financing of the health sector, in addition to fighting specific diseases, is imperative for effective, sustainable scale-up. The less than optimal outcomes from earlier and current support to the health sector have largely been attributed to several factors, namely:

A lack of evidence and country-based budgeting for health outcomes. Given the predominance of disease-specific initiatives, national strategies for maternal, newborn and child health often do not give sufficient attention to a multi-sectoral approach to achieving health outcomes, removing systemic bottlenecks to service delivery or adequately budgeting for health strategies – including the costs of removing bottlenecks to the supply of and demand for primary health-care services.

Slow progress and weak alignment to country processes and harmonization. Linkages between the health sector and broader development processes at country level (public sector and budget reform, poverty reduction strategies, macroeconomic and fiscal planning, etc.) often remain tenuous in low-income countries. Monitoring systems for tracking resource flows, progress and outcomes are often largely inadequate, and there is limited progress in translating global commitments on aid effectiveness into concrete action at country level – most particularly in relation to the provision of predictable long-term financing and the reduction of fragmented aid leading to high transaction costs, in line with the Paris Declaration on Harmonization and Aid Effectiveness.

Insufficient focus of funding in addressing obstacles to strengthening health systems. Despite an increasing commitment by the global community to health goals, countries still experience critical shortages in funding to build up their health systems – including financing for producing and retaining key human resources, providing incentives for performance, building procurement and logistics systems and facilitating transfers to poorer households to address demand-side obstacles to better health. As more and more funds are mobilized for specific diseases such as HIV, an increased imbalance is often observed at country level, with health service delivery and financing mechanisms required to absorb the funds made available for special initiatives often absent. As a result, low levels of execution and effectiveness of disease control programmes are observed. Absent or weak control of government over the behaviour of health service providers, and of beneficiaries of health services over the use of public funds, undermine effective implementation.[23]

Recent international health partnerships propose to leverage greater resources for scaling up for the MDGs. These initiatives seek a focus on results and a clear link between resources allocated and health outcomes. Doing this requires strengthening health systems as a means of achieving development outcomes –

both directly and by influencing other donors – and call for greater coherence in the health aid architecture.[24]

There is a growing agreement about the importance of supporting robust sectoral plans, and about the desirability of ensuring full coherence with existing efforts on health systems strengthening. Key issues related to these new initiatives include development and quality of scaling-up plans, monitoring processes and selection of countries, as well as flow and management of funds.[25]

In this context, a consensus is emerging on five principles for aid:

- Rewarding performance in a predictable way through compacts.

- Aligning development assistance to country systems.

- Results-based financing.

- Establishing benchmarks and outcome indicators for health-systems development.

- Developing innovative and equitable financing strategies.

Rewarding performance in a predictable way through compacts

Along with the renewed emphasis on results, there is an emerging consensus

---

Focus On

Botswana: Going to scale with HIV prevention and treatment using community partnerships

Context and challenge: AIDS is a foremost cause of maternal, newborn and child death in southern Africa. In Botswana, almost 1 in every 4 people aged 15–49 is infected with HIV. The risk to children begins before birth; one third of pregnant women aged 15–24 in Botswana are HIV–positive. Maternal HIV-positive status leads to an increased rate of stillbirths and deaths in the neonatal period and infancy, even if HIV is not transmitted to the child. Women who contract HIV during pregnancy or while breastfeeding have a high risk of passing the infection to their newborn. Moreover, mothers are increasingly at risk of death, leaving behind babies with diminished chances of survival. AIDS is a significant cause of disability and death in babies and children beyond one month.

Interventions and approaches: In Botswana, prevention of mother-to-child transmission of HIV (PMTCT) was initiated in 1999 with strong political commitment and high resource allocation. From the outset, the Government of Botswana planned for national coverage of interventions. Services are provided free of charge to women and children and integrated into existing maternal and child health services. These interventions include safe obstetric practices, counselling, HIV testing, prophylaxis or treatment for

HIV infection as indicated, and testing of babies for HIV infection at six weeks of age. Antiretroviral therapy is also provided to qualifying mothers and their families. Rigorous monitoring and evaluation is implemented and supply chains closely managed.

One of the central success factors in Botswana was the unified coordination mechanism around a single national scale-up plan. PMTCT was fully integrated with maternal and child health services, but ongoing adjustments were made to increase quality and service uptake. Political commitment was important, as was cohesive programme management. Community participation and male involvement were also crucial elements to support women who chose not to breastfeed and to facilitate follow-up paediatric care and support.

Results: In Botswana, the programme expanded to nationwide coverage by 2004. By 2005, 54 per cent of HIV-positive mothers were receiving antiretroviral drugs during pregnancy.

See References, page 108.

Enhanced political commitment and adequate financing by governments are necessary to guarantee access to the continuum of care for mothers, newborns and children. *A child holds his baby sister, Guatemala.*

that resources should be allocated on the basis of such criteria as: need (based on such factors as population size, poverty levels and current state of national health) and peformance (health outcomes and capacity to absorb funds effectively). Performance would be related to key results and policy measures agreed at the country level in a 'compact' that builds on existing results-oriented frameworks, such as those developed by the European Commission, World Bank and African Development Bank and bilateral donors.[26]

These compacts constitute mutual agreements between developing countries and donors based on accountabilities and meeting performance criteria by recipients and provision of predictable financing by donors.

Aligning development assistance to country systems

Alignment of disbursement and implementation to country systems is pivotal to enhancing aid effectiveness. In countries with fiduciary environments (public financial management and procurement) that are considered adequate overall by multilateral and bilateral donors and jointly monitored by partners through the public expenditure and financial accountability mechanism, funding for effective scale-up could flow as sector budget support – providing incremental funding for the implementation of the health-sector component of the national budget, as well as related activities. Monitoring the effectiveness of these funds would be integrated into the monitoring of the existing general and sector budget support. A similar mechanism could

be used in countries with sector-wide approaches and basket fund mechanisms, complementing existing evaluation methods.

There is a growing consensus that resources for the health sector should be channelled through institutions that aim to provide universal coverage, rather than through projects and programmes. Maternal, newborn and child health services must be part of the basket of core health interventions that are covered in any benefit package funded through these institutions. Enhancing resources spent on maternal, newborn and child health may require trade-offs in government expenditures, either within the health budget itself or within the national budget. Such trade-offs need to be negotiated in the context of the overall macroeconomic environment, which can allow for incremental sector spending if health-care requirements are well argued. At the country level, resources also need to be mobilized outside of the public sector through the involvement of the private sector, civil society organizations, communities and households.

Results-based financing

One of the key areas supported by the new scaling-up initiatives is results-based financing. This is an important complement to existing funding flows and a potentially promising approach to surmounting existing obstacles within health systems to achieve health, nutrition and population results. Recent experiences in Afghanistan, Argentina, Cambodia and Rwanda *(see Panel, page 84, on performance-based financing in Rwanda)* have shown positive results, and more rigorous evaluation for the latter is planned.

Strengthening accountability and governance in health-service delivery

Accountability in service delivery may be conceived of as processes through which communities and households can hold providers responsible for the adequacy and effectiveness of the services they offer. For poor and marginalized communities and households, public accountability can be achieved through giving them both voice and suffrage; for policymakers, accountability can be demanded through the social compact in which governments assist, finance and regulate providers of health care, nutrition and environmental health services. When communities are empowered to demand adequate and effective services, families are informed of which services the State has committed to provide and the minimum standards that apply.

Embedding participation in public life and civic education in all maternal, newborn and child survival and development programmes ensures that families are empowered with knowledge of the measures they can take to protect their child's life and enhance the child's early development. Household and community knowledge of available services and the standards of quality required for these services enhance their ability to hold governments and service providers accountable.

Social compacts between governments and providers can also be effective tools for accountability in maternal, newborn and child survival and health when governments make these issues a priority in legislation, budgets, programmes and research – and adequately compensate providers for essential services, while monitoring their performance in delivery.

Strengthening accountability must be tailored to different modes of service delivery. At the primary level of community and family services – including such factors as information and social support for promoting breastfeeding or newborn care services – the ability of households to purchase commodities, access information on services and transform both into better health outcomes is central to increasing demand-side accountability. Community and civil society organizations and commercial networks are often well placed to provide mechanisms for poor and marginalized households that can directly monitor the efficacy of services and exert accountability.

See References, page 108.

Results-based financing offers several advantages over traditional, input-based approaches, including:

- An emphasis on achieving outputs and outcomes relatively quickly within a well defined time period.

- Incentives for performance at key junctures in the service delivery chain.

- Addresses important funding gaps, provides governments with flexible financing to counterbalance funding distortions and gives them the opportunity to focus on priorities, such as targeting the poor.

- By design, results-based financing is essentially a monitoring and

evaluation tool, built on a measurable and targeted strategy that requires baseline, target and progress data at the relevant levels. Consequently, results-based efforts will allow regular review of successes, shortfalls and bottlenecks, enabling midstream adjustments to implementation plans.

- In addition, it supports a broader-range of solutions to health problems beyond those that are officially under the control of the health sector, such as improving roads, water supplies and sanitation.

- Perhaps most importantly, results based financing creates an opportunity to consolidate fragmented aid, thereby reducing high transaction

costs to countries. This can be accomplished through results-based financing arrangements that focus on outputs to which many donors can simultaneously contribute.[27]

Establishing benchmarks and outcome indicators for health-system development

Indicators associated with the health-related MDGs can serve as appropriate tracers or proxy measures for the performance of health systems. New initiatives plan to provide support to governments to achieve agreed outcomes in selected target areas through results-based financing, establishing appropriate incentive frameworks. The objective is to achieve defined output targets for coverage of services that are strongly correlated with positive maternal, newborn and child health and survival outcomes – for example: the proportion of deliveries in an accredited facility; immunization coverage of three doses of diphtheria, tetanus toxoid and pertussis vaccine; or coverage of insecticide-treated mosquito nets in malaria-endemic areas. These outputs and targets would be selected based on the risk factors contributing to mortality and morbidity for each country.

Key outcome indicators can be set in various forms. These parameters can measure either direct outputs, such as the absolute number of children immunized; coverage, such as the percentage of the target population vaccinated, by antigen, in a defined catchment area; or trends, such as increases in the number of children vaccinated or coverage levels achieved over time. A set of core indicators can also be defined for all projects to allow for some cross-country comparison and learning. Countries could also include additional indicators that monitor important elements of their maternal, child and newborn health programmes.

Developing innovative and equitable financing strategies

Investment in human resources and health-system strengthening requires significant resources. Countries where donor support plays a critical role in funding these programmes cannot plan for long-term activities unless financing is secure. Yet, research tracking donor assistance to maternal, newborn and child health found that the 60 priority countries that account for more than 90 per cent of child deaths received only US$1.4 billion in official development assistance in 2004, or just US$3.10 per child.[28]

Performance-based financing in Rwanda

The Government of Rwanda, with support from donors, has recently scaled up several innovative programmes that transfer conditional grants from the central government to municipalities for the purchase of essential health outputs. The health programme includes three principal elements:

Community partnerships in health: This transfers resources (about US$0.25 per capita) directly to municipalities to engage, via a performance-based contract, community-based institutions, non-governmental organizations, health promoters, private health-care providers and other related services to deliver essential interventions at the household and community levels. A performance contract called IMIHIGO – a traditional word that has become synonymous with accountability in government services throughout the country – is signed between the President of Rwanda and district mayors on behalf of their constituencies every year. The services delivered under this approach are simple and low cost, focusing on the promotion of improved health and hygiene practices, behaviour-change interventions, and such preventive services as distribution of insecticide-treated mosquito nets, oral rehydration therapy, nutritional supplementation and safe water systems.

These partnerships were introduced in several districts during 2005 and have been scaled up at the national level since 2006 using treasury funds. The central government signed performance contracts with the 30 municipalities in April 2006 and selected coverage of insecticide-treated nets as the lead performance indicator. Marked results have been achieved since its inception. An evaluation undertaken in June 2007 found that utilization of mosquito nets by children under age five had increased from 4 per cent in 2004 to more than 70 per cent in 2007. The number of cases of malaria has decreased dramatically, emptying paediatric wards, and population-based surveys using blood tests show a dramatic decrease in malaria prevalence. Policymakers rate the situation as unprecedented and are working now at a strategy to eliminate malaria altogether.

Health centres: This strand transfers resources (about US$1 per capita in 2007, or about 15 per cent of government resources apportioned to health) to primary care centres through a performance-based contract. The scheme was initially piloted in two provinces, Butare and Cyangugu, with the support of non-governmental organizations and bilateral aid from 2002. The performance-based contract includes indicators related to adequate coverage (quantity), as well as effective coverage (quality) of services. An evaluation has shown a significant increase in utilization of health services, including immunization and assisted deliveries, in the provinces where the contracts had been implemented compared with provinces that were not covered by the contracts.

The Government of Rwanda subsequently decided to gradually expand the programme to other provinces, incorporating lessons from the pilots. In 2005, budget

While the Strategic Framework suggests that it is possible to fill the gap between present levels and near-universal coverage by 2015, it also shows that scaling up interventions will not be possible without massively increasing investment in maternal, newborn and child health.[29]

Moving towards universal access to a continuum of quality maternal, newborn and child health care, however, is not merely a question of finding money to expand the supply of services or to pay providers. Reaching the health-related MDGs will require that financing strategies focus on overcoming financial barriers to women and children's access to services and give users predictable protection against the financial hardship that may result from paying for care.

This has important implications. Calls for the immediate and universal elimination of user fees for health-care services may prove overly simplistic or unrealistic. Policy decisions regarding user fees should be addressed within the broader context of the health sector budget and the national budgetary framework. Over time, user fees may be phased out in favour of prepayment and pooling schemes, on condition that this is accompanied, from its inception, by structural changes to ensure the long-term sustainability of health financing.

IV. Obtaining national political commitment

Given the level of resources required to ensure access to quality primary health-care services and financial protection, scaling up is as much a political challenge as it is a technical one.

allocations for the programmes were apportioned to two provinces that had undertaken the pilot schemes. The following year, the programme was expanded nationwide and fully transferred to the national budget, and it directly linked service delivery, results and payment.

A steering committee has been established in each province to independently monitor the performance of the health centres using lot quality sampling and satisfaction survey techniques. The results of the independent verification directly affect the amount of funding received by each centre. Again, results from the centres were impressive, with immunization coverage rates of 95 per cent and increases in the annual utilization of services from 0.4 visits per capita in 2004 to 0.7 per capita in 2006 and in assisted deliveries from 29 per cent in 2000 to 52 per cent in 2006. The full impact of these schemes on health outcomes is being evaluated through a randomized controlled prospective design. The programme has also been expanded to all district hospitals of the country.

Health micro-insurance schemes: *Mutuelles* – informal micro-insurance schemes that pool funds from community members to cover a package of basic health services provided by health centres and for the transfer of patients, if needed, to referral hospitals – have been piloted successfully during the past decade. Their aim is to smooth the cost of health services for members, eliminating the hardship of making out-of-pocket payments.

Mutuelles have an important role in intermediating between health centres, district hospitals and the general population. Evaluations show they are more effective when they have strong community participation in their governance structures and make payments to the health centres on a per capita basis, essentially transferring all insurance risk to the health centres.

Initially, the focus was on building administrative and management support and technical capacity, including training and development of appropriate tools. But since 2006, the Rwandan Government has transferred funds (about US$0.15 per capita) to cover premiums for the poorest people in the community, who are identified on the basis of a participatory poverty assessment called *Ubudehe*. Rwanda has systematically supported the expansion of *mutuelles*, which covered about 70 per cent of the population in 2007, up from 7 per cent in 2003. Enrolment of the poor in *mutuelles* is a key indicator in the performance-based contract signed by the mayor and the president. The Government is also engaged in creating municipal pooled funds, as well as a national fund for reinsurance financed by contributions from formal workers.

See References, page 108.

Sustained improvements in maternal, newborn and child health will necessitate long-term commitments that go well beyond the political lifespan of many decision makers. Countries including Brazil, Sri Lanka and Thailand have rooted their impressive results in a step-by-step extension of health-system coverage and nutrition services over many years. During recent decades, Latin America's performance in enhancing health-service coverage, despite periodic economic crises, institutional deficiencies and wide socio-economic disparities, has been noteworthy. All of the countries mentioned went through several distinct phases:

- Building up a cadre of professional health workers as the foundation.

- Developing an accessible network of community-based, primary and referral-level services.

- Consolidating advances by improving the quality of care, all

Focus On: Brazil: Creating a national community-based health-system network

Context and challenge: Brazil is one of 60 countries selected by the Countdown to 2015 group as a priority for child survival in the run-up to the deadline for the Millennium Development Goals. (*For a more detailed explanation of Countdown to 2015, see Chapter 1, page 16.*) These countries represent those with at least 50,000 child deaths or with a rate of under-five mortality of 90 deaths or more per 1,000 live births. In 2006, 74,000 children died before reaching their fifth birthday, according to the latest estimates published by UNICEF.

Although Brazil has made strong and steady progress in reducing mortality rates for children under five, there are clear geographical and ethnic disparities in death rates for infants. According to 2002 data, the aggregate infant mortality rate for the north-east region is twice as high as rates in south, south-east and central-west provinces. In Alagoas, the worst affected state in the north-east region, the infant mortality rate in 2002 was 58 per 1,000 live births, compared to a national average of around 28 per 1,000 births that year. Racial and ethnic disparities in child mortality risks are also evident, and children whose mothers are of indigenous or African descent are threatened by a much higher risk of mortality than children of European-descendent mothers.

The challenge facing Brazil, therefore, is to maintain the downward trend in overall child mortality while simultaneously adopting a strong regional and ethnic focus to health-care provision.

Approach and interventions: After pilot projects in Brazilian cities during the early 1980s, a community health worker network was created with UNICEF support as part of a comprehensive primary-health-care initiative, the Programa Saúde da Família (Family Health Programme). Each community health worker is responsible for visiting families in the community, providing up-to-date information on health, hygiene and childcare, and monitoring and evaluating the growth and health of children under 6 years old, as well as pregnant women. Community health workers also refer residents to local health units and alert family health teams – which usually include a doctor, a nurse, a nurse technician, a social assistant and a dentist – regarding local conditions or crises. Doctors and nurses participating in the Family Health Programme receive competitive salaries to encourage them to work in poor and rural areas. Each team is responsible for around 1,000 families. The teams are jointly financing by federal, state and municipal governments.

The activities of community health workers in the Programa da Saúde include providing education on child development and protection. UNICEF equips workers with Family Information Kits that include flip charts about breastfeeding and the role of all family members in promoting healthy lives for mothers and children. More than 222,280 community health workers cover nearly 110 million people across Brazil, making this network one of the largest in the world. The network is integrated within the national system, and federal, state and municipal governments are fully responsible for funding and administering the programme throughout Brazil.

The use of field trials before implementation of the programme established that it had the potential to generate marked improvements in health. Political commitment to the network ensured its viability. Roles for the community health workers are well defined, including their designation as part

in conjunction with improvements in living conditions and the status of women.

- Prioritizing broad social safety nets that ensured equitable access to health, nutrition and education, making health and nutrition services widely available.

- Reducing barriers to key services and providing primary and secondary schooling to all children.

Even in some of the poorest countries in Latin America, where economic crises, institutional deficiencies and wide socio-economic disparities continue to hinder advances, there has been marked progress towards generalized access to quality health care.

Country ownership and public sector leadership can vastly increase the prospects for successful scaling up. Time and again, it has been shown that when governments take the lead and are committed to expanding successful pilot and small-scale projects,

---

Figure 4.5

Brazil: Wide disparities in infant mortality rates between and within selected regions, by family income and by mother's ethnicity, 2002

	Infant mortality rate (per 1,000 live births)
2000	
Disparities by family income	
20 per cent richest households	15.8
20 per cent poorest households	34.9
Disparities by mother's ethnicity	
White	22.9
Afro-descendent	38
Indian	94
National Average	**30.2**
2002	
Regions/selected states	
Central-West	20.4
Federal District	17.5
Northeast	41.4
Alagoas	57.7
North	27.7
Southeast	20.2
Sao Paolo	17.4
South	17.9
Rio Grande do sol	15.4
National Average	**28.4**

Source: United Nations Children's Fund, 'The State of Brazil's Children 2006: The right to survival and development, UNICEF, Brasilia, 2005, pp. 10-11.

of local health units. Lines of referral and supervision are clear: The unit supports the health workers, and they, in turn, perform outreach for the health system in the communities. The community health workers become a central part of their local communities, and the integration of the network within national, state and municipal governments helps ensure both the sustainability of the programme and its extension into new areas of the national health system.

Results: The introduction of the community health worker programme has contributed to a reduction in infant deaths across the country since 1990. Moreover, the government has focused on the north-east region and on marginalized ethnic groups during recent years. It has also adopted a strong regional focus to child and maternal health care, and almost half of the participants who receive cash benefits from Programa da Saúde live in the north-east.

See References, page 108.

these initiatives can rapidly gain nationwide coverage. Brazil's community health worker programme (*see Panel page 86*) and the Bolsa Familia initiative, Mexico's health, nutrition and education programme, PROGRESA, and Seguro Popular de Salud health insurance scheme, Indonesia's community health workers and Egypt's oral rehydration initiatives, along with many other examples, show the potential for scale-up when governments are willing to commit even scarce funding to health and social welfare programmes.

Ownership is more than just funding, however. Governments must also be committed to creating and sustaining the required technical and administration capacity. Support at each level of health-system administration – federal, provincial and district – is required to coordinate and supervise the expansion. Sustainability issues must also be addressed at the national level, and the programme fully endorsed by the political system – including the legislature – to ensure that it outlasts political transitions and changes.

Governments can provide the capacity and will to creating a national network based on community health. When this has happened, the results are often significant. In the case of China, for example, the Government set itself a tremendous challenge with the launch of the National Iodine Deficiency Disorders Elimination Program, a strategy for ensuring a nationwide supply of commercially marketed iodized salt and promoting universal compliance. At that time, China had the highest number

A new way of working together for multilateral institutions

In New York, 19 July 2007, global health leaders from eight international organizations met informally to discuss ways of strengthening their collaboration to achieve better health outcomes in developing countries. Capitalizing on the recent appointments of several leaders, the objective of the meeting was to review progress made during recent years, assess current trends and future challenges for global health, and agree to collective action, in the context of current opportunities. Several key commitments were recommended, including:

• **Stimulate a global collective sense of urgency for reaching the health-related MDGs.** Participants agreed that, despite important advances in health care for mothers, newborns and children in some countries and for some indicators, the international community – in partnership with national governments – must accelerate and intensify efforts dramatically in order to reach all of the health-related Millennium Development Goals. The eight organizations represented have an important role in stimulating this action. Participants agreed to hold themselves accountable for providing the necessary support to countries to reach the goals and to accelerate action at all levels within each of their own organizations.

Action: The global health leaders agreed to catalyse a greater sense of urgency in their own organizations and support it through budgetary and human resources decisions.

• **Modify institutional ways of doing business.** Achieving the health-related MDGs will require increased collaboration and teamwork. Emphasis was placed on clarifying the core responsibilities of each agency; the need for a coordinated inter-agency approach to providing high-quality, demand-driven technical assistance; and implementation of a collectively supported and robust monitoring and evaluation system. Such approaches need to build on existing structures and programmes at the global, regional and country levels. Each of the organizations agreed to evaluate their personnel, training programmes and incentives structure to reflect this new, collaborative way of doing business, recognizing that new skills will need to be developed, particularly at the country level. The development of a framework for mutual accountability would ensure more clarity on roles, responsibilities and milestones, and a system for monitoring commitments.

Action: The global health leaders agreed to work together to better define their individual and collective accountabilities for better and faster results.

• **Foster a more systematic and robust approach to knowledge management and learning.** Given the significant new investments in global health, opportunities are available to capture knowledge and lessons learned in health programmes. The participants emphasized the opportunity to conduct more systematic mapping of the health sector at the country level, including the role played by the private sector.

Action: The global health leaders agreed to explore means to systematically capture knowledge gained in health

of children unprotected from iodine deficiency, the leading cause of preventable intellectual impairment in the world. Iodine deficiency disorders can be prevented with a single teaspoon of iodine spread over a lifetime. The challenge was to raise public awareness of the vital importance of iodized salt, especially in salt-producing regions where local residents resisted the idea of paying for salt.

With political support from provincial governors, rigorous monitoring and enforcement of iodized salt regulations, as well as a nationwide public health campaign that used posters on buses, newspaper editorials and television documentaries to inform consumers and create demand for fortified salt, adequately iodized salt reached 90 per cent of the households around 2005, up from 51 per cent around 1995.[30]

Addressing the political dimension in creating sustainable continuums of quality care requires more than compelling technical arguments.

It also necessitates a broad understanding of the constraints and opportunities for fostering will and commitment among key political players.

Politicians may need to be convinced that actions in support of the continuum of care satisfy several expedient criteria, including that they:

• Demonstrate visible and tangible results within a relatively short time frame.

programmes and to develop a more robust and coordinated approach to knowledge management in general. Finally, the group agreed to pool resources when their organizations conduct mapping exercises and health sector assessments.

• **Recognition of the important opportunity presented by the renewed interest in health systems.** Participants welcomed the commitment to the health-related MDGs as articulated in several new global initiatives being developed around health-system strengthening. Such support is well aligned with the priorities of the participating organizations. There was strong agreement for adopting a 'systems for outcomes' approach whereby strengthening would be evaluated by its ability to deliver against health outcomes. In addition, the group recognized the key brokering role of the UN agencies in bridging the need for accountability and countries' desires to lead their own development processes. The urgent need for benchmarking health system performance was emphasized. Finally, with the growing number of stakeholders working in global health, the need for closer alignment around an overarching health-sector strategy at the country level was emphasized. In this regard, the global health leaders discussed the experience of programming for HIV and AIDS, which may offer learning opportunities.

Action: The global health leaders agreed to engage emerging global initiatives in a coordinated manner to ensure their organizations effectively support countries through funding and/or technical and policy assistance. In addition, WHO and the World Bank committed to fast-track the benchmarking of health system performance.

• **Recognition that the role of civil society and the private sector will be critical for success.** The private sector has several roles to fulfil in delivering health services, in financing health care and in bringing new technologies to market. Innovations can help accelerate progress, whether they are technologically driven or new programme models, such as micro-venture and performance-based financing. Non-governmental organizations have a long history of delivering services in developing countries, and their field experience is a source of important lessons. Support to developing countries in reaching the health-related MDGs will require strengthening integrated delivery systems across the public and private sectors, and creating opportunities for private sector involvement and investment.

Action: The global health leaders expressed their commitment to involve the private sector and civil society more systematically as the work on the health-related MDGs expands at global, regional and country levels.

The group has agreed to monitor progress towards achieving the commitments made at this meeting.

See References, page 108.

Human rights, community-based health care and child survival

by Paul Farmer and Jim Yong Kim

With 20 years of experience in rural Haiti introducing modern medical care to millions who had not previously enjoyed it, we now know many of the requirements for a successful health-care programme in areas devastated by disease and poverty. To provide primary care alongside specialized treatment for infectious disease, while promoting women's and children's health, community health-care workers must be trained and mobilized to prevent illness and to deliver quality health care. With recent expansion to Lesotho, Malawi and Rwanda, we now see that many of the lessons learned in Haiti are universal in improving the health of children and adults worldwide.

In each of the settings in which Partners In Health works, our goal is to 'do whatever it takes' to improve the health and well-being of those we serve, almost all of whom live in poverty. In each setting, we have learned that health problems do not occur in isolation from other basic needs, such as adequate nutrition, clean water, sanitation, housing and primary education. We have also learned that non-governmental organizations cannot work in isolation but must collaborate with members of the communities served and with local health authorities to strengthen public health so that future generations may come to regard these services as rights rather than privileges.

This rights-based, community-based approach to promoting health leads to a clear vision regarding the health of children

In Haiti, Lesotho, Malawi and Rwanda, Partners In Health – in collaboration with local communities and a wide range of partner organizations, including the Clinton Foundation, ministries of health, UNICEF and the François-Xavier Bagnoud Center for Health and Human Rights – has identified five key components for a comprehensive, community-based child survival programme.

First, we work with public health authorities to roll out the interventions shown to be crucial to improved child survival. These include expanded vaccination campaigns; vitamin A distribution; the use of oral rehydration salts to treat diarrhoeal disease and safe-water programmes to prevent it; an aggressive programme for prevention of mother-to-child transmission of HIV; malaria prevention with mosquito nets, backed by improved community-based and clinical care; nutritional assistance for children suffering from or at risk of malnutrition; and the provision of high-quality in-patient and ambulatory paediatric services for those children who do fall ill. Currently, we are working with the Government of Rwanda and other partners to show how an integrated package of key child survival interventions, including prevention of mother-to-child transmission of HIV, can be rapidly deployed under the Government's strengthened rural-health-care model. With support from the international Joint Learning Initiative on Children and HIV/AIDS, a cross-sectoral, interdisciplinary exercise in collaboration between leading practitioners, policymakers and scholars, practitioners scaling up child survival interventions in rural districts are sharing innovations and results through a collaborative network that will enable them to improve service quality, even as they reach greater numbers of children and families in previously underserved areas.

Second, since the health and well-being of mothers are key determinants of child survival, our efforts promote integrated maternal and child health. Our work on behalf of children is linked to efforts on behalf of their mothers and other family members through family planning programmes, prenatal care and modern obstetrics as part of women's health programmes, efforts to promote adult literacy and poverty alleviation in general.

- Are affordable and cost-effective at scale.

- Fit within existing structures and hierarchies and have the support of professional groups and lobbies.

These political considerations are likely to constrain some of the technical choices that advocates of the continuum prefer, but unless such political concerns are acknowledged and addressed, the strategies they promote are unlikely to succeed.

Stability, in political and macro-economic terms, and sound budgeting are prerequisites for mobilizing the institutional, human and financial resources required to strength health systems and nutrition services. Many of the countries struggling

Third, we initiate and/or strengthen paediatric AIDS prevention and control programmes. As part of an upcoming campaign, and in the manner outlined above, we are launching a major paediatric AIDS initiative in Rwanda in concert with the Clinton Foundation and Rwandan health officials and providers. This initiative will establish a national centre of excellence for paediatric AIDS care. Quality paediatric services will be linked to community-based care for children with HIV and also to prevention efforts within primary and secondary schools in rural Rwanda.

Fourth, we need to launch operational research and training programmes designed to improve the quality of care afforded to rural children. Such research will examine the programmatic features of successful efforts to prevent HIV transmission from mother to child; the diagnosis and management of HIV among infants; paediatric tuberculosis diagnosis and care; the role of community health workers in improving care for chronic paediatric conditions, including AIDS and tuberculosis, and in preventing, diagnosing and providing home-based treatment for such common ailments as malaria and diarrhoea; and assessing the impact of social interventions, including those designed to curb food insecurity and illiteracy, on the health and well-being of children worldwide.

Fifth, we work to advance these efforts in tandem with those designed to promote the basic rights, in particular, the social and economic rights, of the child. The Partners In Health Program on Social and Economic Rights (POSER) disseminates, through tangible projects and through advocacy, a rights-based model of poverty alleviation, using access to health care as a means of meeting and working with the poorest children and families in the communities we serve. POSER backs education, agriculture, housing and water projects to guarantee basic social and economic rights for every child and every family. If we know that hunger and malnutrition are the underlying cause of millions of child deaths each year – and we do – then we must face up to the challenge of prescribing food as an essential medicine for immunization and paediatric care. Similarly, if studies show that education reduces the risk of infection with HIV – as they do – then we must be prepared to invest in access to schooling as a potent and cost-effective element in our formulary for combating HIV and other diseases of poverty.

We now know that without a community-based, comprehensive strategy, efforts to treat children – and subsequently mothers, fathers and siblings – fail to provide the desired outcomes. Working in conjunction with ministries of health, international institutions and other non-profit organizations, we are committed to stemming the tide of childhood death and disease in the areas we serve. From experience in Haiti and now around the world, we know that community-based services to improve health and reduce poverty, linked, when necessary, to excellent clinical resources, offer the highest standard of care in the world today and the key to improving child survival.

Drs. Paul Farmer and Jim Yong Kim are co-founders of Partners In Health, an international health and social justice organization that works in Haiti, Lesotho, Malawi, Peru, the Russian Federation, Rwanda and the United States. Paul Farmer is the Presley Professor of Medical Anthropology at Harvard University and an attending physician at Brigham and Women's Hospital in Boston. Jim Yong Kim is Chair of the Department of Social Medicine at Harvard Medical School, Chief of the Division of Social Medicine and Health Inequalities at Brigham and Women's Hospital, Director of the François-Xavier Bagnoud Center for Health and Human Rights and a former director of the World Health Organization's HIV/AIDS Department.

to meet the MDGs, particularly in sub-Saharan Africa, do not enjoy political or economic stability. Under such circumstances, it is important to mobilize all forms of effective leadership in society, whether at the national level where broad sectoral decisions are made or at various subnational levels (provincial, district) where the interaction with communities takes place.

In contrast to the extensive knowledge of the technical and contextual interventions required to improve maternal, newborn and child health, there is less known on how political commitment to a result-oriented approach to health services delivery is both effected and sustained, particular in settings of low health systems capacity. The international community knows how to set the agenda – witness how the MDGs were derived from the Millennium Declaration and have become the benchmark for human development in the early years of the millennium. But, at the midpoint of the goals, there is still a gap between the intention and action.

Strong leadership and champions are often pivotal to successful scale-up

One of the most intriguing findings of a study on scaling up conducted by the Disease Control Priorities Project, an ongoing effort by many of the world's leading health specialists to assess disease control priorities, is the important role of national champions in generating and sustaining the political will and commitment to take health programmes to scale. These champions are not only strong backers of initiatives, they have also been able to bring together key stakeholders, coordinate activities and sustain momentum for scaling up.

Leadership can come in many different forms: from an individual, such as Fazle Hasan Abed, the founder of BRAC, a successful community health programme that provides essential health-care services to millions in Bangladesh; from the highest levels of national government, as was the case in Mexico, whose PROGRESA programme was championed by President Ernesto Zedillo de Leon, and maintained and expanded by his successors, Vicente Fox and Felipe Calderón; and from international quarters, such as the Expanded Programme on Immunization, the child survival revolution and GOBI (growth monitoring, oral rehydration therapy, breastfeed-

ing and immunization), the multiplicity of global partnerships and programmes for various diseases over the past six decades, and most recently, the Integrated Management of Childhood Illness (IMCI) and the Accelerated Child Survival and Development initiative.

One of the points that emerges from the review of evidence and experience on scaling up is that championing takes time and commitment. Sustained investment in both time and resources is required over many years to steadily take programmes to scale. Key examples of such commitment include Sri Lanka's 50-year project to create a rural health network and Nepal's long-standing campaigns on micronutrient supplementation.[31]

Enshrining national commitments in a legal framework can provide the necessary continuity in support of scaling up the continuum of care beyond the political lifespan of its initial champions. Such a framework makes it possible to translate political commitment into resource mobilization and budgetary measures. This longer-term political agenda requires partnerships between government, civil society organizations and development agencies to maintain the political momentum, overcome resistance to change and mobilize resources. It also requires accountability mechanisms and checks and balances to keep the system on track.

V. Greater harmonization of global health partnerships and programmes

Over the past decade, the aid architecture in health has become even

more complex with the emergence of large global health partnerships (GHPs). Depending on the definition used, it is estimated that there are over 100 GHPs.[32] They are a diverse group, with functions ranging from advocacy to implementation, and are different in nature, scale and scope. The vast majority focus on communicable diseases – particularly AIDS, tuberculosis and malaria. Some GHPs also promote nutrition interventions, such as early and exclusive breastfeeding and vitamin A supplementation, or improved water and sanitation. In recent years, increasing attention has been given to activities focused on achieving MDG 1, which aims to halve hunger and poverty by 2015, through such initiatives as Ending Child Hunger and Undernutrition Initiative, Global Alliance for Improved Nutrition, Micronutrient Initiative and Flour Fortification Initiative.

Although there are a large number of GHPs, only a handful have a major impact on health financing – notably, the GAVI Alliance and the Global Fund to Fight Aids, Tuberculosis and Malaria. Global health partnerships have mobilized important new resources for major health threats, and brought much needed political and technical focus to priority diseases or interventions. They have injected new energy into development assistance by supporting the private sector and encouraging community partnerships to take a more prominent role in the provision of health care.

The rapid creation of new institutions in health is proving challenging for developing countries to keep track of, let alone to manage and coordinate.

Furthermore, new initiatives have the potential to complicate efforts at harmonizing and coordinating actions at the global level in support of maternal, newborn and child survival and health. Given their strong focus on achieving rapid, cost-effective and measurable results, the proliferation of GHPs risks entrenching the 'vertical' nature of health financing by focusing large amounts of new funding on disease-specific programmes and interventions, creating separate financing and delivery silos, and leaving recipient governments with little flexibility to reallocate funds according to their own priorities or to fund health-system costs and investments such as salaries and facilities.

Creating conditions for increased unity in global health programmes and partnerships

In response to the proliferation of global health partnerships and initiatives, a set of best practice principles for global health partnerships has been developed. Based on the Paris Declaration on Aid Effectiveness, the principles were endorsed by participants and have now been adopted by the boards of a number of GHPs. In addition, the OECD Development Assistance Committee has reviewed a 'Good Practice Guidance for aligning global programs at the country level'. This responds to the need identified in the Paris Declaration for taking concrete and effective action to address insufficient integration of global programmes and initiatives into partner countries' broader development agendas. On governance and implementation of global programmes, the good practices address the interlinked roles of financiers (bilateral donors, multilateral institu-

tions and private foundations), partner countries and global programmes.

Global programmes in health, whether in partnerships or through individual actions of single organizations and donors, have become an important tool of development assistance, with bilateral donors, multilateral institutions and private foundations providing rapidly increasing levels of financing for service delivery at the country level. These programmes, which also attract strong public support, call international attention to issues of global importance, encourage innovation and the dissemination of best practices, and provide pooled multi-donor funding (upstream harmonization).

The principles of the Paris Declaration on Aid Effectiveness – with their focus on country ownership, harmonization and alignment, and mutual accountability – apply to global as well as country-based programmes. Country studies confirm that issues of implementation are similar for the two, but that many global programmes face specific challenges. These include lack of field representation and related absence from donor harmonization efforts, inconsistency with government priorities and budgets, parallel mechanisms for coordination, as well as for implementation, and a centrifugal pull on human and financial resources from related national programmes.

The good practices take as their base the principles and related indicators of the Paris Declaration, applying and extending them to reflect the specific case of global programmes. They are intended primarily to improve the

effectiveness of global programmes, current or proposed, that provide significant country-level financing. However, some of the good practices, including those on selectivity and governance, have implications for global programmes in general.

Financiers, partner countries, global programmes and private donors are being invited to apply the guidance on a trial basis. Monitoring of a pilot of good practice application will be carried out as part of the use of health as a tracer sector to monitor the effective implementation of the Paris Declaration on Aid Effectiveness and will be reported at the High Level Forum on Aid Effectiveness to be held in Accra, Ghana, September 2008.

SUMMARY The Millennium Development Goals are not a series of utopian targets. They are the product of tough thinking and hard calculations by some of the world's leading politicians, development specialists, economists and scientists, and they currently represent the world's best hope to accelerate human progress.

Achieving the goals will result in hundreds of millions of children, men and women being relieved of hunger, utilizing safe water and basic sanitation, obtaining an education, and enjoying the same economic advantages and political opportunities that are available to others. Although several regions and countries are lagging behind, the targets are all *reachable* in the time remaining if the political will, the necessary resources and the required strategies are put in place.

Can the political will be mustered? Can frameworks, strategies, actions and resources be galvanized into a unified drive to meet the MDGs on time and in full? The short answer is 'yes' – but only if governments, donors, civil society

Meeting the health-related MDGs will require unified actions and partnerships in support of maternal, newborn and child survival and health. *Children wait in line at a vaccination site, Bangladesh.*

and other stakeholders unite for child survival and commit themselves to ensuring that the health-related MDGs are met.

The challenge is to shake off cynicism and lethargy and put aside the broken promises of the past. In the end, no enterprise is more essential or reward more satisfying than saving the life of a child.

5

Uniting for child survival

The world will not be a perfect place even if the Millennium Development Goals are achieved. Poverty will still exist. Children and their mothers will still die needlessly. And the environment will continue to demand our attention. Nevertheless, according to the estimates from the Millennium Project, the independent advisory body that introduced recommendations for achieving the MDGs to the 2005 World Summit, reaching the goals will mean that the lives of up to 30 million children and 2 million mothers will have been spared. More than 300 million people will no longer go hungry. Hundreds of millions of people will gain access to safe drinking water and basic sanitation facilities. Millions more children will go to school and millions more women will enjoy economic and political opportunities.[1]

The MDGs were not dreamed up by a group of utopians. They are the result of tough thinking and hard calculations by some of the world's leading politicians, development specialists, economists and scientists, and they currently represent humankind's best hope to steer the world on a more sustainable course. They are

reachable targets, well within the realm of possibility – *if* the political will, the necessary resources and the required strategies are put in place. Making the decision to achieve the goals is the essential first step. Action on the additional steps needed to achieve the health-related MDGs – outlined below – can then be accomplished mostly within the framework of existing approaches to maternal, newborn and child health care.

Can this political will be mustered? Can individual and collective frameworks, strategies, actions and resources be galvanized into a unified drive to meet the health-related MDGs in full and on time? *The State of the World's Children 2008* has identified six pivotal actions at the macro level that urgently require unified engagement to intensify efforts for maternal, newborn and child survival and fulfil the right of women and children to health and well-being. These are:

- Work towards creating a supportive environment for maternal, newborn and child survival and health.

- Develop and strengthen the continuum of care across time and location.

- Scale up packages of essential services by strengthening health systems and community partnerships.

- Expand the data, research and evidence base.

- Leverage resources for mothers, newborns and children.

- Make maternal, newborn and child survival a global imperative.

Create a supportive environment for child survival and health

While *The State of the World's Children 2008* has focused mainly on the essential interventions and approaches that have proved effective in saving children's lives, more far-reaching and systemic changes are needed. Providing quality health care to women and children demands an environment in which they can survive and thrive. The most obvious requirement is the absence of conflict. Peace and security are essential for the proper functioning of health programmes, whether they are

Healthy and secure environments are vital conditions for the survival and well-being of mothers and their children. *A woman receives a diploma for completing a child-rearing course, Turkey.*

facility-based services, extension-based services or community partnerships. If paths to conflict resolution cannot be found, it is vitally important to reach and protect children and their families caught in complex emergencies. Although incorporating the concept of children as 'zones of peace' into international law has not been realized, 'days of tranquility', when fighting stops and brigades of health-care workers are able to administer vaccines, have been declared in recent decades in countries as diverse as Afghanistan, Angola, the Democratic Republic

of the Congo, El Salvador, Lebanon, Somalia, Sri Lanka and Sudan.[2]

Equally important is a child's sense of inner security, which can be disrupted by armed conflict, high levels of violence and crime within communities or by living in an embattled home. Infants and young children are acutely sensitive to the world around them. Anticipation of the next crisis, whether it is a landmine explosion or sexual assault by a relative or family friend, can be almost as traumatic and destabilizing as the act itself. Acknowledging children's right to a protective environ-

ment is essential in preventing violence against them, and it must be followed by appropriate legislation and effective enforcement.

Equity is another critical aspect of a supportive environment for children. In far too many countries, to be poor automatically means to be neglected and marginalized by the health system. Others are excluded from essential services and practices on the grounds of gender, disability, race or ethnic origin. Ensuring that health systems and maternal and child survival programmes are rights-based and seek to rectify such inequities is imperative. Moreover, to effectively reach those currently missing out, health programmes must be integrated into strategies that address the root causes, as well as the effects, of marginalization and social exclusion.

Sustained improvements in the health of women and children will also demand greater gender equality and the empowerment of women. No matter how or which health services are provided, many children will miss out unless women have wider decision-making powers within the household. Numerous studies have confirmed the powerful and positive effects of education and economic opportunities on women's well-being, which translate into better care and improved survival prospects for their children.

Develop and strengthen the continuum of care across time and location

Children are most vulnerable at birth and during the first few days of life. Health care, therefore, is crucial during pregnancy, at birth and in the neonatal period. This continuum of care should extend through infancy and early childhood, with packages of essential services delivered to both mother and child at key points during the life cycle. The life cycle approach acknowledges that the continuum will require education, empowerment, knowledge and reproductive health services for girls in adolescence, since many of them will also become mothers – around 13 per cent of babies were born to mothers aged 15–19 in 2005[3] – and on into womanhood. To be effective, the continuum of care must forge strong links between the household, the community and quality outreach and clinical services at primary health facilities, which, in turn, have strong connections to a district hospital. Establishing these links often results in greater use of services. It also means that fewer women and children are likely to fall through the cracks.

The household and community are where childcare practices and care-seeking behaviours are learned and supported. These are often introduced in visits to a health clinic during pregnancy, which can be a woman's first contact with the formal health system. Antenatal care is important because it helps women identify potential risks and plan for a safe pregnancy. If a health clinic is not located nearby, extension services must be provided through staff from outlying and district facilities. Such services typically provide a mix of antenatal, postnatal and child health care.

The district hospital is at the top of the health system for communities and households and must be adequately staffed and equipped to manage any complications during childbirth. At the level of primary care, facilities and staff should be prepared to assist uncomplicated births and offer basic emergency obstetric care and immediate newborn care, including resuscitation. The quality of care provided at all three levels, and strong connections between them, is key to ensuring a continuum of care across time and location.[4]

Scale up packages of essential services by strengthening health systems and community partnerships

The health systems in many of the poorest countries are fragile and fragmented, beset with problems ranging from an acute shortage of skilled staff to lack of financing, equipment and supplies and the inability to generate and use information. Over the medium to long term, the surest way to achieve the health-related Millennium Development Goals is to strengthen national health systems. Community partnerships in primary health care can be effective in scaling up services in areas of a country that are hard to access, and in strengthening health systems. As this report shows, there is a growing body of evidence that packaged interventions can be effectively delivered at the community level throughout the life cycle. Moreover, empowering individuals to assume a measure of responsibility for their own health – and that of their families – can have a profound and lasting impact on development.

Providing community members with the information they need to make changes in their lives can be greatly enhanced by the mass media, which can deliver key health messages at low cost. Moreover, civil society organizations that specialize in participatory approaches can be recruited to promote specific aspects of child survival and health, if given the proper guidelines and carefully monitored. Community mobilization need not be the sole responsibility of overstretched ministries of health. Indeed, local governments and ministries for women's development can play a pivotal role, along with women's organizations and domestic civil society leaders, if brought into the process from the outset.

Although current programmes for child survival emphasize low-tech solutions, cutting-edge technologies could provide an unexpected boon in reaching the hard to reach. For example, simple diagnostic tools have been developed to diagnose malaria, test for HIV, and analyse water quality. With basic training, such tests can be administered out of even the most rudimentary health clinic. Biotechnology is producing safer recombinant vaccines, and research is ongoing to provide vaccines that do not require refrigeration and may be delivered by skin patches, nasal spray or other techniques, rather than by injection. Both of these potential breakthroughs could have enormous repercussions for expanding immunization services.[5]

Although its application to this area is still in the early stages, information technology, too, has a role in child survival and health in developing countries. The growing use of mobile phones, email and the Internet means that eHealth and telemedicine can

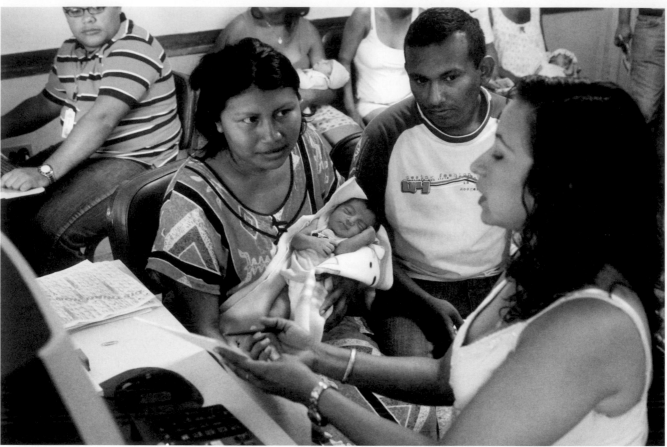

An integrated approach to health systems development is pivotal to advancing child survival and health. *This family participates in the Trio por la Vida ('Trio for Life') programme, which promotes birth registration, breastfeeding and immunization, Venezuela.*

already reach people in remote areas and could have much broader applications. In addition, health-care workers can more easily connect to primary care facilities and, if needed, to departments and referral centres in hospitals.[6]

Expand the evidence base

Understanding a problem is often half the solution. While the broad outlines of the situation of children around the world are clearly defined, the specifics are sometimes vague. The dearth of reliable statistics in many countries makes it difficult for policymakers to establish priorities, measure the effectiveness of pro-

grammes or monitor progress. Even vital registration systems – which record key life events, including birth and death – sometimes cover only portions of a country, if they are available at all. Birth registration, in particular, is essential to protecting children's rights and to generating accurate information about a country's population (*see Chapter 1, page 22*).

Accurate information and situation analysis on the state of health, nutrition, water, sanitation and hygiene, and HIV and AIDS among the world's children are pivotal to formulating strategies to scale up

community partnerships, the continuum of care and health systems for outcomes. The basis for data dissemination, results assessment and strategic planning in developing countries is being provided by a rich array of resources, including: household surveys, such as the Multiple Indicator Cluster Surveys; statistical reviews, such as the *Progress for Children* report card series produced by UNICEF; *The Lancet* series that have covered child, newborn and maternal survival and health; and publications assessing progress towards the Millennium Development Goals that have been produced by the United Nations Development Programme, the World Bank and the World Health Organization, among others. These initiatives are complementing national efforts across the developing world to produce, analyse and disseminate key health data and information related to maternal, newborn and child inputs and outcomes.

With increasing demands for accountability, as a result of both the MDGs and new global health initiatives, the need for a strong base of evidence is imperative. Although there is more than enough information to act, it is also true that there is still a need for more rigorous research and evaluation of what works, systematic sharing of good practices and greater sharing of new information.

Leverage resources for mothers, newborns and children

It is widely acknowledged that the poorest countries, in addition to mobilizing their own domestic resources, will require substantial help from richer nations to achieve the MDGs. According to estimates by the Millennium Project, the total official development assistance (ODA) required for the MDGs was US$135 billion in 2006, but the actual ODA delivered in 2006 totalled US$104 billion[7] (*see Figure 5.1*). On current trends, ODA looks set to rise to around US$200 billion by 2015. These estimated figures are equivalent to about 0.5 per cent of the gross national product (GNP) of donor countries – 0.44 per cent in 2006 and 0.54 per cent in 2015, respectively. When additional costs – for major infrastructure projects, adjusting to climate change and post-conflict reconstruction, for example – are factored in, a more likely target is 0.7 per cent of donor country GNP. The irony is that this amount is completely affordable within commitments already made by donor countries. More than 35 years ago,

major industrialized nations promised to allocate 0.7 per cent of their GNP for ODA.[8] In 2002, the 0.7 per cent target was reconfirmed by all countries in the Monterrey Consensus.

How are we doing? Sixteen of the 22 member countries of the OECD Development Assistance Committee met the 2006 targets for ODA they set in Monterrey. But the remaining six countries must be encouraged to deliver on their promises.[9]

Of course, the needs of countries seeking to achieve the MDGs are different. Based on the best evidence available, UNICEF is currently developing a country-specific list of policy options for achieving the health-related MDGs for consideration by governments and their partners in maternal and child health. It is also helping countries to identify and fill gaps in financial support.

Figure 5.1

Selected financial flows to developing countries

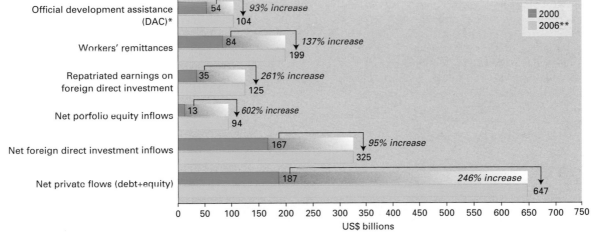

* Refers to official development assistance provided by the members of the OECD Development Assistance Committee.   **Estimate.

Source: World Bank, *Global Development Finance 2007: The globalization of corporate finance in developing countries*, Washington, D.C., 2007, pp. 37, 55.

In sub-Saharan Africa, where the situation of young children is most dire, UNICEF, WHO and the World Bank collaborated in 2006 on an analysis of what it would cost to reduce child mortality there (*see Panel, Chapter 4, page 78*). By scaling up the existing interventions highlighted in this report, deaths of children under five could be reduced by 35 per cent by 2009 at an additional cost of about US$2.50 per capita (or about US$800 per life saved). To fully achieve MDG 4, a reduction in under-five mortality by two thirds by 2015, would require additional strengthening of Africa's health systems, as well as the introduction of new interventions, such as vaccines against rotavirus and pneumococcal infections. The analysis found that it is entirely feasible to save the lives of more than 5 million children and nearly 200,000 mothers a year. What would saving these lives cost? An additional US$10 per capita per year (or less than US$2,000 per life saved).[10]

At the 2005 G8 Summit in Gleneagles, Scotland, the major

Strengthening data collection and monitoring for public health decisions

"It is not because countries are poor that they cannot afford good health information; it is because they are poor that they cannot afford to be without it." – Health Metrics Network, World Health Organization

Sound information is central to public health decisions, informing policy, programmes, budgets and evaluations and forming the basis of accountability for governments to their commitments and to their citizens. In many developing countries, however, underinvestment in health information systems has left gaps in data collection, dissemination and analysis. With health challenges on the rise and the deadline for the health-related Millennium Development Goals drawing ever closer, fulfilling the demand for sound information is imperative.

Before the mid-1990s, critical gaps in data hindered accurate and effective analysis for making such public health decisions. For example, only 38 developing countries had data on whether undernutrition rates among children were rising or falling – a basic indicator of child health and well-being. To help fill these important data gaps and to facilitate monitoring of the 1990 World Summit for Children goals, UNICEF initiated the Multiple Indicator Cluster Surveys (MICS) in 1995. MICS are designed to provide quantitative data on a wide range of topics, including child health and nutrition, child protection, education, HIV and AIDS, and maternal health.

Since 1995, nearly 200 MICS have been conducted in approximately 100 countries and territories. The current round of surveys, implemented in more than 50 countries during 2005–2006, provides data for 21 of 53 MDG sub-indicators. Together with the Demographic and Health Surveys, a complementary initiative sponsored by the United States Agency for International Development (USAID) with which data are harmonized, this is the largest single source of information for MDG monitoring.

Monitoring progress towards the Millennium Development Goals has also stimulated the formation of a series of interagency groups that address specific technical and methodological issues, including standardizing indicators and monitoring tools, building statistical capacity at the country level, developing joint estimates and harmonizing monitoring work between partners. These groups focus on such areas as under-five and maternal mortality, water and sanitation, immunization, malaria, and HIV and AIDS.

There is also an urgent need to improve overall data systems at the national level so they may more reliably report robust and timely data that can be used for informing public health decisions. This is a long-term effort, and the World Health Organization and the Health Metrics Network (HMN), among others, are working closely with countries and other initiatives to improve health information systems. Specifically, the objective is to develop a comprehensive system that would incorporate all the multiple subsystems and data sources that, taken together, contribute to generating health information: surveys, vital registration, censuses, disease surveillance and response, service statistics, health management information, financial data and resource tracking. The development of such a comprehensive system would require enhanced coordination and cooperation between countries and international partners, working together based on one harmonized plan for a unified system. This comprehensive data system would thereby reduce duplication, fragmentation and overlap in data collection and reporting.

See References, page 108.

industrialized nations pledged to double their aid to Africa by 2010. Yet, as of mid-2007, there is little advance in this direction.[11] African countries, too, have been remiss in demonstrating their commitment to their own children. In the Abuja Declaration, adopted at the Organization of African Unity's special summit on AIDS in 2001, African leaders included a commitment to devote 15 per cent of their national budgets to health. Yet six years later, only a few countries have managed to do so.[12]

The resources are available to meet the health-related MDGs. The world is richer than it has ever been. Financial flows to developing countries are at record levels, in terms of private debt inflows, foreign direct investment, portfolio equity and remittances. And yet, while official development assistance has doubled since 2000, its increase has lagged marginally behind other financial flows (*see Figure 5.1, page 99*). Donors have yet to make good on their promise to increase assistance to Africa and will need to step up efforts markedly in the coming years.

Make maternal, newborn and child survival a global imperative

Many have heard the cry for child and maternal survival. Since the early years of the child survival revolution, global partnerships for health, often financed through private sources, have proliferated and reinvigorated the field: including, for example, the Flour Fortification Initiative, the Global Alliance for Improved Nutrition, the GAVI Alliance, the Partnership for Maternal, Newborn & Child Health, Roll Back Malaria

Partnerships and renewed commitment on the part of all stakeholders are required to realize the health needs of all mothers, newborns and children. *A health worker discusses immunization with a mother, United Republic of Tanzania.*

and the Special Programme for Research and Training in Tropical Diseases, among many others.

As a consequence of these and other alliances, public attention to global health issues is at an all-time high. Research and development sponsored by these partnerships are beginning to yield results, with 25 drugs, 8 microbicides and 50 vaccines in the pipeline to address diseases predominantly affecting the poor. A number of these partnerships have proved remarkably effective in offering communities free or reduced-cost medicines whose quality is assured, along with vaccines. Others are improving national policymaking and supporting institutional reforms. Still others are contributing to the establishment of norms and standards in treatment protocols.[13]

Yet, in their single-mindedness to produce results, it has been argued that global partnerships are often donor- and commodity-driven rather than country- and people-centred. Moreover, a frequent focus on single diseases has sometimes meant an over-reliance on vertical interventions and insufficient emphasis on integrating services and strengthening national health systems.[14] The message that has been widely heard – and heeded – is that developing countries must take the lead and 'own' the solutions to their health problems. This will require greater harmonization and alignment with developing countries' own priorities, systems and procedures. Indeed, this was the position adopted in the Paris Declaration on Aid Effectiveness in March 2005, which is providing a framework through which donor

The other side of the mat: Uniting for maternal, newborn and child survival and health

by Melinda French Gates, Co-chair,
Bill & Melinda Gates Foundation

When Bill and I meet people in the developing countries we visit, it's easy to see what we have in common with them, in spite of our different circumstances. Like us, they have hopes for the future. They have parents who love them and children who need them. They have intellectual curiosity, an entrepreneurial spirit and a determination to make life better for themselves and their children.

I am especially moved by the mothers I meet. They invite me into their homes, and we sit on the floor, often on opposite sides of a small mat, talking. I have young children myself, and I try to put myself in their position. What would I do if I were on the other side of the mat? What would I want for my children?

If I were a pregnant mother in Bangladesh, I would want a skilled attendant who knew how to help me deliver my baby safely. If I were a young mother in India, I would want to know the facts: that breastfeeding instead of using formula is one of the best ways to save my newborn from cholera. If I were a mother in Malawi and my daughter got sick with diarrhoea, I would hope that she could get the electrolytes she needed before it was too late.

Those would be my hopes, my dreams, my wishes. But for many, they are not the reality of their daily lives. The reality is this: In 2006, 9.7 million children died before they turned five – most from easily preventable or treatable causes.

In some countries I've visited, mothers don't give their children names for weeks or even months because they don't want to start caring about them. The chance that their children will die in those first weeks is just too high. When I hear such stories, I am jolted back to my side of the mat. How can such widespread tragedy be so common in the developing world?

On my side of the mat, when my kids are sick, they get antibiotics. On the other side of the mat, when their children get sick, they may be receiving a death sentence. Those of us in wealthy countries must try to put ourselves on the other side of the mat.

Fortunately, the story is starting to change. Governments around the world are doing more for children's health. Efforts to treat and prevent the world's most devastating diseases are improving the lives of millions of children.

To keep this momentum going, we must remember that these mothers love their children just as much as we love ours. We must see that these children have boundless potential. And we must help them realize their potential by bringing more governments, more businesses and more individuals to this work – to unite for maternal, newborn and child survival and health. When we do, all mothers will have a chance to see their children grow up happy and strong, and all children will have a chance to make their dreams come true.

and developing country partnerships can fully exploit their potential.

So, where does the world find itself today, just past the midway point to the target date for achieving the Millennium Development Goals? On balance, half of the world's regions are on track to meet MDG 4 and reduce child mortality rates by two thirds between 1990 and 2015. This is without doubt an unprecedented scenario, reflecting advances in maternal and child health in the past century and the commitment of both donors and national governments to unite to ensure that children survive and thrive.

Many developing countries and several regions have managed to make great strides in reducing child mortality, and a few have managed to reduce mortality rates to levels approaching those in some industrialized countries, despite having far lower levels of per capita income. Three regions – Latin America and the Caribbean, East Asia and the Pacific, and Central and Eastern Europe and the Commonwealth of Independent States (CEE/CIS) – have reduced child mortality substantially since 1960, despite bouts of economic and political instability. This success provides a source of hope that child mortality rates will continue to decline at an even faster rate globally if ways can be found to enhance access to quality care for mothers, newborns and children in the developing world.

The challenge is to build on the progress achieved across the developing world in preventive interventions delivered by outreach services, particularly in recent years. Expanded interventions delivered by outreach – notably expanded immunization programmes, enhanced distribution of insecticide-treated mosquito nets, greater distribution of oral rehydration therapy and a broadening of vitamin A supplementation – have enhanced the input side of the child and maternal health balance sheet. Analysis of these results, together with the enhanced frequency of data collection, promises to show a marked impact on child and maternal survival outcomes in the coming years.

Notwithstanding the many initiatives, programmes and policies that have proliferated since the first year of the new millennium, the opportunity to reduce deaths among children under five has never been clearer. What needs to be done for progress in child survival is clear. When it needs to be done, and who needs to be involved is also clear. The need to be *united* – in both word and deed – to ensure the right of mothers, newborns and children to quality primary health care is clearest of all.

The challenge is, therefore, to shake off any cynicism and lethargy and put aside the broken promises of the past. At the midpoint between the inauguration of the MDGs in 2000 and their target date for fulfilment in 2015, much has already been achieved. The basis for action – data, research, evaluation – is already well established. It is time to rally behind the goals of maternal, newborn and child survival and health with renewed energy and sharper vision, and to position these goals at the heart of the international agenda to fulfil the tenets of social justice and honour the sanctity of life.

The means are at hand. It is now a question of will and of action – for there is no enterprise more noble, or reward more precious than saving the life of a child.

References

CHAPTER 1

1 UNICEF estimates, based on the work of the Inter-agency Child Mortality Estimation Group.

2 World Health Organization and United Nations Children's Fund, 'Integration of Vitamin A Supplementation with Immunization: Policy and programme implications, Meeting report (WHO/EPI/GEN/98.07)' WHO, Geneva, 1998, pp. 4-12.

3 Darmstadt, Gary L., et al., 'Evidence-Based, Cost-Effective Interventions: How many newborn babies can we save?', *The Lancet*, vol. 365, no. 9463, 12 March 2005, pp. 977-988.

4 Phillips, James F., Ayaga A. Bawah and Fred N. Binka, 'Accelerating Reproductive and Child Health Programme Impact with Community-Based Services: The Navrongo experiment in Ghana', *Bulletin of the World Health Organization*, vol. 84, no. 12, Dec. 2006, pp. 949-953.

5 United Nations Children's Fund, *Progress for Children: A World Fit for Children statistical review*, Number 6, UNICEF, New York, Dec. 2007, p. 19.

6 WHO Regional Office for Africa, *The Health of the People: The African regional health report*, WHO Press, Geneva, 2006, p. 19.

7 Newell, Marie-Louise, et al., 'Mortality of Infected and Uninfected Infants Born to HIV-Infected Mothers in Africa: A pooled analysis', *The Lancet*, vol. 364, no. 9441, 2 Oct. 2004, pp. 1236-1243.

8 De Cock, Kevin M., et al., 'Prevention of Mother-to-Child HIV Transmission in Resource-Poor Countries: Translating research into policy and practice', *Journal of the American Medical Association*, vol. 283, no. 9, 1 March 2000, pp. 1175-1182.

9 World Health Organization, Joint United Nations Programme on HIV/AIDS and United Nations Children's Fund, *Towards Universal Access: Scaling up priority HIV/AIDS interventions in the health sector – Progress report, April 2007*, WHO, Geneva, 2007, pp. 6, 30.

10 Ngongo, Ngashi, 'PMTCT Report Card 2005: Monitoring progress on the implementation of programs to prevent mother to child transmission of HIV', UNICEF, New York, p. 5.

11 United Nations Children's Fund, *Progress for Children: A World Fit for Children statistical review*, Number 6, UNICEF, New York, Dec. 2007, p. 36.

12 United Nations Children's Fund and Roll Back Malaria Partnership, 'Malaria & Children: Progress in intervention coverage', UNICEF and RBM, New York, 2007, pp. 1, 7.

13 Global Fund to Fight AIDS, Tuberculosis and Malaria, *HIV/AIDS, Tuberculosis and Malaria: The status and impact of the three diseases*, GFATM, Geneva, 2005, p. 39.

14 United Nations Children's Fund, *Progress for Children: A World Fit for Children statistical review*, Number 6, UNICEF, New York, Dec. 2007, pp. 39-41.

15 World Health Organization, 'Health Status: Mortality', *World Health Statistics 2006*, WHO, Geneva, 2007, pp. 29-31.

16 United Nations Children's Fund, *Progress for Children: A report card on water and sanitation, Number 5*, UNICEF, New York, Sept. 2006, p. 3.

17 Black, Robert E., Saul S. Morris and Jennifer Bryce, 'Where and Why Are 10 Million Children Dying Every Year?', *The Lancet*, vol. 361, no. 9376, 28 June 2003, p. 2230.

18 World Health Organization, 'Improving Child Health in the Community', WHO, Geneva, Dec. 2002, p. 7.

19 Countdown to 2015: Child Survival, *Tracking Progress in Child Survival: 2005 report*, UNICEF Health Section, New York, 2005, p. 9.

20 UNICEF estimate, based on data provided by the Inter-agency Child Mortality Estimation Group.

21 Darmstadt, Gary L., et al., 'Evidence-Based, Cost-Effective Interventions: How many lives of newborn babies can we save?', *The Lancet*, <www.thelancet.com>, 3 March 2005, p. 11.

22 World Health Organization, *Making a Difference in Countries: Strategic approach to improving maternal and newborn survival and health*, WHO, Geneva, 2006, p. 9.

23 'Table 1. Basic Indicators', pp. 114-117 of this report.

24 Pinheiro, Paulo Sérgio, *World Report on Violence Against Children*, UN Secretary-General's Study on Violence against Children, New York, 2006, p. 51.

25 United Nations Children's Fund, 'Early Marriage: Child spouses', *Innocenti Digest*, no. 7, UNICEF Innocenti Research Centre, Florence, March 2001, p. 11.

26 Ibid.

27 Ibid.

28 United Nations Children's Fund, *The 'Rights' Start to Life: A statistical analysis of birth registration*, UNICEF, New York, 2005, pp. 1, 13.

29 United Nations Educational, Scientific and Cultural Organization, *EFA Global Monitoring Report 2007: Strong foundations – Early childhood care and education*, UNESCO, Paris, 2006, p. 2.

30 Porterfield, Shirley L., and Timothy D. McBride, 'The Effect of Poverty and Caregiver Education on Perceived Need and Access to Health Services among Children with Special Health Care Needs', *American Journal of Public Health*, vol. 97, no. 2, Feb. 2007, p. 323.

31 Ibid.

32 White, Howard, *Maintaining Momentum to 2015? An impact evaluation of interventions to improve maternal and child health and nutrition in Bangladesh*, World Bank, Washington, D.C., Sept. 2005, p. 25.

33 United Nations Children's Fund, *The State of the World's Children 2006: Excluded and invisible*, UNICEF, New York, Dec. 2005, p. 18.

34 Victora, Cesar G., et al., 'Applying an Equity Lens to Child Health and Mortality: More of the same is not enough', *The Lancet*, vol. 362, no. 9379, 19 July 2003, p. 234.

35 Ibid.

CHAPTER 1 PANELS

The under-five mortality rate: The indispensable gauge of child health
United Nation's Children's Fund, *The State of the World's Children 2007: Women and children – The double dividend of gender equality*, UNICEF, New York, Dec. 2006, pp. 137, 141.

Underlying and structural causes of maternal and child mortality
United Nations Children's Fund, 'UNICEF Joint Health and Nutrition Strategy for 2006-2015 (E/ICEF/2006/8)', UN Economic and Social Council, New York, 15 Nov. 2005, pp. 3-4.

Newborn survival
Darmstadt, Gary L., 'Evidence-Based, Cost-Effective Interventions: How many newborn babies can we save?', *The Lancet*, vol. 365, no. 9463, 12 March 2005, pp. 977-988; The Lancet Series Team, 'Executive Summary of The Lancet Neonatal Survival Series', *The Lancet*, 3 March 2005, p. 1; Lawn, Joy E., Simon Cousens and Jelka Zupan, '4 Million Neonatal Deaths: When? Where? Why?', *The Lancet*, 5 March 2005, vol. 365, no. 9462, pp. 891-900; Save the Children, *State of the World's Mothers 2006: Saving the lives of mothers and newborns*, Save the Children, Westport, CT, May 2006, pp. 3, 8; 'Table 8. Women', pp. 142-145 of this report; World Health Organization, *World Health Report 2005: Make every mother and child count*, WHO, Geneva, 2005, pp. 9-10.

The main proximate causes of child deaths
Mulholland, Kim, 'Childhood Pneumonia Mortality: A permanent global emergency', *The Lancet*, vol. 370, no. 9583, 21 July 2007, pp. 285-289; United Nations Children's Fund, *Progress for Children: A report card on water and sanitation, Number 5*, UNICEF, New York, Sept. 2006, p. 2, and *Progress for Children: A World Fit for Children statistical review, Number 6*, Dec. 2007, pp. 19, 24; UNICEF and World Health Organization, *Pneumonia: The forgotten killer of children*, UNICEF and WHO, New York and Geneva, 2006, p. 5.

Pneumonia: The forgotten killer of children
Mulholland, Kim, 'Childhood Pneumonia Mortality: A permanent global emergency', *The Lancet*, vol. 370, no. 9583, 21 July 2007, pp. 285-289; Sazawal, Sunil, and Robert E. Black, 'Effect of Pneumonia Case Management on Mortality in Neonates, Infants, and Preschool Children: A meta-analysis of community-based trials', *The Lancet Infectious Diseases*, vol. 3, no. 9, Sept. 2003, pp. 547-556; United Nations Children's Fund and World Health Organization, *Pneumonia: The forgotten killer of children*, UNICEF and WHO, New York, and Geneva, 2006, p. 5, 7-9, 14, 26, 27; World Health Organization, 'Evidence Base for the Community Management of Pneumonia (WHO/FCH/CAH/02.23)', WHO Dept. of Child and Adolescent Health and Development, Stockholm, June 2002, pp. 2, 5-6.

The continuum of maternal, newborn and child health care across time and place
Lawn, Joy, and Kate Kerber, editors, *Opportunities for Africa's Newborns: Practical data, policy and programmatic support for newborn care in Africa*, Partnership for Maternal, Newborn & Child Health, Geneva, 2006, p. 3, 5, 9, 24; Le Galès-Camus, Catherine, 'UNICEF Joint Health and Nutrition Strategy for 2006-2015', statement at Executive Board meeting first regular session, New York, 17 Jan. 2006, pp. 3-4; United

Nations Children's Fund, *UNICEF Joint Health and Nutrition Strategy for 2006-2015 (E/ICEF/ 2006/8)*, UN Economic and Social Council, New York, 15 Nov. 2005, p. 3.

Child health in complex emergencies
CIEDRS Working Group, 'Building the Evidence Base on the Provision of Health Care to Children in Complex Emergencies, Draft 4.0', Center for International Emergency, Disaster and Refugee Studies, Johns Hopkins Bloomberg School of Public Health, Baltimore, MD, Sept. 2003, pp. 3-4, 11, 14-15; Collins, Steve, 'Community-Based Therapeutic Care: A new paradigm for selective feeding in nutritional crises – Network paper no. 48', Humanitarian Practice Network, Overseas Development Institute, London, Nov. 2004, p. 24; Collins, Steve, et. al., 'Key Issues in the Success of Community-Based Management of Severe Malnutrition', *Food and Nutrition Bulletin*, vol. 27, no. 3 (suppl.), Sept. 2006, p. 58; UN Millennium Project Task Force on Child Health and Maternal Health, *Who's Got the Power? Transforming health systems for women and children*, Earthscan, London, 2005, p. 77; World Health Organization, *Guide to Health Work-Force Development in Post-Conflict Environments*, WHO, Geneva, 2005, p. 2.

Empowering women to advance maternal, newborn and child health
Perry, Henry, et al., 'Barriers to Immunization among Women and Children in Slums of Zone 3 of Dhaka City, Bangladesh: A qualitative assessment', International Centre for Diarrhoeal Disease Research, Dhaka, April 2007, pp. 16-19; Seidel, Renata, *Behavior Change Perspectives and Communication Guidelines on Six Child Survival Interventions*, Academy for Educational Development and Johns Hopkins Bloomberg School of Public Health, Washington, D.C., Dec. 2005, p. 20; UN Millennium Project Task Force on Child Health and Maternal Health, *Who's Got the Power? Transforming health systems for women and children*, Earthscan, London, 2005, p. 36; WHO Centre for Health Development, 'A Toolkit for Women's Empowerment and Leadership in Health and Welfare', Kobe, Japan, 2005, pp. 26-28; World Health Organization, 'Women's Health in Afghanistan', WHO Dept. of Gender and Women's Health, Family and Community Health Cluster, Geneva, March 2002, pp. 1-2.

Birth registration: An important step towards accessing essential services
'Table 9. Child Protection', pp. 146-147 of this report; UNICEF Innocenti Research Centre, 'Birth Registration and Armed Conflict', *Innocenti Insight*, UNICEF IRC, Florence, 2005, p. vii; United Nations Children's Fund, 'Birth Registration', *Child Protection Information Sheets*, UNICEF, New York, May 2007, pp. 13-14; United Nations Children's Fund, *Progress for Children: A World Fit for Children statistical review, Number 6*, UNICEF, New York, Dec. 2007, p. 42, and The *'Rights' Start to Life: A statistical analysis of birth registration*, 2005, pp. 2, 15-16.

CHAPTER 2

1 Lee, Ronald, 'The Demographic Transition: Three centuries of fundamental change', *Journal of Economic Perspectives*, vol. 17, no. 4, 2003, pp. 167-190.

2 Van Lerberghe, Wim, and Vincent De Brouwere, 'Of Blind Alleys and Things that Have Worked: History's lessons on reducing maternal mortality', *Safe Motherhood Strategies: A review of the evidence*, edited by Wim Van Lerberghe and Vincent De Brouwere, *Studies in Health Services Organisation & Policy*, vol. 17, 2001, pp. 7-34.

3 Claeson, Mariam, and Ronald J. Waldman, 'The Evolution of Child Health Programmes in Developing Countries: From targeting diseases to targeting people', *Bulletin of the World Health Organization*, vol. 78, no. 10, 2000, p. 1235; Oliveira-Cruz, Valeria, Christoph Kurowski and Anne Mills, 'Delivery of Priority Health Services: Searching for synergies within the vertical versus horizontal debate', *Journal of International Development*, vol. 15, 2003, p. 68; and United Nations Children's Fund, *1946-2006: Sixty Years for Children*, UNICEF, New York, 2006, pp. 7-9.

4 Mills, Anne, Fawzia Rasheed and Stephen Tollman, 'Strengthening Health Systems', Chapter 3, *Disease Control Priorities in Developing Countries*, 2nd ed., edited by Dean T. Jamison, et al., Oxford University Press and the World Bank, Washington, D.C., 2006, p. 88.

5 Green, Andrew, *An Introduction to Health Planning in Developing Countries*, 2nd ed., Oxford University Press, New York, 1999; and Morley, David, 'Under-Five Clinics', *Medical Care in Developing Countries: A primer on the medicine of poverty and a symposium from Makerere*, edited by Maurice H. King, Oxford University Press, New York, 1966.

6 Basch, Paul F., *Textbook of International Health*, 2nd ed., Oxford University Press, New York, July 1999.

7 Thieren, Michel, 'Background Paper on the Concept of Universal Access', Technical Meeting for the Development of a Framework for Universal Access to HIV/AIDS Prevention, Treatment and Care in the Health Sector', WHO, Geneva, Oct. 2005; and Vaccine Safety Datalink Group, 'The Use of a Computerized Database to Monitor Vaccine Safety in Viet Nam', *Bulletin of the World Health Organization*, vol. 83, no. 8, Aug. 2005, p. 605.

8 Knippenborg, Rudolf, et al., 'Implementation of the Bamako Initiative: Strategies in Benin and Guinea', *The International Journal of Health Planning and Management*, vol. 12, no. S1, 12 June 1997, pp. S29-S47.

9 Walsh, J. A., and K. S. Warren, 'Selective Primary Health Care: An interim strategy for disease control in developing countries', *New England Journal of Medicine*, vol. 301, no. 18, 1 Nov. 1979, pp. 967-974.

10 Ibid.

11 Claeson, Mariam, and Ronald J. Waldman, 'The Evolution of Child Health Programmes in Developing Countries: From targeting diseases to targeting people', *Bulletin of the World Health Organization*, vol. 78, no. 10, 2000, p. 1235.

12 Ibid.

13 Black, Maggie, 'Children First: The story of UNICEF, past and present', Oxford University Press, New York, 1996, p. 19.

14 Claeson, Mariam, and Ronald J. Waldman, 'The Evolution of Child Health Programmes in Developing Countries: From targeting diseases to targeting people', *Bulletin of the World Health Organization*, vol. 78, no. 10, 2000, p. 1235.

15 UNICEF Statistics, 'Integrated Management of Childhood Illness: An initiative for effective case management', *UNICEF End Decade Databases: IMCI*, <www.childinfo.org/eddb/imci/>, accessed 15 Nov. 2007.

16 World Health Organization and UNICEF, 'Management of Childhood Illness in Developing Countries: Rationale for an integrated strategy', *IMCI Information (WHO/CHS/CAH/98.1A Rev. 1)*, WHO, Geneva, 1999, p. 3.

17 Bryce, Jennifer, et al., 'The Multi-Country Evaluation of the Integrated Management of Childhood Illness Strategy: Lessons for the evaluation of public health interventions', *American Journal of Public Health*, vol. 94, no. 3, March 2004, pp. 406-415; Lucas, Jane E., et al., *Implementing the Household and Community Component of IMCI in the Eastern and Southern Africa Region (ESAR): A state-of-the art review of the human-rights-based approach to programming in the context of accelerated child survival*, UNICEF New York and UNICEF ESARO, 2005, p. xii.

18 Victora, Cesar G., et al., 'Integrated Management of the Sick Child', Chapter 63, *Disease Control Priorities in Developing Countries*, 2nd ed., edited by Dean T. Jamison, et al., Oxford University Press and the World Bank, Washington, D.C., 2006, p. 1189.

19 Armstrong Schellenberg, Joanna R. M., et al., 'Effectiveness and Cost of Facility-Based Integrated Management of Childhood Illness (IMCI) in Tanzania', *The Lancet*, vol. 364, no. 9445, 30 Oct. 2004, p. 1583.

20 Lucas, Jane E., et al., *Implementing the Household and Community Component of IMCI in the Eastern and Southern Africa Region (ESAR): A state-of-the art review of the human-rights-based approach to programming in the context of accelerated child survival*, UNICEF New York and UNICEF ESARO, 2005, p. 86.

21 Victora, Cesar G., et al., 'Integrated Management of the Sick Child', Chapter 63, *Disease Control Priorities in Developing Countries*, 2nd ed., edited by Dean T. Jamison, et al., Oxford University Press and the World Bank, Washington, D.C., 2006, pp. 1188-1189.

22 Martines, Jose, et al., 'Neonatal Survival: A call for action', *The Lancet*, vol. 365, no. 9465, 26 March 2005, p. 1191.

23 Chen, Shaohua, and Martin Ravallion, 'Absolute Poverty Measures for the Developing World, 1981-2004', Development Research Group, World Bank, Washington, D.C., March 2007, p. 12.

24 Bryce, Jennifer, et al., 'Countdown to 2015: Tracking intervention coverage for child survival', *The Lancet*, vol. 368, no. 9541, 23 Sept. 2006, pp. 1070-1071.

25 Jones, Gareth, et al., 'How Many Child Deaths Can We Prevent this Year?', *The Lancet*, vol. 362, no. 9377, 5 July 2003, p. 65; and Lawn, Joy E., et al., 'Newborn Survival', Chapter 27, *Disease Control Priorities in Developing Countries*, 2nd ed., edited by Dean T. Jamison, et al., Oxford University Press and the World Bank, Washington, D.C., 2006, p. 547.

26 Campbell, Oona M. R., and Wendy J. Graham, 'Strategies for Reducing Maternal Mortality: Getting on with what works', *The Lancet*, vol. 368, no. 9543, 28 Sept. 2006, p. 1297.

27 Hill, Zelee, Betty Kirkwood and Karen Edmond, *Family and Community Practices that Promote Child Survival, Growth and Development: A review of the evidence*, World Health Organization, Geneva, 2004, p. 1.

28 Wagstaff, Adam, et al., 'Millennium Development Goals for Health: What will it take to accelerate progress?', Chapter 9, *Disease Control Priorities in Developing Countries*, 2nd ed., edited by Dean T. Jamison, et al., Oxford University Press and the World Bank, Washington, D.C., 2006, pp. 181-194.

CHAPTER 2 PANELS

The Measles Initiative
United Nations Children's Fund, *A World Fit for Children*, UNICEF, New York, 2006, p. 29; Wolfson, Lara J., et al., 'Has the 2005 Measles Mortality Reduction Goal Been Achieved?: A natural history modelling study', *The Lancet*, vol. 369, no. 9557, 20 Jan. 2007, pp. 191-192; World Health Organization, 'World Health Assembly Resolution WHA 52.20: Reducing global measles mortality', WHO, Geneva, 28 May 2003; World Health Organization and United Nations Children's Fund, *Measles: Mortality Reduction and Regional Elimination – Strategic plan 2001-2005*, WHO, Geneva, 2001, pp. 6-7.

National immunization days and child health days
Levine, Ruth, 'Case 4: Reducing Child Mortality with Vitamin A in Nepal', Chapter 4, *Case Studies in Global Health: Millions saved*, Jones and Bartlett Publishers, Sudbury, MA, 2007; Global Polio Eradication Initiative, 'National Immunization Days', <www.polioeradication.org/content/fixed/national.shtml>, accessed 24 Aug. 2007; United Nations Children's Fund, *Annual Report 2006*, UNICEF, New York, June 2007, p. 12, and *1946–2006: Sixty Years for Children*, Nov. 2006, pp. 18-19.

Health sector financing: Sector-wide approaches and the Heavily Indebted Poor Countries Initiative
Gottret, Pablo, and George Schieber, *Health Financing Revisited: A practitioner's guide*, World Bank, Washington, D.C., 2006; Schieber, George, et al., 'Financing Health Systems in the 21st Century', Chapter 12, *Disease Control Priorities in Developing Countries*, 2nd ed., edited by Dean T. Jamison, et al., Oxford University Press and the World Bank, Washington, D.C., 2006, pp. 225-242; World Bank, 'Health and Nutrition Services', Chapter 8, *World Development Report 2004: Making services work for poor people*, World Bank and Oxford University Press, Washington, D.C., 2003, pp. 133-156.

Integrated management of Neonatal and Childhood Illnesses in India
Ramji, Siddarth, 'Integrated Management of Neonatal and Childhood Illness (IMNCI): Implementation challenges in India', *Indian Pediatrics*, vol. 43, no. 12, 17 Dec., 2006, pp. 1029-1031; Sines, Erin, Anne Tinker and Julia Ruben, 'The Maternal-Newborn-Child Health Continuum of Care: A collective effort to save lives', *Policy Perspectives on Newborn Health*, Save the Children and Population Reference Bureau, Washington, D.C., March 2006, p. 2.

The Bamako Initiative
Ebrahim, G. J., 'The Bamako Initiative', *Journal of Tropical Pediatrics*, vol. 39, no. 2, 1993, pp. 66-67; Knippenberg, Rudolf, et al., 'Implementation of the Bamako Initiative: Strategies in Benin and Guinea', *International Journal of Health Planning and Management*, vol. 12, no. S1, 1997, pp. S29-S47; Küchler, Von Felix, 'Manageable Bamako Initiative Schemes', *Bulletin von Medicus Mundi Schweiz*, no. 84, April 2002; Paganini, Agostino, 'The Bamako Initiative Was Not about Money', *Health Policy and Development*, vol. 2, no. 1, 2004, pp. 11-13; World Bank, *World Development Report 2004: Making services work for poor people*, World Bank and Oxford University Press, Washington, D.C., 2003, pp. 72-73, 76-77.

Diagonal approaches: The Mexican way
Frenk, Julio, 'Bridging the Divide: Comprehensive reform to improve health in Mexico', Commission on Social Determinants of Health, Nairobi, 29 June 2006, pp. 4-5; Frenk, Julio, 'Bridging the Divide: Global lessons from evidence-based health policy in Mexico', *The Lancet*, vol. 368, no. 9539, 9 Sept. 2006, pp. 954, 957; Sepúlveda, Jaime, et al., 'Improvement of Child Survival in Mexico: The diagonal approach', *The Lancet*, vol. 368, no. 9551, 2 Dec. 2006, pp. 2017-2027.

Accelerated Child Survival and Development in West Africa
Bryce, Jennifer, et al., 'A Retrospective Evaluation of the Accelerated Child Survival and Development Project in West Africa: Inception Report', submitted to UNICEF and Canadian International Development Agency, 15 Jan. 2007; Bryce, Jennifer, et al., 'Independent Evaluation of Accelerated Child Survival and Development (ACSD)', presentation to the 2nd Global Immunization Meeting, New York, 13-15 Feb. 2007; United Nations Children's Fund, *Accelerated Child Survival and Development in Ghana*, UNICEF Ghana, March 2005, pp. 1-2.

HIV and AIDS in Africa and its impact on women and children
Joint United Nations Programme on HIV/AIDS, United Nations Children's Fund and United States Agency for International Development, *Children on the Brink 2004: A joint report of new orphan estimates and a framework for action*, USAID, Washington, D.C., 2004, p. 10; Joint United Nations Programme on HIV/AIDS, United Nations Population Fund and United Nations Development Fund for Women, *Women and HIV/AIDS: Confronting the crisis*, UNAIDS, UNFPA and UNIFEM, Geneva and New York, 2004, p. 2; Joint United Nations Programme on HIV/AIDS and World Health Organization, 'AIDS Epidemic Update', UNAIDS and WHO, Geneva, Dec. 2006, p. 1.

Partnership for Maternal, Newborn & Child Health
Partnership for Maternal, Newborn & Child Health, <www.who.int/pmnch/en>, accessed 24 Aug. 2007.

CHAPTER 3

1 *Declaration of Alma-Ata*, articles 6-8, International Conference on Primary Health Care, Alma-Ata, USSR, 6-12 Sept. 1978, <www.who.int/hpr/NPH/docs/declaration_almaata.pdf>, accessed 15 Oct. 2007.

2 Adapted from Claeson, Mariam, et al., 'Health, Nutrition and Population', Chapter 18, *A Sourcebook for Poverty Reduction Strategies*, vol. 2, edited by Jeni Klugman, World Bank, Washington, D.C., 2002, pp. 211-212.

3 Zakus, J. David L., and Catherine L. Lysack, 'Revisiting Community Participation', *Health Policy and Planning*, vol. 13, no. 1, Oxford University Press, New York, 1998, pp. 1-12.

4 Gryboski, Kristina, et al., 'Working with the Community for Improved Health', *Health Bulletin No. 3*, Population Reference Bureau, Washington, D.C., June 2006, pp. 1-3.

5 Lehmann, Uta, and David Sanders, 'Community Health Workers: What do we know about them?', World Health Organization, Geneva, Jan. 2007, p. 26.

6 Mason, John B., et al., 'Community Health and Nutrition Programs', Chapter 56, *Disease Control Priorities in Developing Countries*, 2nd ed., edited by Dean T. Jamison et al., Oxford University Press and the World Bank, New York, 2006, pp. 1053.

7 BRAC, <www.brac.net/history.htm>, accessed 22 Oct. 2007; Comprehensive Rural Health Project: Jamkhed, <www.jamkhed.org>, accessed 22 Oct. 2007; and World Health Organization, 'Pakistan's experience in Lady Health Workers (LHWs) Programme (EM/RC51/12)', 51st session, WHO Regional Committee for the Eastern Mediterranean, Cairo, 3-6 Oct. 2004.

8 Wallerstein, Nina B., and Bonnie Duran, 'Using Community-Based Participatory Research to Address Health Disparities', *Health Promotion Practice*, vol. 7, no. 3, July 2006, pp. 312-323.

9 World Health Organization, 'What Is the Effectiveness of Empowerment to Improve Health?'

WHO Europe, Health Evidence Network, Copenhagen, Feb. 2006, p. 5.

10 Rifkin, Susan B., 'Paradigms Lost: Toward a new understanding of community participation in health programmes', *Acta Tropica*, vol. 61, 1996, pp. 88-90.

11 Bhattacharyya, Karabi, et al., *Community Health Worker Incentives and Disincentives: How they affect motivation, retention and sustainability*, Basic Support for Institutionalizing Child Survival Project (BASICS II), United States Agency for International Development, Arlington, VA, Oct. 2001, pp. 1-3, 20-21.

12 Haines, Andy, et al., 'Achieving Child Survival Goals: Potential contribution of community health workers', *The Lancet*, vol. 369, no. 9579, 23 June 2007, p. 2121.

13 Bhattacharyya, Karabi, et al., *Community Health Worker Incentives and Disincentives: How they affect motivation, retention and sustainability*, Basic Support for Institutionalizing Child Survival Project (BASICS II), United States Agency for International Development, Arlington, VA, Oct. 2001, p. 6.

14 Lehmann, Uta, and David Sanders, 'Community Health Workers: What do we know about them?' World Health Organization, Geneva, Jan. 2007, pp. 21-22.

15 Hensher, Martin, Max Price and Sarah Adomakoh, 'Referral Hospitals', Chapter 66, *Disease Control Priorities in Developing Countries*, 2nd ed., edited by Dean T. Jamison et al., Oxford University Press and the World Bank, New York, 2006, p. 1233.

16 Seidel, Renata, *Behavior Change Perspectives and Communication Guidelines on Six Child Survival Interventions*, Academy for Educational Development and Johns Hopkins Bloomberg School of Public Health, Washington, D.C., Dec. 2005.

17 Adventist Development and Relief Agency International, *Final Evaluation Child Survival XVII Baray-Santuk Operational District Kampong Thom Province*, ADRA, Silver Spring, MD, 2006, p. 26.

18 Laughlin, Megan, *The Care Group Difference: A guide to mobilizing community-based volunteer health educators*, World Relief, Baltimore, MD, 2004, p. 5.

19 Kroeger, A., et al., 'Operational Aspects of Bednet Impregnation for Community-Based Malaria Control in Nicaragua, Ecuador, Peru and Colombia', *Tropical Medicine & International Health*, vol. 2, no. 6, June 1997, pp. 590, 593.

20 Perlman, Daniel, Bertha Pooley and Alejandra Villafuerte, 'Como Sera, Pues?: The NGO contribution to neonatal health in Bolivia', The CORE Group, Washington, D.C., April 2006, pp. 1-26.

21 Perry, Henry B., David S. Shanklin and Dirk G. Schroeder, 'Impact of a Community-based Comprehensive Primary Healthcare Programme on Infant and Child Mortality in Bolivia,' *Journal of Health, Population and Nutrition*, vol. 21, no. 4, Dec. 2003, p. 386.

22 England, Sarah, et al., 'Practice and Policies on User Fees for Immunization in Developing Countries', Department of Vaccines and Biologicals, World Health Organization, Geneva, 2001, pp. 10-11.

23 UN Millennium Project, *Investing in Development: A practical plan to achieve the Millennium Development Goals*, United Nations Development Programme, New York, p. 34; and United Nations Children's Fund, World Bank and World Health Organization, 'A Strategic Framework for Reaching the Millennium Development Goal on Child

Survival in Africa', Draft prepared on request of the African Union, 27 Sept. 2006, pp. 25, 26.

[24] Claeson, Mariam, and Ronald J. Waldman, 'The Evolution of Child Health Programmes in Developing Countries: From targeting diseases to targeting people', *Bulletin of the World Health Organization*, vol. 78, no. 10, 2000, p. 1238.

[25] Wagstaff, Adam, and Mariam Claeson, *The Millennium Development Goals for Health: Rising to the challenges*, World Bank, Washington, D.C., 2004, p. 132.

[26] Tollman, Stephen, Jane Doherty and Jo-Ann Mulligan, 'General Primary Care', Chapter 64, *Disease Control Priorities in Developing Countries*, 2nd ed., edited by Dean T. Jamison et al., Oxford University Press and the World Bank, New York, 2006, p. 1195.

[27] United Nations Children's Fund, 'UNICEF Joint Health and Nutrition Strategy for 2006-2015 (E/ICEF/20006/8)', UN Economic and Social Council, New York, 15 Nov. 2005, pp. 1-13.

[28] Mason, John B., et al., 'Community Health and Nutrition Programs', Chapter 56, *Disease Control Priorities in Developing Countries*, 2nd ed., edited by Dean T. Jamison et al., Oxford University Press and the World Bank, New York, 2006, p. 1056.

CHAPTER 3 PANELS

Basic practices for community-based health-care interventions
World Health Organization, *Improving Child Health in the Community*, WHO, Geneva, 2002, pp. 7 8.

Common aspects and challenges of community partnerships in health and nutrition
Mason, John B., et al., 'Community Health and Nutrition Programs', Chapter 56, *Disease Control Priorities in Developing Countries*, 2nd ed., edited by Dean T. Jamison, et al., Oxford University Press and the World Bank, New York, 2006, pp. 1054-1055.

India: Reducing undernutrition through community partnerships
UNICEF India, *Annual Report 2006*, pp. 46-47.

Preventing mother-to-child transmission of HIV: Impact of mothers2mothers programmes in eastern and southern Africa
Baek, Carolyn, et al., *Key Findings from an Evaluation of mothers2mothers in KwaZulu-Natal, South Africa*, Horizons/Population Council, Washington, D.C., 2007, p. 4; mothers2mothers, <www.m2m.org/programmes/where-we-work.html>, accessed 11 Sept 2007; Population Council, 'Helping Mothers Saving Babies: mothers2mothers initiative,' <www.popcouncil.org/pdfs/m2m/m2mDescription.pdf>, accessed 15 Oct. 2007; United Nations Children's Fund, *Children and AIDS: A stocktaking report*, Joint United Nations Programme on HIV/AIDS, UNICEF and World Health Organization, New York, 2007, p. 6; United Nations Children's Fund, *Children: The missing face of AIDS*, UNICEF, New York, 2005, p. 7.

Focus on Mozambique: Reducing under-five mortality through a community-based programme
Bradbury, Kathryn, and Anbrasi Edward, 'Community-Based Solutions for Effective Malaria Control: Lessons from Mozambique', World Relief, The CORE Group and United States Agency for International Development, Washington, D.C., 2005, p. 7; Edward, Anbrasi, et al., 'Examining the Evidence of Under-Five Mortality Reduction in a Community-Based Programme in Gaza, Mozambique', *Transactions of the Royal Society of Tropical Medicine and Hygiene*, vol. 101, no. 8, Aug. 2007, pp. 816-819; 'Table 1. Basic Indicators', 'Table 2. Nutrition', 'Table 3. Health' and 'Table 6. Demographic Indicators', pp. 114-117, 120-121, 122-125 and 134-137 of this report.

Community partnerships in water systems and school sanitation
Rashid, S. M. A., 'Bangladesh: School sanitation and hygiene education – The story of its impact on one village and its school', NGO Forum, <www.schools.watsan.net/redir/content/download/219/1923/file/Bangladesh.doc>, accessed 2 Nov. 2007; 'Safe Water System: A low-cost technology for safe drinking water', March 2006, World Water Forum 4 update, Centers for Disease Control and Prevention, U.S. Department of Health and Human Services, Washington, D.C., pp. 1-2; 'Safe Water System (SWS): Where has the SWS been used? – Afghanistan', Centers for Disease Control and Prevention, U.S. Department of Health and Human Services, <www.cdc.gov/safewater/where_pages/where_afghanistan.htm>, accessed 23 Sept. 2007; Snel, Marielle, *The Worth of School Sanitation and Hygiene Education (SSHE)*, IRC International Water and Sanitation Centre, Delft, the Netherlands, 2004, pp. 57-64.

CHAPTER 4

[1] Dormstadt, Gary, et al, 'Evidence-Based, Cost-Effective Interventions: How many newborn babies can we save?', *The Lancet*, vol. 265, no. 9463, 12 March 2005, p. 977.

[2] United Nations Population Fund, United Nations Children's Fund, World Bank and World Health Organization, 'Building Strategies to Scale-up Access: A discussion paper for the Oslo debate on the Global Business Plan', UNFPA, UNICEF, World Bank and WHO, New York, 24 March 2007, pp. 4-5, 10-11.

[3] Ibid., p. 5.

[4] United Nations Children's Fund, World Bank and World Health Organization, 'A Strategic Framework for Reaching the Millennium Development Goals on Child Survival in Africa', Draft prepared on request of the African Union, 27 Sept 2006 , p. 18.

[5] Ibid., p. 24.

[6] Seidel, Renata, *Behavior Change Perspectives and Communication Guidelines on Six Child Survival Interventions*, Academy for Educational Development and Johns Hopkins Bloomberg School of Public Health, Washington, D.C., Dec. 2005, p. 10.

[7] United Nations Children's Fund, World Bank and World Health Organization, 'A Strategic Framework for Reaching the Millennium Development Goals on Child Survival in Africa', Draft prepared on request of the African Union, 27 Sept. 2006, p. 24.

[8] High-Level Forum Secretariat, 'High-Level Forum on the Health MDGs', World Health Organization and World Bank, Geneva and Washington, D.C., <www.hlfhealthmdgs.org>, accessed 16 Nov. 2007.

[9] United Nations Children's Fund, *Accelerated Child Survival and Development in Ghana*, UNICEF Ghana, Accra-North, March 2005, pp. 1-2.

[10] United Nations Children's Fund, World Bank and World Health Organization, 'A Strategic Framework for Reaching the Millennium Development Goals on Child Survival in Africa', Draft prepared on request of the African Union, 27 Sept. 2006, pp. 24-28.

[11] Mills, Anne, Fawzia Rasheed and Stephen Tollman, 'Strengthening Health Systems', Chapter 3, *Disease Control Priorities in Developing Countries*, 2nd ed., edited by Dean T. Jamison, et al., Oxford University Press and the World Bank, Washington, D.C., 2006, p. 101.

[12] Ibid., p. 90.

[13] Perry, Henry, et al., 'The Census-Based Impact-Oriented Approach: Its effectiveness in promoting

child health in Bolivia', *Health Policy and Planning*, vol. 13, no. 2, 1998, p. 140.

[14] United Nations Children's Fund, World Bank and World Health Organization, 'A Strategic Framework for Reaching the Millennium Development Goals on Child Survival in Africa', Draft prepared on request of the African Union, 27 Sept. 2006, p. 5.

[15] Ibid., pp. 5, 28-30.

[16] Haines, Andy, et al., 'Achieving Child Survival Goals: Potential contribution of community health workers', *The Lancet*, vol. 369, no. 9579, 23 June 2007, p. 2121.

[17] Bhattacharyya, Karabi, et al., 'Community Health Worker Incentives and Disincentives: How they affect motivation, retention and sustainability', Basic Support for Institutionalizing Child Survival Project (BASIC II) for USAID, Arlington, VA, Oct. 2001, p. 19.

[18] World Health Organization, *World Health Report 2005: Make every mother and child count*, WHO, Geneva, 2005, pp. 21-22.

[19] Ibid., pp. 25-30.

[20] Bodart, Claude, 'The Influence of Health Sector Reform and External Assistance in Burkina Faso', *Health Policy and Planning*, vol. 16, no. 1, March 2001, p. 74.

[21] World Health Organization, *World Health Report 2005: Make every mother and child count*, WHO, Geneva, 2005, p. 33.

[22] Mills, Anne, Fawzia Rasheed and Stephen Tollman, 'Strengthening Health Systems', Chapter 3, *Disease Control Priorities in Developing Countries*, 2nd ed., edited by Dean T. Jamison, et al., Oxford University Press and the World Bank, Washington, D.C., p. 91.

[23] United Nations Population Fund, United Nations Children's Fund, World Bank and World Health Organization, 'Building Strategies to Scale-up Access: A discussion paper for the Oslo debate on the Global Business Plan', UNFPA, UNICEF, World Bank and WHO, New York, 24 March 2007, pp. 4-8.

[24] World Bank, *The Millennium Development Goals for Health: Rising to the challenges*, World Bank, Geneva, 2004, p. ix.

[25] United Nations Children's Fund, World Bank and World Health Organization, 'A Strategic Framework for Reaching the Millennium Development Goals on Child Survival in Africa', Draft prepared on request of the African Union, 27 Sept. 2006, p. 40.

[26] 'International Health Partnership: A global compact' for achieving the health Millennium Development Goals', agreement signed by all partners at the launch of the International Health Partnership, London, 5 Sept. 2007.

[27] Soeters, Robert, Christian Habineza and Peter Bob Peerenboom, 'Performance-Based Financing and Changing the District Health System: Experience from Rwanda', *Bulletin of the World Health Organization*, vol. 84, no. 11, Nov. 2006, pp. 885, 887.

[28] Powell-Jackson, Timothy, et al., 'Countdown to 2015: Tracking donor assistance to maternal, newborn, and child health', *The Lancet*, vol. 368, no. 9541, Sept. 2006, p. 25.

[29] United Nations Children's Fund, World Bank and World Health Organization, 'A Strategic Framework for Reaching the Millennium Development Goals on Child Survival in Africa', Draft prepared on request of the African Union, 27 Sept. 2006.

[30] Center for Global Development, 'Case 15: Preventing iodine deficiency disease in China',

Millions Saved: Proven successes in global health, <www.cgdev.org> accessed 16 Nov. 2007; and United Nations Children's Fund, *Progress for Children: A World Fit for Children statistical review*, UNICEF, New York, Dec. 2007, p. 8.

31 Levine, Ruth, 'Case 6: Saving mothers' lives in Sri Lanka', *Case Studies in Global Health: Millions saved*, Jones and Bartlett Publisher, Sudbury, MA, 2007, pp. 41-48; and MOST: The USAID Micronutrient Program, *Cost Analysis of the National Vitamin A Supplementation Programs in Ghana, Nepal, and Zambia: Synthesis of three studies*, USAID, Washington, D.C., 2004, p. 4.

32 Overseas Development Institute, 'Global Health: Making partnerships work', Briefing paper no. 15, ODI, London, Jan. 2007, p. 1.

CHAPTER 4 PANELS

Scaling up: Adequate nutrition for mothers, newborns and children
Basic Support for Institutionalizing Child Survival Project, *Basics II Country Report: Benin, BASICS II*, United States Agency for International Development, Arlington, VA, 2004, pp. 7-15; Collins, Steve, et al., 'Key Issues in the Success of Community-Based Management of Severe Malnutrition', *Food and Nutrition Bulletin*, vol. 27, no. 3, 2006, pp. S49-S51; Collins, Steve, et al., 'Management of severe acute malnutrition in children', The Lancet, vol. 368, no. 9551, 2 Dec. 2006, p. 1992; World Bank, *Repositioning Nutrition as Central to Development: A strategy for large-scale action*, World Bank, Washington, D.C., 2006, pp. 10-11; and World Health Organization, World Food Programme, United Nations System Standing Committee on Nutrition and United Nations Children's Fund, 'Community-Based Management of Severe Acute Malnutrition', WHO, WFP, SCN and UNICEF, Geneva, Rome, New York, May 2007, p. 2.

'Marginal Budgeting for Bottlenecks'
United Nations Children's Fund, World Bank and World Health Organization, 'A Strategic Framework for Reaching the Millennium Development Goals on Child Survival in Africa', draft prepared on request of the African Union, 27 Sept. 2006, p. 25.

Scaling up: Safe water, adequate sanitation and improved hygiene practices
Black, Robert E., Saul S. Morris and Jennifer Bryce, ' Where and why are 10 million children dying every year?', *The Lancet*, vol. 361, 28 June 2003, p. 2227; Curtis, Val, and Sandy Cairncross, 'Effect of Washing Hands with Soap on Diarrhoea Risk in the Community: A systematic review', *The Lancet Infectious Diseases*, vol. 3, no. 5, May 2003, p. 275; Favin, Michael, *Promoting Hygiene Behavior Change within C-IMCI: The Peru and Nicaragua experience, Activity Report 143*, Environmental Health Project, Washington, D.C., Oct. 2004, p. xi; IRC International Water and Sanitation Centre and United Nations Children's Fund, *Water, Sanitation and Hygiene Education for Schools*, final report from Oxford Roundtable, 24-26 Jan. 2005, UNICEF and IRC, New York, p. 32; Lane, Jon, 'Ghana, Lesotho and South Africa: Regional expansion of water supply in rural areas', case study from 'Reducing Poverty, Sustaining Growth: What works, what doesn't, and why – A global exchange for scaling up success', paper offered at Scaling Up Poverty Reduction conference in Shanghai, 25-27 May 2004, World Bank Group, 2004, pp. 1-10; Pan American Health Organization, 'Rotavirus Update', *Immunization Newsletter*, vol. 27, no. 3, June 2005, pp. 1-2; Slaymaker, Tom, and Karin Christiansen, 'Community- Based Approaches and

Service Delivery: Issues and options in difficult environments and partnerships', Overseas Development Institute, London, Feb. 2005, p. 26; United Nations Children's Fund, *Progress for Children: A report card on water and sanitation, Number 5*, UNICEF, New York, Sept. 2006, pp. 3, 22, 30; Water and Sanitation Program, 'Community-Led Total Sanitation in Rural Areas: An approach that works', WSP, New Delhi, Feb. 2007, pp. 4, 6-9.

The urgent need to address the health worker crisis in Africa
The Health Workforce in Africa, Challenges and Prospects, ' A Report of the Africa Working Group of the Joint Learning Initiative on Human Resources for Health and Development', Sept. 2006, p. 3; UN Millennium Project Task Force on Child Health and Maternal Health, *Who's Got the Power? Transforming health systems for women and children*, Earthscan, London, 2005, p. 77; World Health Organization, 'Guide to Health Work-Force Development in Post-Conflict Environments', WHO, Geneva, 2005, pp. 6-13, 52- 77, 119-122; World Health Organization, 'Working together for health', *The World Health Report 2006*, WHO, Geneva, 2006.

The investment case for child survival and other health-related Millennium Development Goals in sub-Saharan Africa
United Nations Children's Fund, World Bank and World Health Organization, 'A Strategic Framework for Reaching the Millennium Development Goals on Child Survival in Africa', Draft prepared on request of the African Union, 27 Sept. 2006, pp. 5-6, 38-43.

Focus on Botswana: Going to scale with HIV prevention and treatment using community partnerships
Botswana Progress Report, 'A World Fit for Children 2007', Government of Botswana, July 2007, pp. 11-12, 15, 18; Kak, Lily, et al., 'Prevention of Mother-to-Child transmission of HIV/AIDS Programmes', Chapter 7, *Opportunities for Africa's Newborns*, Partnership for Maternal, Newborn & Child Health, Cape Town, 2006, pp. 113-127; and United Nations Children's Fund, *Progress for Children: A statistical review, Number 6*, UNICEF, New York, Dec. 2007, pp. 30, 34, 60.

Strengthening accountability and governance in health-service delivery
World Bank, *World Development Report 2004: Making services work for poor people*, World Bank, Washington, D.C., 2003, pp. 133-156.

Performance-based financing in Rwanda
Sekabaraga, Claude, Louis Rusa and Agnes Soucat, 'What it Takes to Scale up for Better Health: The experience of Rwanda 2004-2007', Background paper to 'Innovations in service delivery', 2007.

Focus on Brazil: Creating a national community based health system network
United Nations Children's Fund, *The State of Brazil's Children 2006: The right to survival and development*, UNICEF, Brasilia, 2005, pp. 10-11.

A new way of working together for multilateral institutions
United Nations Children's Fund, 'Informal Meeting of Global Health Leaders: Final summary', UNICEF, New York, July 2007.

CHAPTER 5

1 UN Millennium Project, *Investing in Development: A practical plan to achieve the Millennium Development Goals*, Earthscan, London, 2005, pp. 1-2.

2 United Nations Children's Fund, *The State of the World's Children 2005: Childhood under threat*, UNICEF, New York, 2004, pp. 57-58; UNICEF, *Children Affected by Armed Conflict: UNICEF actions*, May 2002, p. 15; and UNICEF, *Outlook Special Edition: Crisis in Middle East*, Aug. 2006, p. 2.

3 Derived from UN Department of Economic and Social Affairs, Population Division databases, *World Population Prospects: The 2006 revision* and *World Urbanization Prospects: The 2005 revision*, <http://esa.un.org/unpp>, accessed 30 Sept. 2007.

4 World Health Organization, *World Health Report 2006: Working together for health*, WHO, Geneva, 2006, p. 119; Sines, Erin, Anne Tinker and Julia Ruben, 'The Maternal-Newborn-Child Health Continuum of Care: A collective effort to save lives', *Policy Perspectives on Newborn Health*, Save the Children and Population Reference Bureau, Washington, D.C., March 2006, pp. 2-3.

5 Juma, Calestous, and Lee Yee-Cheong, 'Reinventing Global Health: The role of science, technology, and innovation', *The Lancet*, vol. 365, no. 9464, 19 March 2005, pp. 1105-1106; Acharya, Tara, Abdallah S. Daar and Peter A. Singer, 'Biotechnology and the UN's Millennium Development Goals', *Nature Biotechnology*, vol. 21, no. 12, Dec. 2003, pp. 1434-1436.

6 Department of Essential Health Technologies, World Health Organization, 'Strategy for 2004-2007: eHealth for health-care delivery', WHO, Geneva, 2004, p. 2.

7 UN Millennium Project, *Investing in Development: A practical plan to achieve the Millennium Development Goals*, Earthscan, London, 2005, p. 240; United Nations, *The Millennium Development Goals Report 2007*, UN, New York, June 2007, p. 28.

8 United Nations, *Report on the World Social Situation 2005: The inequality predicament*, UN, New York, 2005, p. 114.

9 United Nations, *The Millennium Development Goals Report 2007*, UN, New York, June 2007, p. 28.

10 Gautum, Kul C., 'Pre-Conference Report on Diseases of Poverty, Child Survival and MDGs', presented at the BioVision 2007 Pre-Conference on Diseases of Poverty, Lyon, France, 12 March 2007.

11 United Nations, *The Millennium Development Goals Report 2007*, UN, New York, June 2007, p. 29.

12 Martines, Jose, et al., 'Neonatal Survival: A call for action', *The Lancet*, vol. 365, no. 9465, 26 March 2005, pp. 1193-1194.

13 Buse, Kent, and Andrew M. Harmer, 'Seven Habits of Highly Effective Global Public-Private Health Partnerships: Practice and potential', *Social Science & Medicine*, vol. 64, no. 2, Jan. 2007, p. 261.

CHAPTER 5 PANEL

Strengthening data collection and monitoring for public health decisions
United Nations Children's Fund, *Progress for Children: A World Fit for Children statistical review, Number 6*, UNICEF, New York, Dec. 2007, p. 68; Health Metrics Network, *Framework and Standards for Country Health Information Systems*, 2nd ed., WHO, Geneva, 2007, pp. 5, 17, 60.

STATISTICAL TABLES

Economic and social statistics on the countries and territories of the world, with particular reference to children's well-being.

STATISTICAL TABLES

General note on the data

The data presented in the following statistical tables are based on internationally comparable and statistically sound data, and are accompanied by definitions, sources and explanations of symbols. Data from the responsible United Nations organization have been used wherever possible, such as for the economic and demographic indicators. In the absence of such internationally standardized estimates, the tables draw on other sources, particularly data received from the appropriate UNICEF field office. More detailed information on methodology and sources of the data presented is available at <www.childinfo.org>.

Several of the indicators, such as the data for life expectancy, total fertility rates, and crude birth and death rates, are part of the regular work on estimates and projections undertaken by the United Nations Population Division. These and other internationally produced estimates are revised periodically, which explains why some data will differ from earlier UNICEF publications. This report includes the latest estimates and projections from the *World Population Prospects 2006*.

Data quality is likely to be adversely affected for countries that have recently suffered from human-caused or natural disasters. This is particularly true where basic country infrastructure has been fragmented or major population movements have occurred.

Mortality estimates

Each year, UNICEF includes in *The State of the World's Children* mortality estimates, such as the infant mortality rate, under-five mortality rate and under-five deaths, for at least two reference years, if possible. These figures represent the best estimates available at the time the report is produced and are based on the work of the Inter-agency Group for Child Mortality Estimation, which includes UNICEF, the World Health Organization (WHO), the World Bank and the United Nations Population Division. This group updates these estimates every year, undertaking a detailed review of all newly available data points. At times, this review will result in adjustments to previously reported estimates. Therefore, estimates published in consecutive editions of *The State of the World's Children* may not be comparable and should not be used for analysing mortality trends over time. It is important to note that comparable under-five mortality estimates for the periods 1970, 1990 and the latest year are available in Table 10. In

addition, the full time series for all countries is published at <www.childinfo.org>. This time series is based on the most recent estimates produced by the Inter-agency Group for Child Mortality Estimation.

In addition, updated maternal mortality estimates for the year 2005 are presented in this report. These estimates, based on the work of a WHO/UNICEF/United Nations Population Fund UNFPA/World Bank inter-agency group, were jointly published by the group in *Maternal Mortality in 2005*, WHO, Geneva, 2007. These model-based estimates use a dual approach to adjust these data to take into account the frequent under-reporting and misclassification of maternal deaths.

Multiple Indicator Cluster Surveys (MICS)

For more than a decade, UNICEF has supported countries in collecting statistically sound and internationally comparable data through the Multiple Indicator Cluster Surveys (MICS). Since 1995, nearly 200 surveys have been conducted in approximately 100 countries, and the latest round of MICS surveys was conducted in over 50 countries in 2005–2006, allowing for a new and more comprehensive assessment of the situation of children and women globally. The UNICEF-supported MICS, along with the Demographic and Health Surveys, are among the largest sources of data for monitoring progress towards the Millennium Development Goals and may be used for reporting on 21 of the 53 MDG indicators. These data are also used for monitoring other internationally agreed commitments, such as the World Fit for Children Plan of Action and the global goals on AIDS and malaria. They have been incorporated into the statistical tables appearing in this report and have also been used to inform the report's analyses. More information on these data is available at <www.childinfo.org>.

Revisions

Several statistical tables have been revised this year.

Table 2. Nutrition: The vitamin A supplementation coverage rate is now reported for children aged 6–59 months receiving two high-dose vitamin A supplements, in addition to the previously reported indicator of children aged 6–59 months receiving at least one dose in the last six months. Full coverage is defined as receiving two high-dose vitamin A supplements in the previous calendar year.

Table 3. Health: There are two major changes in this year's child health indicators.

Immunization – A new methodology has been developed by WHO and UNICEF to estimate protection at birth (PAB) against tetanus, and the figures presented in this year's report are therefore not comparable to estimates published in previous editions.

This new methodology tracks cohorts of women from infancy through life, using both WHO/UNICEF estimates of coverage by three doses of diphtheria, pertussis and tetanus vaccine (DPT3) and reported and survey-based estimates of the proportion of pregnant women who are routinely vaccinated with tetanus toxoid (TT). Adjustments are then made to account for the proportion of women who were reached with TT in supplementary immunization activities. Reported data may also be adjusted to take into account coverage patterns in other years and/or results available through surveys. The duration of protection is then calculated based on published WHO estimates of the duration of protection by all doses ever received. The end result is the probability that a child is protected against tetanus as a result of maternal immunization if she or he is born in a given year.

Antibiotic use for suspected pneumonia – Data now include estimates of the percentage of children under five with suspected pneumonia who receive antibiotics, in addition to the previously reported estimates of children with suspected pneumonia taken to appropriate health providers. The recently implemented Multiple Indicator Cluster Surveys have provided a wealth of new data on antibiotic use for childhood pneumonia.

Table 4. HIV and AIDS: The data on estimated adult HIV prevalence and the estimated number of people living with HIV are based on Joint United Nations Programme on HIV/AIDS (UNAIDS) and WHO estimates generated in 2005. These estimates were scheduled to be updated at the end of 2007, but the new figures were not available at the time of publishing this report.

Global surveillance of HIV and AIDS and sexually transmitted infections is a joint effort of WHO and UNAIDS. In countries with a generalized epidemic, national estimates of HIV prevalence are based on data generated by surveillance systems that focus on pregnant women attending selected sentinel antenatal clinics. More recently,

an increasing number of countries are implementing HIV testing as part of their nationally representative population-based surveys. When available, the results of this population survey are included in the estimation of a country's adult HIV prevalence. In countries with a low-level or concentrated epidemic, national estimates of HIV prevalence are primarily based on surveillance data collected from populations at high risk (commercial sex workers, men who have sex with men, injecting drug users) and on estimates of the size of populations at high and low risk. More information on these estimates is available at <www.epidem.org>.

Table 5. Education: The adult literacy rate has been replaced by the youth literacy rate (ages 15–24 years), disaggregated by gender.

Table 8. Women: There are three major changes to this year's table:

Female primary and secondary school enrolment/attendance – Previously, this table reported the gross enrolment ratio (females as a percentage of males) for both primary and secondary education. This year, those figures have been replaced by the net attendance ratio (females as a percentage of males) for both levels of education, and these data are presented alongside the net enrolment ratio (females as a percentage of males) for both levels. The net enrolment/attendance ratios better reflect levels of school participation in both primary and secondary education.

Institutional deliveries – In addition to presenting the proportion of births attended by skilled health personnel, this year's table presents the proportion of births taking place in health facilities.

Maternal mortality – As mentioned above, updated maternal mortality estimates for the year 2005 presented in this report are based on the work of the WHO/UNICEF/UNFPA/World Bank inter-agency group and are published in *Maternal Mortality in 2005*, WHO, Geneva, 2007. These maternal mortality estimates are adjusted to take into account the under-reporting and misclassification of maternal deaths. More information is available at <www.childinfo.org>.

Table 9. Child Protection: Three new indicators have been included in this table, which is largely based on the wealth

STATISTICAL TABLES

Economic and social statistics on the countries and territories of the world, with particular reference to children's well-being.

General note on the data (continued)

of new child protection data that has recently become available through MICS, DHS and other national-level surveys.

Attitudes towards domestic violence – This indicator is defined as the percentage of girls and women aged 15–49 who responded that a husband or partner is justified in hitting or beating his wife under certain circumstances. Respondents were asked whether a husband or partner is justified in hitting or beating his wife under certain circumstances, i.e., if his wife neglects the children, goes out without telling him, argues with him, refuses sexual relations, or burns the food.

Child disability – This indicator is defined as the percentage of children aged 2–9 years who screened positive on at least one of the questions on disability (i.e., cognitive, motor, seizure, vision or hearing). Questions on disability are addressed to the parent or caretaker of the child, who is asked to provide a personal assessment of the child's physical and mental development and functioning. Data on the prevalence of disability refer to the percentage of children who screened positive on these questions and therefore must be considered an indication of the percentage of children who are likely to have a disability and who may require further medical and developmental assessment.

Child discipline – This indicator is defined as the percentage of children aged 2–14 years who experience any psychological or physical punishment. Psychological punishment includes shouting, yelling and screaming at the child, and addressing him or her with offensive names. Physical or corporal punishment comprises actions intended to cause physical pain or discomfort but not injury. Minor physical punishment includes shaking the child and slapping or hitting him or her on the hand, arm, leg or bottom. Severe physical punishment includes hitting the child on the face, head or ears, or hitting the child hard or repeatedly.

Explanation of symbols

Because the aim of these statistical tables is to provide a broad picture of the situation of children and women worldwide, detailed data qualifications and footnotes are seen as more appropriate for inclusion elsewhere. The following symbols are common across all tables; symbols specific to a particular table are included in the table footnotes.

-    Data are not available.

x   Data refer to years or periods other than those specified in the column heading, differ from the standard definition or refer to only part of a country. Such data are not included in the calculation of regional and global averages.

y   Data refer to years or periods other than those specified in the column heading, differ from the standard definition or refer to only part of a country. Such data are included in the calculation of regional and global averages.

*   Data refer to the most recent year available during the period specified in the column heading.

§   Includes territories within each country category or regional group. Countries and territories in each country category or regional group are listed on page 148.

Under-five mortality rankings

The following list ranks countries and territories in descending order of their estimated 2006 under-five mortality rate (U5MR), a critical indicator of the well-being of children. Countries and territories are listed alphabetically in the tables on the following pages.

Country	Under-5 mortality rate (2006) Value	Rank	Country	Under-5 mortality rate (2006) Value	Rank	Country	Under-5 mortality rate (2006) Value	Rank
Sierra Leone	270	1	Turkmenistan	51	67	Saint Lucia	14	130
Angola	260	2	Iraq	46	68	Syrian Arab Republic	14	130
Afghanistan	257	3	Mongolia	43	69	Belarus	13	135
Niger	253	4	Uzbekistan	43	69	Seychelles	13	135
Liberia	235	5	Guatemala	41	71	Sri Lanka	13	135
Mali	217	6	Kyrgyzstan	41	71	Barbados	12	138
Chad	209	7	Micronesia (Federated States of)	41	71	Costa Rica	12	138
Equatorial Guinea	206	8	Suriname	39	74	Malaysia	12	138
Congo, Democratic Republic of the	205	9	Algeria	38	75	Oman	12	138
Burkina Faso	204	10	Trinidad and Tobago	38	75	Uruguay	12	138
Guinea-Bissau	200	11	Tuvalu	38	75	Antigua and Barbuda	11	143
Nigeria	191	12	Morocco	37	78	Kuwait	11	143
Zambia	182	13	Nicaragua	36	79	Palau	11	143
Burundi	181	14	Vanuatu	36	79	Bahrain	10	146
Central African Republic	175	15	Egypt	35	81	Montenegro	10	146
Swaziland	164	16	Mexico	35	81	Brunei Darussalam	9	148
Guinea	161	17	Cape Verde	34	83	Chile	9	148
Rwanda	160	18	Indonesia	34	83	Latvia	9	148
Cameroon	149	19	Iran (Islamic Republic of)	34	83	Lithuania	8	151
Benin	148	20	Georgia	32	86	Serbia	8	151
Somalia	145	21	Philippines	32	86	Slovakia	8	151
Mozambique	138	22	Jamaica	31	88	Thailand	8	151
Uganda	134	23	Lebanon	30	89	United Arab Emirates	8	151
Lesotho	132	24	Maldives	30	89	United States	8	151
Djibouti	130	25	Nauru	30	89	Cuba	7	157
Côte d'Ivoire	127	26	Dominican Republic	29	92	Estonia	7	157
Congo	126	27	Kazakhstan	29	92	Hungary	7	157
Mauritania	125	28	Samoa	28	94	Poland	7	157
Botswana	124	29	Honduras	27	95	Australia	6	161
Ethiopia	123	30	Turkey	26	96	Canada	6	161
Kenya	121	31	El Salvador	25	97	Croatia	6	161
Ghana	120	32	Jordan	25	97	Malta	6	161
Malawi	120	32	Peru	25	97	New Zealand	6	161
Tanzania, United Republic of	118	34	Saudi Arabia	25	97	United Kingdom	6	161
Senegal	116	35	Armenia	24	101	Austria	5	167
Madagascar	115	36	China	24	101	Denmark	5	167
Gambia	113	37	Ecuador	24	101	Ireland	5	167
Togo	108	38	Tonga	24	101	Israel	5	167
Zimbabwe	105	39	Ukraine	24	101	Korea, Republic of	5	167
Myanmar	104	40	Panama	23	106	Netherlands	5	167
Yemen	100	41	Tunisia	23	106	Portugal	5	167
Pakistan	97	42	Occupied Palestinian Territory	22	108	Switzerland	5	167
Sao Tome and Principe	96	43	Paraguay	22	108	Belgium	4	175
Gabon	91	44	Colombia	21	110	Cyprus	4	175
Sudan	89	45	Qatar	21	110	Czech Republic	4	175
Azerbaijan	88	46	Venezuela (Bolivarian Republic of)	21	110	Finland	4	175
Cambodia	82	47	Brazil	20	113	France	4	175
Haiti	80	48	Grenada	20	113	Germany	4	175
India	76	49	Saint Vincent and the Grenadines	20	113	Greece	4	175
Lao People's Democratic Republic	75	50	Cook Islands	19	116	Italy	4	175
Eritrea	74	51	Moldova, Republic of	19	116	Japan	4	175
Papua New Guinea	73	52	Saint Kitts and Nevis	19	116	Luxembourg	4	175
Solomon Islands	73	52	Fiji	18	119	Monaco	4	175
Bhutan	70	54	Libyan Arab Jamahiriya	18	119	Norway	4	175
Bangladesh	69	55	Romania	18	119	Slovenia	4	175
South Africa	69	55	Albania	17	122	Spain	4	175
Comoros	68	57	The former Yugoslav Republic of Macedonia	17	122	Andorra	3	189
Tajikistan	68	57	Viet Nam	17	122	Iceland	3	189
Kiribati	64	59	Argentina	16	125	Liechtenstein	3	189
Guyana	62	60	Belize	16	125	San Marino	3	189
Bolivia	61	61	Russian Federation	16	125	Singapore	3	189
Namibia	61	61	Bosnia and Herzegovina	15	128	Sweden	3	189
Nepal	59	63	Dominica	15	128	Holy See	–	–
Marshall Islands	56	64	Bahamas	14	130	Niue	–	–
Korea, Democratic People's Republic of	55	65	Bulgaria	14	130			
Timor-Leste	55	65	Mauritius	14	130			

TABLE 1. BASIC INDICATORS

Countries and territories	Under-5 mortality rank	Under-5 mortality rate 1990	Under-5 mortality rate 2006	Infant mortality rate (under 1) 1990	Infant mortality rate (under 1) 2006	Neonatal mortality rate 2000	Total population (thousands) 2006	Annual no. of births (thousands) 2006	Annual no. of under-5 deaths (thousands) 2006	GNI per capita (US$) 2006	Life expectancy at birth (years) 2006	Total adult literacy rate 2000-2005*	Primary school net enrolment/ attendance (%) 2000-2006*	% share of household income 1995-2004* lowest 40%	% share of household income 1995-2004* highest 20%
Afghanistan	3	260	257	168	165	60	26088	1272	327	250x	43	28	53s	-	-
Albania	122	45	17	37	15	12	3172	52	1	2960	76	99	94	21	40
Algeria	75	69	38	54	33	20	33351	694	26	3030	72	70	97	19	43
Andorra	189	6	3	5	3	4	74	0	0	d	-	-	80	-	-
Angola	2	260	260	154	154	54	16557	792	206	1980	42	67	58s	-	-
Antigua and Barbuda	143	-	11	-	10	8	84	0	0	11210	-	-	-	-	-
Argentina	125	29	16	25	14	10	39134	690	11	5150	75	97	99	11	55
Armenia	101	56	24	47	21	17	3010	36	1	1930	72	99	99s	21	43
Australia	161	10	6	8	5	3	20530	255	2	35990	81	-	97	18x	41x
Austria	167	10	5	8	4	3	8327	77	0	39590	80	-	97	22	38
Azerbaijan	46	105	88	84	73	36	8406	129	11	1850	67	99x	85	19	45
Bahamas	130	29	14	22	13	10	327	6	0	14920x	73	-	91	-	-
Bahrain	146	19	10	15	9	11	739	13	0	14370x	75	87	97	-	-
Bangladesh	55	149	69	100	52	36	155991	4013	277	480	63	48	81s	21	43
Barbados	138	17	12	15	11	8	293	3	0	d	77	-	98	-	-
Belarus	135	24	13	20	12	5	9742	91	1	3380	69	100x	89	22	38
Belgium	175	10	4	8	4	3	10430	110	0	38600	79	-	99	21	41
Belize	125	43	16	35	14	18	282	7	0	3650	76	70x	95	-	-
Benin	20	185	148	111	88	38	8760	358	53	540	56	35	54s	19	44
Bhutan	54	166	70	107	63	38	649	21	1	1410	65	-	70s	-	-
Bolivia	61	125	61	89	50	27	9354	264	16	1100	65	87	78s	7	63
Bosnia and Herzegovina	128	22	15	18	13	11	3926	35	1	2980	75	97	91s	24	36
Botswana	29	58	124	45	90	40	1858	47	6	5900	49	81	85	7x	70x
Brazil	113	57	20	48	19	15	189323	3720	74	4730	72	89	95	9	61
Brunei Darussalam	148	11	9	10	8	4	382	8	0	24100x	77	93	93	-	-
Bulgaria	130	18	14	14	12	8	7693	69	1	3990	73	98	93	22	38
Burkina Faso	10	206	204	123	122	36	14359	641	131	460	52	24	45	18	47
Burundi	14	190	181	114	109	41	8173	381	69	100	49	59	71s	15	48
Cambodia	47	116	82	85	65	40	14197	377	31	480	59	74	75s	17	50
Cameroon	19	139	149	85	87	40	18175	649	97	1080	50	68	84s	15	51
Canada	161	8	6	7	5	4	32577	338	2	36170	80	-	100	20	40
Cape Verde	83	60	34	45	25	10	519	15	1	2130	71	81	90	-	-
Central African Republic	15	173	175	114	115	48	4265	157	27	360	44	49	59s	7x	65x
Chad	7	201	209	120	124	45	10468	482	101	480	50	26	36s	-	-
Chile	148	21	9	18	8	6	16465	249	2	6980	78	96	90	11	60
China	101	45	24	36	20	21	1320864	17309	415	2010	73	91	99	13	52
Colombia	110	35	21	26	17	14	45558	884	19	2740	73	93	87	9	63
Comoros	57	120	68	88	51	29	818	28	2	660	65	-	72	-	-
Congo	27	103	126	67	79	32	3689	132	17	950x	54	85	86s	-	-
Congo, Democratic Republic of the	9	205	205	129	129	47	60644	3026	620	130	46	67	52s	-	-
Cook Islands	116	32	19	26	16	12	14	0	0	-	-	-	77	-	-
Costa Rica	138	18	12	16	11	7	4399	80	1	4980	79	95	92	12	54
Côte d'Ivoire	26	153	127	105	90	65	18914	684	87	870	48	49	62s	14	51
Croatia	161	12	6	10	5	5	4556	41	0	9330	76	98	87	21	40
Cuba	157	13	7	11	5	4	11267	121	1	1170x	78	100	97	-	-
Cyprus	175	12	4	11	3	4	846	10	0	18430x	79	97	99	-	-
Czech Republic	175	13	4	11	3	2	10189	93	0	12680	76	-	92	25	36
Denmark	167	9	5	7	4	4	5430	62	0	51700	78	-	95	23	36
Djibouti	25	175	130	116	86	38	819	24	3	1060	54	-	79s	-	-
Dominica	128	17	15	15	13	7	68	0	0	3960	-	-	84	-	-
Dominican Republic	92	65	29	50	25	19	9615	231	7	2850	72	87	88	12	57
Ecuador	101	57	24	43	21	16	13202	285	7	2840	75	91	98	11	58
Egypt	81	91	35	67	29	21	74166	1828	64	1350	71	71	94	21	44
El Salvador	97	60	25	47	22	16	6762	159	4	2540	72	81	93	10	56
Equatorial Guinea	8	170	206	103	124	40	496	19	4	8250	51	87	81	-	-
Eritrea	51	147	74	88	48	25	4692	186	14	200	57	-	67s	-	-
Estonia	157	16	7	12	5	6	1340	14	0	11410	71	100	95	18	43
Ethiopia	30	204	123	122	77	51	81021	3159	389	180	52	36	45s	22	39
Fiji	119	22	18	19	16	9	833	18	0	3300	69	-	96	-	-
Finland	175	7	4	6	3	2	5261	58	0	40650	79	-	98	24	37
France	175	9	4	7	4	3	61330	763	3	36550	80	-	99	20	40
Gabon	44	92	91	60	60	31	1311	34	3	5000	56	84	94s	-	-
Gambia	37	153	113	103	84	46	1663	60	7	310	59	-	61s	13	53

	Under-5 mortality rank	Under-5 mortality rate		Infant mortality rate (under 1)		Neonatal mortality rate 2000	Total population (thousands) 2006	Annual no. of births (thousands) 2006	Annual no. of under-5 deaths (thousands) 2006	GNI per capita (US$) 2006	Life expectancy at birth (years) 2006	Total adult literacy rate 2000-2005*	Primary school net enrolment/ attendance (%) 2000-2006*	% share of household income 1995-2004*	
		1990	2006	1990	2006									lowest 40%	highest 20%
Georgia	86	46	32	39	28	25	4433	48	2	1560	71	-	93	16	46
Germany	175	9	4	7	4	3	82641	683	3	36620	79	-	96	22	37
Ghana	32	120	120	76	76	27	23008	700	84	520	59	58	75s	16	47
Greece	175	11	4	9	4	4	11123	103	0	21690	79	96	99	19	41
Grenada	113	37	20	30	16	13	106	2	0	4420	68	-	84	-	-
Guatemala	71	82	41	60	31	19	13029	445	18	2640	70	69	94	10	59
Guinea	17	235	161	139	98	48	9181	374	60	410	55	30	51s	18	46
Guinea-Bissau	11	240	200	142	119	48	1646	82	16	190	46	-	54s	14x	53x
Guyana	60	88	62	64	46	25	739	13	1	1130	66	-	96s	14	50
Haiti	48	152	80	105	60	34	9446	269	22	480	60	-	50s	9	63
Holy See	-	-	-	-	-	-	1	-	-	-	-	-	-	-	-
Honduras	95	58	27	45	23	18	6969	199	5	1200	70	80	79s	11	58
Hungary	157	17	7	15	6	6	10058	93	1	10950	73	-	89	23	37
Iceland	189	7	3	5	2	2	298	4	0	50580	82	-	99	-	-
India	49	115	76	82	57	43	1151751	27195	2067	820	64	61	84s	19	45
Indonesia	83	91	34	60	26	18	228864	4427	151	1420	70	90	96	20	43
Iran (Islamic Republic of)	83	72	34	54	30	22	70270	1407	48	3000	71	82	95	15	50
Iraq	68	53	46	42	37	63	28506	937	43	2170x	58	74	88	-	-
Ireland	167	10	5	8	4	4	4221	66	0	45580	79	-	96	20	42
Israel	167	12	5	10	4	4	6810	137	1	18580x	80	-	97	16	45
Italy	175	9	4	8	4	3	58779	544	2	32020	80	98	99	18	42
Jamaica	88	33	31	28	26	10	2699	55	2	3480	72	80	97s	14	52
Japan	175	6	4	5	3	2	127953	1087	4	38410	82	-	100	25x	36x
Jordan	97	40	25	33	21	17	5729	152	4	2660	72	91	99s	18	46
Kazakhstan	92	60	29	51	26	32	15314	289	8	3790	66	100x	98s	19	41
Kenya	31	97	121	64	79	29	36553	1447	175	580	53	74	79	16	49
Kiribati	59	88	64	65	47	27	94	0	0	1230	-	-	97	-	-
Korea, Democratic People's Republic of	65	55	55	42	42	22	23708	321	18	a	67	-	-	-	-
Korea, Republic of	167	9	5	8	5	3	48050	455	2	17690	78	-	100	21	37
Kuwait	143	16	11	14	9	6	2779	50	1	30630x	77	93	87	-	-
Kyrgyzstan	71	75	41	63	36	31	5259	113	5	490	66	99x	92s	22	39
Lao People's Democratic Republic	50	163	75	120	59	35	5759	156	12	500	64	69	84	20	43
Latvia	148	18	9	14	8	7	2289	21	0	8100	72	100	88	18	45
Lebanon	89	37	30	32	26	20	4055	74	2	5490	72	-	92	-	-
Lesotho	24	101	132	81	102	28	1995	59	8	1030	42	82	87	6	66
Liberia	5	235	235	157	157	66	3579	184	43	140	45	52	66	-	-
Libyan Arab Jamahiriya	119	41	18	35	17	11	6039	144	3	7380	74	84	-	-	-
Liechtenstein	189	10	3	9	3	-	35	0	0	d	-	-	88	-	-
Lithuania	151	13	8	10	7	5	3408	30	0	7870	73	100	89	18	43
Luxembourg	175	10	4	8	4	4	461	5	0	76040	79	-	95	21	39
Madagascar	36	168	115	103	72	33	19159	714	82	280	50	59	76s	13	54
Malawi	32	221	120	131	76	40	13571	566	68	170	47	64x	87s	18	47
Malaysia	138	22	12	16	10	5	26114	556	7	5490	74	89	95	13	54
Maldives	89	111	30	78	26	37	300	7	0	2680	68	96	79	-	-
Mali	6	250	217	140	119	55	11968	579	126	440	54	24	51	16	47
Malta	161	11	6	10	5	5	405	4	0	13610x	79	88x	86	-	-
Marshall Islands	64	92	56	63	50	26	58	0	0	3000	-	-	90	-	-
Mauritania	28	133	125	85	78	70	3044	102	13	740	64	51	72	17	46
Mauritius	130	23	14	21	13	12	1252	19	0	5450	73	84	95	-	-
Mexico	81	53	35	42	29	15	105342	2109	74	7870	76	92	98	13	55
Micronesia (Federated States of)	71	58	41	45	33	12	111	3	0	2380	68	-	92	-	-
Moldova, Republic of	116	37	19	30	16	16	3833	44	1	1100	69	99	86	20	41
Monaco	175	9	4	7	3	3	33	0	0	d	-	-	-	-	-
Mongolia	69	109	43	79	34	26	2605	49	2	880	66	98	97s	20	40
Montenegro	146	16	10	15	9	-	601	8	0	3860	74	96	97s	-	-
Morocco	78	89	37	69	34	21	30853	635	23	1900	71	52	86	17	47
Mozambique	22	235	138	158	96	48	20971	856	118	340	42	39x	60s	15	54
Myanmar	40	130	104	91	74	40	48379	897	93	220x	61	90	84s	-	-
Namibia	61	86	61	60	45	25	2047	53	3	3230	52	85	72	4x	79x
Nauru	89	-	30	-	25	14	10	0	0	-	-	-	60	-	-
Nepal	63	142	59	99	46	40	27641	791	47	290	63	49	87	15	55

TABLE 1. BASIC INDICATORS

	Under-5 mortality rank	Under-5 mortality rate		Infant mortality rate (under 1)		Neonatal mortality rate 2000	Total population (thousands) 2006	Annual no. of births (thousands) 2006	Annual no. of under-5 deaths (thousands) 2006	GNI per capita (US$) 2006	Life expectancy at birth (years) 2006	Total adult literacy rate 2000-2005*	Primary school net enrolment/ attendance (%) 2000-2006*	% share of household income 1995-2004*	
		1990	2006	1990	2006									lowest 40%	highest 20%
Netherlands	167	9	5	7	4	4	16379	188	1	42670	79	-	99	21	39
New Zealand	161	11	6	9	5	4	4140	57	0	27250	80	-	99	18	44
Nicaragua	79	68	36	52	29	18	5532	139	5	1000	72	77	87	15	49
Niger	4	320	253	191	148	43	13737	683	173	260	56	29	40	10	53
Nigeria	12	230	191	120	99	53	144720	5909	1129	640	47	69	68	15	49
Niue	-	-	-	-	-	13	2	0	-	-	-	-	90	-	-
Norway	175	9	4	7	3	3	4669	56	0	66530	80	-	98	24	37
Occupied Palestinian Territory	108	40	22	34	20	-	3889	143	3	1230x	73	92	80	-	-
Oman	138	32	12	25	10	6	2546	57	1	9070x	75	81	73	-	-
Pakistan	42	130	97	100	78	57	160943	4358	423	770	65	50	68	22	40
Palau	143	21	11	18	10	14	20	0	0	7990	-	-	96	-	-
Panama	106	34	23	27	18	11	3288	70	2	4890	75	92	99	9	60
Papua New Guinea	52	94	73	69	54	32	6202	191	14	770	57	57	-	12	57
Paraguay	108	41	22	33	19	16	6016	153	3	1400	71	94	88	9	62
Peru	97	78	25	58	21	16	27589	584	15	2920	71	88	97	11	57
Philippines	86	62	32	41	24	15	86264	2295	73	1420	71	93	94	15	51
Poland	157	18	7	16	6	6	38140	358	3	8190	75	-	96	19	42
Portugal	167	14	5	11	3	3	10579	113	1	18100	78	94	98	17	46
Qatar	110	26	21	21	18	5	821	13	0	12000x	75	89	96	-	-
Romania	119	31	18	23	16	9	21532	213	4	4850	72	97	93	21	39
Russian Federation	125	27	16	23	14	9	143221	1506	24	5780	65	99	92	17	47
Rwanda	18	176	160	106	98	45	9464	420	67	250	46	65	86s	14	53
Saint Kitts and Nevis	116	36	19	30	17	12	50	1	0	8840	-	-	93	-	-
Saint Lucia	130	21	14	17	12	10	163	3	0	5110	73	-	97	15	48
Saint Vincent and the Grenadines	113	25	20	20	17	11	120	2	0	3930	71	-	90	-	-
Samoa	94	50	28	40	23	13	185	5	0	2270	71	99	90	-	-
San Marino	189	14	3	13	3	2	31	0	0	d	-	-	-	-	-
Sao Tome and Principe	43	100	96	65	63	38	155	5	0	780	65	85	97	-	-
Saudi Arabia	97	44	25	35	21	12	24175	612	15	12510x	72	83	78	-	-
Senegal	35	149	116	72	60	31	12072	435	50	750	63	39	58s	17	48
Serbia	151	-	8	-	7	-	9851	126	1	3910	74	96	96	-	-
Seychelles	135	19	13	17	12	9	86	3	0	8650	-	92	99	-	-
Sierra Leone	1	290	270	169	159	56	5743	262	71	240	42	35	69s	3x	63x
Singapore	189	9	3	7	2	1	4382	37	0	29320	80	89x	-	14	49
Slovakia	151	14	8	12	7	5	5388	53	0	9870	74	-	92	24	35
Slovenia	175	10	4	8	3	4	2001	18	0	18890	78	100	98	23	36
Solomon Islands	52	121	73	86	55	12	484	15	1	680	63	-	63	-	-
Somalia	21	203	145	121	90	49	8445	371	54	130x	47	-	22s	-	-
South Africa	55	60	69	45	56	21	48282	1102	76	5390	50	82x	87	10	62
Spain	175	9	4	7	4	3	43887	468	2	27570	81	97x	99	19	42
Sri Lanka	135	32	13	26	11	11	19207	295	4	1300	72	91	97	17	48
Sudan	45	120	89	74	61	29	37707	1225	109	810	58	61	58s	-	-
Suriname	74	48	39	35	29	18	455	9	0	3200	70	90	94	-	-
Swaziland	16	110	164	78	112	38	1134	33	5	2430	40	80	80	13	56
Sweden	189	7	3	6	3	2	9078	101	0	43580	81	-	96	23	37
Switzerland	167	9	5	7	4	3	7455	69	0	57230	81	-	93	20	41
Syrian Arab Republic	130	38	14	31	12	9	19408	529	7	1570	74	81	95	-	-
Tajikistan	57	115	68	91	56	38	6640	185	13	390	66	100	89s	20	41
Tanzania, United Republic of	34	161	118	102	74	43	39459	1589	188	350	52	69	73s	19	42
Thailand	151	31	8	26	7	13	63444	936	7	2990	70	93	98s	16	49
The former Yugoslav Republic of Macedonia	122	38	17	33	15	9	2036	23	0	3060	74	96	92	17	46
Timor-Leste	65	177	55	133	47	40	1114	46	3	840	60	-	75s,y	-	-
Togo	38	149	108	88	69	40	6410	242	26	350	58	53	78	-	-
Tonga	101	32	24	26	20	10	100	3	0	2170	73	99x	95	-	-
Trinidad and Tobago	75	34	38	30	33	13	1328	20	1	13340	69	98	98s	16x	46x
Tunisia	106	52	23	41	19	14	10215	172	4	2970	74	74	97	16	47
Turkey	96	82	26	67	24	22	73922	1378	36	5400	72	87	89	15	50
Turkmenistan	67	99	51	81	45	35	4899	108	6	1340x	63	99x	99s	16	47
Tuvalu	75	54	38	42	31	22	10	0	0	-	-	-	100	-	-
Uganda	23	160	134	93	78	32	29899	1406	188	300	50	67	82s	15	53
Ukraine	101	25	24	22	20	9	46557	417	10	1950	68	99	97s	23	38

	Under-5 mortality rank	Under-5 mortality rate		Infant mortality rate (under 1)		Neonatal mortality rate 2000	Total population (thousands) 2006	Annual no. of births (thousands) 2006	Annual no. of under-5 deaths (thousands) 2006	GNI per capita (US$) 2006	Life expectancy at birth (years) 2006	Total adult literacy rate 2000-2005*	Primary school net enrolment/attendance (%) 2000-2006*	% share of household income 1995-2004*	
		1990	2006	1990	2006									lowest 40%	highest 20%
United Arab Emirates	151	15	8	13	8	5	4248	69	1	23950x	78	89	71	-	-
United Kingdom	161	10	6	8	5	4	60512	715	4	40180	79	-	99	18	44
United States	151	12	8	10	6	5	302841	4248	34	44970	78	-	92	16	46
Uruguay	138	23	12	20	11	7	3331	51	1	5310	76	97x	93	14	50
Uzbekistan	69	74	43	61	38	27	26981	619	27	610	67	-	100s	19	45
Vanuatu	79	62	36	48	30	19	221	6	0	1710	70	74	94	-	-
Venezuela (Bolivarian Republic of)	110	33	21	27	18	12	27191	595	12	6070	73	93	91	12	52
Viet Nam	122	53	17	38	15	15	86206	1654	28	690	74	90x	94s	20	44
Yemen	41	139	100	98	75	37	21732	839	84	760	62	54	75	20	41
Zambia	13	180	182	101	102	40	11696	470	86	630	41	68x	57s	11	55
Zimbabwe	39	76	105	52	68	33	13228	372	39	340x	42	89	82	13	56

SUMMARY INDICATORS

Sub-Saharan Africa	187	160	111	95	44	748886	29889	4786	851	50	58	66	13	55	
Eastern and Southern Africa	165	131	102	83	40	370361	14074	1844	1171	50	60	70	11	58	
West and Central Africa	208	186	119	107	48	378525	15815	2942	553	50	57	62	16	49	
Middle East and North Africa	79	46	58	36	26	382048	9617	442	2104	69	73	85	17	46	
South Asia	123	83	87	62	44	1542571	37942	3149	777	64	58	82	19	46	
East Asia and Pacific	55	29	41	23	20	1968675	29764	863	2371	72	91	97	17	46	
Latin America and Caribbean	55	27	43	22	15	559525	11418	308	4847	73	90	93	12	56	
CEE/CIS	53	27	43	24	18	405584	5529	149	4264	68	97	92	20	42	
Industrialized countries§	10	6	9	5	4	969949	11003	66	37217	79	-	96	21	40	
Developing countries§	103	79	70	54	33	5358223	121685	9614	1967	66	76	84	15	50	
Least developed countries§	180	142	113	90	43	785444	28061	4070	438	55	55	65	15	50	
World	93	72	64	49	30	6577236	135163	9733	7406	68	78	86	20	42	

§ Also includes territories within each country category or regional group. Countries and territories in each country category or regional group are listed on page 148.

DEFINITIONS OF THE INDICATORS

Under-five mortality rate – Probability of dying between birth and exactly five years of age, expressed per 1,000 live births.

Infant mortality rate – Probability of dying between birth and exactly one year of age, expressed per 1,000 live births.

Neonatal mortality rate – Probability of dying during the first 28 completed days of life, expressed per 1,000 live births.

GNI per capita – Gross national income (GNI) is the sum of value added by all resident producers, plus any product taxes (less subsidies) not included in the valuation of output, plus net receipts of primary income (compensation of employees and property income) from abroad. GNI per capita is gross national income divided by midyear population. GNI per capita in US dollars is converted using the World Bank Atlas method.

Life expectancy at birth – Number of years newborn children would live if subject to the mortality risks prevailing for the cross section of population at the time of their birth.

Adult literacy rate – Number of literate persons aged 15 and above, expressed as a percentage of the total population in that age group.

Primary school net enrolment/attendance ratios – Number of children enrolled in or attending primary school, expressed as a percentage of the total number of children of primary school age. The indicator is either the primary school net enrolment ratio or the primary school net attendance ratio. In general, if both indicators are available, the primary school net enrolment ratio is preferred unless the data for primary school attendance is considered to be of superior quality. Definitions for both the primary school net enrolment ratio and the primary school net attendance ratio are given in Table 5, p. 130.

Income share – Percentage of income received by the 20 per cent of households with the highest income and by the 40 per cent of households with the lowest income.

MAIN DATA SOURCES

Under-five and infant mortality rates – UNICEF, World Health Organization, United Nations Population Division and United Nations Statistics Division.

Neonatal mortality rate – World Health Organization using vital registration systems and household surveys.

Total population – United Nations Population Division.

Births – United Nations Population Division.

Under-five deaths – UNICEF.

GNI per capita – World Bank.

Life expectancy – United Nations Population Division.

Adult literacy – UNESCO Institute for Statistics (UIS), including the Education for All 2000 Assessment.

School enrolment/attendance – UIS, Multiple Indicator Cluster Surveys (MICS) and Demographic and Health Surveys (DHS).

Household income – World Bank.

NOTES

a: low income ($905 or less).
b: lower-middle income ($906 to $3,595).
c: upper-middle income ($3,596 to $11,115).
d: high income ($11,116 or more).

- Data not available.

x Data refer to years or periods other than those specified in the column heading, differ from the standard definition or refer to only part of a country. Such data are not included in the calculation of regional and global averages.

y Data refer to years or periods other than those specified in the column heading, differ from the standard definition or refer to only part of a country. Such data are included in the calculation of regional and global averages.

* Data refer to the most recent year available during the period specified in the column heading.

s National household survey data.

TABLE 2. NUTRITION

Countries and territories	% of infants with low birthweight 1999-2006*	% of children (2000-2006*) who are: exclusively breastfed (<6 months)	breastfed with complementary food (6-9 months)	still breastfeeding (20-23 months)	% of under-fives (2000-2006*) suffering from: underweight moderate & severe	underweight severe	wasting moderate & severe	stunting moderate & severe	Vitamin A supplement coverage rate (6-59 months) 2005 at least one dose‡ (%)	full coverage△ (%)	% of households consuming iodized salt 2000-2006*
Afghanistan	-	-	29	54	39	12	7	54	95	91	28
Albania	7	2	38	20	8	1	7	22	-	-	62
Algeria	6	7	39	22	4	1	3	11	-	-	61
Andorra	-	-	-	-	-	-	-	-	-	-	-
Angola	12	11	77	37	31	8	6	45	79	65	35
Antigua and Barbuda	5	-	-	-	-	-	-	-	-	-	-
Argentina	7	-	-	-	4	-	1	4	-	-	90x
Armenia	8	33	57	15	4	0	5	13	-	-	97
Australia	7	-	-	-	-	-	-	-	-	-	-
Austria	7	-	-	-	-	-	-	-	-	-	-
Azerbaijan	12	7	39	16	7	1	2	13	29	29w	26
Bahamas	7	-	-	-	-	-	-	-	-	-	-
Bahrain	8	34x,k	65x	41x	9x	2x	5x	10x	-	-	-
Bangladesh	22	37	52	89	48	13	13	43	83	82	84
Barbados	13	-	-	-	-	-	-	-	-	-	-
Belarus	4	9	38	4	1	0	1	3	-	-	55
Belgium	8	-	-	-	-	-	-	-	-	-	-
Belize	6	24x,k	54x	23x	7	-	1	18	-	-	90x
Benin	16	70	50	57	23	5	7	38	94	92	72
Bhutan	15	-	-	-	19x	3x	3x	40x	-	-	96
Bolivia	7	54	74	46	8	1	1	27	39	39	90
Bosnia and Herzegovina	5	18	29	10	2	0	3	7	-	-	62
Botswana	10	34	57	11	13	2	5	23	-	-	66
Brazil	8	-	30x	17x	6x	1x	2x	11x	-	-	88
Brunei Darussalam	10	-	-	-	-	-	-	-	-	-	-
Bulgaria	10	-	-	-	-	-	-	-	-	-	100
Burkina Faso	16	7	50	85	37	14	23	35	95	95	34
Burundi	11	45	88	-	39	14	7	53	69	17	98
Cambodia	11	60	82	54	36	7	7	37	79	65	73
Cameroon	11	21	64	21	19	5	6	30	95	95	49
Canada	6	-	-	-	-	-	-	-	-	-	-
Cape Verde	13	57x,k	64x	13x	-	-	-	-	-	-	0x
Central African Republic	13	23	55	47	29	8	10	38	-	-	62
Chad	22	2	77	65	37	14	14	41	95	93	56
Chile	6	63	47	-	1	-	0	1	-	-	100
China	2	51	32	15	7	-	-	11	-	-	90
Colombia	9	47	65	32	7	1	1	12	-	-	92x
Comoros	25	21	34	45	25	-	8	44	-	-	82
Congo	13	19	78	21	14	3	7	26	90	9	82
Congo, Democratic Republic of the	12	24	79	52	31	9	13	38	92	87	72
Cook Islands	3	19x,k	-	-	10x	-	-	-	-	-	-
Costa Rica	7	35x,k	47x	12x	5x	0x	2x	6x	-	-	97x
Côte d'Ivoire	17	4	54	37	20	4	7	34	95	89	84
Croatia	6	23x	-	-	1x	-	1x	1x	-	-	90x
Cuba	5	41	42	9	4	0	2	5	-	-	88
Cyprus	-	-	-	-	-	-	-	-	-	-	-
Czech Republic	7	-	-	-	-	-	-	-	-	-	-
Denmark	5	-	-	-	-	-	-	-	-	-	-
Djibouti	10	1	23	18	29	10	21	33	52	0	0
Dominica	10	-	-	-	-	-	-	-	-	-	-
Dominican Republic	11	4	36	15	5	1	1	7	-	-	19
Ecuador	16	40	77	23	9	1	2	23	-	-	99x
Egypt	14	38	67	37	6	1	4	18	-	-	78
El Salvador	7	24	76	43	10	1	1	19	-	-	62
Equatorial Guinea	13	24	-	-	19	4	7	39	-	-	33
Eritrea	14	52	43	62	40	12	13	38	57	50	68
Estonia	4	-	-	-	-	-	-	-	-	-	-
Ethiopia	20	49	54	-	38	11	11	47	59	59	20
Fiji	10	47x,k	-	-	-	-	-	-	-	-	31x
Finland	4	-	-	-	-	-	-	-	-	-	-
France	7	-	-	-	-	-	-	-	-	-	-

	% of infants with low birthweight 1999-2006*	% of children (2000-2006*) who are:			% of under-fives (2000-2006*) suffering from:					Vitamin A supplement coverage rate (6-59 months) 2005		% of households consuming iodized salt 2000-2006*
		exclusively breastfed (<6 months)	breastfed with complementary food (6-9 months)	still breastfeeding (20-23 months)	underweight		wasting	stunting		at least one dose‡ (%)	full coverage△ (%)	
					moderate & severe	severe	moderate & severe	moderate & severe				
Gabon	14	6	62	9	12	2	3	21		-	-	36
Gambia	20	41	44	53	20	4	6	22		95	16	7
Georgia	7	18x,k	12x	12x	3x	0x	2x	12x		-	-	91
Germany	7	-	-	-	-	-	-	-		-	-	-
Ghana	9	54	58	56	18	3	5	22		95	95	32
Greece	8	-	-	-	-	-	-	-		-	-	-
Grenada	9	39x,k	-	-	-	-	-	-		-	-	-
Guatemala	12	51	67	47	23	4	2	49		44	36w	67
Guinea	12	27	41	71	26	7	9	35		95	95	51
Guinea-Bissau	24	16	35	61	19	4	7	41		-	-	1
Guyana	13	11	42	31	14	3	11	11		-	-	-
Haiti	25	41	87	35	22	6	9	24		42	42	3
Holy See	-	-	-	-	-	-	-	-		-	-	-
Honduras	10	30	69	48	11	1	1	25		40	40	80x
Hungary	9	-	-	-	-	-	-	-		-	-	-
Iceland	4	-	-	-	-	-	-	-		-	-	-
India	30	46	56	-	43	16	20	48		64	64w	51
Indonesia	9	40	75	59	28	9	-	-		76	76	73
Iran (Islamic Republic of)	7	44	-	0	11x	2x	5x	15x		-	-	99
Iraq	15	25	51	36	8	1	5	21		-	-	28
Ireland	6	-	-	-	-	-	-	-		-	-	-
Israel	8	-	-	-	-	-	-	-		-	-	-
Italy	6	-	-	-	-	-	-	-		-	-	-
Jamaica	12	15	36	24	4	-	4	3		-	-	100x
Japan	8	-	-	-	-	-	-	-		-	-	-
Jordan	12	27	70	12	4	1	2	9		-	-	88
Kazakhstan	6	17	39	16	4	1	4	13		-	-	92
Kenya	10	13	84	57	20	4	6	30		69	69	91
Kiribati	5	80x,k	-	-	13x	-	-	-		62	60	-
Korea, Democratic People's Republic of	7	65	31	37	23	8	7	37		95	95	40
Korea, Republic of	4	-	-	-	-	-	-	-		-	-	-
Kuwait	7	12x,k	26x	9x	10x	3x	11x	24x		-	-	-
Kyrgyzstan	5	32	49	26	3	0	4	14		88	87	76
Lao People's Democratic Republic	14	23	10	47	40	13	15	42		63	62	75
Latvia	5	-	-	-	-	-	-	-		-	-	-
Lebanon	6	27k	35	11	4	-	5	11		-	-	92
Lesotho	13	36	79	60	20	4	4	38		9	2	91
Liberia	-	35	70	45	26	8	6	39		95	79	-
Libyan Arab Jamahiriya	7	-	-	23x	5x	1x	3x	15x		-	-	90x
Liechtenstein	-	-	-	-	-	-	-	-		-	-	-
Lithuania	4	-	-	-	-	-	-	-		-	-	-
Luxembourg	8	-	-	-	-	-	-	-		-	-	-
Madagascar	17	67	78	64	42	11	13	48		95	95	75
Malawi	13	56	89	73	19	3	3	46		94	86	48
Malaysia	9	29x,k	-	12x	8	1	-	-		-	-	-
Maldives	22	10	85	-	30	7	13	25		-	-	44
Mali	23	25	32	69	33	11	11	38		66	66	74
Malta	6	-	-	-	-	-	-	-		-	-	-
Marshall Islands	12	63x,k	-	-	-	-	-	-		6	6	-
Mauritania	-	20	78	57	32	10	13	35		96	57	2
Mauritius	14	21k	-	-	15x	2x	14x	10x		-	-	0x
Mexico	8	38x,k	36x	21x	5	-	2	13		68	63	91
Micronesia (Federated States of)	18	60x,k	-	-	15x	-	-	-		89	73	-
Moldova, Republic of	6	46	18	2	4	1	4	8		-	-	60
Monaco	-	-	-	-	-	-	-	-		-	-	-
Mongolia	6	57	57	65	6	1	2	21		92	92	83
Montenegro	4	19	35	13	3	1	3	5		-	-	71
Morocco	15	31	66	15	10	2	9	18		-	-	59
Mozambique	15	30	80	65	24	6	4	41		95	16	54
Myanmar	15	15k	66	67	32	7	9	32		95	95	60
Namibia	14	19	57	37	24	5	9	24		68	0	63

TABLE 2. NUTRITION

	% of infants with low birthweight 1999-2006*	% of children (2000-2006*) who are:			% of under-fives (2000-2006*) suffering from:				Vitamin A supplement coverage rate (6-59 months) 2005		% of households consuming iodized salt 2000-2006*
		exclusively breastfed (<6 months)	breastfed with complementary food (6-9 months)	still breastfeeding (20-23 months)	underweight moderate & severe	underweight severe	wasting moderate & severe	stunting moderate & severe	at least one dose‡ (%)	full coverage△ (%)	
Nauru	-	-	-	-	-	-	-	-	-	-	-
Nepal	21	53	75	95	39	11	13	49	96	96	63
Netherlands	-	-	-	-	-	-	-	-	-	-	-
New Zealand	6	-	-	-	-	-	-	-	-	-	83x
Nicaragua	12	31	68	39	10	2	2	20	98	0	97
Niger	13	14	62	62	44	15	10	50	94	94	46
Nigeria	14	17	64	34	29	9	9	38	73	73	97
Niue	0	-	-	-	-	-	-	-	-	-	-
Norway	5	-	-	-	-	-	-	-	-	-	-
Occupied Palestinian Territory	7	27	-	-	3	0	1	10	-	-	86
Oman	8	-	92	73	18x	1x	7x	10x	-	-	61x
Pakistan	19	16x,k	31x	56x	38	13	13	37	95	95	17
Palau	9	59x,k	-	-	-	-	-	-	-	-	-
Panama	10	25x	38x	21x	8x	1x	1x	18x	4	4	95x
Papua New Guinea	11	59x	74x	66x	-	-	-	-	90	0	-
Paraguay	9	22	60	-	5	-	1	14	-	-	88
Peru	11	64	81	41	8	0	1	24	-	-	91
Philippines	20	34	58	32	28	-	6	30	85	85	56
Poland	6	-	-	-	-	-	-	-	-	-	-
Portugal	8	-	-	-	-	-	-	-	-	-	-
Qatar	10	12x,k	48x	21x	6x	-	2x	8x	-	-	-
Romania	8	16	41	-	3	0	2	10	-	-	74
Russian Federation	6	-	-	-	3x	1x	4x	13x	-	-	35
Rwanda	6	88	69	77	23	4	4	45	100	99	88
Saint Kitts and Nevis	9	56x,k	-	-	-	-	-	-	-	-	-
Saint Lucia	12	-	-	-	-	-	-	-	-	-	-
Saint Vincent and the Grenadines	5	-	-	-	-	-	-	-	-	-	-
Samoa	4	-	-	-	-	-	-	-	-	-	-
San Marino	-	-	-	-	-	-	-	-	-	-	-
Sao Tome and Principe	8	60	60	18	9	1	8	23	33	28	37
Saudi Arabia	11	31x,k	60x	30x	14x	3x	11x	20x	-	-	-
Senegal	19	34	61	42	17	3	8	16	95	86	41
Serbia	5	15	39	8	2	0	3	6	-	-	73
Seychelles	-	-	-	-	-	-	-	-	-	-	-
Sierra Leone	24	8	52	57	30	8	9	40	95	95	45
Singapore	8	-	-	-	3	0	2	2	-	-	-
Slovakia	7	-	-	-	-	-	-	-	-	-	-
Slovenia	6	-	-	-	-	-	-	-	-	-	-
Solomon Islands	13	65k	-	-	-	-	-	-	-	-	-
Somalia	11	9	15	35	36	12	11	38	-	-	1
South Africa	15	7y	46y	-	12x	2x	3x	25x	33	29	62x
Spain	6	-	-	-	-	-	-	-	-	-	-
Sri Lanka	22	53	-	73	29	-	14	14	64	61w	94
Sudan	31	16	47	40	41	15	16	43	90	90	1
Suriname	13	9	25	11	13	2	7	10	-	-	-
Swaziland	9	24	60	25	10	2	1	30	59	40	59
Sweden	4	-	-	-	-	-	-	-	-	-	-
Switzerland	6	-	-	-	-	-	-	-	-	-	-
Syrian Arab Republic	9	29	37	16	10	2	9	22	-	-	79
Tajikistan	10	25	15	34	17	4	7	27	98	98	46
Tanzania, United Republic of	10	41	91	55	22	4	3	38	95	95	43
Thailand	9	5	43	19	9	0	4	12	-	-	58
The former Yugoslav Republic of Macedonia	6	37x	8x	10x	2	0	2	9	-	-	94
Timor-Leste	12	31	82	35	46	15	12	49	91	35	72
Togo	12	28	35	44	26	7	14	24	95	92	25
Tonga	3	62x,k	-	-	-	-	-	-	-	-	-
Trinidad and Tobago	19	13	43	22	6	1	4	4	-	-	28
Tunisia	7	47	-	22	4	1	2	12	-	-	97
Turkey	16	21	38	24	4	1	1	12	-	-	64
Turkmenistan	4	11	54	37	11	2	6	15	-	-	87
Tuvalu	5	-	-	-	-	-	-	-	-	-	-

| | % of infants with low birthweight 1999-2006* | % of children (2000-2006*) who are: | | | % of under-fives (2000-2006*) suffering from: | | | | | | Vitamin A supplement coverage rate (6-59 months) 2005 | | % of households consuming iodized salt 2000-2006* |
| | | exclusively breastfed (<6 months) | breastfed with complementary food (6-9 months) | still breastfeeding (20-23 months) | underweight | | wasting | stunting | | | | | |
					moderate & severe	severe	moderate & severe	moderate & severe			at least one dose‡ (%)	full coverageᐃ (%)	
Uganda	12	60	80	54	20	5	5	32			78	78	95
Ukraine	4	6	83	11	1	0	0	3			-	-	18
United Arab Emirates	15	34x,k	52x	29x	14x	3x	15x	17x			-	-	-
United Kingdom	8	-	-	-	-	-	-	-			-	-	-
United States	8	-	-	-	2	0	0	1			-	-	-
Uruguay	8	-	-	-	5	1	2	11			-	-	-
Uzbekistan	5	26	45	38	5	1	3	15			82	82	53
Vanuatu	6	50x,k	-	-	-	-	-	-			-	-	-
Venezuela (Bolivarian Republic of)	9	7x,k	50x	31x	5	1	4	13			-	-	90x
Viet Nam	7	17	70	23	25	3	7	30			99	99w	93
Yemen	32	12	76	-	46	15	12	53			15	15w	30
Zambia	12	40	87	58	20	-	6	50			66	66	77
Zimbabwe	11	22	79	28	17	3	6	29			81	81	93x

SUMMARY INDICATORS

Sub-Saharan Africa	14	30	67	50	28	8	9	38			79	73	64
Eastern and Southern Africa	14	39	71	56	28	7	7	41			73	64	54
West and Central Africa	14	21	63	46	28	9	10	36			85	82	72
Middle East and North Africa	16	28	57	25	17	5	8	25			-	-	64
South Asia	29	45	55	-	42	15	18	46			71	71	51
East Asia and Pacific	6	43	45	27	14	-	-	16			84	82**	84
Latin America and Caribbean	9	-	-	-	7	-	2	16			-	-	85
CEE/CIS	6	19	44	23	5	1	2	12			-	-	50
Industrialized countries§	7	-	-	-	-	-	-	-			-	-	-
Developing countries§	16	38	56	40	26	10	11	32			75	72**	69
Least developed countries§	17	35	64	63	35	10	10	42			82	77	55
World	15	38	56	39	25	9	11	31			75	72**	68

§ Also includes territories within each country category or regional group. Countries and territories in each country category or regional group are listed on page 140.

DEFINITIONS OF THE INDICATORS

Low birthweight – Weight less than 2,500 grams at birth.

Underweight – Moderate and severe: below minus two standard deviations from median weight for age of reference population; severe: below minus three standard deviations from median weight for age of reference population.

Wasting – Moderate and severe: below minus two standard deviations from median weight for height of reference population.

Stunting – Moderate and severe: below minus two standard deviations from median height for age of reference population.

Vitamin A – Percentage of children aged 6-59 months who received vitamin A supplements in 2005.

Iodized salt consumption – Percentage of households consuming adequately iodized salt (15 parts per million or more).

MAIN DATA SOURCES

Low birthweight – Demographic and Health Surveys (DHS), Multiple Indicator Cluster Surveys (MICS), other national household surveys and data from routine reporting systems.

Breastfeeding – DHS, MICS and UNICEF.

Underweight, wasting and stunting – DHS, MICS, World Health Organization (WHO) and UNICEF.

Vitamin A – UNICEF and WHO.

Salt iodization – MICS, DHS and UNICEF.

NOTES

-    Data not available.
- x   Data refer to years or periods other than those specified in the column heading, differ from the standard definition or refer to only part of a country. Such data are not included in the calculation of regional and global averages.
- y   Data refer to years or periods other than those specified in the column heading, differ from the standard definition or refer to only part of a country. Such data are included in the calculation of regional and global averages.
- *   Data refer to the most recent year available during the period specified in the column heading.
- k   Refers to exclusive breastfeeding for less than four months.
- w   Identifies countries with national vitamin A supplementation programmes targeted towards a reduced age range. Coverage figure is reported as targeted.
- ‡   Refers to the percentage of children who received at least one dose in 2005 (the most recent coverage point at the time of reporting).
- ᐃ   The percentage of children reached with two doses in 2005 is reported as the lower percentage of two coverage points. '0' (zero) indicates that only one dose was delivered in 2005.
- **   Excludes China.

TABLE 3. HEALTH

Countries and territories	% of population using improved drinking-water sources 2004 total	urban	rural	% of population using adequate sanitation facilities 2004 total	urban	rural	% of routine EPI vaccines financed by government 2006 total	TB BCG	DPT DPT1β	DPT3β	Polio polio3	Measles measles	HepB HepB3	Hib Hib3	% newborns protected against tetanus	% under-fives with suspected pneumonia taken to an appropriate health-care provider 2000-2006*	% under-fives with suspected pneumonia receiving antibiotics 2000-2006*	% under-fives with diarrhoea receiving oral rehydration and continued feeding 2000-2006*	Malaria 2003-2006* % under-fives sleeping under a mosquito net	% under-fives sleeping under a treated mosquito net	% under-fives with fever receiving anti-malarial drugs
Afghanistan	39	63	31	34	49	29	0	90	90	77	77	68	-	-	88	28	-	48	-	-	-
Albania	96	99	94	91	99	84	-	98	98	98	97	97	98	-	87	45	38	50	-	-	-
Algeria	85	88	80	92	99	82	100	99	98	95	95	91	80	-	70	53	59	24	-	-	-
Andorra	100	100	100	100	100	100	-	-	97	93	93	91	84	93	-	-	-	-	-	-	-
Angola	53	75	40	31	56	16	67	65	66	44	44	48	-	-	80	58	-	32	-	-	-
Antigua and Barbuda	91	95	89	95	98	94	100	-	99	99	99	99	99	99	-	-	-	-	-	-	-
Argentina	96	98	80	91	92	83	-	99	93	91	92	97	84	91	-	-	-	-	-	-	-
Armenia	92	99	80	83	96	61	30	91	95	87	87	92	78	-	-	36	11	59	-	-	-
Australia	100	100	100	100	100	100	-	-	97	92	92	94	94	94	-	-	-	-	-	-	-
Austria	100	100	100	100	100	100	88	-	94	83	83	80	83	83	-	-	-	-	-	-	-
Azerbaijan	77	95	59	54	73	36	70	99	97	95	97	96	93	-	-	36	-	40	12x	1x	1x
Bahamas	97	98	86	100	100	100	100	-	95	95	94	88	96	95	65	-	-	-	-	-	-
Bahrain	-	100	-	-	100	-	100	-	99	98	98	99	98	97	92	-	-	-	-	-	-
Bangladesh	74	82	72	39	51	35	63	96	96	88	88	81	88	-	92	30	22	49	-	-	-
Barbados	100	100	100	100	99	100	100	-	81	84	85	92	84	84	-	-	-	-	-	-	-
Belarus	100	100	100	84	93	61	100	99	99	99	97	97	98	-	-	90	67	54	-	-	-
Belgium	-	100	-	-	-	-	-	-	98	97	97	88	78	95	94	-	-	-	-	-	-
Belize	91	100	82	47	71	25	100	97	96	98	98	99	98	98	80	66x	-	-	-	-	-
Benin	67	78	57	33	59	11	10	99	99	93	93	89	93	93	84	35	-	42	47	20	54
Bhutan	62	86	60	70	65	70	-	92	98	95	96	90	95	-	88	-	-	-	-	-	-
Bolivia	85	95	68	46	60	22	69	93	94	81	79	81	81	81	-	52	-	54	-	-	-
Bosnia and Herzegovina	97	99	96	95	99	92	85	97	94	87	91	90	82	85	85	91	73	53	-	-	-
Botswana	95	100	90	42	57	25	100	99	98	97	97	90	85	-	71	14	-	7	-	-	-
Brazil	90	96	57	75	83	37	-	99	99	96	99	99	97	99	84	46x	15x	28x	-	-	-
Brunei Darussalam	-	-	-	-	-	-	-	96	99	99	99	97	99	99	92	-	-	-	-	-	-
Bulgaria	99	100	97	99	100	96	100	98	97	95	96	96	96	-	65	-	-	-	-	-	-
Burkina Faso	61	94	54	13	42	6	17	99	99	95	94	88	76	76	-	39	15	42	18	10	48
Burundi	79	92	77	36	47	35	1	84	86	74	64	75	74	74	84	38	26	23	13	8	30
Cambodia	41	64	35	17	53	8	0	87	85	80	80	78	80	-	80	48	-	59	88	4	0
Cameroon	66	86	44	51	58	43	20	85	87	81	78	73	81	-	52	35	38	22	27	13	58
Canada	100	100	99	100	100	99	-	-	97	94	94	94	14	94	82	-	-	-	-	-	-
Cape Verde	80	86	73	43	61	19	90	70	74	72	72	65	69	-	-	-	-	-	-	-	-
Central African Republic	75	93	61	27	47	12	0	70	65	40	40	35	-	-	74	32	39	47	33	15	57
Chad	42	41	43	9	24	4	55	40	45	20	36	23	-	-	60	12	-	27	27x	1x	32x
Chile	95	100	58	91	95	62	100	98	95	94	94	91	94	94	-	-	-	-	-	-	-
China	77	93	67	44	69	28	-	92	94	93	94	93	91	-	-	-	-	-	-	-	-
Colombia	93	99	71	86	96	54	100	88	95	86	86	88	86	86	88	62	-	39	24x	-	-
Comoros	86	92	82	33	41	29	0	84	78	69	69	66	69	-	77	49	-	31	36x	9x	63x
Congo	58	84	27	27	28	25	75	84	81	79	79	66	-	-	84	48	-	39	68	6	48
Congo, Democratic Republic of the	46	82	29	30	42	25	0	87	87	77	78	73	-	-	77	36	-	17	12x	1x	52x
Cook Islands	94	98	88	100	100	100	100	99	99	99	99	99	99	-	-	-	-	-	-	-	-
Costa Rica	97	100	92	92	89	97	-	88	89	91	91	89	90	89	-	-	-	-	-	-	-
Côte d'Ivoire	84	97	74	37	46	29	28	77	95	77	76	73	77	-	-	35	19	45	17	6	36
Croatia	100	100	100	100	100	100	100	98	96	96	96	96	-	96	-	-	-	-	-	-	-
Cuba	91	95	78	98	99	95	99	99	96	89	99	96	89	97	-	-	-	-	-	-	-
Cyprus	100	100	100	100	100	100	36	-	99	97	97	87	93	90	-	-	-	-	-	-	-
Czech Republic	100	100	100	98	99	97	-	99	98	98	98	97	98	97	-	-	-	-	-	-	-
Denmark	100	100	100	-	-	-	100	-	93	93	93	90	-	93	-	-	-	-	-	-	-
Djibouti	73	76	59	82	88	50	-	88	76	72	72	67	-	-	77	62	43	33	9	1	10
Dominica	97	100	90	84	86	75	100	99	99	95	88	99	7	7	-	-	-	-	-	-	-
Dominican Republic	95	97	91	78	81	73	69	95	93	81	85	99	74	69	85	63	-	42	-	-	-
Ecuador	94	97	89	89	94	82	100	99	99	98	97	97	98	98	66	-	-	-	-	-	-
Egypt	98	99	97	70	86	58	100	99	98	98	98	98	98	-	86	63	-	27	-	-	-
El Salvador	84	94	70	62	77	39	100	93	98	96	96	98	96	96	91	62	-	-	-	-	-
Equatorial Guinea	43	45	42	53	60	46	0	73	65	33	39	51	-	-	59	-	-	36	15x	1x	49x
Eritrea	60	74	57	9	32	3	10	99	99	97	96	95	97	-	79	44	-	54	12x	4x	4x
Estonia	100	100	99	97	97	96	100	99	98	95	95	96	95	88	-	-	-	-	-	-	-
Ethiopia	22	81	11	13	44	7	0	72	80	72	69	63	-	-	80	19	-	15	2	2	3
Fiji	47	43	51	72	87	55	100	93	84	81	83	99	81	81	93	-	-	-	-	-	-
Finland	100	100	100	100	100	100	100	98	99	97	97	97	-	98	-	-	-	-	-	-	-
France	100	100	100	-	-	-	-	84	98	98	98	87	29	87	-	-	-	-	-	-	-

	% of population using improved drinking-water sources 2004			% of population using adequate sanitation facilities 2004			% of routine EPI vaccines financed by government 2006	Immunization 2006 1-year-old children immunized against:							% newborns protected against tetanus$^\lambda$	% under-fives with suspected pneumonia taken to an appropriate health-care provider$^\pm$	% under-fives with suspected pneumonia receiving antibiotics$^\pm$	% under-fives with diarrhoea receiving oral rehydration and continued feeding	Malaria 2003-2006*		
								TB	DPT	DPT	Polio	Measles	HepB	Hib					% under-fives sleeping under a mosquito net	% under-fives sleeping under a treated mosquito net	% under-fives with fever receiving anti-malarial drugs
	total	urban	rural	total	urban	rural	total	BCG	DPT1$^\beta$	DPT3$^\beta$	polio3	measles	HepB3	Hib3		2000-2006*		2000-2006*			
Gabon	88	95	47	36	37	30	100	89	69	38	31	55	38	-	63	48	-	44	-	-	-
Gambia	82	95	77	53	72	46	35	99	95	95	95	95	95	95	94	69	61	38	63	49	63
Georgia	82	96	67	94	96	91	71	95	99	87	88	95	83	-	87	99	-	-	-	-	-
Germany	100	100	100	100	100	100	-	-	96	90	96	94	86	94	-	-	-	-	-	-	-
Ghana	75	88	64	18	27	11	-	99	87	84	84	85	84	84	-	59	33	29	33	22	61
Greece	-	-	-	-	-	-	-	88	96	88	87	88	88	88	69	-	-	-	-	-	-
Grenada	95	97	93	96	96	97	100	-	87	91	91	98	91	91	-	-	-	-	-	-	-
Guatemala	95	99	92	86	90	82	-	96	93	80	81	95	80	80	91	64	-	22x	6x	1x	-
Guinea	50	78	35	18	31	11	40	90	99	71	70	67	-	-	79	42	-	38	12	0	44
Guinea-Bissau	59	79	49	35	57	23	-	87	85	77	74	60	-	-	91	57	42	25	73	39	46
Guyana	83	83	83	70	86	60	100	96	95	93	92	90	93	93	31	78	-	40	74	6	1
Haiti	54	52	56	30	57	14	-	75	83	53	52	58	-	-	94	31	3	43	-	-	5
Holy See	-	-	-	-	-	-	-	-	-	-	-	-	-	-	-	-	-	-	-	-	-
Honduras	87	95	81	69	87	54	100	90	95	87	87	91	87	87	-	56	54	49	-	-	1
Hungary	99	100	98	95	100	85	100	99	99	99	99	99	-	99	-	-	-	-	-	-	-
Iceland	100	100	100	100	100	100	-	-	97	97	97	95	-	97	86	-	-	-	-	-	-
India	86	95	83	33	59	22	100	78	78	55	58	59	6	-	83	69	-	32	-	-	12x
Indonesia	77	87	69	55	73	40	87	82	88	70	70	72	70	-	87	61	-	56	32x	0x	1
Iran (Islamic Republic of)	94	99	84	-	-	-	100	99	99	99	99	99	99	-	-	93	-	-	-	-	-
Iraq	81	97	50	79	95	48	100	91	83	60	63	60	75	-	89	82	82	64	7x	0x	1x
Ireland	-	100	-	-	-	-	100	93	97	91	91	86	-	91	-	-	-	-	-	-	-
Israel	100	100	100	-	100	-	-	-	98	95	93	95	95	96	-	-	-	-	-	-	-
Italy	-	-	-	-	-	-	-	-	97	96	97	87	96	95	52	-	-	-	-	-	-
Jamaica	93	98	88	80	91	69	-	90	86	85	86	87	87	87	72	75	52	39	-	-	-
Japan	100	100	100	100	100	100	-	-	99	99	97	99	-	-	86	-	-	-	-	-	-
Jordan	97	99	91	93	94	87	100	95	99	98	98	99	98	98	-	78	-	44	-	-	-
Kazakhstan	86	97	73	72	87	52	100	99	99	99	99	99	99	-	-	71	32	48	-	-	-
Kenya	61	83	46	43	46	41	80	92	90	80	77	77	80	80	74	49	-	33	15	5	27
Kiribati	65	77	53	40	59	22	100	99	98	86	86	61	88	-	-	-	-	-	-	-	-
Korea, Democratic People's Republic of	100	100	100	59	58	60	-	96	91	89	98	96	96	-	-	93	-	-	-	-	-
Korea, Republic of	92	97	71	-	-	-	-	98	98	98	98	99	99	-	-	-	-	-	-	-	-
Kuwait	-	-	-	-	-	-	-	-	99	99	99	99	99	99	90	-	-	-	-	-	-
Kyrgyzstan	77	98	66	59	75	51	40	99	96	92	93	97	90	-	82	62	45	22	-	-	-
Lao People's Democratic Republic	51	79	43	30	67	20	0	61	68	57	56	48	57	-	52	36	-	37	82x	18x	9x
Latvia	99	100	96	78	82	71	100	99	99	98	98	95	97	99	-	-	-	-	-	-	-
Lebanon	100	100	100	98	100	87	100	-	98	92	92	96	88	92	72	74	-	-	-	-	-
Lesotho	79	92	76	37	61	32	1	96	95	83	80	85	85	-	72	59	-	53	-	-	-
Liberia	61	72	52	27	49	7	0	89	99	88	87	94	-	-	-	70	-	-	11	3	-
Libyan Arab Jamahiriya	-	-	-	97	97	96	100	98	98	98	98	98	98	-	-	-	-	-	-	-	-
Liechtenstein	-	-	-	-	-	-	-	-	-	-	-	-	-	-	-	-	-	-	-	-	-
Lithuania	-	-	-	-	-	-	100	99	99	94	94	97	95	94	-	-	-	-	-	-	-
Luxembourg	100	100	100	-	-	-	-	-	99	99	99	95	95	98	-	-	-	-	-	-	-
Madagascar	50	77	35	34	48	26	18	72	71	61	63	59	61	-	67	48	-	47	30x	0x	34
Malawi	73	98	61	61	62	61	20	99	99	99	99	85	99	99	84	51	29	26	29	23	24
Malaysia	99	100	96	94	95	93	100	99	88	96	96	90	87	89	88	-	-	-	-	-	-
Maldives	83	98	76	59	100	42	75	99	99	98	98	97	98	-	85	22	-	-	-	-	-
Mali	50	78	36	46	59	39	77	85	95	85	83	86	90	16	-	36	-	45	-	-	-
Malta	100	100	100	-	100	-	70	-	85	85	83	94	86	83	62	-	-	-	-	-	-
Marshall Islands	87	82	96	82	93	58	100	92	90	74	95	96	97	60	-	-	-	-	-	-	-
Mauritania	53	59	44	34	49	8	100	86	85	68	68	62	68	-	94	41	-	9	31	2	33
Mauritius	100	100	100	94	95	94	100	97	96	97	98	99	97	96	-	-	-	-	-	-	-
Mexico	97	100	87	79	91	41	100	99	99	98	98	96	98	98	87	-	-	-	-	-	-
Micronesia (Federated States of)	94	95	94	28	61	14	100	55	86	67	81	83	84	59	-	-	-	-	-	-	-
Moldova, Republic of	92	97	88	68	86	52	-	99	97	97	98	96	98	-	-	60	-	48	-	-	-
Monaco	100	100	-	100	100	-	-	90	99	99	99	99	99	99	-	-	-	-	-	-	-
Mongolia	62	87	30	59	75	37	-	98	99	99	98	99	98	56	87	63	71	47	-	-	-
Montenegro	-	-	-	-	-	-	-	98	95	90	90	90	90	90	85	89	57	64	-	-	-
Morocco	81	99	56	73	88	52	100	95	99	97	97	95	95	10	-	38	-	46	-	-	-
Mozambique	43	72	26	32	53	19	-	87	88	72	70	77	72	-	85	55	-	47	10	-	15
Myanmar	78	80	77	77	88	72	-	85	86	82	82	78	75	-	87	66	-	65	-	-	-
Namibia	87	98	81	25	50	13	100	88	90	74	74	63	-	-	81	53	-	39	7x	-	14x

TABLE 3. HEALTH

| | % of population using improved drinking-water sources 2004 | | | % of population using adequate sanitation facilities 2004 | | | % of routine EPI vaccines financed by government 2006 | Immunization 2006 1-year-old children immunized against: | | | | | | | % new-borns protected against tetanus[λ] | % under-fives with suspected pneumonia taken to an appropriate health-care provider[±] | % under-fives with suspected pneumonia receiving antibiotics[±] | % under-fives with diarrhoea receiving oral rehy-dration and continued feeding | Malaria 2003-2006* | | |
| | | | | | | | | TB | DPT | | Polio | Measles | HepB | Hib | | | | | % under-fives sleeping under a mosquito net | % under-fives sleeping under a treated mosquito net | % under-fives with fever receiving anti-malarial drugs |
	total	urban	rural	total	urban	rural	total	BCG	DPT1[β]	DPT3[β]	polio3	measles	HepB3	Hib3		2000-2006*		2000-2006*			
Nauru	-	-	-	-	-	-	0	99	98	72	45	99	99	-	-	-	-	-	-	-	-
Nepal	90	96	89	35	62	30	18	93	93	89	91	85	69	-	83	43	25	43	-	-	-
Netherlands	100	100	100	100	100	100	100	-	98	98	98	96	-	97	-	-	-	-	-	-	-
New Zealand	-	100	-	-	-	-	100	-	92	89	89	82	87	80	-	-	-	-	-	-	-
Nicaragua	79	90	63	47	56	34	83	99	94	87	88	99	87	87	94	57	-	49	-	-	2x
Niger	46	80	36	13	43	4	19	64	58	39	55	47	-	-	53	27	-	43	15	7	33
Nigeria	48	67	31	44	53	36	100	69	72	54	61	62	41	-	71	33	-	28	6	1	34
Niue	100	100	100	100	100	100	100	99	99	99	99	99	99	99	-	-	-	-	-	-	-
Norway	100	100	100	-	-	-	100	-	97	93	93	91	-	94	-	-	-	-	-	-	-
Occupied Palestinian Territory	92	94	88	73	78	61	-	99	98	96	96	99	97	-	-	65	-	-	-	-	-
Oman	-	-	-	-	97	-	-	99	98	98	98	96	99	98	94	-	-	-	-	-	-
Pakistan	91	96	89	59	92	41	100	89	90	83	83	80	83	-	80	66x	16x	-	-	-	-
Palau	85	79	94	80	96	52	100	-	98	98	98	98	98	98	-	-	-	-	-	-	-
Panama	90	99	79	73	89	51	100	99	99	99	99	94	99	99	-	-	-	-	-	-	-
Papua New Guinea	39	88	32	44	67	41	100	75	85	75	75	65	70	-	81	75x	-	-	-	-	-
Paraguay	86	99	68	80	94	61	100	75	90	73	72	88	73	73	82	51x	29x	-	-	-	-
Peru	83	89	65	63	74	32	96	99	98	94	95	99	94	94	64	68	-	57	-	-	-
Philippines	85	87	82	72	80	59	100	91	90	88	88	92	77	-	57	55	-	76	-	-	-
Poland	-	-	-	-	-	-	-	94	99	99	99	99	98	31	-	-	-	-	-	-	-
Portugal	-	-	-	-	-	-	-	89	94	93	93	99	94	93	-	-	-	-	-	-	-
Qatar	100	100	100	100	100	100	100	99	99	96	95	99	96	96	-	-	-	-	-	-	-
Romania	57	91	16	-	89	-	100	99	98	97	97	95	99	-	-	-	-	-	-	-	-
Russian Federation	97	100	88	87	93	70	-	97	98	99	99	99	99	-	-	-	-	-	-	-	-
Rwanda	74	92	69	42	56	38	28	98	99	99	99	95	99	99	82	28	-	24	16	13	12
Saint Kitts and Nevis	100	99	99	95	96	96	100	99	99	99	99	99	99	99	-	-	-	-	-	-	-
Saint Lucia	98	98	98	89	89	89	-	94	94	85	85	94	85	85	-	-	-	-	-	-	-
Saint Vincent and the Grenadines	-	-	93	-	-	96	100	99	99	99	99	99	99	99	-	-	-	-	-	-	-
Samoa	88	90	87	100	100	100	100	84	80	56	57	54	56	-	-	-	-	-	-	-	-
San Marino	-	-	-	-	-	-	-	-	94	95	95	94	95	95	-	-	-	-	-	-	-
Sao Tome and Principe	79	89	73	25	32	20	0	98	99	99	97	85	75	-	-	47	-	63	53	42	25
Saudi Arabia	-	97	-	-	100	-	100	95	97	96	96	95	96	96	56	-	-	-	-	-	-
Senegal	76	92	60	57	79	34	37	99	99	89	89	80	89	89	86	47	-	43	14	7	27
Serbia	-	-	-	-	-	-	-	99	97	92	97	88	93	42	-	93	57	31	-	-	-
Seychelles	88	100	75	-	-	100	100	99	99	99	99	99	99	-	-	-	-	-	-	-	-
Sierra Leone	57	75	46	39	53	30	-	82	77	64	64	67	-	-	-	48	21	31	20	5	52
Singapore	100	100	-	100	100	-	-	98	96	95	95	93	94	-	4	-	-	-	-	-	-
Slovakia	100	100	99	99	100	98	100	98	99	99	99	98	99	99	73	-	-	-	-	-	-
Slovenia	-	-	-	-	-	-	70	-	98	97	97	96	-	97	74	-	-	-	-	-	-
Solomon Islands	70	94	65	31	98	18	-	84	96	91	91	84	93	-	74	-	-	-	-	-	-
Somalia	29	32	27	26	48	14	0	50	40	35	35	35	-	-	-	13	32	7	18	9	8
South Africa	88	99	73	65	79	46	100	97	99	99	99	85	99	99	88	75x	-	37x	-	-	-
Spain	100	100	100	100	100	100	100	-	98	98	98	97	81	98	72	-	-	-	-	-	-
Sri Lanka	79	98	74	91	98	89	68	99	99	99	98	99	98	-	93	-	-	-	-	-	-
Sudan	70	78	64	34	50	24	0	77	91	78	77	73	60	-	-	57	-	38	23x	0x	50x
Suriname	92	98	73	94	99	76	-	-	94	84	84	83	84	84	-	58	-	43	77x	3x	-
Swaziland	62	87	54	48	59	44	100	78	73	68	67	57	68	-	-	60	-	24	0x	0x	26x
Sweden	100	100	100	100	100	100	-	17	99	99	99	99	-	99	86	-	-	-	-	-	-
Switzerland	100	100	100	100	100	100	5	-	98	95	94	86	-	92	93	-	-	-	-	-	-
Syrian Arab Republic	93	98	87	90	99	81	100	99	99	99	99	98	98	99	87	77	71	34	-	-	-
Tajikistan	59	92	48	51	70	45	5	94	93	86	81	87	86	-	88	64	41	22	2	1	2
Tanzania, United Republic of	62	85	49	47	53	43	83	99	94	90	91	93	90	-	-	59	-	53	31	16	58
Thailand	99	98	100	99	98	99	100	99	99	98	98	96	96	-	-	84	65	46	-	-	-
The former Yugoslav Republic of Macedonia	-	-	-	-	-	-	-	92	95	93	92	94	89	-	88	93	74	45	-	-	-
Timor-Leste	58	77	56	36	66	33	0	72	75	67	66	64	-	-	63	24	-	-	48x	8x	47x
Togo	52	80	36	35	71	15	100	96	91	87	87	83	-	-	84	23	26	22	41	38	48
Tonga	100	100	100	96	98	96	75	99	99	99	99	99	99	99	-	-	-	-	-	-	-
Trinidad and Tobago	91	92	88	100	100	100	100	-	93	92	89	89	89	89	-	74	34	32	-	-	-
Tunisia	93	99	82	85	96	65	100	99	99	99	99	98	99	-	89	43	-	-	-	-	-
Turkey	96	98	93	88	96	72	-	88	92	90	90	98	82	-	67	41	-	19x	-	-	-
Turkmenistan	72	93	54	62	77	50	-	99	99	98	98	99	98	-	-	83	50	25	-	-	-
Tuvalu	100	94	92	90	93	84	10	99	99	97	97	84	97	-	-	-	-	-	-	-	-

	% of population using improved drinking-water sources 2004			% of population using adequate sanitation facilities 2004			% of routine EPI vaccines financed by government 2006	Immunization 2006 — 1-year-old children immunized against:							% new-borns protected against tetanus$^\lambda$	% under-fives with suspected pneumonia taken to an appropriate health-care provider$^\pm$ 2000-2006*	% under-fives with suspected pneumonia receiving antibiotics$^\pm$	% under-fives with diarrhoea receiving oral rehydration and continued feeding 2000-2006*	Malaria 2003-2006*		
								TB	DPT		Polio	Measles	HepB	Hib					% under-fives sleeping under a mosquito net	% under-fives sleeping under a treated mosquito net	% under-fives with fever receiving anti-malarial drugs
	total	urban	rural	total	urban	rural	total	BCG	DPT1$^\beta$	DPT3$^\beta$	polio3	measles	HepB3	Hib3		2000-2006*		2000-2006*			
Uganda	60	87	56	43	54	41	8	85	89	80	81	89	80	80	88	67	-	29	22	10	62
Ukraine	96	99	91	96	98	93	99	97	98	98	99	98	96	11	-	-	-	-	-	-	-
United Arab Emirates	100	100	100	98	98	95	-	98	97	94	94	92	92	94	-	-	-	-	-	-	-
United Kingdom	100	100	100	-	-	-	100	-	97	92	92	85	-	92	-	-	-	-	-	-	-
United States	100	100	100	100	100	100	-	-	99	96	92	93	92	94	-	-	-	-	-	-	-
Uruguay	100	100	100	100	100	99	100	99	99	95	95	94	95	95	-	-	-	-	-	-	-
Uzbekistan	82	95	75	67	78	61	64	98	96	95	94	95	97	-	87	68	56	28	-	-	-
Vanuatu	60	86	52	50	78	42	100	92	90	85	85	99	85	-	52	-	-	-	-	-	-
Venezuela (Bolivarian Republic of)	83	85	70	68	71	48	-	83	78	71	73	55	71	71	88	72	-	51	-	-	-
Viet Nam	85	99	80	61	92	50	80	95	94	94	94	93	93	-	61	71	-	65	94	5	3
Yemen	67	71	65	43	86	28	100	70	92	85	85	80	85	85	-	47	-	18x	-	-	-
Zambia	58	90	40	55	59	52	85	94	94	80	80	84	80	80	90	69	-	48	27	23	58
Zimbabwe	81	98	72	53	63	47	0	99	95	90	90	90	90	-	80	50x	-	80x	7	3	5

SUMMARY INDICATORS

	total	urban	rural	total	urban	rural	total	BCG	DPT1	DPT3	polio3	measles	HepB3	Hib3							
Sub-Saharan Africa	55	81	41	37	53	28	49	82	83	72	74	72	48	24	77	40	-	30	15	8	34
Eastern and Southern Africa	56	86	42	38	58	30	43	85	86	78	77	76	58	36	81	44	-	32	15	9	28
West and Central Africa	55	76	40	36	49	26	55	79	81	67	70	68	38	13	72	36	-	29	16	7	40
Middle East and North Africa	88	95	78	74	90	53	88	92	95	91	91	89	88	24	81	66	-	38	-	-	-
South Asia	85	94	81	37	63	27	91	82	82	63	66	65	25	-	84	62	-	35	-	-	-
East Asia and Pacific	79	92	70	51	73	36	-	91	92	89	89	89	86	2	-	64**	-	61**	-	-	-
Latin America and Caribbean	91	96	73	77	86	49	96	96	96	92	92	93	89	90	84	-	-	-	-	-	-
CEE/CIS	91	98	79	84	93	70	-	95	96	95	95	97	92	3	-	57	-	-	-	-	-
Industrialized countries§	100	100	100	100	100	99	-	-	98	96	94	93	64	82	-	-	-	-	-	-	-
Developing countries§	80	92	70	50	73	33	78	86	88	78	79	78	59	17	80	56**	-	38**	-	-	-
Least developed countries§	59	79	51	36	55	29	33	85	87	77	77	74	50	17	82	40	-	37	-	-	-
World	83	95	73	59	80	39	78	87	89	79	80	80	60	22	80	56**	-	38**	-	-	-

§ Also includes territories within each country category or regional group. Countries and territories in each country category or regional group are listed on page 148.

DEFINITIONS OF THE INDICATORS

Government funding of vaccines – Percentage of vaccines that are routinely administered in a country to protect children and are financed by the national government (including loans).

EPI – Expanded programme on immunization: The immunizations in this programme include those against tuberculosis (TB), diphtheria, pertussis (whooping cough) and tetanus (DPT), polio and measles, as well as vaccination of pregnant women to protect babies against neonatal tetanus. Other vaccines, e.g., against hepatitis B (HepB), *Haemophilus influenzae* type b (Hib) or yellow fever, may be included in the programme in some countries.

BCG – Percentage of infants who received bacille Calmette-Guérin (vaccine against tuberculosis).

DPT1 – Percentage of infants who received their first dose of diphtheria, pertussis and tetanus vaccine.

DPT3 – Percentage of infants who received three doses of diphtheria, pertussis and tetanus vaccine.

HepB3 – Percentage of infants who received three doses of hepatitis B vaccine.

Hib3 – Percentage of infants who received three doses of *Haemophilus influenzae* type b vaccine.

% under-fives with suspected pneumonia receiving antibiotics – Percentage of children (aged 0-4) with suspected pneumonia in the two weeks preceding the survey who are receiving antibiotics.

% under-fives with suspected pneumonia taken to an appropriate health-care provider – Percentage of children (aged 0-4) with suspected pneumonia in the two weeks preceding the survey who were taken to an appropriate health-care provider.

% under-fives with diarrhoea receiving oral rehydration and continued feeding – Percentage of children (aged 0-4) with diarrhoea in the two weeks preceding the survey who received either oral rehydration therapy (oral rehydration solutions or recommended home-made fluids) or increased fluids and continued feeding.

Malaria:

% under-fives sleeping under a mosquito net – Percentage of children (aged 0-4) who slept under a mosquito net.

% under-fives sleeping under a treated mosquito net – Percentage of children (aged 0-4) who slept under an insecticide-treated mosquito net.

% under-fives with fever receiving antimalarial drugs – Percentage of children (aged 0-4) who were ill with fever in the two weeks preceding the survey and received any appropriate (locally defined) antimalarial drugs.

MAIN DATA SOURCES

Use of improved drinking-water sources and adequate sanitation facilities – UNICEF, World Health Organization (WHO), Multiple Indicator Cluster Surveys (MICS) and Demographic and Health Surveys (DHS).

Government funding of vaccines – UNICEF and WHO.

Immunization – UNICEF and WHO.

Suspected pneumonia – DHS, MICS and other national household surveys.

Oral rehydration DHS and MICS.

Malaria – DHS and MICS.

NOTES

- Data not available.

x Data refer to years or periods other than those specified in the column heading, differ from the standard definition or refer to only part of a country. Such data are not included in the calculation of regional and global averages.

* Data refer to the most recent year available during the period specified in the column heading.

β Coverage for DPT1 should be at least as high as DPT3. Discrepancies where DPT1 coverage is less than DPT3 reflect deficiencies in the data collection and reporting process. UNICEF and WHO are working with national and territorial systems to eliminate these discrepancies.

± In this year's report, as in last year's, we use the term 'suspected pneumonia' instead of 'acute respiratory infections (ARI)', which was employed in previous editions. However, the data collection methodology has not changed, and estimates presented here are comparable to those in previous reports. For a more detailed discussion regarding this update, please see the *General note on the data* on page 110.

λ In this year's report, WHO and UNICEF have employed a model to calculate the percentage of births that can be considered to be protected against tetanus because pregnant women were given two doses or more of tetanus toxoid (TT) vaccine. The model aims to improve the accuracy of this indicator by capturing or including other potential scenarios where women might be protected (e.g., women who receive doses of TT in supplemental immunization activities). A fuller explanation of the methodology can be found in the *General note on the data*, page 110.

** Excludes China.

TABLE 4. HIV/AIDS

Countries and territories	Estimated adult HIV prevalence rate (aged 15-49), end-2005	Estimated number of people (all ages) living with HIV, 2005 (thousands) estimate	low estimate - high estimate	Estimated number of women (aged 15+) living with HIV, 2005 (thousands)	HIV prevalence rate in young pregnant women (aged 15-24) in capital city year	median	Estimated number of children (aged 0-14) living with HIV, 2005 (thousands)	HIV prevalence among young people (aged 15-24), 2005 male	female	% who have comprehensive knowledge of HIV, 2000-2006* male	female	% who used condom at last high-risk sex, 2000-2006* male	female	Orphans Children (aged 0-17) orphaned by AIDS, 2005 estimate (thousands)	orphaned due to all causes, 2005 estimate (thousands)	Orphan school attendance ratio 2000-2006*
Afghanistan	<0.1	<1.0	<2.0	<0.1	-	-	-	-	-	-	-	-	-	-	1600	-
Albania	-	-	<1.0	-	-	-	-	-	-	-	6	-	-	-	-	-
Algeria	0.1	19	9.0 - 59	4.1	-	-	-	-	-	-	13	-	-	-	-	-
Andorra	-	-	-	-	-	-	-	-	-	-	-	-	-	-	-	-
Angola	3.7	320	200 - 450	170	2004	2.8	35	0.9	2.5	-	-	-	-	160	1200	90
Antigua and Barbuda	-	-	-	-	-	-	-	-	-	-	-	-	-	-	-	-
Argentina	0.6	130	80 - 220	36	-	-	-	-	-	-	-	-	-	-	690	-
Armenia	0.1	2.9	1.8 - 5.8	<1.0	-	-	-	-	-	15	23	86	-	-	-	-
Australia	0.1	16	9.7 - 27	<1.0	-	-	-	-	-	-	-	-	-	-	-	-
Austria	0.3	12	7.2 - 20	2.3	-	-	-	-	-	-	-	-	-	-	-	-
Azerbaijan	0.1	5.4	2.6 - 17	<1.0	-	-	-	-	-	-	2	-	-	-	-	-
Bahamas	3.3	6.8	3.3 - 22	3.8	-	-	<0.5	-	-	-	-	-	-	-	8	-
Bahrain	-	<1.0	<2.0	-	-	-	-	-	-	-	-	-	-	-	-	-
Bangladesh	<0.1	11	6.4 - 18	1.4	-	-	-	-	-	-	16	-	-	-	4400	-
Barbados	1.5	2.7	1.5 - 4.2	<1.0	-	-	<0.1	-	-	-	-	-	-	-	3	-
Belarus	0.3	20	11 - 47	5.1	-	-	-	-	-	-	34	-	-	-	-	-
Belgium	0.3	14	8.1 - 22	5.4	-	-	-	-	-	-	-	-	-	-	-	-
Belize	2.5	3.7	2.0 - 5.7	1.0	-	-	<0.1	-	-	-	-	-	-	-	5	-
Benin	1.8	87	57 - 120	45	2003	1.7 - 2.1	9.8	0.4	1.1	14	8	44	17	62	370	-
Bhutan	<0.1	<0.5	<2.0	<0.1	-	-	-	-	-	-	-	-	-	-	78	-
Bolivia	0.1	7.0	3.8 - 17	1.9	-	-	-	-	-	18	15	37	20	-	310	74
Bosnia and Herzegovina	<0.1	<0.5	<1.0	-	-	-	-	-	-	-	48	-	71	-	-	-
Botswana	24.1	270	260 - 350	140	2005	33.5	14	5.7	15.3	33	40	88	75	120	150	99
Brazil	0.5	620	370 - 1000	220	-	-	-	-	-	67	67	71	58	-	3700	-
Brunei Darussalam	<0.1	<0.1	<0.2	<0.1	-	-	-	-	-	-	-	-	-	-	4	-
Bulgaria	<0.1	<0.5	<1.0	-	-	-	-	-	-	15	17	70	57	-	-	-
Burkina Faso	2.0	150	120 - 190	80	2005	1.8	17	0.5	1.4	23	19r	67	64r	120	710	71
Burundi	3.3	150	130 - 180	79	2004	8.6	20	0.8	2.3	-	30	-	25	120	600	86
Cambodia	1.6	130	74 - 210	59	2002	2.7	-	0.1h	0.3h	45	50	84	-	-	470	80
Cameroon	5.4	510	460 - 560	290	2002	7.0	43	1.4h	4.8h	34	32r	57	62r	240	1000	87
Canada	0.3	60	48 - 72	9.6	-	-	-	-	-	-	-	-	-	-	-	-
Cape Verde	-	-	-	-	-	-	-	-	-	-	-	-	-	-	-	-
Central African Republic	10.7	250	110 - 390	130	2002	14.0	24	2.5	7.3	-	17	-	41	140	330	96
Chad	3.5	180	88 - 300	90	2005	3.6	16	0.9	2.2	20	8	25	17	57	600	105
Chile	0.3	28	17 - 56	7.6	-	-	-	-	-	-	-	-	-	-	200	-
China	0.1	650	390 - 1100	180	-	-	-	-	-	-	-	-	-	-	20600	-
Colombia	0.6	160	100 - 320	45	-	-	-	-	-	-	-	-	30	-	870	-
Comoros	<0.1	<0.5	<1.0	<0.1	-	-	<0.1	<0.1	<0.1	-	10	-	-	-	33	59
Congo	5.3	120	75 - 160	61	2002	3.0	15	1.2	3.7	22	10	38	20	110	270	90
Congo, Democratic Republic of the	3.2	1000	560 - 1500	520	2003	3.2	120	0.8	2.2	-	-	-	-	680	4200	72
Cook Islands	-	-	-	-	-	-	-	-	-	-	-	-	-	-	-	-
Costa Rica	0.3	7.4	3.6 - 24	2.0	2002	5.2	-	-	-	-	-	-	-	-	44	-
Côte d'Ivoire	7.1	750	470 - 1000	400	2002	5.2	74	0.3h	2.4h	28	18	53	39	450	1400	121
Croatia	<0.1	<0.5	<1.0	-	-	-	-	-	-	-	-	-	-	-	-	-
Cuba	0.1	4.8	2.3 - 15	2.6	-	-	-	-	-	-	52	-	-	-	120	-
Cyprus	-	<0.5	<1.0	-	-	-	-	-	-	-	-	-	-	-	-	-
Czech Republic	0.1	1.5	0.9 - 2.5	<1.0	-	-	-	-	-	-	-	-	-	-	-	-
Denmark	0.2	5.6	3.4 - 9.3	1.3	-	-	-	-	-	-	-	-	-	-	-	-
Djibouti	3.1	15	3.9 - 34	8.4	-	-	1.2	0.7	2.1	22	18	50	26	6	48	82
Dominica	-	-	-	-	-	-	-	-	-	-	-	-	-	-	-	-
Dominican Republic	1.1	66	56 - 77	31	-	-	3.6	0.4h	0.7h	-	36	52	29	-	220	93
Ecuador	0.3	23	11 - 74	12	-	-	-	-	-	-	-	-	-	-	230	-
Egypt	<0.1	5.3	2.9 - 13	<1.0	-	-	-	-	-	-	4	-	-	-	-	-
El Salvador	0.9	36	22 - 72	9.9	-	-	-	-	-	-	-	-	-	-	150	-
Equatorial Guinea	3.2	8.9	7.3 - 11	4.7	-	-	<1.0	0.7	2.3	-	4	-	-	5	29	95
Eritrea	2.4	59	33 - 95	31	-	-	6.6	0.6	1.6	-	37	-	-	36	280	83
Estonia	1.3	10	4.8 - 32	2.4	-	-	-	-	-	-	-	-	-	-	-	-
Ethiopia	-	-	420 - 1300	-	2003	11.5	-	0.3h	1.2h	33	21	50	28	-	4800	60
Fiji	0.1	<1.0	0.3 - 2.1	<0.5	-	-	-	-	-	-	-	-	-	-	25	-
Finland	0.1	1.9	1.1 - 3.1	<1.0	-	-	-	-	-	-	-	-	-	-	-	-
France	0.4	130	78 - 210	45	-	-	-	-	-	-	-	-	-	-	-	-
Gabon	7.9	60	40 - 87	33	-	-	3.9	1.8	5.4	22	24	48	33	20	65	98
Gambia	2.4	20	10 - 33	11	-	-	1.2	0.6	1.7	-	39	-	54	4	64	87

	Estimated adult HIV prevalence rate (aged 15-49), end-2005	Estimated number of people (all ages) living with HIV, 2005 (thousands)		Mother-to-child transmission			Paediatric infections	Prevention among young people						Orphans		
				Estimated number of women (aged 15+) living with HIV, 2005 (thousands)	HIV prevalence rate in young pregnant women (aged 15-24) in capital city		Estimated number of children (aged 0-14) living with HIV, 2005 (thousands)	HIV prevalence among young people (aged 15-24), 2005		% who have comprehensive knowledge of HIV, 2000-2006*		% who used condom at last high-risk sex, 2000-2006*		Children (aged 0-17)		Orphan school attendance ratio
		estimate	low estimate - high estimate		year	median		male	female	male	female	male	female	orphaned by AIDS, 2005 (estimate thousands)	orphaned due to all causes, 2005 (estimate thousands)	2000-2006*
Georgia	0.2	5.6	2.7 - 18	<1.0	-	-	-	-	-	-	-	-	-	-	-	-
Germany	0.1	49	29 - 81	15	-	-	-	-	-	-	-	-	-	-	-	-
Ghana	2.3	320	270 - 380	180	2003	3.9	25	0.1h	1.2h	44	34r	52	42r	170	1000	79p
Greece	0.2	9.3	5.6 - 15	2.0	-	-	-	-	-	-	-	-	-	-	-	-
Grenada	-	-	-	-	-	-	-	-	-	-	-	-	-	-	-	-
Guatemala	0.9	61	37 - 100	16	-	-	-	-	-	-	-	-	-	-	370	98
Guinea	1.5	85	69 - 100	53	2004	4.4	7.0	0.6h	1.2h	23	17	37	26	28	370	73
Guinea-Bissau	3.8	32	18 - 50	17	-	-	3.2	0.9	2.5	-	18	-	39	11	100	97
Guyana	2.4	12	4.7 - 23	6.6	-	-	<1.0	-	-	47	53	68	62	-	26	-
Haiti	3.8	190	120 - 270	96	2000	3.7	17	0.6h	1.5h	40	32	43	29	-	490	86
Holy See	-	-	-	-	-	-	-	-	-	-	-	-	-	-	-	-
Honduras	1.5	63	35 - 99	16	-	-	2.4	-	-	-	30	-	24	-	180	-
Hungary	0.1	3.2	1.9 - 5.3	<1.0	-	-	-	-	-	-	-	-	-	-	-	-
Iceland	0.2	<0.5	<1.0	<0.1	-	-	-	-	-	-	-	-	-	-	-	-
India#	0.9	2500	2000 - 3100	1600	-	-	-	-	-	43	24	37	22	-	25700	84
Indonesia	0.1	170	100 - 290	29	-	-	-	-	-	-	7	-	-	-	5300	82
Iran (Islamic Republic of)	0.2	66	36 - 160	11	-	-	-	-	-	-	-	-	-	-	1500	-
Iraq	-	-	-	-	-	-	-	-	-	-	3	-	-	-	-	84
Ireland	0.2	5.0	3.0 - 8.3	1.8	-	-	-	-	-	-	-	-	-	-	-	-
Israel	-	4.0	2.2 - 9.8	-	-	-	-	-	-	-	-	-	-	-	-	-
Italy	0.5	150	90 - 250	50	-	-	-	-	-	-	-	-	-	-	-	-
Jamaica	1.5	25	14 - 39	6.9	-	-	<0.5	-	-	-	60	-	-	-	55	101
Japan	<0.1	17	10 - 29	9.9	-	-	-	-	-	-	-	-	-	-	-	-
Jordan	-	<1.0	<2.0	-	-	-	-	-	-	-	-	-	-	-	-	-
Kazakhstan	0.1	12	11 - 77	6.8	-	-	-	-	-	-	22	65	32	-	-	98
Kenya	6.1	1300	1100 - 1500	740	-	-	150	1.3h	5.9h	47	34	47	25	1100	2300	95
Kiribati	-	-	-	-	-	-	-	-	-	-	-	-	-	-	-	-
Korea, Democratic People's Republic of	-	-	-	-	-	-	-	-	-	-	-	-	-	-	-	-
Korea, Republic of	<0.1	13	7.9 - 25	7.4	-	-	-	-	-	-	-	-	-	-	450	-
Kuwait	-	<1.0	<2.0	-	-	-	-	-	-	-	-	-	-	-	-	-
Kyrgyzstan	0.1	4.0	1.9 - 13	<1.0	-	-	-	-	-	-	20	-	56	-	-	-
Lao People's Democratic Republic	0.1	3.7	1.8 - 12	<1.0	-	-	-	-	-	-	-	-	-	-	290	-
Latvia	0.8	10	6.1 - 17	2.2	-	-	-	-	-	-	-	-	-	-	-	-
Lebanon	0.1	2.9	1.4 - 9.2	<1.0	-	-	-	-	-	-	-	-	-	-	-	-
Lesotho	23.2	270	250 - 290	150	2004	27.3	18	6.0h	15.4h	18	26	53	53	97	150	95
Liberia	-	-	-	-	-	-	-	-	-	-	-	-	-	-	250	-
Libyan Arab Jamahiriya	-	-	-	-	-	-	-	-	-	-	-	-	-	-	-	-
Liechtenstein	-	-	-	-	-	-	-	-	-	-	-	-	-	-	-	-
Lithuania	0.2	3.3	1.6 - 10	<1.0	-	-	-	-	-	-	-	-	-	-	-	-
Luxembourg	0.2	<1.0	<1.0	-	-	-	-	-	-	-	-	-	-	-	-	-
Madagascar	0.5	49	16 - 110	13	-	-	1.6	0.6	0.3	16	19	12	5	13	900	76
Malawi	14.1	940	480 - 1400	500	2001	15.0	91	2.1h	9.1h	36	41r	47	40r	550	950	96
Malaysia	0.5	69	33 - 220	17	-	-	-	-	-	-	-	-	-	-	480	-
Maldives	-	-	-	-	-	-	-	-	-	-	-	-	-	-	-	-
Mali	1.7	130	96 - 160	66	2002	2.5	16	0.4	1.2	15	9	35	17	94	710	104
Malta	0.1	<0.5	<1.0	-	-	-	-	-	-	-	-	-	-	-	-	-
Marshall Islands	-	-	-	-	-	-	-	-	-	-	-	-	-	-	-	-
Mauritania	0.7	12	7.3 - 23	6.3	-	-	1.1	0.2	0.5	-	-	-	-	7	170	-
Mauritius	0.6	4.1	1.9 - 13	<1.0	-	-	-	-	-	-	-	-	-	-	23	-
Mexico	0.3	180	99 - 440	42	-	-	-	-	-	-	-	-	-	-	1600	-
Micronesia (Federated States of)	-	-	-	-	-	-	-	-	-	-	-	-	-	-	-	-
Moldova, Republic of	1.1	29	15 - 69	16	-	-	-	-	-	54	42	63	44	-	-	-
Monaco	-	-	-	-	-	-	-	-	-	-	-	-	-	-	-	-
Mongolia	<0.1	<0.5	<2.0	<0.1	-	-	-	-	-	-	35	-	-	-	79	96
Montenegro	-	-	-	-	-	-	-	-	-	-	30	-	66	-	-	-
Morocco	0.1	19	12 - 38	4.0	-	-	-	-	-	-	12	-	-	-	-	-
Mozambique	16.1	1800	1400 - 2200	960	2002	14.7	140	3.6	10.7	33	20	33	29	510	1500	80
Myanmar	1.3	360	200 - 570	110	-	-	-	-	-	-	-	-	-	-	1700	-
Namibia	19.6	230	110 - 360	130	2004	7.5	17	4.4	13.4	41	31	69	48	85	140	92
Nauru	-	-	-	-	-	-	-	-	-	-	-	-	-	-	-	-
Nepal	0.5	75	41 - 180	16	-	-	-	-	-	44	28	78	-	-	970	-

TABLE 4. HIV/AIDS

	Estimated adult HIV prevalence rate (aged 15-49), end-2005	Estimated number of people (all ages) living with HIV, 2005 (thousands) estimate	low estimate - high estimate	Mother-to-child transmission: Estimated number of women (aged 15+) living with HIV, 2005 (thousands)	HIV prevalence rate in young pregnant women (aged 15-24) in capital city year	median	Paediatric infections: Estimated number of children (aged 0-14) living with HIV, 2005 (thousands)	HIV prevalence among young people (aged 15-24), 2005 male	female	% who have comprehensive knowledge of HIV, 2000-2006* male	female	% who used condom at last high-risk sex, 2000-2006* male	female	Orphans: Children (aged 0-17) orphaned by AIDS, 2005 estimate (thousands)	orphaned due to all causes, 2005 estimate (thousands)	Orphan school attendance ratio 2000-2006*
Netherlands	0.2	18	11 - 29	5.9	-	-	-	-	-	-	-	-	-	-	-	-
New Zealand	0.1	1.4	0.8 - 2.3	-	-	-	-	-	-	-	-	-	-	-	-	-
Nicaragua	0.2	7.3	3.9 - 18	1.7	-	-	-	-	-	-	-	-	17	-	130	-
Niger	1.1	79	39 - 130	42	-	-	8.9	0.1h	0.5h	16	13	37	18	46	800	-
Nigeria	3.9	2900	1700 - 4200	1600	-	-	240	0.9	2.7	21	18	46	24	930	8600	64p
Niue	-	-	-	-	-	-	-	-	-	-	-	-	-	-	-	-
Norway	0.1	2.5	1.5 - 4.1	<1.0	-	-	-	-	-	-	-	-	-	-	-	-
Occupied Palestinian Territory	-	-	-	-	-	-	-	-	-	-	-	-	-	-	-	-
Oman	-	-	-	-	-	-	-	-	-	-	-	-	-	-	-	-
Pakistan	0.1	85	46 - 210	14	-	-	-	-	-	-	-	-	-	-	4400	-
Palau	-	-	-	-	-	-	-	-	-	-	-	-	-	-	-	-
Panama	0.9	17	11 - 34	4.3	-	-	-	-	-	-	-	-	-	-	53	-
Papua New Guinea	1.8	60	32 - 140	34	-	-	-	-	-	-	-	-	-	-	350	-
Paraguay	0.4	13	6.2 - 41	3.5	-	-	-	-	-	-	-	-	-	-	150	-
Peru	0.6	93	56 - 150	26	-	-	-	-	-	-	-	-	32	-	660	85p
Philippines	<0.1	12	7.3 - 20	3.4	-	-	-	-	-	-	-	-	-	-	2000	-
Poland	0.1	25	15 - 41	7.5	-	-	-	-	-	-	-	-	-	-	-	-
Portugal	0.4	32	19 - 53	1.3	-	-	-	-	-	-	-	-	-	-	-	-
Qatar	-	-	-	-	-	-	-	-	-	-	-	-	-	-	-	-
Romania	<0.1	7.0	3.4 - 22	-	-	-	-	-	-	3	6	-	-	-	-	-
Russian Federation	1.1	940	560 - 1600	210	-	-	-	-	-	-	-	-	-	-	-	-
Rwanda	3.1	190	180 - 210	91	2003	10.3	27	0.4h	1.5h	54	51	40	26	210	820	82
Saint Kitts and Nevis	-	-	-	-	-	-	-	-	-	-	-	-	-	-	-	-
Saint Lucia	-	-	-	-	-	-	-	-	-	-	-	-	-	-	-	-
Saint Vincent and the Grenadines	-	-	-	-	-	-	-	-	-	-	-	-	-	-	-	-
Samoa	-	-	-	-	-	-	-	-	-	-	-	-	-	-	-	-
San Marino	-	-	-	-	-	-	-	-	-	-	-	-	-	-	-	-
Sao Tome and Principe	-	-	-	-	-	-	-	-	-	-	44	-	56	-	-	109
Saudi Arabia	-	-	-	-	-	-	-	-	-	-	-	-	-	-	-	-
Senegal	0.9	61	29 - 100	33	2005	0.9	5.0	0.2h	0.6h	24	19	52	36	25	560	83p
Serbia	-	-	-	-	-	-	-	-	-	-	42	-	74	-	-	-
Seychelles	-	-	-	-	-	-	-	-	-	-	-	-	-	-	-	-
Sierra Leone	1.6	48	27 - 73	26	2003	3.2	5.2	0.4	1.1	-	17	-	20	31	340	83
Singapore	0.3	5.5	3.1 - 14	1.5	-	-	-	-	-	-	-	-	-	-	26	-
Slovakia	<0.1	<0.5	<1.0	-	-	-	-	-	-	-	-	-	-	-	-	-
Slovenia	<0.1	<0.5	<1.0	-	-	-	-	-	-	-	-	-	-	-	-	-
Solomon Islands	-	-	-	-	-	-	-	-	-	-	-	-	-	-	-	-
Somalia	0.9	44	23 - 81	23	-	-	4.5	0.2	0.6	-	4	-	-	23	630	87
South Africa	18.8	5500	4900 - 6100	3100	2004	25.2	240	4.4h	16.9h	-	-	-	-	1200	2500	-
Spain	0.6	140	84 - 230	32	-	-	-	-	-	-	-	-	-	-	-	-
Sri Lanka	<0.1	5.0	3.0 - 8.3	<1.0	-	-	-	-	-	-	-	-	-	-	310	-
Sudan	1.6	350	170 - 580	180	-	-	30	-	-	-	-	-	-	-	1700	96
Suriname	1.9	5.2	2.8 - 8.1	1.4	-	-	<0.1	-	-	-	41	-	49	-	10	97
Swaziland	33.4	220	150 - 290	120	2004	37.3	15	7.7	22.7	52	52	70	54	63	95	97
Sweden	0.2	8.0	4.8 - 13	2.5	-	-	-	-	-	-	-	-	-	-	-	-
Switzerland	0.4	17	9.9 - 27	5.9	-	-	-	-	-	-	-	-	-	-	-	-
Syrian Arab Republic	-	-	-	-	-	-	-	-	-	-	7	-	-	-	-	106
Tajikistan	0.1	4.9	2.4 - 16	<0.5	-	-	-	-	-	-	2	-	-	-	-	-
Tanzania, United Republic of	6.5	1400	1300 - 1600	710	2003	8.2	110	3.0h	4.0h	40	45	46	34	1100	2400	102
Thailand	1.4	580	330 - 920	220	-	-	16	-	-	-	46	-	-	-	1200	99
The former Yugoslav Republic of Macedonia	<0.1	<0.5	<1.0	-	-	-	-	-	-	-	27	-	70	-	-	-
Timor-Leste	-	-	-	-	-	-	-	-	-	-	-	-	-	-	-	-
Togo	3.2	110	65 - 160	61	2004	9.3	9.7	0.8	2.2	-	28	-	50	88	280	94
Tonga	-	-	-	-	-	-	-	-	-	-	-	-	-	-	-	-
Trinidad and Tobago	2.6	27	15 - 42	15	-	-	<1.0	-	-	-	54	-	51	-	28	101
Tunisia	0.1	8.7	4.7 - 21	1.9	-	-	-	-	-	-	-	-	-	-	-	-
Turkey	-	<2.0	<5.0	-	-	-	-	-	-	-	-	-	-	-	-	-
Turkmenistan	<0.1	<0.5	<1.0	-	-	-	-	-	-	-	5	-	-	-	-	-
Tuvalu	-	-	-	-	-	-	-	-	-	-	-	-	-	-	-	-
Uganda	6.7	1000	850 - 1200	520	2005	5.2	110	1.1h	4.3h	35	30	55	53	1000	2300	94
Ukraine	1.4	410	250 - 680	200	-	-	-	-	-	-	28	-	-	-	-	98

	Estimated adult HIV prevalence rate (aged 15-49), end-2005	Estimated number of people (all ages) living with HIV, 2005 (thousands)		Estimated number of women (aged 15+) living with HIV, 2005 (thousands)	HIV prevalence rate in young pregnant women (aged 15-24) in capital city		Estimated number of children (aged 0-14) living with HIV, 2005 (thousands)	HIV prevalence among young people (aged 15-24), 2005		% who have comprehensive knowledge of HIV, 2000-2006*		% who used condom at last high-risk sex, 2000-2006*		Children (aged 0-17)		Orphan school attendance ratio
		estimate	low estimate - high estimate		year	median		male	female	male	female	male	female	orphaned by AIDS, 2005 (estimate thousands)	orphaned due to all causes, 2005 (estimate thousands)	2000-2006*
United Arab Emirates	-	-	-	-	-	-	-	-	-	-	-	-	-	-	-	-
United Kingdom	0.2	68	41 - 110	21	-	-	-	-	-	-	-	-	-	-	-	-
United States	0.6	1200	720 - 2000	300	-	-	-	-	-	-	-	-	-	-	-	-
Uruguay	0.5	9.6	4.6 - 30	5.3	-	-	-	-	-	-	-	-	-	-	55	-
Uzbekistan	0.2	31	15 - 99	4.1	-	-	-	-	-	7	31r	50	61r	-	-	-
Vanuatu	-	-	-	-	-	-	-	-	-	-	-	-	-	-	-	-
Venezuela (Bolivian Republic of)	0.7	110	54 - 350	31	-	-	-	-	-	-	-	-	-	-	480	-
Viet Nam	0.5	260	150 - 430	84	-	-	-	0.8h	0h	50	42r	68	-	-	1800	84
Yemen	-	-	-	-	-	-	-	-	-	-	-	-	-	-	-	-
Zambia	17.0	1100	1100 - 1200	570	2004	20.7	130	3.0h	11.1h	46	41	38	26	710	1200	103
Zimbabwe	20.1	1700	1100 - 2200	890	2004	18.6	160	4.2h	11.0h	46	44	68	42	1100	1400	95

SUMMARY INDICATORS

		estimate	low estimate - high estimate		year	median		male	female	male	female	male	female			
Sub-Saharan Africa	6.1	24500	21600 - 27400	13200	-	9.7	2000	1.4	4.3	31	25	47	31	12000	46600	80
Eastern and Southern Africa	8.6	17500	15800 - 19200	9400	-	13.5	1400	2.1	6.2	37	31	46	32	8700	24300	84
West and Central Africa	3.5	6900	5300 - 8700	3700	-	4.0	650	0.7	2.3	24	19	47	31	3300	22200	76
Middle East and North Africa	0.2	510	320 - 830	210	-	-	33	-	-	-	-	-	-	-	-	-
South Asia#	0.7	5900	3600 - 9700	1600	-	-	130	-	-	43	23	38	22	-	37500	84
East Asia and Pacific	0.2	2300	1800 - 3200	750	-	-	50	-	-	-	-	-	-	-	34800	-
Latin America and Caribbean	0.6	1900	1500 - 2800	640	-	-	54	-	-	-	-	-	47	-	10700	-
CEE/CIS	0.6	1500	1000 - 2300	450	-	-	9	-	-	-	-	-	-	-	-	-
Industrialized countries§	0.4	2000	1400 - 3000	530	-	-	13	-	-	-	-	-	-	-	-	-
Developing countries§	1.1	35100	30300 - 41900	16400	-	-	2300	-	-	-	25	-	-	-	-	-
Least developed countries§	2.7	11700	10100 - 13500	6000	-	7.5	1100	1.1	2.9	-	24	-	-	-	-	82
World	1.0	38600	33400 - 46000	17300	-	-	2300	-	-	-	25	-	-	15200	132700	-

§ Also includes territories within each country category or regional group. Countries and territories in each country category or regional group are listed on page 148.

DEFINITIONS OF THE INDICATORS

Estimated adult HIV prevalence rate – Percentage of adults (aged 15-49) living with HIV as of end-2005.

Estimated number of people (all ages) living with HIV – Estimated number of people (all ages) living with HIV as of end-2005.

Estimated number of women (aged 15+) living with HIV – Estimated number of women (aged 15+) living with HIV as of end-2005.

HIV prevalence rate in young pregnant women (aged 15-24) in capital city – Percentage of blood samples taken from pregnant women (aged 15-24) who test positive for HIV during 'unlinked anonymous' sentinel surveillance at selected antenatal clinics.

Estimated number of children (aged 0-14) living with HIV – Estimated number of children (aged 0-14) living with HIV as of end-2005.

HIV prevalence among young men and women – Percentage of young men and women (aged 15-24) living with HIV as of end-2005.

Comprehensive knowledge of HIV – Percentage of young men and women (aged 15-24) who correctly identify the two major ways of preventing the sexual transmission of HIV (using condoms and limiting sex to one faithful, uninfected partner), who reject the two most common local misconceptions about HIV transmission and who know that a healthy-looking person can be HIV-infected.

Condom use at last high-risk sex – Percentage of young men and women (aged 15-24) who say they used a condom the last time they had sex with a non-marital, non-cohabiting partner, of those who have had sex with such a partner during the past 12 months.

Children orphaned by AIDS – Estimated number of children (aged 0-17) as of end-2005 who have lost one or both parents to AIDS.

Children orphaned due to all causes – Estimated number of children (aged 0-17) as of end-2005 who have lost one or both parents due to any cause.

Orphan school attendance ratio – Percentage of children (aged 10-14) who have lost both biological parents and who are currently attending school as a percentage of non-orphaned children of the same age who live with at least one parent and who are attending school.

MAIN DATA SOURCES

Estimated adult HIV prevalence rate – Joint United Nations Programme on HIV/AIDS (UNAIDS), *Report on the Global AIDS Epidemic*, 2006.

Estimated number of people (all ages) living with HIV – UNAIDS, *Report on the Global AIDS Epidemic*, 2006.

Estimated number of women (aged 15+) living with HIV – UNAIDS, *Report on the Global AIDS Epidemic*, 2006.

HIV prevalence rate in young pregnant women (aged 15-24) in capital city – UNAIDS, *Report on the Global AIDS Epidemic*, 2006.

Estimated number of children (aged 0-14) living with HIV – UNAIDS, *Report on the Global AIDS Epidemic*, 2006.

HIV prevalence among young men and women – UNAIDS, *Report on the Global AIDS Epidemic*, 2006, AIDS Indicator Surveys (AIS), Demographic and Health Surveys (DHS), 2001-2006.

Comprehensive knowledge of HIV – AIS, Behavioural Surveillance Surveys (BSS), DHS, Multiple Indicator Cluster Surveys (MICS) and Reproductive Health Surveys (RHS), 2000-2006; 'HIV/AIDS Survey Indicators Database', <www.measuredhs.com/hivdata>.

Condom use at last high-risk sex – AIS, BSS, DHS and RHS, 2000-2006; 'HIV/AIDS Survey Indicators Database', <www.measuredhs.com/hivdata>.

Children orphaned by AIDS – UNAIDS, UNICEF and United States Agency for International Development (USAID), *Africa's Orphaned and Vulnerable Generations*, 2006.

Children orphaned due to all causes – UNAIDS, UNICEF and USAID, *Africa's Orphaned and Vulnerable Generations*, 2006.

Orphan school attendance ratio – AIS, DHS and MICS, 2000-2006; 'HIV/AIDS Survey Indicators Database', <www.measuredhs.com/hivdata>.

NOTES

- Data not available.
* Data refer to the most recent year available during the period specified in the column heading.
p Proportion of orphans (aged 10-14) attending school is based on small denominators (typically 25-49 unweighted cases).
The revised adult HIV prevalence data for India were not available at the time of publication; India's most recent data on the 'Estimated number of people (all ages) living with HIV' are excluded from the regional summaries.
r Refers to year of female data more recent than male.
h Data are from DHS and AIS conducted between 2001 and 2006.

TABLE 5. EDUCATION

Countries and territories	Youth (15-24 years) literacy rate 2000-2006* male	female	Number per 100 population 2005 phones	Internet users	Primary school enrolment ratio 2000-2006* gross male	female	net male	female	Primary school attendance ratio (2000-2006*) net male	female	% of primary school entrants reaching grade 5 2000-2006* admin. data	survey data	Secondary school enrolment ratio 2000-2006* gross male	female	net male	female	Secondary school attendance ratio (2000-2006*) net male	female
Afghanistan	51	18	4	1	108	64	-	-	66	40	-	92	24	8	-	-	18	6
Albania	99	100	60	6	106	105	94	94	92	92	90y	9	79	77	75	73	79	77
Algeria	94	86	49	6	116	107	98	95	97	96	96	95	80	86	65	68	57	65
Andorra	-	-	149	33	89	85	82	79	-	-	-	-	84	93	73	80	-	-
Angola	84	63	11	1	69x	59x	-	-	58	59	-	75	19	15	-	-	22	20
Antigua and Barbuda	-	-	150	36	-	-	-	-	-	-	-	-	-	-	-	-	-	-
Argentina	99	99	82	18	113	112	99	98	-	-	97	-	83	89	76	82	-	-
Armenia	100	100	30	5	92	96	77	81	99	98	-	100	87	89	83	86	93	95
Australia	-	-	142	70	104	104	96	97	-	-	-	-	152	145	86	87	-	-
Austria	-	-	152	49	106	106	96	98	-	-	99y	-	105	100	-	-	-	-
Azerbaijan	100x	100x	40	8	97	96	85	84	91	91	98y	99	84	81	79	76	87	84
Bahamas	-	-	112	32	101	101	90	92	-	-	99	-	90	91	83	85	-	-
Bahrain	97	97	130	21	105	104	97	97	86	87	99	99	96	102	87	93	77	85
Bangladesh	67	60	7	0	107	111	93	96	79	84	65	94	47	48	44	45	36	41
Barbados	-	-	127	59	108	108	98	98	-	-	98	-	113	113	96	97	-	-
Belarus	100x	100x	76	35	103	100	91	88	93	94	99y	100	95	96	88	89	95	97
Belgium	-	-	135	46	104	104	99	99	-	-	-	-	112	108	97	98	-	-
Belize	76x	77x	57	14	130	125	93	96	-	-	91	-	84	85	71	72	-	-
Benin	59	33	11	6	107	85	86	70	60	47	52	92	41	23	23	11	19	12
Bhutan	-	-	9	3	-	-	80	79	74	67	93	-	-	-	-	-	-	-
Bolivia	99	96	33	5	113	113	94	96	78	77	85	50	90	87	73	72	57	56
Bosnia and Herzegovina	100	100	66	21	-	-	-	-	92	89	-	100	-	-	-	-	89	89
Botswana	92	96	54	3	107	105	85	84	83	86	91	96y	72	75	57	62	36	44
Brazil	96	98	68	21	146	135	95	95	95	95	81y	84x,y	101	111	75	81	42x	50x
Brunei Darussalam	99	99	85	36	108	107	93	94	-	-	100	-	94	98	85	90	-	-
Bulgaria	98	98	113	21	103	102	94	93	-	-	92y	-	106	101	89	87	-	-
Burkina Faso	40	27	5	0	64	51	50	40	49	44	76	91	16	12	13	9	17	15
Burundi	77	70	2	1	91	78	63	58	72	70	67	87	16	12	-	-	8	6
Cambodia	88	79	8	0	139	129	93	90	73	76	56	95	35	24	27	22	24	21
Cameroon	-	-	14	2	126	107	-	-	86	81	64	91	49	39	-	-	45	42
Canada	-	-	117	68	100	99	99	100	-	-	93	-	119	116	-	-	-	-
Cape Verde	96	97	32	6	111	105	91	89	97	96	78	-	65	70	55	60	-	-
Central African Republic	70	47	3	0	67	44	44	37	64	54	-	73	-	-	13	9	16	10
Chad	56	23	2	0	92	62	72	50	41	31	33	64y	23	8	16	5	13	7
Chile	99	99	90	29	106	101	91	89	-	-	100	-	90	91	-	-	-	-
China	99	99	57	8	114	112	99	99	-	-	-	-	74	75	-	-	-	-
Colombia	98	98	65	10	113	111	87	87	90	92	81	89	74	82	53	58	64	72
Comoros	-	-	4	3	91	80	80	65	31	31	80	25	40	30	-	-	10	11
Congo	98	97	13	1	91	84	40	48	86	87	66	95	42	35	-	-	39	42
Congo, Democratic Republic of the	78	63	5	0	69	54	-	-	55	49	-	54	28	16	-	-	18	15
Cook Islands	-	-	-	-	83	81	78	77	-	-	-	-	72	73	62	68	-	-
Costa Rica	97	98	58	21	110	109	91	93	87	89	87	-	77	82	58	64	59	65
Côte d'Ivoire	71	52	14	1	80	63	62	50	66	57	88	92	32	18	26	15	32	22
Croatia	100	100	122	32	95	94	88	87	-	-	100y	-	88	89	84	86	-	-
Cuba	100	100	9	2	104	99	96	96	-	-	97	99y	94	94	87	88	-	-
Cyprus	100	100	136	39	101	101	99	99	-	-	99	-	96	98	93	95	-	-
Czech Republic	-	-	147	27	102	100	91	93	-	-	98	-	95	97	-	-	-	-
Denmark	-	-	162	53	98	99	95	96	-	-	93	-	122	126	91	93	-	-
Djibouti	-	-	8	1	44	36	37	30	80	78	77x	96	29	19	27	18	50	42
Dominica	-	-	88	-	93	92	83	85	-	-	93	-	109	106	92	92	-	-
Dominican Republic	93	95	51	17	116	110	87	88	84	88	86	91	64	78	47	59	27	39
Ecuador	96	97	60	7	117	117	97	98	-	-	76	-	61	61	52	53	-	-
Egypt	90	79	34	7	104	97	96	91	96	94	95	99	89	82	85	79	72	67
El Salvador	87	90	49	9	115	111	93	93	-	-	69	-	62	64	52	54	-	-
Equatorial Guinea	95	95	21	1	117	111	85	77	61	60	33	72y	38	22	-	-	23	22
Eritrea	-	-	2	2	71	57	51	43	69	64	79	82y	40	23	30	20	23	21
Estonia	100	100	142	52	102	99	95	95	-	-	99	-	100	101	90	93	-	-
Ethiopia	62	39	1	0	107	94	71	66	45	45	68y	78	41	28	38	26	30	23
Fiji	-	-	37	8	107	105	97	96	-	-	99	-	85	91	80	85	-	-
Finland	-	-	141	53	100	99	98	98	-	-	100	-	108	113	95	95	-	-
France	-	-	135	43	112	110	99	99	-	-	98x	-	116	116	98	100	-	-

| | Youth (15-24 years) literacy rate 2000-2006* | | Number per 100 population 2005 | | Primary school enrolment ratio 2000-2006* | | | | Primary school attendance ratio (2000-2006*) net | | % of primary school entrants reaching grade 5 2000-2006* | | Secondary school enrolment ratio 2000-2006* | | | | Secondary school attendance ratio (2000-2006*) net | |
| | | | | | gross | | net | | | | | | gross | | net | | | |
	male	female	phones	Internet users	male	female	male	female	male	female	admin. data	survey data	male	female	male	female	male	female
Gabon	97	95	50	5	130	129	77	77	94	94	69	91y	49	42	-	-	34	36
Gambia	-	-	19	4	79	84	78	77	60	62	-	97	51	42	49	41	39	34
Georgia	-	-	39	6	93	94	93	93	99y	100y	98y	-	82	83	81	81	-	-
Germany	-	-	162	43	101	101	96	96	-	-	99y	-	101	99	-	-	-	-
Ghana	76	66	14	2	94	93	69	70	75	75	63	90	50	43	40	36	45	45
Greece	99	99	149	18	101	101	99	99	-	-	99	-	103	101	90	92	-	-
Grenada	-	-	72	19	94	91	84	83	-	-	79	-	99	102	78	80	-	-
Guatemala	86	78	46	8	118	109	96	92	80	76	68	73x,y	54	49	35	32	23x	24x
Guinea	59	34	3	1	88	74	70	61	55	48	76	97	39	21	31	17	27	17
Guinea-Bissau	-	-	8	2	84	56	53	38	54	53	-	80	23	13	11	6	8	7
Guyana	-	-	52	21	133	131	-	-	96	96	64	97	101	103	-	-	66	73
Haiti	-	-	8	7	-	-	-	-	48	51	-	89	-	-	-	-	18	21
Holy See	-	-	-	-	-	-	-	-	-	-	-	-	-	-	-	-	-	-
Honduras	87	91	25	4	113	113	90	92	77	80	70	83	59	73	-	-	29	36
Hungary	-	-	126	30	99	97	90	88	-	-	98y	-	97	96	90	90	-	-
Iceland	-	-	169	62	101	98	100	97	-	-	100	-	107	109	87	89	-	-
India	84	68	13	5	123	116	92	86	84	85	73	95y	63	50	-	-	64	58
Indonesia	99	99	27	7	119	115	97	94	94	95	90	96y	64	63	59	58	54	56
Iran (Islamic Republic of)	98	97	38	11	100	122	91	100	94	91	88	-	83	78	79	75	-	-
Iraq	89x	81x	6	0	108	89	94	81	91	80	81	95	54	36	44	31	46	34
Ireland	-	-	152	34	108	106	96	96	-	-	100	-	108	118	85	91	-	-
Israel	-	-	155	24	109	110	97	98	-	-	100	-	93	92	89	89	-	-
Italy	100	100	167	48	103	102	99	98	-	-	100	-	100	99	92	93	-	-
Jamaica	-	-	118	46	95	94	90	90	97	98	90	99	86	89	77	80	88	92
Japan	-	-	121	67	100	100	100	100	-	-	-	-	102	102	99	100	-	-
Jordan	99	99	66	13	96	96	88	90	99	99	96	99y	87	88	77	80	85	89
Kazakhstan	100x	100x	55	4	110	108	92	90	99	98	100y	100	100	97	92	91	97	97
Kenya	80	81	14	3	114	110	78	79	79	79	83	98	50	48	42	42	12	13
Kiribati	-	-	-	2	111	113	96	98	-	-	82	-	82	93	65	71	-	-
Korea, Democratic People's Republic of	-	-	-	-	-	-	-	-	-	-	-	-	-	-	-	-	-	-
Korea, Republic of	-	-	135	68	105	104	100	99	-	-	99	-	96	96	94	94	-	-
Kuwait	100	100	108	26	99	97	87	86	-	-	99y	-	92	98	76	80	-	-
Kyrgyzstan	100x	100x	19	5	98	97	87	86	91	93	97y	99	86	87	80	81	90	92
Lao People's Democratic Republic	83	75	12	0	123	108	86	81	81	77	63	92	53	40	41	35	40	33
Latvia	100	100	113	45	94	90	86	89	-	-	98y	-	98	99	-	-	-	-
Lebanon	-	-	46	20	108	105	93	92	97	97	93	96	85	93	-	-	61	68
Lesotho	-	-	17	3	132	132	84	89	82	88	73	91	34	43	19	30	16	27
Liberia	65	70	-	-	115	83	74	58	-	-	-	-	37	27	22	12	-	-
Libyan Arab Jamahiriya	100	97	20	4	106	105	-	-	-	-	-	-	96	115	-	-	-	-
Liechtenstein	-	-	137	63	106	107	87	89	-	-	98y	-	120	104	62	69	-	-
Lithuania	100	100	150	26	95	95	89	89	-	-	92	-	97	96	91	91	-	-
Luxembourg	-	-	207	68	100	100	95	95	-	-	92	-	91	97	79	85	-	-
Madagascar	59	57	3	1	141	136	93	92	74	77	43	93	14x	14x	11x	11x	17	21
Malawi	82x	71x	4	0	121	124	92	97	86	88	42	87	31	25	25	22	27	26
Malaysia	97	97	92	42	96	96	96	95	-	-	98	-	72	81	71	81	-	-
Maldives	98	98	-	-	95	93	79	79	-	-	92	-	68	78	60	66	-	-
Mali	32x	17x	8	1	74	59	56	45	45	33	87	93	29	18	-	-	15	11
Malta	94x	98x	131	32	101	95	88	84	-	-	99	-	98	101	84	83	-	-
Marshall Islands	-	-	9	-	105	101	90	89	-	-	-	-	75	78	72	77	-	-
Mauritania	68	56	26	1	93	94	72	72	46	42	57	69y	22	19	17	14	15	9
Mauritius	94	95	81	24	102	102	94	96	-	-	97	-	89	88	81	82	-	-
Mexico	98	98	62	17	110	108	98	98	97	97	94	-	78	83	64	66	-	-
Micronesia (Federated States of)	-	-	24	13	116	113	-	-	-	-	-	-	83	88	-	-	-	-
Moldova, Republic of	100	100	48	13	93	92	86	86	84	85	91y	100	80	83	75	77	82	85
Monaco	-	-	145	51	-	-	-	-	-	-	-	-	-	-	-	-	-	-
Mongolia	97	98	27	10	92	94	83	85	96	98	91y	96	86	98	79	90	85	91
Montenegro	-	-	-	-	98	98	-	-	98	97	-	97	88	89	-	-	90	92
Morocco	81	61	45	15	111	99	89	83	91	87	79	86y	54	46	38	32	39	36
Mozambique	60x	37x	8	1	111	94	81	74	63	57	62	84	16	11	8	6	8	7

TABLE 5. EDUCATION

	Youth (15-24 years) literacy rate 2000-2006*		Number per 100 population 2005		Primary school enrolment ratio 2000-2006*				Primary school attendance ratio (2000-2006*) net		% of primary school entrants reaching grade 5 2000-2006*		Secondary school enrolment ratio 2000-2006*				Secondary school attendance ratio (2000-2006*) net	
					gross		net						gross		net			
	male	female	phones	Internet users	male	female	male	female	male	female	admin. data	survey data	male	female	male	female	male	female
Myanmar	96	93	1	0	99	101	89	91	83	84	70	100	41	40	38	37	51	48
Namibia	91	94	31	4	99	100	69	74	78	78	86	95	52	60	33	44	29	40
Nauru	-	-	-	-	84	83	-	-	-	-	31	-	46	50	-	-	-	-
Nepal	81	60	3	1	129	123	90	83	86	82	79	95	46	40	-	-	46	38
Netherlands	-	-	144	74	108	106	99	98	-	-	99	-	120	117	86	88	-	-
New Zealand	-	-	131	68	102	102	99	99	-	-	-	-	119	127	90	93	-	-
Nicaragua	84	89	23	2	113	110	88	86	77	84	54	63	62	71	40	46	35	47
Niger	52	23	2	0	54	39	46	33	36	25	65	89	10	7	9	6	6	6
Nigeria	87	81	15	4	111	95	72	64	66	58	73	97	37	31	29	25	38	33
Niue	-	-	-	-	78	97	-	-	-	-	-	-	104	94	91x	96x	-	-
Norway	-	-	149	58	98	98	98	98	-	-	100	-	114	114	97	97	-	-
Occupied Palestinian Territory	99	99	39	7	89	88	80	80	91	92	98y	99	96	103	92	98	-	-
Oman	98	97	62	11	81	82	73	74	-	-	100	-	90	86	77	77	-	-
Pakistan	77	53	12	7	99	75	77	59	62	51	70	90	31	23	24	18	23	18
Palau	-	-	-	-	108	101	98	95	-	-	-	-	97	105	-	-	-	-
Panama	97	96	67	6	113	109	99	98	-	-	85	-	68	73	61	67	-	-
Papua New Guinea	69	64	2	2	80	70	-	-	-	-	68	-	29	23	-	-	-	-
Paraguay	96	96	36	3	106	103	87	88	95	96	81	90x,y	63	64	-	-	81	80
Peru	98	96	28	16	113	112	96	97	94	94	90	95	91	92	70	69	70	70
Philippines	94	97	45	5	113	112	93	95	88	89	75	93	81	90	55	66	55	70
Poland	-	-	106	26	98	98	96	97	-	-	99	-	100	99	92	94	-	-
Portugal	100	100	149	27	117	112	98	98	-	-	-	-	94	104	79	87	-	-
Qatar	95	98	119	28	107	106	96	96	-	-	-	-	101	99	91	89	-	-
Romania	98	98	82	22	108	106	93	92	-	-	95y	-	85	86	79	82	-	-
Russian Federation	100	100	112	15	129	129	92	93	-	-	-	-	93	91	-	-	-	-
Rwanda	79	77	3	1	119	121	72	75	84	87	46	84	15	13	11	10	5	5
Saint Kitts and Nevis	-	-	83	-	97	102	91	96	-	-	87	-	95	93	87	85	-	-
Saint Lucia	-	-	-	34	111	107	98	96	-	-	96	-	71	85	61	76	-	-
Saint Vincent and the Grenadines	-	-	78	8	117	105	92	88	-	-	88	-	67	83	57	71	-	-
Samoa	99	99	24	3	100	100	90	91	-	-	94	-	76	85	62	70	-	-
San Marino	-	-	-	-	-	-	-	-	-	-	-	-	-	-	-	-	-	-
Sao Tome and Principe	96	95	12	15	135	132	97	96	94	95	76	87	43	46	30	34	39	41
Saudi Arabia	97	95	73	12	91	91	77	79	-	-	96	-	89	86	63	68	-	-
Senegal	59	41	17	5	80	77	70	67	58	59	73	95	24	18	19	15	20	16
Serbia	-	-	-	-	98	98	-	-	98	98	-	100	88	89	-	-	90	93
Seychelles	99	99	97	26	115	116	99	100	-	-	99	-	106	105	94	100	-	-
Sierra Leone	60	37	-	0	171	139	-	-	69	69	-	92	35	26	-	-	22	17
Singapore	99x	99x	143	40	-	-	-	-	-	-	-	-	-	-	-	-	-	-
Slovakia	-	-	106	35	99	98	91	92	-	-	97y	-	94	95	-	-	-	-
Slovenia	100	100	131	55	102	101	99	98	-	-	99y	-	100	100	94	95	-	-
Solomon Islands	-	-	3	1	99	94	65	62	-	-	-	-	32	27	28	24	-	-
Somalia	-	-	7	1	-	-	-	-	24	20	56y	92	-	-	-	-	8	4
South Africa	94x	94x	82	11	106	102	87	87	80	83	82	98x,y	90	97	58	65	41x	48x
Spain	100x	100x	142	40	108	105	100	99	-	-	100	-	121	127	97	100	-	-
Sri Lanka	95	96	22	2	102	101	99	98	-	-	100	-	82	83	-	-	-	-
Sudan	85	71	7	8	65	56	47	39	60	57	79	71	35	33	-	-	19	20
Suriname	96	94	70	7	120	120	93	96	94	93	-	93	75	100	63	87	55	66
Swaziland	87	90	23	4	111	104	80	81	73	72	77	89	46	44	31	35	24	33
Sweden	-	-	171	76	97	97	96	96	-	-	-	-	103	103	99	100	-	-
Switzerland	-	-	161	51	102	101	93	93	-	-	-	-	98	91	87	81	-	-
Syrian Arab Republic	95	90	31	6	127	121	97	92	97	96	92	99	70	65	64	60	64	65
Tajikistan	100	100	8	0	103	99	99	96	89	88	98y	99	89	74	86	73	89	74
Tanzania, United Republic of	81	76	9	1	112	109	99	97	71	75	85	96	7x	5x	-	-	8	8
Thailand	98	98	59	11	98	94	90	86	98	98	-	99	69	72	62	66	77	84
The former Yugoslav Republic of Macedonia	99	99	88	8	98	98	92	92	97	93	98y	100	85	83	83	81	79	78
Timor-Leste	-	-	-	-	157	145	-	-	76y	74y	-	-	52	52	-	-	-	-
Togo	84	64	10	6	109	92	84	72	82	76	75	92	54	27	30	14	45	32
Tonga	99x	99x	44	3	118	112	97	93	-	-	89	-	94	102	61	75	-	-
Trinidad and Tobago	100	100	86	12	102	99	90	90	98	98	91	99	79	82	68	70	84	90
Tunisia	96	92	69	9	111	108	97	97	95	93	97	92y	80	88	62	68	-	-
Turkey	98	93	86	15	96	91	92	87	91	87	97	97x,y	83	68	72	61	53	47

| | Youth (15-24 years) literacy rate 2000-2006* | | Number per 100 population 2005 | | Primary school enrolment ratio 2000-2006* | | | | Primary school attendance ratio (2000-2006*) net | | % of primary school entrants reaching grade 5 2000-2006* | | Secondary school enrolment ratio 2000-2006* | | | | Secondary school attendance ratio (2000-2006*) net | |
| | | | | | gross | | net | | | | | | gross | | net | | | |
	male	female	phones	Internet users	male	female	male	female	male	female	admin. data	survey data	male	female	male	female	male	female
Turkmenistan	100x	100x	10	1	-	-	-	-	99	99	-	100	-	-	-	-	84	84
Tuvalu	-	-	-	-	95	102	-	-	-	-	70	100	87	81	-	-	-	-
Uganda	83	71	5	2	119	119	-	-	82	81	48	89	21	17	16	14	16	16
Ukraine	100	100	90	10	107	107	83	83	96	98	-	100	92	85	82	77	90	93
United Arab Emirates	98	96	128	29	85	82	71	70	-	-	97	-	62	66	56	59	-	-
United Kingdom	-	-	167	54	107	107	99	99	-	-	-	-	104	107	94	97	-	-
United States	-	-	130	66	100	99	92	93	-	-	-	-	94	96	88	90	-	-
Uruguay	98x	99x	66	21	110	108	92	93	-	-	91	-	98	113	-	-	-	-
Uzbekistan	-	-	9	3	100	99	-	-	100	100	96y	100	96	93	-	-	91	90
Vanuatu	-	-	9	3	120	116	95	93	-	-	78	-	44	38	42	36	-	-
Venezuela (Bolivarian Republic of)	96	98	60	13	106	104	91	92	91	93	91	96	70	79	59	68	30	43
Viet Nam	94x	94x	30	13	98	91	97	92	94	94	87	98	77	75	71	68	77	78
Yemen	91	59	14	1	102	75	87	63	68	41	73	88x,y	62	31	46	21	35x	13x
Zambia	73x	66x	9	3	114	108	89	89	55	58	94	88	31	25	29	23	17	19
Zimbabwe	98	98	8	8	97	95	81	82	85	87	70	88	38	35	35	33	45	45

SUMMARY INDICATORS

	male	female	phones	Internet users	male	female	male	female	male	female	admin. data	survey data	male	female	male	female	male	female
Sub-Saharan Africa	76	64	14	3	102	91	75	70	64	60	70	86	37	30	30	25	25	22
Eastern and Southern Africa	75	64	17	3	110	104	83	81	66	67	69	87	41	35	35	30	20	19
West and Central Africa	76	64	11	2	95	79	68	59	62	55	71	86	34	25	26	20	30	25
Middle East and North Africa	92	83	37	9	100	94	86	81	89	86	88	91	74	68	67	62	54	52
South Asia	81	65	12	5	118	109	90	83	81	79	72	94	56	46	-	-	55	50
East Asia and Pacific	99	98	52	10	112	110	98	97	91	92	84**	96**	72	72	61**	62**	60**	63**
Latin America and Caribbean	96	97	61	16	120	115	95	94	90	91	85	-	85	82	67	71	-	-
CEE/CIS	99	98	84	14	105	102	91	89	93	91	97	-	90	86	80	75	80	78
Industrialized countries§	-	-	138	55	102	101	95	96	-	-	-	-	102	103	92	93	-	-
Developing countries§	90	84	35	8	111	105	90	86	80	78	77**	92**	63	59	52**	50**	50**	46**
Least developed countries§	74	59	6	1	100	91	80	75	65	63	67	85	36	29	33	28	26	24
World	91	85	53	15	110	104	91	87	80	78	78**	92**	68	64	59**	58**	50**	47**

§ Also includes territories within each country category or regional group. Countries and territories in each country category or regional group are listed on page 148.

DEFINITIONS OF THE INDICATORS

Youth literacy rate – Number of literate persons aged 15-24, expressed as a percentage of the total population in that age group.

Primary school gross enrolment ratio – Number of children enrolled in primary school, regardless of age, expressed as a percentage of the total number of children of official primary school age.

Secondary school gross enrolment ratio – Number of children enrolled in secondary school, regardless of age, expressed as a percentage of the total number of children of official secondary school age.

Primary school net enrolment ratio – Number of children enrolled in primary school who are of official primary school age, expressed as a percentage of the total number of children of official primary school age.

Secondary school net enrolment ratio – Number of children enrolled in secondary school who are of official secondary school age, expressed as a percentage of the total number of children of official secondary school age.

Primary school net attendance ratio – Number of children attending primary or secondary school who are of official primary school age, expressed as a percentage of the total number of children of official primary school age.

Secondary school net attendance ratio – Number of children attending secondary or tertiary school who are of official secondary school age, expressed as a percentage of the total number of children of official secondary school age.

Primary school entrants reaching grade five – Percentage of children entering the first grade of primary school who eventually reach grade five.

MAIN DATA SOURCES

Youth literacy – UNESCO Institute for Statistics (UIS).

Phone and Internet use – International Telecommunications Union, Geneva.

Primary and secondary school enrolment – UIS.

Primary and secondary school attendance – Demographic and Health Surveys (DHS) and Multiple Indicator Cluster Surveys (MICS).

Reaching grade five – Administrative data: UIS. Survey data: DHS and MICS.

NOTES

-    Data not available.

x   Data refer to years or periods other than those specified in the column heading, differ from the standard definition or refer to only part of a country. Such data are not included in the calculation of regional and global averages.

y   Data refer to years or periods other than those specified in the column heading, differ from the standard definition or refer to only part of a country. Such data are included in the calculation of regional and global averages.

*   Data refer to the most recent year available during the period specified in the column heading.

**   Excludes China.

TABLE 6. DEMOGRAPHIC INDICATORS

Countries and territories	Population (thousands) 2006 under 18	Population (thousands) 2006 under 5	Population annual growth rate (%) 1970-1990	Population annual growth rate (%) 1990-2006	Crude death rate 1970	Crude death rate 1990	Crude death rate 2006	Crude birth rate 1970	Crude birth rate 1990	Crude birth rate 2006	Life expectancy 1970	Life expectancy 1990	Life expectancy 2006	Total fertility rate 2006	% of population urbanized 2006	Average annual growth rate of urban population (%) 1970-1990	Average annual growth rate of urban population (%) 1990-2006
Afghanistan	13982	4823	0.3	4.5	29	23	20	52	52	49	35	41	43	7.2	23	2.9	6.0
Albania	1003	250	2.2	-0.2	8	6	6	33	24	16	67	72	76	2.1	46	2.9	1.2
Algeria	11870	3213	3.0	1.7	16	7	5	49	32	21	53	67	72	2.4	64	4.4	3.0
Andorra	14	4	3.9	2.1	-	-	-	-	-	-	-	-	-	-	91	3.8	1.9
Angola	8797	3082	2.7	2.8	27	24	21	52	53	48	37	40	42	6.5	54	7.3	5.2
Antigua and Barbuda	28	8	-0.6	1.9	-	-	-	-	-	-	-	-	-	-	38	-0.3	2.4
Argentina	12277	3346	1.5	1.1	9	8	8	23	22	18	66	71	75	2.3	90	2.0	1.4
Armenia	789	164	1.7	-1.0	5	8	9	23	21	12	70	68	72	1.3	64	2.3	-1.4
Australia	4803	1267	1.4	1.2	9	7	7	20	15	12	71	77	81	1.8	88	1.4	1.4
Austria	1584	394	0.2	0.5	13	11	9	15	12	9	70	76	80	1.4	66	0.2	0.5
Azerbaijan	2604	547	1.7	1.0	7	7	7	29	27	15	65	66	67	1.7	52	2.0	0.7
Bahamas	106	28	2.0	1.6	7	6	6	31	24	17	66	70	73	2.0	91	3.1	2.1
Bahrain	226	65	4.0	2.5	9	4	3	40	29	18	62	72	75	2.4	97	4.3	3.1
Bangladesh	64194	18951	2.4	2.0	20	12	8	45	35	26	44	54	63	2.9	25	7.2	3.6
Barbados	67	17	0.6	0.5	9	8	7	22	16	11	69	75	77	1.5	53	1.0	1.6
Belarus	1936	455	0.6	-0.3	7	11	15	16	14	9	71	71	69	1.2	73	2.7	0.2
Belgium	2138	561	0.2	0.3	12	11	10	14	12	11	71	76	79	1.6	97	0.3	0.4
Belize	123	36	2.1	2.6	8	5	4	40	35	26	66	72	76	3.0	48	1.7	2.7
Benin	4437	1488	3.0	3.3	22	15	12	47	47	41	46	53	56	5.6	40	6.7	4.3
Bhutan	252	61	3.0	1.1	23	14	7	47	38	19	41	52	65	2.3	11	6.1	4.0
Bolivia	4131	1243	2.3	2.1	20	11	8	46	36	28	46	59	65	3.6	65	4.0	3.1
Bosnia and Herzegovina	842	195	0.9	-0.6	7	7	9	23	15	9	66	72	75	1.2	46	2.8	0.5
Botswana	784	216	3.3	1.9	13	7	15	45	35	25	55	64	49	3.0	58	11.8	4.0
Brazil	62408	18092	2.2	1.5	10	7	6	35	24	20	59	66	72	2.3	85	3.7	2.3
Brunei Darussalam	131	40	3.4	2.5	7	3	3	36	28	22	67	74	77	2.4	74	3.7	3.2
Bulgaria	1331	341	0.2	-0.9	9	12	15	16	12	9	71	71	73	1.3	70	1.4	-0.5
Burkina Faso	7573	2605	2.4	3.0	24	17	15	51	49	45	42	50	52	6.1	19	6.8	4.9
Burundi	4249	1461	2.4	2.3	20	19	16	44	48	46	44	46	49	6.8	10	7.3	5.4
Cambodia	6261	1690	1.7	2.4	20	12	9	42	44	26	44	55	59	3.3	20	2.0	5.4
Cameroon	8791	2851	2.9	2.5	19	13	15	45	42	36	46	55	50	4.5	56	6.4	4.4
Canada	6948	1716	1.2	1.0	7	7	7	17	14	10	73	77	80	1.5	80	1.3	1.3
Cape Verde	240	73	1.4	2.4	12	8	5	40	39	30	56	66	71	3.5	58	5.5	4.1
Central African Republic	2107	668	2.4	2.2	22	16	19	42	42	37	42	50	44	4.7	38	3.9	2.4
Chad	5528	1943	2.5	3.4	21	16	16	46	48	46	45	52	50	6.3	26	5.5	4.7
Chile	4897	1233	1.6	1.4	10	6	5	29	23	15	62	73	78	1.9	88	2.1	1.7
China	348276	84390	1.6	0.9	8	7	7	33	21	13	62	68	73	1.7	41	3.9	3.4
Colombia	16233	4438	2.2	1.7	9	6	6	38	27	19	61	68	73	2.3	73	3.2	2.0
Comoros	395	129	3.3	2.8	18	11	7	50	41	34	48	56	65	4.5	38	5.1	4.6
Congo	1788	587	3.0	2.6	14	11	12	44	39	36	54	57	54	4.6	61	4.7	3.3
Congo, Democratic Republic of the	32671	11843	3.1	2.9	20	18	18	48	49	50	45	47	46	6.7	33	2.6	3.9
Cook Islands	5	2	-0.9	-1.7	-	-	-	-	-	-	-	-	-	-	73	-0.5	-0.2
Costa Rica	1490	393	2.6	2.2	7	4	4	33	27	18	67	75	79	2.1	62	4.0	3.5
Côte d'Ivoire	9179	2849	4.4	2.5	18	13	16	51	45	36	49	54	48	4.6	45	6.1	3.3
Croatia	859	205	0.4	0.1	10	11	12	15	12	9	69	72	76	1.3	57	1.9	0.4
Cuba	2630	652	1.0	0.4	7	7	8	29	17	11	70	74	78	1.5	75	2.0	0.5
Cyprus	202	49	0.5	1.4	10	8	7	19	19	12	71	76	79	1.6	69	3.0	1.6
Czech Republic	1857	466	0.2	-0.1	12	12	11	16	12	9	70	72	76	1.2	73	2.1	-0.2
Denmark	1210	321	0.2	0.3	10	12	10	16	12	11	73	75	78	1.8	86	0.5	0.4
Djibouti	368	107	6.2	2.4	21	14	12	49	42	29	43	51	54	4.1	87	7.3	3.2
Dominica	23	6	0.3	-0.1	-	-	-	-	-	-	-	-	-	-	73	2.1	0.3
Dominican Republic	3760	1110	2.3	1.7	11	6	6	42	29	24	58	67	72	2.9	68	3.9	3.0
Ecuador	5064	1414	2.7	1.6	12	6	5	42	29	22	58	68	75	2.6	63	4.4	2.4
Egypt	29263	8634	2.2	1.9	17	9	6	41	32	25	50	62	71	3.0	43	2.4	1.8
El Salvador	2685	775	1.8	1.8	12	7	6	44	30	23	57	65	72	2.7	60	2.9	3.0
Equatorial Guinea	241	81	0.8	2.4	25	19	15	41	42	39	40	47	51	5.4	39	2.0	3.1
Eritrea	2330	808	2.7	2.5	21	16	10	47	41	40	43	48	57	5.2	20	3.8	3.9
Estonia	261	67	0.7	-1.0	11	13	14	15	14	11	71	69	71	1.5	69	1.1	-1.2
Ethiopia	41299	13439	2.7	2.9	21	18	13	49	47	39	43	47	52	5.4	16	4.6	4.4
Fiji	321	90	1.6	0.9	8	6	7	34	29	22	60	67	69	2.8	51	2.5	2.2

	Population (thousands) 2006		Population annual growth rate (%)		Crude death rate			Crude birth rate			Life expectancy			Total fertility rate 2006	% of population urbanized 2006	Average annual growth rate of urban population (%)	
	under 18	under 5	1970-1990	1990-2006	1970	1990	2006	1970	1990	2006	1970	1990	2006			1970-1990	1990-2006
Finland	1097	286	0.4	0.3	10	10	10	14	13	11	70	75	79	1.8	61	1.4	0.3
France	13555	3834	0.6	0.5	11	9	9	17	13	12	72	77	80	1.9	77	0.8	0.7
Gabon	554	158	2.8	2.2	20	11	12	34	36	26	47	61	56	3.1	84	6.6	3.5
Gambia	784	261	3.5	3.4	28	15	11	50	43	36	37	51	59	4.8	55	6.8	5.7
Georgia	1043	237	0.7	-1.3	9	9	12	19	16	11	67	71	71	1.4	52	1.5	-1.6
Germany	14517	3548	0.1	0.2	12	11	10	14	11	8	71	75	79	1.4	75	0.1	0.4
Ghana	10452	3195	2.7	2.4	16	11	10	45	40	30	49	57	59	4.0	49	3.9	4.2
Greece	1917	513	0.7	0.6	8	9	10	17	10	9	72	77	79	1.3	59	1.3	0.6
Grenada	43	10	0.1	0.6	9	10	8	28	28	18	64	66	68	2.3	31	0.1	0.3
Guatemala	6463	2066	2.5	2.4	15	9	6	44	39	34	52	62	70	4.3	48	3.2	3.3
Guinea	4576	1544	2.3	2.6	27	19	12	50	47	41	38	47	55	5.6	33	5.1	3.7
Guinea-Bissau	889	322	2.8	3.0	29	23	19	49	50	50	36	42	46	7.1	30	5.9	3.3
Guyana	268	73	0.1	0.1	11	9	9	38	25	18	60	62	66	2.4	28	0.2	-0.2
Haiti	4190	1244	2.1	1.8	18	13	10	39	37	28	47	54	60	3.7	39	4.1	3.6
Holy See	-	-	-	-	-	-	-	-	-	-	-	-	-	-	-	-	-
Honduras	3235	943	3.0	2.2	15	7	6	47	38	28	52	66	70	3.4	47	4.6	3.2
Hungary	1935	475	0.0	-0.2	11	14	13	15	12	9	69	69	73	1.3	67	0.5	-0.1
Iceland	78	21	1.1	1.0	7	7	6	21	17	14	74	78	82	2.0	93	1.4	1.1
India	445361	126843	2.2	1.8	16	10	8	38	32	24	49	59	64	2.9	29	3.5	2.6
Indonesia	76870	21720	2.1	1.4	17	9	6	41	26	19	48	61	70	2.2	49	5.0	4.4
Iran (Islamic Republic of)	24682	6270	3.4	1.3	14	7	5	43	35	20	54	64	71	2.0	67	4.9	2.5
Iraq	13691	4223	3.0	2.7	12	8	10	46	39	33	56	63	58	4.4	67	4.1	2.4
Ireland	1047	315	0.9	1.1	11	9	7	22	15	16	71	75	79	2.0	61	1.3	1.6
Israel	2231	679	2.2	2.6	7	6	5	27	22	20	71	76	80	2.8	92	2.6	2.7
Italy	9886	2729	0.3	0.2	10	10	10	17	10	9	72	77	80	1.4	68	0.4	0.3
Jamaica	1011	277	1.2	0.8	8	7	7	35	25	20	68	72	72	2.5	53	2.1	1.3
Japan	21393	5622	0.8	0.2	7	7	9	19	10	9	72	79	82	1.3	66	1.7	0.5
Jordan	2460	718	3.5	3.5	16	6	4	52	36	26	54	67	72	3.2	83	4.8	4.4
Kazakhstan	4595	1253	1.2	-0.5	9	9	10	26	23	19	62	67	66	2.2	58	1.7	-0.3
Kenya	18155	6161	3.7	2.8	15	10	12	51	42	39	52	60	53	5.0	21	6.5	3.7
Kiribati	35	10	2.5	1.7	-	-	-	-	-	-	-	-	-	-	50	4.0	4.0
Korea, Democratic People's Republic of	6744	1606	1.7	1.0	7	6	10	35	21	14	62	71	67	1.9	62	2.1	1.4
Korea, Republic of	10616	2369	1.5	0.7	9	6	6	31	16	9	60	71	78	1.2	81	4.5	1.3
Kuwait	769	236	5.3	1.6	6	2	2	48	24	18	66	75	77	2.2	98	6.0	1.6
Kyrgyzstan	1959	504	2.0	1.1	11	8	8	31	31	21	60	66	66	2.5	36	2.0	0.8
Lao People's Democratic Republic	2682	715	2.3	2.2	19	13	7	44	43	27	46	54	64	3.3	21	4.7	4.1
Latvia	427	102	0.6	-0.9	11	13	14	14	14	9	70	69	72	1.3	68	1.3	-1.1
Lebanon	1367	363	1.0	1.9	9	7	7	33	26	18	65	69	72	2.2	87	2.7	2.2
Lesotho	952	272	2.2	1.4	17	11	19	43	36	30	49	59	42	3.5	19	5.7	2.0
Liberia	1922	690	2.2	3.2	22	21	19	49	50	50	42	43	45	6.8	59	4.9	4.9
Libyan Arab Jamahiriya	2154	676	3.9	2.0	16	5	4	49	26	24	51	68	74	2.8	85	6.7	2.5
Liechtenstein	7	2	1.5	1.2	-	-	-	-	-	-	-	-	-	-	22	1.6	1.5
Lithuania	713	151	0.8	-0.5	9	11	12	17	15	9	71	71	73	1.3	66	2.4	-0.6
Luxembourg	101	27	0.6	1.2	12	11	9	13	13	12	70	75	79	1.7	83	1.0	1.3
Madagascar	9613	3142	2.8	2.9	21	15	10	47	44	37	44	51	59	4.9	27	5.3	3.8
Malawi	7286	2425	3.7	2.3	24	18	16	56	50	42	41	49	47	5.7	18	7.0	4.8
Malaysia	9623	2758	2.6	2.3	9	5	4	37	30	21	61	70	74	2.7	68	4.5	4.3
Maldives	123	30	2.9	2.1	17	9	6	40	40	23	50	60	68	2.6	30	6.8	3.0
Mali	6528	2247	2.3	2.8	26	20	15	52	52	48	39	47	54	6.6	31	4.7	4.6
Malta	85	20	0.9	0.7	9	8	8	17	15	10	70	76	79	1.4	96	0.9	1.1
Marshall Islands	22	6	4.2	1.3	-	-	-	-	-	-	-	-	-	-	67	4.3	1.5
Mauritania	1415	456	2.6	2.8	18	11	8	45	40	33	47	57	64	4.5	41	7.6	2.9
Mauritius	360	94	1.2	1.1	7	6	7	28	20	15	62	69	73	1.9	42	1.4	0.8
Mexico	37911	10445	2.4	1.4	10	5	5	44	28	20	61	70	76	2.3	76	3.4	1.7
Micronesia (Federated States of)	50	14	2.2	0.9	9	7	6	41	34	27	62	66	68	3.9	22	2.4	0.0
Moldova, Republic of	975	213	1.0	-0.8	10	10	12	18	19	11	65	68	69	1.4	47	2.9	-0.8
Monaco	6	2	1.2	0.5	-	-	-	-	-	-	-	-	-	-	100	1.2	0.5
Mongolia	918	233	2.8	1.0	14	9	7	42	33	19	53	61	66	1.9	57	4.0	1.0
Montenegro	145	38	0.6	0.1	3	5	9	10	11	13	69	75	74	1.8	-	-	-

TABLE 6. DEMOGRAPHIC INDICATORS

	Population (thousands) 2006		Population annual growth rate (%)		Crude death rate			Crude birth rate			Life expectancy			Total fertility rate 2006	% of population urbanized 2006	Average annual growth rate of urban population (%)	
	under 18	under 5	1970-1990	1990-2006	1970	1990	2006	1970	1990	2006	1970	1990	2006			1970-1990	1990-2006
Morocco	11135	2978	2.4	1.4	17	8	6	47	30	21	52	64	71	2.4	59	4.1	2.6
Mozambique	10674	3670	1.8	2.7	25	20	20	48	43	41	39	43	42	5.2	35	8.3	5.9
Myanmar	15772	4146	2.1	1.2	15	11	10	40	27	19	51	59	61	2.1	31	2.5	2.6
Namibia	942	248	3.0	2.3	15	9	13	43	42	26	53	62	52	3.3	36	4.1	3.9
Nauru	4	1	1.7	0.6	-	-	-	-	-	-	-	-	-	-	100	1.7	0.6
Nepal	12487	3626	2.3	2.3	21	13	8	42	39	29	43	54	63	3.4	16	6.3	6.1
Netherlands	3592	987	0.7	0.6	8	9	9	17	13	12	74	77	79	1.7	81	1.2	1.6
New Zealand	1066	284	1.0	1.2	9	8	7	22	17	14	71	75	80	2.0	86	1.2	1.3
Nicaragua	2446	671	2.7	1.8	13	7	5	47	37	25	54	64	72	2.8	59	3.3	2.5
Niger	7455	2713	3.1	3.5	26	22	14	58	56	50	40	46	56	7.3	17	5.9	4.1
Nigeria	73703	24503	2.8	2.7	22	18	17	47	47	41	42	47	47	5.5	49	5.3	4.8
Niue	1	0	-	-	-	-	-	-	-	-	-	-	-	-	37	-	-
Norway	1092	284	0.4	0.6	10	11	9	17	14	12	74	77	80	1.8	77	0.9	1.1
Occupied Palestinian Territory	2039	673	3.4	3.7	19	7	4	49	46	37	54	68	73	5.3	72	4.5	4.0
Oman	1014	269	4.5	2.0	17	4	3	50	38	22	49	70	75	3.1	71	9.3	2.6
Pakistan	70673	19012	3.2	2.2	16	11	7	43	42	27	51	60	65	3.6	35	4.2	3.1
Palau	8	2	1.4	1.9	-	-	-	-	-	-	-	-	-	-	68	2.2	1.8
Panama	1172	344	2.4	1.9	8	5	5	38	26	21	65	72	75	2.6	72	3.0	3.7
Papua New Guinea	2899	898	2.4	2.5	19	11	10	42	37	31	43	54	57	4.0	13	3.9	2.7
Paraguay	2522	731	2.7	2.2	7	6	6	37	33	25	65	68	71	3.2	59	4.0	3.4
Peru	10318	2815	2.5	1.5	14	7	6	42	30	21	53	65	71	2.5	73	3.4	1.8
Philippines	36430	11027	2.6	2.1	11	7	5	40	33	27	57	65	71	3.3	63	4.5	3.8
Poland	7684	1765	0.8	0.0	8	10	10	17	15	9	70	71	75	1.2	62	1.6	0.1
Portugal	1996	557	0.7	0.4	11	10	11	21	12	11	67	74	78	1.5	58	1.8	1.6
Qatar	204	64	7.2	3.5	13	3	2	34	23	17	60	69	75	2.7	96	7.4	3.7
Romania	4276	1058	0.7	-0.5	9	11	12	21	14	10	68	69	72	1.3	54	2.2	-0.5
Russian Federation	27839	7195	0.7	-0.2	9	12	16	14	14	11	69	68	65	1.3	73	1.5	-0.3
Rwanda	4844	1617	3.3	1.6	20	33	17	53	49	44	44	33	46	6.0	20	5.9	9.9
Saint Kitts and Nevis	17	5	-0.5	1.3	-	-	-	-	-	-	-	-	-	-	32	-0.4	0.7
Saint Lucia	55	15	1.4	1.1	8	7	7	41	25	19	64	71	73	2.2	28	2.4	0.7
Saint Vincent and the Grenadines	42	12	0.9	0.6	11	7	7	40	25	20	61	69	71	2.2	46	3.0	1.4
Samoa	88	25	0.6	0.9	10	7	5	39	34	26	55	65	71	4.1	23	0.8	1.3
San Marino	6	2	1.2	1.5	-	-	-	-	-	-	-	-	-	-	89	3.1	1.4
Sao Tome and Principe	75	23	2.3	1.8	13	10	8	47	38	33	55	62	65	4.0	59	4.2	3.7
Saudi Arabia	9671	2879	5.2	2.5	18	5	4	48	36	25	52	68	72	3.5	81	7.5	2.8
Senegal	5888	1913	2.9	2.7	21	12	9	48	43	36	45	57	63	4.9	42	4.2	3.1
Serbia	2222	605	0.8	0.2	9	10	11	18	15	13	68	71	74	1.8	-	-	-
Seychelles	44	15	1.6	1.1	-	-	-	-	-	-	-	-	-	-	50	4.8	1.2
Sierra Leone	2827	999	2.1	2.1	29	26	23	47	48	46	35	39	42	6.5	41	4.8	4.1
Singapore	1010	207	1.9	2.3	5	5	5	23	18	9	69	75	80	1.3	100	1.9	2.3
Slovakia	1114	259	0.7	0.2	10	10	10	19	15	10	70	72	74	1.2	56	2.3	0.1
Slovenia	349	89	0.7	0.2	10	10	10	17	11	9	69	73	78	1.3	51	2.3	0.3
Solomon Islands	226	70	3.3	2.7	10	12	7	46	40	31	54	57	63	4.0	17	5.5	4.2
Somalia	4261	1507	3.1	1.4	24	22	17	51	46	44	40	42	47	6.2	36	4.5	2.6
South Africa	18349	5254	2.4	1.7	14	8	16	38	29	23	53	62	50	2.7	60	2.9	2.6
Spain	7671	2268	0.7	0.8	9	8	9	20	10	11	72	77	81	1.4	77	1.4	0.9
Sri Lanka	5576	1483	1.6	0.7	8	7	7	31	21	15	65	70	72	1.9	15	1.0	-0.1
Sudan	17697	5483	2.9	2.3	20	14	10	47	41	32	44	53	58	4.4	42	5.3	5.1
Suriname	160	45	0.4	0.8	8	6	7	37	24	20	63	68	70	2.5	74	2.4	1.3
Swaziland	536	147	3.2	1.7	18	10	20	50	41	29	48	59	40	3.6	24	7.5	2.1
Sweden	1925	499	0.3	0.4	10	11	10	14	14	11	74	78	81	1.8	84	0.4	0.5
Switzerland	1500	362	0.5	0.5	9	9	8	16	12	9	73	78	81	1.4	76	1.6	1.2
Syrian Arab Republic	8342	2500	3.5	2.6	13	5	3	47	37	27	55	68	74	3.2	51	4.1	2.9
Tajikistan	3090	858	2.9	1.4	10	8	6	40	39	28	60	63	66	3.5	25	2.2	-0.2
Tanzania, United Republic of	20171	6953	3.1	2.7	18	15	13	48	44	40	47	51	52	5.3	25	7.5	4.4
Thailand	16522	4514	1.9	1.0	10	7	9	37	19	15	59	67	70	1.8	33	3.6	1.6
The former Yugoslav Republic of Macedonia	486	117	1.0	0.4	8	8	8	24	17	11	66	71	74	1.5	70	2.0	1.6
Timor-Leste	570	190	1.0	2.6	22	18	9	46	43	42	40	46	60	6.7	27	3.4	4.1
Togo	3192	1045	3.1	3.0	18	12	10	48	44	38	48	58	58	5.0	41	4.9	4.9

	Population (thousands) 2006		Population annual growth rate (%)		Crude death rate			Crude birth rate			Life expectancy			Total fertility rate 2006	% of population urbanized 2006	Average annual growth rate of urban population (%)	
	under 18	under 5	1970-1990	1990-2006	1970	1990	2006	1970	1990	2006	1970	1990	2006			1970-1990	1990-2006
Tonga	44	12	-0.2	0.3	6	6	6	37	30	25	65	70	73	3.8	24	0.4	0.7
Trinidad and Tobago	365	93	1.2	0.5	7	7	8	27	21	15	66	70	69	1.6	13	-0.5	2.9
Tunisia	3225	823	2.4	1.4	14	6	6	39	27	17	54	69	74	1.9	66	3.8	2.0
Turkey	24632	6630	2.3	1.6	12	8	6	39	26	19	56	65	72	2.2	68	4.5	2.4
Turkmenistan	1865	491	2.6	1.8	11	8	8	37	35	22	58	63	63	2.6	47	2.3	2.0
Tuvalu	4	1	1.3	0.7	-	-	-	-	-	-	-	-	-	-	57	4.6	2.7
Uganda	16828	5840	3.2	3.2	16	15	14	49	50	47	50	51	50	6.6	13	5.7	4.1
Ukraine	8676	2001	0.4	-0.6	9	13	16	15	13	9	71	70	68	1.2	68	1.4	-0.5
United Arab Emirates	976	315	10.6	5.1	11	3	1	36	27	16	61	73	78	2.3	77	10.5	5.0
United Kingdom	13155	3467	0.1	0.3	12	11	10	16	14	12	72	76	79	1.8	90	0.8	0.4
United States	75757	20776	1.0	1.0	9	9	8	16	16	14	71	75	78	2.1	81	1.1	1.5
Uruguay	943	254	0.5	0.4	10	10	9	21	18	15	69	72	76	2.1	92	0.9	0.7
Uzbekistan	10673	2861	2.7	1.7	10	7	7	36	35	23	63	67	67	2.6	37	3.1	1.2
Vanuatu	102	31	2.8	2.4	14	7	5	43	37	29	53	64	70	3.9	24	4.9	4.0
Venezuela (Bolivarian Republic of)	10052	2880	3.0	2.0	7	5	5	37	29	22	65	71	73	2.6	94	3.8	2.7
Viet Nam	30570	8101	2.2	1.7	18	8	5	41	31	19	49	65	74	2.2	27	2.7	3.4
Yemen	11482	3639	3.3	3.6	27	13	8	56	51	38	38	54	62	5.6	28	5.5	5.3
Zambia	6164	2012	3.2	2.3	17	16	20	49	44	40	49	49	41	5.3	35	4.5	1.6
Zimbabwe	6199	1703	3.5	1.5	13	8	19	48	37	28	55	63	42	3.3	36	6.1	2.9

SUMMARY INDICATORS

	under 18	under 5	1970-1990	1990-2006	1970	1990	2006	1970	1990	2006	1970	1990	2006	2006	2006	1970-1990	1990-2006
Sub-Saharan Africa	376047	125254	2.9	2.6	20	16	15	48	45	40	45	50	50	5.3	35	4.7	4.1
Eastern and Southern Africa	183232	60197	2.9	2.5	19	15	15	47	43	38	46	51	50	5.0	29	4.7	3.7
West and Central Africa	192816	65057	2.9	2.7	22	17	16	48	47	42	43	49	50	5.6	42	4.8	4.3
Middle East and North Africa	152632	44126	3.0	2.0	16	8	6	45	35	25	51	63	69	3.1	58	4.4	2.8
South Asia	612647	174830	2.3	1.9	17	11	8	39	33	25	49	59	64	3.0	29	3.8	2.8
East Asia and Pacific	566804	144870	1.8	1.1	10	7	7	35	22	15	59	67	72	1.9	43	3.9	3.4
Latin America and Caribbean	197134	55715	2.2	1.5	10	7	6	37	27	20	60	68	73	2.4	78	3.3	2.1
CEE/CIS	101837	26218	1.0	0.2	9	11	12	20	18	14	67	68	68	1.7	62	2.0	0.2
Industrialized countries§	204920	54768	0.7	0.6	10	9	9	17	13	11	71	76	79	1.7	76	1.0	0.9
Developing countries§	1958948	559069	2.2	1.6	13	9	8	38	29	23	55	63	66	2.8	43	3.8	2.9
Least developed countries§	376727	122114	2.5	2.5	21	16	13	47	42	36	44	51	55	4.7	27	4.9	4.1
World	2212024	625781	1.8	1.4	12	9	9	32	26	21	59	65	68	2.6	49	2.7	2.2

§ Also includes territories within each country category or regional group. Countries and territories in each country category or regional group are listed on page 148.

DEFINITIONS OF THE INDICATORS

Life expectancy at birth – Number of years newborn children would live if subject to the mortality risks prevailing for the cross section of population at the time of their birth.

Crude death rate – Annual number of deaths per 1,000 population.

Crude birth rate – Annual number of births per 1,000 population.

Total fertility rate – Number of children who would be born per woman if she lived to the end of her childbearing years and bore children at each age in accordance with prevailing age-specific fertility rates.

Urban population – Percentage of population living in urban areas as defined according to the national definition used in the most recent population census.

MAIN DATA SOURCES

Child population – United Nations Population Division.

Crude death and birth rates – United Nations Population Division.

Life expectancy – United Nations Population Division.

Fertility – United Nations Population Division.

Urban population – United Nations Population Division.

NOTES   Data not available.

TABLE 7. ECONOMIC INDICATORS

Countries and territories	GNI per capita (US$) 2006	GDP per capita average annual growth rate (%) 1970-1990	GDP per capita average annual growth rate (%) 1990-2006	Average annual rate of inflation (%) 1990-2006	% of population below US$1 a day 1995-2005*	% of central government expenditure (1995-2005*) allocated to: health	education	defence	ODA inflow in millions US$ 2005	ODA inflow as a % of recipient GNI 2005	Debt service as a % of exports of goods and services 1990	Debt service as a % of exports of goods and services 2005
Afghanistan	250x	1.6x	-	-	-	-	-	-	2775	40	-	-
Albania	2960	-0.7x	5.2	20	<2	4	2	4	319	4	4x	2x
Algeria	3030	2	1.3	13	<2	4	24	17	371	0	62	19x
Andorra	d	-	-	-	-	-	-	-	-	-	-	-
Angola	1980	0.4x	2.1	361	-	6x	15x	34x	442	2	7	9
Antigua and Barbuda	11210	6.5x	1.8	2	-	-	-	-	7	1	-	-
Argentina	5150	-1	1.3	6	7	5	5	3	100	0	30	12
Armenia	1930	-	5.2	78	<2	-	-	-	193	4	-	5x
Australia	35990	2	2.5	2	-	15	10	6	-	-	-	-
Austria	39590	2	1.9	1	-	14	10	2	-	-	-	-
Azerbaijan	1850	-	1.5	78	4	1	4	12	223	2	-	4x
Bahamas	14920x	2	0.4x	3x	-	16	20	3	-	-	-	-
Bahrain	14370x	-1.3x	2.3x	2x	-	8	15	14	0	0	-	-
Bangladesh	480	1	3	4	41	7	17	10	1321	2	17	5
Barbados	d	2	1.5x	3x	-	-	-	-	-2	0	14	5
Belarus	3380	-	2.8	180	<2	3	4	3	54	0	-	1x
Belgium	38600	2	1.8	2	-	16	3	3	-	-	-	-
Belize	3650	3	2.3	1	-	8	20	5	13	1	5	34
Benin	540	0	1.4	6	31	6x	31x	17x	349	8	7	6x
Bhutan	1410	4.7x	4.8	8	-	9	13	-	90	11	5x	5x
Bolivia	1100	-1	1.3	7	23	10	21	5	583	6	31	13
Bosnia and Herzegovina	2980	-	11.6x	5x	-	-	-	-	546	5	-	3x
Botswana	5900	8	4.8	8	28x	5	26	8	71	1	4	1
Brazil	4730	2	1.1	81	8	6	6	3	192	0	19	26
Brunei Darussalam	24100x	-2.1x	-0.8x	0x	-	-	-	-	-	-	-	-
Bulgaria	3990	3.4x	2	55	<2	12	5	6	-	-	19	28
Burkina Faso	460	1	1.5	5	27	7x	17x	14x	660	13	6	10x
Burundi	100	1	-2.6	12	55	2	15	23	365	50	41	41
Cambodia	480	-	5.8x	3x	34	-	-	-	538	9	-	0x
Cameroon	1080	3	0.7	4	17	3	12	10	414	3	18	11x
Canada	36170	2	2.2	2	-	9	2	6	-	-	-	-
Cape Verde	2130	-	3.3	4	-	-	-	-	161	16	5	6
Central African Republic	360	-1	-0.6	3	67x	-	-	-	95	7	8	12x
Chad	480	-1	2.4	7	-	8x	8x	-	380	10	2	7x
Chile	6980	2	3.7	6	<2	14	17	7	152	0	20	15
China	2010	7	8.8	5	10	0	2	12	1757	0	10	3
Colombia	2740	2	0.8	15	7	9	20	13	511	0	39	34
Comoros	660	0.1x	-0.4	4	-	-	-	-	25	6	2	3x
Congo	950x	3	-0.8	8	-	4	4	10	1449	38	32	2
Congo, Democratic Republic of the	130	-2	-4.7	385	-	0	0	18	1828	26	5x	0x
Cook Islands	-	-	-	-	-	-	-	-	8	0	-	-
Costa Rica	4980	1	2.4	13	3	21	22	0	30	0	21	5
Côte d'Ivoire	870	-2	-0.5	6	15	4x	21x	4x	119	1	26	4
Croatia	9330	-	2.8	37	<2	13	8	4	125	0	-	27x
Cuba	1170x	-	3.5x	4x	-	23x	10x	-	88	0	-	-
Cyprus	18430x	5.9x	2.3x	4x	-	6	12	4	-	-	-	-
Czech Republic	12680	-	2.1	8	<2	16	10	4	-	-	-	10x
Denmark	51700	2	1.9	2	-	1	12	5	-	-	-	-
Djibouti	1060	-	-2.4	3	-	-	-	-	79	10	-	4x
Dominica	3960	4.7x	1.4	2	-	-	-	-	15	5	4	13
Dominican Republic	2850	2	3.7	11	3	10	13	4	77	0	7	6
Ecuador	2840	1	1	5	18	11x	18x	13x	210	1	27	28
Egypt	1350	4	2.4	7	3	3	15	9	926	1	18	6
El Salvador	2540	-2	1.6	5	19	13	15	3	199	1	14	7
Equatorial Guinea	8250	-	21.6	13	-	-	-	-	39	1	2	0x
Eritrea	200	-	0x	12x	-	-	-	-	355	47	-	13x
Estonia	11410	1.5x	4.9	26	<2	16	7	5	-	-	-	15x
Ethiopia	180	-	1.9	4	23	1	5	17	1937	17	33	4
Fiji	3300	0.6x	1.4x	3x	-	9	18	6	64	2	12	6x
Finland	40650	3	2.6	2	-	3	10	4	-	-	-	-
France	36550	2	1.6	1	-	16x	7x	6x	-	-	-	-

	GNI per capita (US$) 2006	GDP per capita average annual growth rate (%)		Average annual rate of inflation (%) 1990-2006	% of population below US$1 a day 1995-2005*	% of central government expenditure (1995-2005*) allocated to:			ODA inflow in millions US$ 2005	ODA inflow as a % of recipient GNI 2005	Debt service as a % of exports of goods and services	
		1970-1990	1990-2006			health	education	defence			1990	2005
Gabon	5000	0	-1	6	-	-	-	-	54	1	4	11x
Gambia	310	1	0.3	8	59	7x	12x	4x	58	13	18	11
Georgia	1560	3	1	116	7	3	4	9	310	5	-	8x
Germany	36620	2.2x	1.4	1	-	19	1	4	-	-	-	-
Ghana	520	-2	2.1	25	45	7x	22x	5x	1120	11	21	6
Greece	21690	1	2.7	6	-	7	11	8	-	-	-	-
Grenada	4420	4.9x	2.3	2	-	10x	17x	-	45	9	2	6
Guatemala	2640	0	1.2	9	14	11x	17x	11x	254	1	11	5
Guinea	410	0.3x	1.3	8	-	3x	11x	29x	182	5	18	17x
Guinea-Bissau	190	0	-2.5	17	-	1x	3x	4x	79	28	21	11x
Guyana	1130	-2	3	8	<2x	-	-	-	137	18	-	5x
Haiti	480	0	-2	19	54	-	-	-	515	13	5	3
Holy See	-	-	-	-	-	-	-	-	-	-	-	-
Honduras	1200	1	0.6	14	15	10x	19x	7x	681	8	30	7
Hungary	10950	3	3.2	14	<2	6	5	3	-	-	30	30
Iceland	50580	3	2.3	4	-	26	10	-	-	-	-	-
India	820	2	4.4	6	34	2	2	13	1724	0	25	18x
Indonesia	1420	5	2.2	15	8	1	4	7	2524	1	31	20x
Iran (Islamic Republic of)	3000	-2	2.5	23	<2	6	7	14	104	0	1	4x
Iraq	2170x	-4.3x	-	-	-	-	-	-	21654	0	-	-
Ireland	45580	3	6	4	-	16	14	3	-	-	-	-
Israel	18580x	2	1.5x	7x	-	13	15	19	-	-	-	-
Italy	32020	3	1.3	3	-	3	10	3	-	-	-	-
Jamaica	3480	-1	0.7	16	<2	7	15	2	36	-	20	16
Japan	38410	3	0.9	-1	-	2x	6x	4x	-	-	18	5
Jordan	2660	2.5x	1.8	?	<2	10	16	19	622	5	18x	7x
Kazakhstan	3790	-	2.6	83	<2	4	4	5	229	1	-	38x
Kenya	580	1	0	11	23	7	26	6	768	4	26	4
Kiribati	1230	-5	1.9	2	-	-	-	-	28	22	-	22x
Korea, Democratic People's Republic of	a	-	-	-	-	-	-	-	81	0	-	-
Korea, Republic of	17690	6	4.5	4	<2	0	14	10	-	-	10x	10x
Kuwait	30630x	-6.8x	0.6x	4x	-	6	12	15	-	-	-	-
Kyrgyzstan	490	-	-0.9	51	<2	11	20	10	268	12	-	11x
Lao People's Democratic Republic	500	-	4.1	26	27	-	-	-	296	12	8	8x
Latvia	8100	3	4.2	23	<2	11	6	4	-	-	-	18x
Lebanon	5490	-	2.5	9	-	2	7	11	243	1	1x	63x
Lesotho	1030	3	2.3	8	36	6	25	5	69	4	4	5
Liberia	140	-4	2.2	44	36x	5x	11x	9x	236	54	-	0x
Libyan Arab Jamahiriya	7380	-4.8x	-	-	-	-	-	-	24	0	-	-
Liechtenstein	d	-	-	-	-	-	-	-	-	-	-	-
Lithuania	7870	-	2.5	32	<2	10	7	4	-	-	-	13x
Luxembourg	76040	3	3.3	2	-	13	10	1	-	-	-	-
Madagascar	280	-2	-0.5	15	61	8	13	5	929	17	32	14
Malawi	170	0	1.1	28	21	7x	12x	5x	575	28	23	6x
Malaysia	5490	4	3.2	3	<2	6	23	11	32	0	12	5
Maldives	2680	-	4.2x	1x	-	9	14	10	67	9	4	7
Mali	440	-1	2.2	5	36	2x	9x	8x	691	13	8	5x
Malta	13610x	7	2.7x	3x	-	14	13	2	0	0	0x	3x
Marshall Islands	3000	-	-2.2	5	-	-	-	-	57	31	-	-
Mauritania	740	-1	0.5	8	26	4x	23x	-	190	11	24	20x
Mauritius	5450	5.1x	3.7	6	-	9	16	1	32	0	6	6
Mexico	7870	2	1.5	14	3	5	25	3	189	0	16	17
Micronesia (Federated States of)	2380	-	-0.2	2	-	-	-	-	106	42	-	-
Moldova, Republic of	1100	1.8x	-2	57	<2	13	9	1	192	6	-	10x
Monaco	d	-	-	-	-	-	-	-	-	-	-	-
Mongolia	880	-	3.3x	11x	11	6	9	9	212	12	-	2x
Montenegro	3860	-	2.6x	-	-	-	-	-	-	-	-	-
Morocco	1900	2	1.6	2	<2	3	18	13	652	1	18	11
Mozambique	340	-1x	4.4	21	36	5x	10x	35x	1286	21	21	3
Myanmar	220x	2	6.6x	24x	-	5	15	22	145	0	17	3x
Namibia	3230	-2.3x	1.5	9	35x	10x	22x	7x	123	2	12	4

TABLE 7. ECONOMIC INDICATORS

	GNI per capita (US$) 2006	GDP per capita average annual growth rate (%)		Average annual rate of inflation (%) 1990-2006	% of population below US$1 a day 1995-2005*	% of central government expenditure (1995-2005*) allocated to:			ODA inflow in millions US$ 2005	ODA inflow as a % of recipient GNI 2005	Debt service as a % of exports of goods and services	
		1970-1990	1990-2006			health	education	defence			1990	2005
Nauru	-	-	-	-	-	-	-	-	9	0	-	-
Nepal	290	1	1.9	6	24	5	18	11	428	6	12x	5x
Netherlands	42670	2	1.8	2	-	10	11	4	-	-	-	-
New Zealand	27250	1	2.1	2	-	18	20	3	-	-	-	-
Nicaragua	1000	-4	1.9	22	45	13x	15x	6x	740	15	2	6
Niger	260	-2	-0.5	4	61	-	-	-	515	15	12	6x
Nigeria	640	-1	0.7	22	71	1x	3x	3x	6437	9	22	16
Niue	-	-	-	-	-	-	-	-	21	0	-	-
Norway	66530	3	2.6	3	-	16	6	5	-	-	-	-
Occupied Palestinian Territory	1230x	-	-2.8x	4x	-	-	-	-	1102	25	-	-
Oman	9070x	3	1.8x	1x	-	7	15	33	31	0	12	7
Pakistan	770	3	1.4	10	17	1	1	20	1666	2	16	9
Palau	7990	-	-	3x	-	-	-	-	23	15	-	-
Panama	4890	0	2.3	2	7	18	16	-	20	0	3	17
Papua New Guinea	770	-1	0.2	8	-	7	22	4	266	6	37	9
Paraguay	1400	3	-0.5	11	14	7x	22x	11x	51	1	12	11
Peru	2920	-1	2.3	14	11	13	7	-	398	1	6	25
Philippines	1420	1	1.7	7	15	2	19	5	562	1	23	16
Poland	8190	-	4.3	14	<2	11	12	4	-	-	4	28
Portugal	18100	3	1.9	4	<2x	16	16	3	-	-	-	-
Qatar	12000x	-	-	-	-	-	-	-	-	-	-	-
Romania	4850	0.9x	2	62	<2	14	7	5	-	-	0	17
Russian Federation	5780	-	0.6	78	<2	9	4	13	-	-	-	9x
Rwanda	250	1	0.3	9	60	5x	26x	-	576	28	10	7
Saint Kitts and Nevis	8840	6.3x	2.8	3	-	-	-	-	4	1	3	23
Saint Lucia	5110	5.3x	1.1	2	-	-	-	-	11	1	2	6
Saint Vincent and the Grenadines	3930	3	1.7	3	-	12	16	-	5	1	3	11
Samoa	2270	-0.1x	2.5	6	-	-	-	-	44	12	5	5
San Marino	d	-	-	-	-	18	9	-	-	-	-	-
Sao Tome and Principe	780	-	0.5x	34x	-	-	-	-	32	47	28	31x
Saudi Arabia	12510x	-2	0.1x	3x	-	6x	14x	36x	26	0	-	-
Senegal	750	0	1.2	4	17	3	14	7	689	8	14	9x
Serbia	3910	-	-	-	-	-	-	-	-	-	-	-
Seychelles	8650	3	1.4	2	-	10	9	4	19	3	7	6
Sierra Leone	240	0	-0.8	20	57x	10x	13x	10x	343	28	8	8
Singapore	29320	6	3.7	0	-	6	22	29	-	-	-	-
Slovakia	9870	-	2.9	8	<2	18	4	5	-	-	-	13x
Slovenia	18890	-	3.3	16	<2	15	13	3	0	0	10x	16x
Solomon Islands	680	3	-2.3	8	-	-	-	-	198	67	10	7x
Somalia	130x	-1	-	-	-	1x	2x	38x	236	0	25x	-
South Africa	5390	0	0.8	9	11	-	-	-	700	0	-	6x
Spain	27570	2	2.5	4	-	15	2	4	-	-	-	-
Sri Lanka	1300	3	3.8	9	6	6	10	18	1189	5	10	4
Sudan	810	0	3.7	37	-	1	8	28	1829	8	4	6
Suriname	3200	-2.2x	1.4	55	-	-	-	-	44	4	-	-
Swaziland	2430	2	0.4	11	48	8	20	8	46	2	6	2
Sweden	43580	2	2.2	2	-	3	6	5	-	-	-	-
Switzerland	57230	1	0.7	1	-	0	4	6	-	-	-	-
Syrian Arab Republic	1570	2	1.4	7	-	2	9	24	78	0	20	2
Tajikistan	390	-	-3.1	109	7	2	4	9	241	11	-	6x
Tanzania, United Republic of	350	-	1.6	15	58	6x	8x	16x	1505	12	25	2
Thailand	2990	5	2.8	3	<2	8	20	6	-171	0	14	14
The former Yugoslav Republic of Macedonia	3060	-	0.2	34	<2	-	-	-	230	4	-	9x
Timor-Leste	840	-	-	-	-	-	-	-	185	31	-	-
Togo	350	-1	-0.1	4	-	5x	20x	11x	87	4	8	0x
Tonga	2170	-	1.9	4	-	7x	13x	-	32	14	2	2x
Trinidad and Tobago	13340	1	4.7	5	12x	8	17	2	-2	0	18	4x
Tunisia	2970	3	3.3	4	<2	5	20	5	376	1	22	12
Turkey	5400	2	1.9	57	3	3	10	8	464	0	27	29
Turkmenistan	1340x	-	-6.8x	408x	12x	-	-	-	28	0	-	30x
Tuvalu	-	-	-	-	-	-	-	-	9	0	-	-

	GNI per capita (US$) 2006	GDP per capita average annual growth rate (%)		Average annual rate of inflation (%) 1990-2006	% of population below US$1 a day 1995-2005*	% of central government expenditure (1995-2005*) allocated to:			ODA inflow in millions US$ 2005	ODA inflow as a % of recipient GNI 2005	Debt service as a % of exports of goods and services	
		1970-1990	1990-2006			health	education	defence			1990	2005
Uganda	300	-	3.1	8	85x	2x	15x	26x	1198	15	47	7
Ukraine	1950	-	-1.5	104	<2	3	6	3	410	1	-	10x
United Arab Emirates	23950x	-4.8x	-0.9x	3x	-	7	17	30	-	-	-	-
United Kingdom	40180	2	2.5	3	-	15	4	7	-	-	-	-
United States	44970	2	2.1	2	-	24	3	20	-	-	-	-
Uruguay	5310	1	1.2	20	<2	7	8	4	15	0	31	27
Uzbekistan	610	-	0.7	117	<2	-	-	-	172	1	-	21x
Vanuatu	1710	-0.5x	-0.3	3	-	-	-	-	39	12	2	1
Venezuela (Bolivarian Republic of)	6070	-2	-0.6	36	19	8	21	5	49	0	22	9
Viet Nam	690	-	6	10	<2x	4	14	-	1905	4	7x	3x
Yemen	760	-	1.5	18	16	4	22	19	336	3	4	2
Zambia	630	-2	0	35	64	13	14	4	945	16	13	22x
Zimbabwe	340x	0	-2.4	76	56	8	24	7	368	8	19	6x

SUMMARY INDICATORS

Sub-Saharan Africa	851	-	1.1	35	43	-	-	-	28779	5	11	10
Eastern and Southern Africa	1171	-	1.2	38	34	-	-	-	12571	4	6	6
West and Central Africa	553	-	1	29	52	-	-	-	16208	9	20	15
Middle East and North Africa	2104	0	2.2	15	4	5	13	15	28451	3	21	14
South Asia	777	2	3.9	6	32	2	3	14	9260	1	21	-
East Asia and Pacific	2371	6	6.7	5	9	1	7	11	8968	0	16	6
Latin America and Caribbean	4847	1	1.4	37	9	7	15	4	5363	0	20	18
CEE/CIS	4264	-	1.1	74	2	7	6	9	4006	0	-	18
Industrialized countries§	37217	2	1.9	2	-	18	4	12	-	-	-	-
Developing countries§	1967	3	4.1	19	20	3	9	10	82952	1	18	13
Least developed countries§	438	-	2.3	62	38	5	14	14	25979	10	13	8
World	7406	2	2.3	8	19	14	5	11	84828	0	18	14

§ Also includes territories within each country category or regional group. Countries and territories in each country category or regional group are listed on page 148.

DEFINITIONS OF THE INDICATORS

GNI per capita – Gross national income (GNI) is the sum of value added by all resident producers plus any product taxes (less subsidies) not included in the valuation of output plus net receipts of primary income (compensation of employees and property income) from abroad. GNI per capita is gross national income divided by midyear population. GNI per capita in US dollars is converted using the World Bank Atlas method.

GDP per capita – Gross domestic product (GDP) is the sum of value added by all resident producers plus any product taxes (less subsidies) not included in the valuation of output. GDP per capita is gross domestic product divided by midyear population. Growth is calculated from constant price GDP data in local currency.

% of population below US$1 a day – Percentage of the population living on less than US$1.08 a day at 1993 international prices (equivalent to US$1 a day in 1985 prices, adjusted for purchasing power parity). As a result of revisions in purchasing power parity exchange rates, poverty rates for individual countries cannot be compared with poverty rates reported in previous editions.

ODA – Net official development assistance.

Debt service – Sum of interest payments and repayments of principal on external public and publicly guaranteed long-term debts.

MAIN DATA SOURCES

GNI per capita – World Bank.

GDP per capita – World Bank.

Rate of inflation – World Bank.

% of population below US$1 a day – World Bank.

Expenditure on health, education and defence – International Monetary Fund (IMF).

ODA – Organisation for Economic Co-operation and Development (OECD).

Debt service – World Bank.

NOTES

a: low income ($905 or less).
b: lower-middle income ($906 to $3,595).
c: upper-middle income ($3,596 to $11,115).
d: high income ($11,116 or more).

- Data not available.

x Data refer to years or periods other than those specified in the column heading, differ from the standard definition or refer to only part of a country. Such data are not included in the calculation of regional and global averages.

* Data refer to the most recent year available during the period specified in the column heading.

TABLE 8. WOMEN

Countries and territories	Life expectancy: females as a % of males 2006	Adult literacy rate: females as a % of males 2000-2006*	Enrolment and attendance ratios: females as a % of males net primary school 2000-2006* enrolled	attending	net secondary school 2000-2006* enrolled	attending	Contraceptive prevalence (%) 2000-2006*	Antenatal care coverage (%) 2000-2006*	Skilled attendant at delivery (%) 2000-2006*	Institutional deliveries (%) 2000-2006*	Maternal mortality ratio† 2000-2006* reported	2005 adjusted	Lifetime risk of maternal death. 1 in:
Afghanistan	100	30	-	61	-	33	10	16	14	13	1600	1800	8
Albania	109	99	100	100	97	97	60	97	100	98	17	92	490
Algeria	104	75	97	99	105	114	61	89	95	95	120x	180	220
Andorra	-	-	96	-	110	-	-	-	-	-	-	-	-
Angola	108	65	-	102	-	91	6	66	45	16x	-	1400	12
Antigua and Barbuda	-	-	-	-	-	-	53x	100	100	-	0	-	-
Argentina	111	100	99	-	108	-	-	99	99	99	39	77	530
Armenia	110	99	105	99	104	102	53	93	98	97	27	76	980
Australia	106	-	101	-	101	-	-	100x	100x	-	-	4	13300
Austria	107	-	102	-	-	-	51x	100x	100x	-	-	4	21500
Azerbaijan	112	98x	99	100	96	97	55	70	100	74	26	82	670
Bahamas	108	-	102	-	102	-	-	-	99	-	-	16	2700
Bahrain	104	94	100	101	107	110	62x	97x	98x	98x	46x	32	1300
Bangladesh	103	76	103	106	102	114	58	48	20	16	320	570	51
Barbados	108	-	100	-	101	-	55x	100	100	-	0x	16	4400
Belarus	119	99x	97	101	101	102	73	99	100	100	10	18	4800
Belgium	108	-	100	-	101	-	78x	-	-	-	-	8	7800
Belize	108	100x	103	-	101	-	56x	96	84x	77	130	52	560
Benin	104	48	81	78	48	63	17	88	78	78	500x	840	20
Bhutan	105	-	99	91	-	-	31	51	56	37	260	440	55
Bolivia	107	87	102	99	99	98	58	79	67	57	230	290	89
Bosnia and Herzegovina	107	95	-	97	-	100	36	99	100	100	3	3	29000
Botswana	101	103	99	104	109	122	48	97	94	80x	330x	380	130
Brazil	111	101	100	100x	108	119x	77x	97	88x	97	76	110	370
Brunei Darussalam	106	95	101	-	106	-	-	100x	99x	-	0x	13	2900
Bulgaria	110	99	99	-	98	-	86x	-	99	-	10	11	7400
Burkina Faso	106	55	80	90	69	88	17	85	54	51	480x	700	22
Burundi	106	78	92	97	-	75	9	92	34	29	620	1100	16
Cambodia	109	75	97	104	81	88	40	69	44	22	470	540	48
Cameroon	102	78	-	94	-	93	29	82	63	61	670	1000	24
Canada	106	-	101	-	-	-	75x	-	98	-	-	7	11000
Cape Verde	109	86	98	99x	109	-	53x	99	89x	49x	76	210	120
Central African Republic	106	52	84	84	69	63	19	69	53	51	540	980	25
Chad	106	32	69	76	31	54	3	39	14	13	1100	1500	11
Chile	108	100	98	-	-	-	56x	95x	100	100	17	16	3200
China	105	92	100	-	-	-	87	90	98	83	48	45	1300
Colombia	111	100	100	102	109	113	78	94	96	92	78	130	290
Comoros	107	-	81	100	-	110	26	75	62	43x	380	400	52
Congo	105	87	120	101	-	108	44	86	83	82	780	740	22
Congo, Democratic Republic of the	106	67	-	89	-	83	31	68	61	-	1300	1100	13
Cook Islands	-	-	99	-	110	-	44	-	98	-	6x	-	-
Costa Rica	106	100	102	102	110	110	96	92	99	94	36	30	1400
Côte d'Ivoire	104	64	81	86	58	69	13	85	57	54	540	810	27
Croatia	110	98	99	-	102	-	-	-	100	-	7	7	10500
Cuba	105	100	98	-	101	-	77	100	100	-	37	45	1400
Cyprus	106	96	100	-	102	-	-	-	-	-	0x	10	6400
Czech Republic	109	-	102	-	-	-	69x	99x	100	-	5	4	18100
Denmark	106	-	101	-	102	-	-	-	-	-	10x	3	17800
Djibouti	105	-	81	98	67	84	9	67	61	74	74x	650	35
Dominica	-	-	102	-	100	-	50x	100	100	-	0	-	-
Dominican Republic	109	100	101	105	126	144	61	99	96	95	92	150	230
Ecuador	108	98	101	-	102	-	73	84	99x	74	110	210	170
Egypt	107	71	95	98	93	93	59	70	74	65	84	130	230
El Salvador	109	96	100	-	104	-	67	86	92	69	71	170	190
Equatorial Guinea	105	87	91	98	-	96	-	86	65	-	-	680	28
Eritrea	109	-	84	93	67	91	8	70	28	26	1000x	450	44
Estonia	117	100	100	-	103	-	70x	-	100	-	29	25	2900
Ethiopia	105	46	93	100	68	77	15	28	6	5	670	720	27
Fiji	107	-	99	-	106	-	44	-	99	-	38x	210	160
Finland	108	-	100	-	100	-	-	100x	100x	100	6x	7	8500
France	109	-	100	-	102	-	75x	99x	99x	-	10x	8	6900

| | Life expectancy: females as a % of males 2006 | Adult literacy rate: females as a % of males 2000-2006* | Enrolment and attendance ratios: females as a % of males | | | | Contraceptive prevalence (%) 2000-2006* | Antenatal care coverage (%) 2000-2006* | Skilled attendant at delivery (%) 2000-2006* | Institutional deliveries (%) 2000-2006* | Maternal mortality ratio[†] | | |
| | | | net primary school 2000-2006* | | net secondary school 2000-2006* | | | | | | | | 2005 | |
			enrolled	attending	enrolled	attending					2000-2006* reported	adjusted	Lifetime risk of maternal death. 1 in:
Gabon	102	91	100	100	-	106	33	94	86	85	520	520	53
Gambia	104	-	99	103	84	87	18	98	57	55	730	690	32
Georgia	112	-	100	101x,y	100	-	47	94	99	92	23	66	1100
Germany	107	-	100	-	-	-	75x	-	-	-	8x	4	19200
Ghana	101	76	101	100	90	100	17	92	50	49	210x	560	45
Greece	106	96	100	-	102	-	-	-	-	-	1x	3	25900
Grenada	105	-	99	-	103	-	54	100	100	-	0	-	-
Guatemala	111	84	96	95	91	104x	43	84	41	42	150	290	71
Guinea	106	42	87	87	55	63	9	82	38	31	980	910	19
Guinea-Bissau	107	-	72	98	55	88	10	78	39	36	410	1100	13
Guyana	109	-	-	100	-	111	35	90	94	-	120	470	90
Haiti	106	-	-	106	-	117	32	85	26	25	630	670	44
Holy See	-	-	-	-	-	-	-	-	-	-	-	-	-
Honduras	111	100	102	104	-	124	65	92	67	67	110x	280	93
Hungary	112	-	98	-	100	-	77x	-	100	-	4	6	13300
Iceland	104	-	97	-	102	-	-	-	-	-	-	4	12700
India	105	66	93	101	-	91	56	74	47	41	300	450	70
Indonesia	106	93	97	101	98	104	57	92	72	40	310	420	97
Iran (Islamic Republic of)	105	88	110	97	95	-	74	77x	90	84	37x	140	300
Iraq	107	76	86	88	70	74	50	84	89	63	290x	300	72
Ireland	106	-	100	-	107	-	-	-	100	100	6x	1	47600
Israel	105	-	101	-	100	-	-	-	-	-	5x	4	7800
Italy	108	99	99	-	101	-	60x	-	-	-	7x	3	26600
Jamaica	108	116	100	101	104	105	69	91	97	94	95	170	240
Japan	109	-	100	-	101	-	56	-	100x	-	8x	6	11600
Jordan	105	92	102	100	104	105	56	99	100	97	41x	62	450
Kazakhstan	118	99x	98	99	99	100	51	100	100	100	70	140	360
Kenya	104	90	101	100	100	108	39	88	42	40	410	560	39
Kiribati	-	-	102	-	109	-	21x	88x	85x	-	56	-	-
Korea, Democratic People's Republic of	106	-	-	-	-	-	62x	-	97	-	110u	370	140
Korea, Republic of	110	-	99	-	100	-	81x	-	100x	-	20x	14	6100
Kuwait	105	97	99	-	105	-	50x	95x	98	98x	5x	4	9600
Kyrgyzstan	113	99x	99	102	101	102	48	97	98	97	100	150	240
Lao People's Democratic Republic	104	79	94	95	85	83	32	27	19	-	410	660	33
Latvia	116	100	103	-	-	-	48x	-	100	-	10	10	8500
Lebanon	106	-	99	100	-	111	58	96	98x	-	100x	150	290
Lesotho	101	122	106	107	158	169	37	90	55	52	760	960	45
Liberia	104	79	78	-	55	-	10	85	51	36	580x	1200	12
Libyan Arab Jamahiriya	107	81	-	-	-	-	45x	81x	94x	-	77x	97	350
Liechtenstein	-	-	102	-	111	-	-	-	-	-	-	-	-
Lithuania	117	100	100	-	100	-	47x	-	100	-	16	11	7800
Luxembourg	108	-	100	-	108	-	-	-	100	-	0x	12	5000
Madagascar	106	87	99	104	100x	124	27	80	51	32	470	510	38
Malawi	101	72x	105	102	88	96	42	92	54	54	980	1100	18
Malaysia	107	92	99	-	114	-	55x	79	98	98	28	62	560
Maldives	102	100	100	-	110	-	39	81	84	-	140	120	200
Mali	109	48x	80	73	-	73	8	57	41	38	580	970	15
Malta	105	103x	95	-	99	-	-	-	98x	-	-	8	8300
Marshall Islands	-	-	99	-	107	-	34	-	95x	-	74	-	-
Mauritania	106	72	100	91	82	60	8	64	57	49	750	820	22
Mauritius	110	92	102	-	101	-	76	-	98	98	22	15	3300
Mexico	107	97	100	100	103	-	74	86x	86x	86	62	60	670
Micronesia (Federated States of)	102	-	-	-	-	-	45x	-	88	-	270x	-	-
Moldova, Republic of	111	99	100	101	103	104	68	98	100	99	19	22	3700
Monaco	-	-	-	-	-	-	-	-	-	-	-	-	-
Mongolia	110	100	102	102	114	107	66	99	99	99	93	46	840
Montenegro	106	95	-	99	-	102	39	97	99	100	-	-	-
Morocco	106	61	93	96	84	92	63	68	63	61	230	240	150
Mozambique	103	45x	91	90	75	88	17	85	48	48	410	520	45
Myanmar	111	91	102	101	97	94	34	76	57	16	320	380	110
Namibia	102	97	107	100	133	138	44	91	76	75	270	210	170

TABLE 8. WOMEN

	Life expectancy: females as a % of males 2006	Adult literacy rate: females as a % of males 2000-2006*	Enrolment and attendance ratios: females as a % of males net primary school 2000-2006* enrolled	attending	net secondary school 2000-2006* enrolled	attending	Contraceptive prevalence (%) 2000-2006*	Antenatal care coverage (%) 2000-2006*	Skilled attendant at delivery (%) 2000-2006*	Institutional deliveries (%) 2000-2006*	Maternal mortality ratio† 2000-2006* reported	2005 adjusted	Lifetime risk of maternal death. 1 in:
Nauru	-	-	-	-	-	-	-	-	-	-	-	-	-
Nepal	101	56	92	95	-	83	48	44	19	18	280	830	31
Netherlands	106	-	99	-	102	-	79x	-	100x	-	7x	6	10200
New Zealand	105	-	100	-	103	-	75x	95x	100x	-	15x	9	5900
Nicaragua	109	100	98	109	115	134	69	86	67	66	87	170	150
Niger	97	35	72	69	67	100	11	46	33	17	650	1800	7
Nigeria	102	77	89	88	86	87	13	58	35	33	-	1100	18
Niue	-	-	-	-	105x	-	-	-	100	-	-	-	-
Norway	106	-	100	-	100	-	-	-	-	-	6x	7	7700
Occupied Palestinian Territory	104	91	100	101	107	-	50	99	99	97	-	-	-
Oman	104	85	101	-	100	-	32	100	95	94	15	64	420
Pakistan	101	55	77	82	75	78	28	36	31	28	530x	320	74
Palau	-	-	97	-	-	-	17	-	100	-	0x	-	-
Panama	107	98	99	-	110	-	-	72	93	92	40	130	270
Papua New Guinea	111	81	-	-	-	-	26x	78x	41	-	370x	470	55
Paraguay	106	99	101	101	-	99	73	94	77	74	170	150	170
Peru	107	88	101	100	99	100	71	92	73	70	190	240	140
Philippines	106	102	102	101	120	127	49	88	60	38	170x	230	140
Poland	112	-	101	-	102	-	49x	-	100	-	4	8	10600
Portugal	108	96	100	-	110	-	-	-	100	-	8x	11	6400
Qatar	102	100	100	-	98	-	43x	-	99x	98x	10x	12	2700
Romania	110	98	99	-	104	-	70	94	99	98	17	24	3200
Russian Federation	123	99	101	-	-	-	-	-	99	-	23	28	2700
Rwanda	107	85	104	104	91	100	17	94	39	28	750	1300	16
Saint Kitts and Nevis	-	-	105	-	98	-	54	100	100	-	0	-	-
Saint Lucia	105	-	98	-	125	-	47x	99	100	-	35	-	-
Saint Vincent and the Grenadines	106	-	96	-	125	-	48	95	100	-	0	-	-
Samoa	109	99	101	-	113	-	43x	-	100x	-	29	-	-
San Marino	-	-	-	-	-	-	-	-	-	-	-	-	-
Sao Tome and Principe	106	85	99	101	113	105	30	97	81	78	150	-	-
Saudi Arabia	106	86	103	-	108	-	32x	90x	91x	91x	-	18	1400
Senegal	107	57	96	102	79	80	12	87	52	62	430	980	21
Serbia	107	95	-	100	-	103	41	98	99	99	-	-	-
Seychelles	-	101	101	-	106	-	-	-	-	-	57	-	-
Sierra Leone	108	51	-	100	-	77	5	81	43	19	1800	2100	8
Singapore	105	87x	-	-	-	-	62x	-	100x	-	6x	14	6200
Slovakia	111	-	101	-	-	-	74x	-	100	-	6	6	13800
Slovenia	110	100	99	-	101	-	74x	98x	100	-	17x	6	14200
Solomon Islands	103	-	95	-	86	-	7	-	85x	-	140x	220	100
Somalia	105	-	-	83	-	50	15	26	33	9	1000	1400	12
South Africa	104	96x	100	104x	112	117x	60	92	92	-	150x	400	110
Spain	109	97x	99	-	103	-	81x	-	-	-	6x	4	16400
Sri Lanka	111	97	99	-	-	-	70	95	96	97	43	58	850
Sudan	105	73	83	95	-	105	7	60	87	-	550x	450	53
Suriname	110	95	103	99	138	120	42	91	85	-	150	72	530
Swaziland	101	96	101	99	113	138	48	90	74	-	230x	390	120
Sweden	106	-	100	-	101	-	-	-	-	-	5x	3	17400
Switzerland	107	-	100	-	93	-	82x	-	-	-	5x	5	13800
Syrian Arab Republic	105	84	95	99	94	102	58	84	93	70	65	130	210
Tajikistan	108	99	97	99	85	83	38	77	83	62	97	170	160
Tanzania, United Republic of	104	79	98	106	-	100	26	78	43	47	580	950	24
Thailand	114	96	96	100	106	109	77	98	97	97	24	110	500
The former Yugoslav Republic of Macedonia	107	96	100	96	98	99	-	81	99	98	13	10	6500
Timor-Leste	103	-	-	97y	-	-	10	61	18	10	-	380	35
Togo	106	57	86	93	47	71	17	84	62	63	480x	510	38
Tonga	103	100x	96	-	123	-	33	-	95	-	78	-	-
Trinidad and Tobago	106	99	100	100	103	107	43	96	98	97	45x	45	1400
Tunisia	106	78	100	98	110	-	66	92	90	89	69x	100	500
Turkey	107	84	95	96	85	89	71	81	83	78	29	44	880

	Life expectancy: females as a % of males 2006	Adult literacy rate: females as a % of males 2000-2006*	Enrolment and attendance ratios: females as a % of males				Contraceptive prevalence (%) 2000-2006*	Antenatal care coverage (%) 2000-2006*	Skilled attendant at delivery (%) 2000-2006*	Institutional deliveries (%) 2000-2006*	Maternal mortality ratio†		
			net primary school 2000-2006*		net secondary school 2000-2006*						2000-2006* reported	2005 adjusted	2005 Lifetime risk of maternal death. 1 in:
			enrolled	attending	enrolled	attending							
Turkmenistan	115	99x	-	100	-	100	48	99	100	98	14	130	290
Tuvalu	-	-	-	-	-	-	32	-	100	-	-	-	-
Uganda	102	75	-	99	88	100	24	94	42	41	510	550	25
Ukraine	119	99	100	102	94	103	66	99	100	100	13	18	5200
United Arab Emirates	106	99	99	-	105	-	28x	97x	99x	99x	3x	37	1000
United Kingdom	106	-	100	-	103	-	84	-	99x	-	7x	8	8200
United States	107	-	101	-	102	-	76x	-	99x	-	8x	11	4800
Uruguay	110	101x	101	-	-	-	84x	94x	100x	-	26x	20	2100
Uzbekistan	110	-	-	100	-	99	65	99	100	97	28	24	1400
Vanuatu	106	-	98	-	86	-	28	-	88x	-	68x	-	-
Venezuela (Bolivarian Republic of)	108	100	101	102	115	143	77x	94	95	95	60	57	610
Viet Nam	105	93x	95	100	96	101	76	91	88	64	160	150	280
Yemen	105	48	72	60x	46	37x	23	41	27	20	370	430	39
Zambia	101	79x	100	105	79	112	34	93	43	44	730	830	27
Zimbabwe	97	92	101	102	94	100	60	95	80	68	560	880	43

SUMMARY INDICATORS

Sub-Saharan Africa	104	72	93	95	84	87	23	69	43	36	-	920	22
Eastern and Southern Africa	104	74	98	101	88	91	30	71	40	32	-	760	29
West and Central Africa	104	69	87	89	78	85	17	67	46	39	-	1100	17
Middle East and North Africa	105	77	94	97	93	96	55	72	79	68	-	210	140
South Asia	104	66	92	98	-	90	53	65	41	36	-	500	59
East Asia and Pacific	106	92	99	101**	102**	105**	79	89	87	69	-	150	350
Latin America and Caribbean	109	99	99	101	106	-	70	94	-	86	-	130	280
CEE/CIS	115	96	98	98	94	97	63	90	95	89	-	46	1300
Industrialized countries§	108	-	101	-	102	-	-	-	99	-	-	8	8000
Developing countries§	105	83	96	98**	97**	93**	61	75	59	53	-	450	76
Least developed countries§	105	68	94	97	85	93	30	61	38	27	-	870	24
World	106	86	96	98**	98**	94**	61	75	63	59	-	400	92

§ Also includes territories within each country category or regional group. Countries and territories in each country category or regional group are listed on page 148.

DEFINITIONS OF THE INDICATORS

Life expectancy at birth – Number of years newborn children would live if subject to the mortality risks prevailing for the cross section of population at the time of their birth.

Adult literacy rate – Number of literate persons aged 15 and above, expressed as a percentage of the total population in that age group.

Enrolment and attendance ratios: females as a % of males – Girls' net enrolment and attendance ratios divided by those of boys, as a percentage.

Primary or secondary school net enrolment ratio – Number of children enrolled in primary or secondary school who are of official primary or secondary school age, expressed as a percentage of the total number of children of official primary or secondary school age.

Primary school net attendance ratio – Number of children attending primary or secondary school who are of official primary school age, expressed as a percentage of the total number of children of official primary school age.

Secondary school net attendance ratio – Number of children attending secondary or tertiary school who are of official secondary school age, expressed as a percentage of the total number of children of official secondary school age.

Contraceptive prevalence – Percentage of women in union aged 15-49 currently using contraception.

Antenatal care – Percentage of women 15-49 years old attended at least once during pregnancy by skilled health personnel (doctors, nurses or midwives).

Skilled attendant at delivery – Percentage of births attended by skilled health personnel (doctors, nurses or midwives).

Institutional deliveries – Proportion of women 15-49 years old who gave birth in the two years preceding the survey and delivered in a health facility.

Maternal mortality ratio – Annual number of deaths of women from pregnancy-related causes per 100,000 live births. This 'reported' column shows country-reported figures that are not adjusted for under-reporting and misclassification.

Lifetime risk of maternal death – Lifetime risk of maternal death takes into account both the probability of becoming pregnant and the probability of dying as a result of that pregnancy accumulated across a woman's reproductive years.

MAIN DATA SOURCES

Life expectancy – United Nations Population Division.

Adult literacy – UNESCO Institute for Statistics (UIS).

Primary and secondary school enrolment – UIS.

Primary and secondary school attendance – Demographic and Health Surveys (DHS) and Multiple Indicator Cluster Surveys (MICS).

Contraceptive prevalence – DHS, MICS, United Nations Population Division and UNICEF.

Antenatal care – DHS, MICS, World Health Organization (WHO) and UNICEF.

Skilled attendant at delivery – DHS, MICS, WHO and UNICEF.

Institutional deliveries – DHS, MICS, WHO and UNICEF.

Maternal mortality – WHO and UNICEF.

Lifetime risk – WHO and UNICEF.

---

† The maternal mortality data in the column headed 'reported' are those reported by national authorities. Periodically, UNICEF, WHO, UNFPA and the World Bank evaluate these data and make adjustments to account for the well-documented problems of under-reporting and misclassification of maternal deaths and to develop estimates for countries with no data. The column with 'adjusted' estimates for the year 2005 reflects the most recent of these reviews.

NOTES
- Data not available.

x Data refer to years or periods other than those specified in the column heading, differ from the standard definition or refer to only part of a country. Such data are not included in the calculation of regional and global averages.

y Data refer to years or periods other than those specified in the column heading, differ from the standard definition or refer to only part of a country. Such data are included in the calculation of regional and global averages.

* Data refer to the most recent year available during the period specified in the column heading.

** Excludes China.

TABLE 9. CHILD PROTECTION

Countries and territories	Child labour (5-14 years) 1999-2006* total	male	female	Child marriage 1987-2006* total	urban	rural	Birth registration 1999-2006 total	urban	rural	Female genital mutilation/cutting 2000-2006* women[a] (15-49 years) total	urban	rural	daughters[b] total	Attitude towards domestic violence 1999-2006* total	Child disability 1999-2006* total	Child discipline 2005-2006* total
Afghanistan	30	28	33	43	-	-	6	12	4	-	-	-	-	-	-	-
Albania	12	14	9	8	7	8	98	97	98	-	-	-	-	30	11	49
Algeria	5	6	4	2	2	2	99	99	99	-	-	-	-	68	1y	86
Angola	24	22	25	-	-	-	29	34	19	-	-	-	-	-	-	-
Argentina	7y	8y	5y	-	-	-	91y	-	-	-	-	-	-	-	-	-
Armenia	-	-	-	10	7	16	96	97	95	-	-	-	-	22	-	-
Azerbaijan	11	11	11	-	-	-	97	98	96	-	-	-	-	-	-	-
Bahrain	5	6	3	-	-	-	-	-	-	-	-	-	-	-	-	-
Bangladesh	13	18	8	64	58	69	10	13	9	-	-	-	-	-	18	-
Belarus	5	6	4	7	6	10	-	-	-	-	-	-	-	-	-	83
Belize	40	39	42	-	-	-	93y	92y	94y	-	-	-	-	-	-	-
Benin	26y	23y	29y	37	25	45	70	78	66	17	13	20	6	60	-	-
Bhutan	19y	16y	22y	-	-	-	-	-	-	-	-	-	-	-	-	-
Bolivia	22	22	22	26	22	37	82	83	79	-	-	-	-	-	-	-
Bosnia and Herzegovina	5	7	4	6	2	7	100	99	100	-	-	-	-	5	7	36
Botswana	-	-	-	10	13	9	58	66	52	-	-	-	-	-	-	-
Brazil	6y	8y	4y	24	22	30	89y	-	-	-	-	-	-	-	-	-
Burkina Faso	47y	46y	48y	48	29	61	64	86	58	73	76	71	25	71	-	83
Burundi	19	19	19	18	14	18	60	62	60	-	-	-	-	-	-	-
Cambodia	45y	45y	45y	23	-	-	66	71	66	-	-	-	-	55	-	-
Cameroon	31	31	30	36	23	57	70	86	58	1	1	2	1	56	23	92
Cape Verde	3y	4y	3y	-	-	-	-	-	-	-	-	-	-	-	-	-
Central African Republic	47	44	49	61	57	64	49	72	36	26	21	29	7	-	31	88
Chad	53	54	51	72	65	73	9	36	3	45	47	44	21	-	3y	-
Chile	3	3	2	-	-	-	96y	-	-	-	-	-	-	-	-	-
China	-	-	-	-	-	-	-	-	-	-	-	-	-	-	3y	-
Colombia	5	6	4	23	19	38	90	97	77	-	-	-	-	-	-	-
Comoros	27	26	28	30	23	33	83	87	83	-	-	-	-	-	-	-
Congo	-	-	-	31	24	40	81y	88y	75y	-	-	-	-	76	-	-
Congo, Democratic Republic of the	32	29	34	-	-	-	34	30	36	-	-	-	-	-	-	-
Costa Rica	5	6	3	-	-	-	-	-	-	-	-	-	-	-	-	-
Côte d'Ivoire	35	36	34	35	27	43	55	79	41	36	34	39	9	65	-	90
Cuba	-	-	-	-	-	-	100y	100y	100y	-	-	-	-	-	-	-
Djibouti	8	8	8	5	5	13	89	90	82	93	93	96	49	-	35	70
Dominican Republic	10	12	7	41	-	-	78	82	70	-	-	-	-	9	-	-
Ecuador	12	12	13	26y	21y	34y	-	-	-	-	-	-	-	-	-	-
Egypt	7	8	5	17	-	-	-	-	-	96	92	98	28y	50	8y	92y
El Salvador	6y	9y	4y	27	-	-	-	-	-	-	-	-	-	-	-	-
Equatorial Guinea	28	28	28	-	-	-	32	43	24	-	-	-	-	-	-	-
Eritrea	-	-	-	47	31	60	-	-	-	89	86	91	63	-	-	-
Ethiopia	53	59	46	49	27	55	7	29	5	74	69	76	38	81	-	-
Gabon	-	-	-	34	30	49	89	90	87	-	-	-	-	-	-	-
Gambia	25	20	29	36	24	45	55	57	54	78	72	83	64	74	-	84
Georgia	-	-	-	16	-	-	93y	97y	89y	-	-	-	-	30y	-	-
Ghana	34	34	34	22	15	28	51	69	42	4	2	6	1	47	16	89
Guatemala	29	25	32	34	25	44	-	-	-	-	-	-	-	-	-	-
Guinea	25	26	24	63	45	75	43	78	33	96	94	96	57	86	-	-
Guinea-Bissau	39	41	37	24	14	32	39	53	33	45	39	48	35	52	-	80
Guyana	19	21	17	30	-	-	97	99	96	-	-	-	-	-	-	-
Haiti	-	-	-	30	-	-	81	-	-	-	-	-	-	29	-	-
Honduras	16	16	15	39	33	46	94	95	93	-	-	-	-	16	-	-
India	12	-	-	45	28	53	41	59	35	-	-	-	-	54	-	-
Indonesia	4y	5y	4y	24	15	33	55	69	43	-	-	-	-	25	-	-
Iraq	11	12	9	17	16	19	95	95	96	-	-	-	-	59	15	84
Jamaica	6	7	5	9	7	11	89	88	89	-	-	-	-	6	15	87
Jordan	-	-	-	11	11	12	-	-	-	-	-	-	-	-	-	-
Kazakhstan	2	2	2	7	6	9	99	99	99	-	-	-	-	10	-	52
Kenya	26	27	25	25	19	27	48y	64y	44y	32	21	36	21	68	-	-
Korea, Democratic People's Republic of	-	-	-	-	-	-	99	99	99	-	-	-	-	-	-	-
Kyrgyzstan	4	4	3	10	7	14	94	96	93	-	-	-	-	38	-	51
Lao People's Democratic Republic	25	24	26	-	-	-	59	71	56	-	-	-	-	-	-	-
Lebanon	7	8	6	11	-	-	-	-	-	-	-	-	-	-	-	-
Lesotho	23	25	21	23	13	26	26	39	24	-	-	-	-	-	-	-
Liberia	-	-	-	40	-	-	-	-	-	-	-	-	-	-	-	-
Madagascar	32	36	28	39	29	42	75	87	72	-	-	-	-	28	-	-
Malawi	29	28	29	51	38	53	-	-	-	-	-	-	-	28	-	-
Maldives	-	-	-	-	-	-	73	-	-	-	-	-	-	-	-	-
Mali	34	35	33	65	46	74	47y	84y	34y	92	90	93	73	89	-	-
Mauritania	4y	5y	3y	37	32	42	55	72	42	71	65	77	66	-	-	-
Mexico	16y	15y	16y	28y	31y	21y	-	-	-	-	-	-	-	-	-	-
Moldova, Republic of	32	32	33	19	16	22	98	98	98	-	-	-	-	21	-	-
Mongolia	18	19	17	9	7	12	98	98	99	-	-	-	-	20	17	79
Montenegro	10	12	8	5	5	5	98	98	99	-	-	-	-	11	13	61
Morocco	11y	13y	9y	16	12	21	85	92	80	-	-	-	-	-	-	-
Mozambique	-	-	-	56	41	66	-	-	-	-	-	-	-	-	-	-
Myanmar	-	-	-	-	-	-	65y	66y	64y	-	-	-	-	-	-	-
Namibia	13y	15y	12y	10	9	10	71	82	64	-	-	-	-	-	-	-
Nepal	31y	30y	33y	51	-	-	35	-	-	-	-	-	-	23	-	-
Nicaragua	15	18	11	43	36	55	81	90	73	-	-	-	-	17	-	-
Niger	38y	39y	38y	75	-	-	32	71	25	2	2	2	1	70	-	-
Nigeria	13y	-	-	43	27	52	33y	52y	25y	19	28	14	10	65	-	-
Occupied Palestinian Territory	-	-	-	19	-	-	96y	97y	96y	-	-	-	-	-	-	95y
Pakistan	-	-	-	32	21	37	-	-	-	-	-	-	-	-	-	-

Countries and territories	Child labour (5-14 years) 1999-2006*			Child marriage 1987-2006*			Birth registration 1999-2006◊			Female genital mutilation/cutting 2000-2006*				Attitude towards domestic violence 1999-2006*	Child disability 1999-2006*	Child discipline 2005-2006*
										women[a] (15-49 years)			daughters[b]			
	total	male	female	total	urban	rural	total	urban	rural	total	urban	rural	total	total	total	total
Panama	3	5	2	-	-	-	-	-	-	-	-	-	-	-	-	-
Paraguay	15	17	12	24	18	32	-	-	-	-	-	-	-	-	-	-
Peru	19	20	19	17	13	30	93	93	92	-	-	-	-	-	-	-
Philippines	12	13	11	14	10	22	83	87	78	-	-	-	-	24	-	-
Portugal	3y	4y	3y	-	-	-	-	-	-	-	-	-	-	-	-	-
Romania	1	1	1	-	-	-	-	-	-	-	-	-	-	-	-	-
Rwanda	35	36	35	13	9	14	82	79	83	-	-	-	-	48	2y	-
Sao Tome and Principe	8	8	7	33	31	37	69	70	67	-	-	-	-	32	16	-
Senegal	22	24	21	39	23	55	55	75	44	28	22	34	20	65	-	73
Serbia	4	5	4	6	4	8	99	99	99	-	-	-	-	6	11	73
Sierra Leone	48	49	48	56	34	66	48	62	44	94	86	97	35	85	23	92
Somalia	49	45	54	45	35	52	3	6	2	98	97	98	46	76y	-	-
South Africa	-	-	-	8	5	12	-	-	-	-	-	-	-	-	-	-
Sri Lanka	8	9	7	12y	-	-	-	-	-	-	-	-	-	-	-	-
Sudan	13	14	12	27y	19y	34y	64	82	46	90	92	88	58	-	-	-
Suriname	-	-	-	-	-	-	95	94	94	-	-	-	-	-	-	-
Swaziland	9	9	9	-	-	-	53	72	50	-	-	-	-	-	-	-
Syrian Arab Republic	4	5	3	13	15	12	95	96	95	-	-	-	-	-	-	87
Tajikistan	10	9	11	13	13	13	88	85	90	-	-	-	-	74y	-	74
Tanzania, United Republic of	36	37	34	41	23	49	8	22	4	15	7	18	4	60	-	-
Thailand	8	8	8	20	12	23	99	100	99	-	-	-	-	-	12	-
The former Yugoslav Republic of Macedonia	6	7	5	4	3	4	94	95	93	-	-	-	-	21	10	69
Timor-Leste	4	4	4	-	-	-	53y	-	-	-	-	-	-	-	-	-
Togo	29	29	30	24	15	36	78	93	69	6	4	7	1	53	-	90
Trinidad and Tobago	1	1	1	8	-	-	96	-	-	-	-	-	-	8	-	75
Tunisia	-	-	-	10y	7y	14y	-	-	-	-	-	-	-	-	-	-
Turkey	5	4	6	18	-	-	-	-	-	-	-	-	-	39	-	-
Turkmenistan	-	-	-	7	9	6	96	96	95	-	-	-	-	38y	-	-
Uganda	36	37	36	54	34	59	4	11	3	-	-	-	-	77	-	-
Ukraine	7	8	7	6	6	10	100	100	100	-	-	-	-	5	-	70
Uzbekistan	2	2	2	7	9	7	100	100	100	-	-	-	-	70	2	-
Venezuela (Bolivarian Republic of)	8	9	6	-	-	-	92	-	-	-	-	-	-	64	-	93
Viet Nam	16	15	16	10	3	13	87	94	85	-	-	-	-	-	-	-
Yemen	11y	11y	12y	37	-	-	-	-	-	23	26	22	20	-	-	-
Zambia	12y	11y	12y	42	32	49	10	16	6	1	1	1	-	85	-	-
Zimbabwe	13y	12y	14y	29	21	36	42	56	35	-	-	-	-	51	-	-

SUMMARY INDICATORS

	total	male	female	total	urban	rural	total	urban	rural	total	urban	rural	total	total	total	total
Sub-Saharan Africa	35	36	34	40	24	47	34	52	28	36	31	40	19	66	-	-
Eastern and Southern Africa	36	38	33	36	20	44	24	39	21	-	-	-	-	66	-	-
West and Central Africa	34	33	34	44	27	53	41	58	35	28	29	29	15	65	-	-
Middle East and North Africa	9	10	8	17	11	19	-	-	-	-	-	-	-	-	-	-
South Asia	13	-	-	45	30	53	36	52	30	-	-	-	-	53	-	-
East Asia and Pacific	10**	11**	10**	19**	12**	25**	72**	80**	67**	-	-	-	-	34**	-	-
Latin America and Caribbean	11	12	10	26	24	31	89	93	83	-	-	-	-	-	-	-
CEE/CIS	5	5	5	11	7	9	-	-	-	-	-	-	-	31	-	-
Industrialized countries§	-	-	-	-	-	-	-	-	-	-	-	-	-	-	-	-
Developing countries§	16**	19**	17**	34**	23**	45**	49**	64**	37**	-	-	-	-	51**	-	-
Least developed countries§	29	31	28	49	37	57	30	43	24	-	-	-	-	-	-	-
World	-	-	-	-	-	-	-	-	-	-	-	-	-	-	-	-

§ Also includes territories within each country category or regional group. Countries and territories in each country category or regional group are listed on page 148.

DEFINITIONS OF THE INDICATORS

Child labour – Percentage of children 5-14 years old involved in child labour at the moment of the survey. A child is considered to be involved in child labour under the following conditions: (a) children 5-11 years old who, during the week preceding the survey, did at least one hour of economic activity or at least 28 hours of domestic work, or (b) children 12-14 years old who, during the week preceding the survey, did at least 14 hours of economic activity or at least 28 hours of domestic work.

Child labour background variables – Sex of the child; urban or rural place of residence; poorest 20 per cent or richest 20 per cent of the population constructed from household assets (a more detailed description of the household wealth estimation procedure can be found at www.childinfo.org); mother's education reflecting mothers with and without some level of education.

Child marriage – Percentage of women 20-24 years old who were married or in union before they were 18 years old.

Birth registration – Percentage of children less than five years old who were registered at the moment of the survey. The numerator of this indicator includes children whose birth certificate was seen by the interviewer or whose mother or caretaker says the birth has been registered. MICS data refer to children alive at the time of the survey.

Female genital mutilation/cutting – (a) Women – the percentage of women 15-49 years old who have been mutilated/cut. (b) Daughters – the percentage of women 15-49 years old with at least one mutilated/cut daughter. Female genital mutilation/cutting (FGM/C) is the cutting or alteration of the female genitalia for social reasons.

Attitudes towards domestic violence – Percentage of women 15-49 years old who consider a husband to be justified in hitting or beating his wife for at least one of the specified reasons. Women were asked whether a husband is justified in hitting or beating his wife under a series of circumstances, i.e., if his wife burns the food, argues with him, goes out without telling him, neglects the children or refuses sexual relations.

Child disability – Percentage of children 2-9 years old with at least one reported disability (i.e., cognitive, motor, seizure, vision or hearing).

Child discipline – Percentage of children 2-14 years old that experience any psychological or physical punishment.

MAIN DATA SOURCES

Child labour – Multiple Indicator Cluster Surveys (MICS) and Demographic and Health Surveys (DHS).

Child marriage – MICS, DHS and other national surveys.

Birth registration – MICS, DHS, other national surveys and vital registration systems.

Female genital mutilation/cutting – MICS, DHS and other national surveys.

Attitudes towards domestic violence – MICS, DHS and other national surveys.

Child disability – MICS, DHS and other national surveys.

Child discipline – MICS, DHS and other national surveys.

NOTES
-    Data not available.
- y   Data refer to years or periods other than those specified in the column heading, differ from the standard definition or refer to only part of a country. Such data are included in the calculation of regional and global averages.
- *   Data refer to the most recent year available during the period specified in the column heading.
- ◊   The global and regional estimates for birth registration included in this table are based on the sub-set of countries for which data are available for the period 1999-2006. Global and regional estimates for a wider set of countries are available for the period 1997-2006 and can be found at www.childinfo.org/areas/birthregistration.
- **   Excludes China.

Summary indicators

Averages given at the end of each table are calculated using data from the countries and territories as grouped below.

Sub-Saharan Africa

Angola; Benin; Botswana; Burkina Faso; Burundi; Cameroon; Cape Verde; Central African Republic; Chad; Comoros; Congo; Congo, Democratic Republic of the; Côte d'Ivoire; Equatorial Guinea; Eritrea; Ethiopia; Gabon; Gambia; Ghana; Guinea; Guinea-Bissau; Kenya; Lesotho; Liberia; Madagascar; Malawi; Mali; Mauritania; Mauritius; Mozambique; Namibia; Niger; Nigeria; Rwanda; Sao Tome and Principe; Senegal; Seychelles; Sierra Leone; Somalia; South Africa; Swaziland; Tanzania, United Republic of; Togo; Uganda; Zambia; Zimbabwe

Middle East and North Africa

Algeria; Bahrain; Djibouti; Egypt; Iran (Islamic Republic of); Iraq; Jordan; Kuwait; Lebanon; Libyan Arab Jamahiriya; Morocco; Occupied Palestinian Territory; Oman; Qatar; Saudi Arabia; Sudan; Syrian Arab Republic; Tunisia; United Arab Emirates; Yemen

South Asia

Afghanistan; Bangladesh; Bhutan; India; Maldives; Nepal; Pakistan; Sri Lanka

East Asia and Pacific

Brunei Darussalam; Cambodia; China; Cook Islands; Fiji; Indonesia; Kiribati; Korea, Democratic People's Republic of; Korea, Republic of; Lao People's Democratic Republic; Malaysia; Marshall Islands; Micronesia (Federated States of); Mongolia; Myanmar; Nauru; Niue; Palau; Papua New Guinea; Philippines; Samoa; Singapore; Solomon Islands; Thailand; Timor-Leste; Tonga; Tuvalu; Vanuatu; Viet Nam

Latin America and Caribbean

Antigua and Barbuda; Argentina; Bahamas; Barbados; Belize; Bolivia; Brazil; Chile; Colombia; Costa Rica; Cuba; Dominica; Dominican Republic; Ecuador; El Salvador; Grenada; Guatemala; Guyana; Haiti; Honduras; Jamaica; Mexico; Nicaragua; Panama; Paraguay; Peru; Saint Kitts and Nevis; Saint Lucia; Saint Vincent and the Grenadines; Suriname; Trinidad and Tobago; Uruguay; Venezuela (Bolivarian Republic of)

CEE/CIS

Albania; Armenia; Azerbaijan; Belarus; Bosnia and Herzegovina; Bulgaria; Croatia; Georgia; Kazakhstan; Kyrgyzstan; Moldova, Republic of; Montenegro; Romania; Russian Federation; Serbia; Tajikistan; the former Yugoslav Republic of Macedonia; Turkey; Turkmenistan; Ukraine; Uzbekistan

Industrialized countries/territories

Andorra; Australia; Austria; Belgium; Canada; Cyprus; Czech Republic; Denmark; Estonia; Finland; France; Germany; Greece; Holy See; Hungary; Iceland; Ireland; Israel; Italy; Japan; Latvia; Liechtenstein; Lithuania; Luxembourg; Malta; Monaco; Netherlands; New Zealand; Norway; Poland; Portugal; San Marino; Slovakia; Slovenia; Spain; Sweden; Switzerland; United Kingdom; United States

Developing countries/territories

Afghanistan; Algeria; Angola; Antigua and Barbuda; Argentina; Armenia; Azerbaijan; Bahamas; Bahrain; Bangladesh; Barbados; Belize; Benin; Bhutan; Bolivia; Botswana; Brazil; Brunei Darussalam; Burkina Faso; Burundi; Cambodia; Cameroon; Cape Verde; Central African Republic; Chad; Chile; China; Colombia; Comoros; Congo; Congo, Democratic Republic of the; Cook Islands; Costa Rica; Côte d'Ivoire; Cuba; Cyprus; Djibouti; Dominica; Dominican Republic; Ecuador; Egypt; El Salvador; Equatorial Guinea; Eritrea; Ethiopia; Fiji; Gabon; Gambia; Georgia; Ghana; Grenada; Guatemala; Guinea; Guinea-Bissau; Guyana; Haiti; Honduras; India; Indonesia; Iran (Islamic Republic of); Iraq; Israel; Jamaica; Jordan; Kazakhstan; Kenya; Kiribati; Korea, Democratic People's Republic of; Korea, Republic of; Kuwait; Kyrgyzstan; Lao People's Democratic Republic; Lebanon; Lesotho; Liberia; Libyan Arab Jamahiriya; Madagascar; Malawi; Malaysia; Maldives; Mali; Marshall Islands; Mauritania; Mauritius; Mexico; Micronesia (Federated States of); Mongolia; Morocco; Mozambique; Myanmar; Namibia; Nauru; Nepal; Nicaragua; Niger; Nigeria; Niue; Occupied Palestinian Territory; Oman; Pakistan; Palau; Panama; Papua New Guinea; Paraguay; Peru; Philippines; Qatar; Rwanda; Saint Kitts and Nevis; Saint Lucia; Saint Vincent/Grenadines; Samoa; Sao Tome and Principe; Saudi Arabia; Senegal; Seychelles; Sierra Leone; Singapore; Solomon Islands; Somalia; South Africa; Sri Lanka; Sudan; Suriname; Swaziland; Syrian Arab Republic; Tajikistan; Tanzania, United Republic of; Thailand; Timor-Leste; Togo; Tonga; Trinidad and Tobago; Tunisia; Turkey; Turkmenistan; Tuvalu; Uganda; United Arab Emirates; Uruguay; Uzbekistan; Vanuatu; Venezuela (Bolivarian Republic of); Viet Nam; Yemen; Zambia; Zimbabwe

Least developed countries/territories

Afghanistan; Angola; Bangladesh; Benin; Bhutan; Burkina Faso; Burundi; Cambodia; Cape Verde; Central African Republic; Chad; Comoros; Congo, Democratic Republic of the; Djibouti; Equatorial Guinea; Eritrea; Ethiopia; Gambia; Guinea; Guinea-Bissau; Haiti; Kiribati; Lao People's Democratic Republic; Lesotho; Liberia; Madagascar; Malawi; Maldives; Mali; Mauritania; Mozambique; Myanmar; Nepal; Niger; Rwanda; Samoa; Sao Tome and Principe; Senegal; Sierra Leone; Solomon Islands; Somalia; Sudan; Tanzania, United Republic of; Timor-Leste; Togo; Tuvalu; Uganda; Vanuatu; Yemen; Zambia

Measuring human development
An introduction to Table 10

If development is to be measured by a comprehensive and inclusive assessment, then the need arises for a method of measuring human as well as economic progress. From UNICEF's point of view, there is a need for an agreed method of measuring the level of child well-being and its rate of change.

The under-five mortality rate (U5MR) is used in Table 10 (*pages 150–153*) as the principal indicator of such progress. In 2006, for the first time since records have been kept, the number of children dying before their fifth birthday fell below 10 million, to 9.7 million – an important milestone in child survival. Around 1960, approximately 20 million children were dying every year – highlighting an important long-term decline in the global number of under-five deaths.

The U5MR has several advantages. First, it measures an end result of the development process rather than an 'input', such as school enrolment level, per capita calorie availability or the number of doctors per thousand population – all of which are means to an end.

Second, the U5MR is known to be the result of a wide variety of inputs: antibiotics to treat pneumonia; insecticide-treated mosquito nets to prevent malaria; the nutritional health and the health knowledge of mothers; the level of immunization and oral rehydration therapy use; the availability of maternal and child health services, including prenatal care; income and food availability in the family; the availability of safe drinking water and basic sanitation; and the overall safety of the child's environment.

Third, the U5MR is less susceptible to the fallacy of the average than, for example, per capita gross national income (GNI). This is because the natural scale does not allow the children of the rich to be one thousand times as likely to survive, even if the human-made scale does permit them to have one thousand times as much income. In other words, it is much more difficult for a wealthy minor-

ity to affect a nation's U5MR, and it therefore presents a more accurate, if far from perfect, picture of the health status of the majority of children and of society as a whole.

The speed of progress in reducing the U5MR can be measured by calculating its average annual rate of reduction (AARR). Unlike the comparison of absolute changes, the AARR reflects the fact that the lower limits to U5MR are approached only with increasing difficulty. As lower levels of under-five mortality are reached, for example, the same absolute reduction obviously represents a greater percentage reduction. The AARR therefore shows a higher rate of progress for a 10-point reduction, for example, if that reduction happens at a lower level of under-five mortality. A fall in the U5MR of 10 points from 100 to 90 represents a reduction of 10 per cent, whereas the same 10-point fall from 20 to 10 represents a reduction of 50 per cent. (A negative value for the percentage reduction indicates an increase in the U5MR over the period specified.)

When used in conjunction with gross domestic product (GDP) growth rates, the U5MR and its rate of reduction can therefore give a picture of the progress being made by any country, territory or region, and over any period of time, towards the satisfaction of some of the most essential of human needs.

As Table 10 shows, there is no fixed relationship between the annual reduction rate of the U5MR and the annual rate of growth in per capita GDP. Such comparisons help to shed light on the relationship between economic advances and human development.

Finally, the table gives the total fertility rate for each country and territory and the corresponding average annual rate of reduction. It is clear that many of the nations that have achieved significant reductions in their U5MR have also achieved significant reductions in fertility.

TABLE 10. THE RATE OF PROGRESS

Countries and territories	Under-5 mortality rank	Under-5 mortality rate			Average annual rate of reduction (%)⊖		Reduction since 1990 (%)⊖	GDP per capita average annual growth rate (%)		Total fertility rate			Average annual rate of reduction (%)	
		1970	1990	2006	1970-1990	1990-2006		1970-1990	1990-2006	1970	1990	2006	1970-1990	1990-2006
Afghanistan	3	320	260	257	1.0	0.1	1	1.6x	-	7.7	8.0	7.2	-0.2	0.6
Albania	122	109	45	17	4.4	6.1	62	-0.7x	5.2	4.9	2.9	2.1	2.6	2.0
Algeria	75	220	69	38	5.8	3.7	45	2	1.3	7.4	4.7	2.4	2.3	4.2
Andorra	189	-	6	3	-	4.3	50	-	-	-	-	-	-	-
Angola	2	300	260	260	0.7	0.0	0	0.4x	2.1	7.3	7.2	6.5	0.1	0.6
Antigua and Barbuda	143	-	-	11	-	-	-	6.5x	1.8	-	-	-	-	-
Argentina	125	71	29	16	4.5	3.7	45	-1	1.3	3.1	3.0	2.3	0.1	1.7
Armenia	101	-	56	24	-	5.3	57	-	5.2	3.2	2.5	1.3	1.2	4.0
Australia	161	20	10	6	3.5	3.2	40	2	2.5	2.7	1.9	1.8	1.9	0.3
Austria	167	33	10	5	6.0	4.3	50	2	1.9	2.3	1.5	1.4	2.3	0.2
Azerbaijan	46	-	105	88	-	1.1	16	-	1.5	4.6	3.0	1.7	2.2	3.4
Bahamas	130	49	29	14	2.6	4.6	52	2	0.4x	3.6	2.6	2.0	1.6	1.5
Bahrain	146	82	19	10	7.3	4.0	47	-1.3x	2.3x	6.5	3.7	2.4	2.8	2.9
Bangladesh	55	239	149	69	2.4	4.8	54	1	3	6.4	4.4	2.9	1.9	2.5
Barbados	138	54	17	12	5.8	2.2	29	2	1.5x	3.1	1.7	1.5	3.1	0.7
Belarus	135	-	24	13	-	3.8	46	-	2.8	2.3	1.9	1.2	1.0	2.8
Belgium	175	29	10	4	5.3	5.7	60	2	1.8	2.2	1.6	1.6	1.7	-0.2
Belize	125	-	43	16	-	6.2	63	3	2.3	6.3	4.5	3.0	1.7	2.4
Benin	20	252	185	148	1.5	1.4	20	0	1.4	7.0	6.8	5.6	0.2	1.2
Bhutan	54	267	166	70	2.4	5.4	58	4.7x	4.8	6.7	5.9	2.3	0.6	5.8
Bolivia	61	243	125	61	3.3	4.5	51	-1	1.3	6.6	4.9	3.6	1.5	1.9
Bosnia and Herzegovina	128	82	22	15	6.6	2.4	32	-	11.6x	2.9	1.7	1.2	2.6	2.1
Botswana	29	142	58	124	4.5	-4.7	-114	8	4.8	6.6	4.7	3.0	1.7	2.9
Brazil	113	136	57	20	4.3	6.5	65	2	1.1	5.0	2.8	2.3	2.9	1.3
Brunei Darussalam	148	78	11	9	9.8	1.3	18	-2.1x	-0.8x	5.7	3.2	2.4	2.8	2.0
Bulgaria	130	32	18	14	2.9	1.6	22	3.4x	2	2.2	1.7	1.3	1.2	1.7
Burkina Faso	10	287	206	204	1.7	0.1	1	1	1.5	7.6	7.3	6.1	0.2	1.1
Burundi	14	244	190	181	1.3	0.3	5	1	-2.6	6.8	6.8	6.8	0.0	0.0
Cambodia	47	-	116	82	-	2.2	29	-	5.8x	5.9	5.8	3.3	0.1	3.6
Cameroon	19	215	139	149	2.2	-0.4	-7	3	0.7	6.2	5.9	4.5	0.2	1.7
Canada	161	23	8	6	5.3	1.8	25	2	2.2	2.2	1.7	1.5	1.5	0.6
Cape Verde	83	-	60	34	-	3.5	43	-	3.3	7.0	5.5	3.5	1.2	2.8
Central African Republic	15	232	173	175	1.5	-0.1	-1	-1	-0.6	5.7	5.7	4.7	0.0	1.2
Chad	7	-	201	209	-	-0.2	-4	-1	2.4	6.5	6.7	6.3	-0.1	0.3
Chile	148	98	21	9	7.7	5.3	57	2	3.7	4.0	2.6	1.9	2.1	1.9
China	101	118	45	24	4.8	3.9	47	7	8.8	5.6	2.2	1.7	4.7	1.6
Colombia	110	105	35	21	5.5	3.2	40	2	0.8	5.6	3.0	2.3	3.1	1.7
Comoros	57	215	120	68	2.9	3.5	43	0.1x	-0.4	7.1	6.1	4.5	0.7	2.0
Congo	27	142	103	126	1.6	-1.3	-22	3	-0.8	6.3	5.4	4.6	0.8	1.0
Congo, Democratic Republic of the	9	245	205	205	0.9	0.0	0	-2	-4.7	6.4	6.7	6.7	-0.3	0.0
Cook Islands	116	-	32	19	-	3.3	41	-	-	-	-	-	-	-
Costa Rica	138	83	18	12	7.6	2.5	33	1	2.4	5.0	3.2	2.1	2.3	2.5
Côte d'Ivoire	26	237	153	127	2.2	1.2	17	-2	-0.5	7.4	6.6	4.6	0.5	2.2
Croatia	161	42	12	6	6.3	4.3	50	-	2.8	2.0	1.7	1.3	0.9	1.4
Cuba	157	43	13	7	6.0	3.9	46	-	3.5x	4.0	1.8	1.5	4.2	0.8
Cyprus	175	33	12	4	5.1	6.9	67	5.9x	2.3x	2.6	2.4	1.6	0.4	2.6
Czech Republic	175	24	13	4	3.1	7.4	69	-	2.1	2.0	1.8	1.2	0.5	2.5
Denmark	167	19	9	5	3.7	3.7	44	2	1.9	2.1	1.7	1.8	1.2	-0.5
Djibouti	25	-	175	130	-	1.9	26	-	-2.4	7.4	6.2	4.1	0.9	2.5
Dominica	128	-	17	15	-	0.8	12	4.7x	1.4	-	-	-	-	-
Dominican Republic	92	127	65	29	3.3	5.0	55	2	3.7	6.2	3.3	2.9	3.1	0.9
Ecuador	101	140	57	24	4.5	5.4	58	1	1	6.3	3.7	2.6	2.7	2.0
Egypt	81	235	91	35	4.7	6.0	62	4	2.4	6.2	4.4	3.0	1.7	2.4
El Salvador	97	162	60	25	5.0	5.5	58	-2	1.6	6.4	3.7	2.7	2.7	1.9
Equatorial Guinea	8	-	170	206	-	-1.2	-21	-	21.6	5.7	5.9	5.4	-0.2	0.5
Eritrea	51	237	147	74	2.4	4.3	50	-	0x	6.6	6.2	5.2	0.3	1.1
Estonia	157	26	16	7	2.4	5.2	56	1.5x	4.9	2.1	1.9	1.5	0.4	1.8
Ethiopia	30	241	204	123	0.8	3.2	40	-	1.9	6.8	6.8	5.4	0.0	1.4
Fiji	119	65	22	18	5.4	1.3	18	0.6x	1.4x	4.5	3.4	2.8	1.5	1.2
Finland	175	16	7	4	4.1	3.5	43	3	2.6	1.9	1.7	1.8	0.3	-0.2
France	175	24	9	4	4.9	5.1	56	2	1.6	2.5	1.8	1.9	1.7	-0.5

	Under-5 mortality rank	Under-5 mortality rate			Average annual rate of reduction (%)[e]		Reduction since 1990 (%)[e]	GDP per capita average annual growth rate (%)		Total fertility rate			Average annual rate of reduction (%)	
		1970	1990	2006	1970-1990	1990-2006		1970-1990	1990-2006	1970	1990	2006	1970-1990	1990-2006
Gabon	44	-	92	91	-	0.1	1	0	-1	4.8	4.8	3.1	0.0	2.6
Gambia	37	311	153	113	3.5	1.9	26	1	0.3	6.7	6.0	4.8	0.5	1.4
Georgia	86	-	46	32	-	2.3	30	3	1	2.6	2.1	1.4	1.0	2.5
Germany	175	26	9	4	5.3	5.1	56	2.2x	1.4	2.0	1.4	1.4	1.9	0.1
Ghana	32	183	120	120	2.1	0.0	0	-2	2.1	6.7	5.8	4.0	0.7	2.3
Greece	175	54	11	4	8.0	6.3	64	1	2.7	2.4	1.4	1.3	2.5	0.5
Grenada	113	-	37	20	-	3.8	46	4.9x	2.3	4.6	3.7	2.3	1.1	3.0
Guatemala	71	168	82	41	3.6	4.3	50	0	1.2	6.2	5.6	4.3	0.6	1.6
Guinea	17	338	235	161	1.8	2.4	31	0.3x	1.3	7.0	6.7	5.6	0.2	1.1
Guinea-Bissau	11	-	240	200	-	1.1	17	0	-2.5	6.8	7.1	7.1	-0.2	0.0
Guyana	60	-	88	62	-	2.2	30	-2	3	5.6	2.6	2.4	3.8	0.6
Haiti	48	222	152	80	1.9	4.0	47	0	-2	5.8	5.4	3.7	0.3	2.5
Holy See	-	-	-	-	-	-	-	-	-	-	-	-	-	-
Honduras	95	170	58	27	5.4	4.8	53	1	0.6	7.3	5.1	3.4	1.7	2.6
Hungary	157	39	17	7	4.2	5.5	59	3	3.2	2.0	1.8	1.3	0.6	2.2
Iceland	189	14	7	3	3.5	5.3	57	3	2.3	3.0	2.2	2.0	1.6	0.4
India	49	192	115	76	2.6	2.6	34	2	4.4	5.4	4.0	2.9	1.5	2.0
Indonesia	83	172	91	34	3.2	6.2	63	5	2.2	5.5	3.1	2.2	2.8	2.1
Iran (Islamic Republic of)	83	191	72	34	4.9	4.7	53	-2	2.5	6.6	5.0	2.0	1.3	5.6
Iraq	68	125	53	46	4.3	0.9	13	-4.3x	-	7.2	5.9	4.4	1.0	1.8
Ireland	167	27	10	5	5.0	4.3	50	3	6	3.9	2.1	2.0	3.1	0.4
Israel	167	27	12	5	4.1	5.5	58	2	1.5x	3.8	3.0	2.8	1.2	0.4
Italy	175	33	9	4	6.5	5.1	56	3	1.3	2.4	1.3	1.4	3.1	-0.2
Jamaica	88	62	33	31	3.2	0.4	6	-1	0.7	5.5	2.9	2.5	3.1	1.0
Japan	175	21	6	4	6.3	2.5	33	3	0.9	2.1	1.6	1.3	1.3	1.4
Jordan	97	107	40	25	4.9	2.9	38	2.5x	1.8	7.9	5.5	3.2	1.8	3.4
Kazakhstan	92	-	60	29	-	4.5	52	-	2.6	3.5	2.8	2.2	1.1	1.5
Kenya	31	156	97	121	2.4	-1.4	-25	1	0	8.1	5.9	5.0	1.6	1.1
Kiribati	59	-	88	64	-	2.0	27	-5	1.9	-	-	-	-	-
Korea, Democratic People's Republic of	65	70	55	55	1.2	0.0	0	-	-	4.0	2.4	1.9	2.6	1.6
Korea, Republic of	167	54	9	5	9.0	3.7	44	6	4.5	4.5	1.6	1.2	5.2	1.9
Kuwait	143	59	16	11	6.5	2.3	31	-6.8x	0.6x	7.2	3.5	2.2	3.6	3.0
Kyrgyzstan	71	-	75	41	-	3.8	45	-	-0.9	4.9	3.9	2.5	1.2	2.8
Lao People's Democratic Republic	50	218	163	75	1.5	4.9	54	-	4.1	6.4	6.2	3.3	0.2	4.0
Latvia	148	26	18	9	1.8	4.3	50	3	4.2	1.9	1.9	1.3	0.0	2.5
Lebanon	89	54	37	30	1.9	1.3	19	-	2.5	5.1	3.1	2.2	2.4	2.2
Lesotho	24	186	101	132	3.1	-1.7	-31	3	2.3	5.8	4.9	3.5	0.8	2.2
Liberia	5	263	235	235	0.6	0.0	0	-4	2.2	6.9	6.9	6.8	0.0	0.1
Libyan Arab Jamahiriya	119	160	41	18	6.8	5.1	56	-4.8x	-	7.6	4.8	2.8	2.3	3.4
Liechtenstein	189	-	10	3	-	7.5	70	-	-	-	-	-	-	-
Lithuania	151	28	13	8	3.8	3.0	38	-	2.5	2.3	2.0	1.3	0.7	2.9
Luxembourg	175	26	10	4	4.8	5.7	60	3	3.3	2.0	1.6	1.7	1.1	-0.4
Madagascar	36	180	168	115	0.3	2.4	32	-2	-0.5	6.8	6.2	4.9	0.4	1.5
Malawi	32	341	221	120	2.2	3.8	46	0	1.1	7.3	7.0	5.7	0.2	1.2
Malaysia	138	70	22	12	5.8	3.8	45	4	3.2	5.6	3.7	2.7	2.0	2.1
Maldives	89	264	111	30	4.3	8.2	73	-	4.2x	7.0	6.2	2.6	0.6	5.4
Mali	6	400	250	217	2.4	0.9	13	-1	2.2	7.5	7.4	6.6	0.0	0.8
Malta	161	32	11	6	5.3	3.8	45	7	2.7x	2.1	2.0	1.4	0.0	2.5
Marshall Islands	64	-	92	56	-	3.1	39	-	-2.2	-	-	-	-	-
Mauritania	28	250	133	125	3.2	0.4	6	-1	0.5	6.6	5.8	4.5	0.6	1.6
Mauritius	130	86	23	14	6.6	3.1	39	5.1x	3.7	3.7	2.2	1.9	2.5	1.1
Mexico	81	110	53	35	3.7	2.6	34	2	1.5	6.7	3.4	2.3	3.4	2.5
Micronesia (Federated States of)	71	-	58	41	-	2.2	29	-	-0.2	6.9	5.0	3.9	1.7	1.5
Moldova, Republic of	116	65	37	19	2.8	4.2	49	1.8x	-2	2.6	2.4	1.4	0.3	3.3
Monaco	175	-	9	4	-	5.1	56	-	-	-	-	-	-	-
Mongolia	69	-	109	43	-	5.8	61	-	3.3x	7.5	4.1	1.9	3.0	4.8
Montenegro	146	-	16	10	-	2.9	38	-	2.6x	2.4	2.0	1.8	0.9	0.6
Morocco	78	184	89	37	3.6	5.5	58	2	1.6	7.1	4.0	2.4	2.8	3.3
Mozambique	22	278	235	138	0.8	3.3	41	-1x	4.4	6.6	6.2	5.2	0.3	1.1

TABLE 10. THE RATE OF PROGRESS

	Under-5 mortality rank	Under-5 mortality rate			Average annual rate of reduction (%)⊖		Reduction since 1990 (%)⊖	GDP per capita average annual growth rate (%)		Total fertility rate			Average annual rate of reduction (%)	
		1970	1990	2006	1970-1990	1990-2006		1970-1990	1990-2006	1970	1990	2006	1970-1990	1990-2006
Myanmar	40	179	130	104	1.6	1.4	20	2	6.6x	6.1	3.4	2.1	2.8	3.1
Namibia	61	135	86	61	2.3	2.1	29	-2.3x	1.5	6.5	5.8	3.3	0.5	3.6
Nauru	89	-	-	30	-	-	-	-	-	-	-	-	-	-
Nepal	63	238	142	59	2.6	5.5	58	1	1.9	5.9	5.2	3.4	0.6	2.7
Netherlands	167	15	9	5	2.6	3.7	44	2	1.8	2.4	1.6	1.7	2.2	-0.6
New Zealand	161	20	11	6	3.0	3.8	45	1	2.1	3.1	2.1	2.0	2.0	0.3
Nicaragua	79	165	68	36	4.4	4.0	47	-4	1.9	6.9	4.8	2.8	1.9	3.3
Niger	4	330	320	253	0.2	1.5	21	-2	-0.5	8.1	7.9	7.3	0.1	0.5
Nigeria	12	265	230	191	0.7	1.2	17	-1	0.7	6.9	6.8	5.5	0.1	1.3
Niue	-	-	-	-	-	-	-	-	-	-	-	-	-	-
Norway	175	15	9	4	2.6	5.1	56	3	2.6	2.5	1.9	1.8	1.5	0.1
Occupied Palestinian Territory	108	-	40	22	-	3.7	45	-	-2.8x	7.9	6.4	5.3	1.0	1.3
Oman	138	200	32	12	9.2	6.1	63	3	1.8x	7.2	6.6	3.1	0.4	4.7
Pakistan	42	181	130	97	1.7	1.8	25	3	1.4	6.6	6.3	3.6	0.2	3.5
Palau	143	-	21	11	-	4.0	48	-	-	-	-	-	-	-
Panama	106	68	34	23	3.5	2.4	32	0	2.3	5.3	3.0	2.6	2.8	0.9
Papua New Guinea	52	158	94	73	2.6	1.6	22	-1	0.2	6.2	4.8	4.0	1.2	1.2
Paraguay	108	78	41	22	3.2	3.9	46	3	-0.5	5.7	4.5	3.2	1.2	2.2
Peru	97	174	78	25	4.0	7.1	68	-1	2.3	6.3	3.9	2.5	2.4	2.7
Philippines	86	90	62	32	1.9	4.1	48	1	1.7	6.3	4.3	3.3	1.8	1.7
Poland	157	36	18	7	3.5	5.9	61	-	4.3	2.2	2.0	1.2	0.4	3.2
Portugal	167	62	14	5	7.4	6.4	64	3	1.9	2.8	1.5	1.5	3.0	0.3
Qatar	110	65	26	21	4.6	1.3	19	-	-	6.9	4.4	2.7	2.3	3.0
Romania	119	57	31	18	3.0	3.4	42	0.9x	2	2.9	1.9	1.3	2.0	2.4
Russian Federation	125	40	27	16	2.0	3.3	41	-	0.6	2.0	1.9	1.3	0.3	2.1
Rwanda	18	209	176	160	0.9	0.6	9	1	0.3	8.2	7.6	6.0	0.4	1.5
Saint Kitts and Nevis	116	-	36	19	-	4.0	47	6.3x	2.8	-	-	-	-	-
Saint Lucia	130	-	21	14	-	2.5	33	5.3x	1.1	6.1	3.3	2.2	3.0	2.6
Saint Vincent and the Grenadines	113	-	25	20	-	1.4	20	3	1.7	6.0	3.0	2.2	3.5	1.9
Samoa	94	101	50	28	3.5	3.6	44	-0.1x	2.5	6.1	4.8	4.1	1.2	1.0
San Marino	189	-	14	3	-	9.6	79	-	-	-	-	-	-	-
Sao Tome and Principe	43	106	100	96	0.3	0.3	4	-	0.5x	6.5	5.4	4.0	0.9	1.9
Saudi Arabia	97	185	44	25	7.2	3.5	43	-2	0.1x	7.3	5.8	3.5	1.1	3.3
Senegal	35	276	149	116	3.1	1.6	22	0	1.2	7.0	6.6	4.9	0.3	1.9
Serbia	151	-	-	8	-	-	-	-	-	2.4	2.1	1.8	0.6	1.1
Seychelles	135	59	19	13	5.7	2.4	32	3	1.4	-	-	-	-	-
Sierra Leone	1	368	290	270	1.2	0.4	7	0	-0.8	6.5	6.5	6.5	0.0	0.0
Singapore	189	27	9	3	5.5	6.9	67	6	3.7	3.0	1.8	1.3	2.7	2.0
Slovakia	151	29	14	8	3.6	3.5	43	-	2.9	2.5	2.0	1.2	1.0	3.2
Slovenia	175	29	10	4	5.3	5.7	60	-	3.3	2.3	1.5	1.3	2.0	1.1
Solomon Islands	52	-	121	73	-	3.2	40	3	-2.3	6.9	5.9	4.0	0.8	2.4
Somalia	21	-	203	145	-	2.1	29	-1	-	7.3	6.8	6.2	0.3	0.6
South Africa	55	-	60	69	-	-0.9	-15	0	0.8	5.6	3.6	2.7	2.2	1.8
Spain	175	34	9	4	6.6	5.1	56	2	2.5	2.9	1.3	1.4	3.9	-0.1
Sri Lanka	135	100	32	13	5.7	5.6	59	3	3.8	4.4	2.5	1.9	2.7	1.8
Sudan	45	172	120	89	1.8	1.9	26	0	3.7	6.6	6.0	4.4	0.5	1.9
Suriname	74	-	48	39	-	1.3	19	-2.2x	1.4	5.7	2.7	2.5	3.6	0.6
Swaziland	16	196	110	164	2.9	-2.5	-49	2	0.4	6.9	5.7	3.6	0.9	3.0
Sweden	189	15	7	3	3.8	5.3	57	2	2.2	2.0	2.0	1.8	0.1	0.8
Switzerland	167	18	9	5	3.5	3.7	44	1	0.7	2.0	1.5	1.4	1.4	0.5
Syrian Arab Republic	130	128	38	14	6.1	6.2	63	2	1.4	7.6	5.5	3.2	1.6	3.5
Tajikistan	57	140	115	68	1.0	3.3	41	-	-3.1	6.9	5.2	3.5	1.4	2.5
Tanzania, United Republic of	34	218	161	118	1.5	1.9	27	-	1.6	6.8	6.1	5.3	0.5	0.9
Thailand	151	102	31	8	6.0	8.5	74	5	2.8	5.5	2.1	1.8	4.8	0.8
The former Yugoslav Republic of Macedonia	122	119	38	17	5.7	5.0	55	-	0.2	3.2	1.9	1.5	2.4	1.8
Timor-Leste	65	-	177	55	-	7.3	69	-	-	6.3	5.3	6.7	0.8	-1.4
Togo	38	219	149	108	1.9	2.0	28	-1	-0.1	7.0	6.4	5.0	0.5	1.6
Tonga	101	50	32	24	2.2	1.8	25	-	1.9	5.9	4.6	3.8	1.3	1.2
Trinidad and Tobago	75	54	34	38	2.3	-0.7	-12	1	4.7	3.5	2.4	1.6	1.8	2.6

	Under-5 mortality rank	Under-5 mortality rate			Average annual rate of reduction (%)[e]		Reduction since 1990 (%)[e]	GDP per capita average annual growth rate (%)		Total fertility rate			Average annual rate of reduction (%)	
		1970	1990	2006	1970-1990	1990-2006		1970-1990	1990-2006	1970	1990	2006	1970-1990	1990-2006
Tunisia	106	201	52	23	6.8	5.1	56	3	3.3	6.6	3.6	1.9	3.0	3.9
Turkey	96	201	82	26	4.5	7.2	68	2	1.9	5.5	3.0	2.2	3.0	2.2
Turkmenistan	67	-	99	51	-	4.1	48	-	-6.8x	6.3	4.3	2.6	1.9	3.3
Tuvalu	75	-	54	38	-	2.2	30	-	-	-	-	-	-	-
Uganda	23	170	160	134	0.3	1.1	16	-	3.1	7.1	7.1	6.6	0.0	0.5
Ukraine	101	36	25	24	1.8	0.3	4	-	-1.5	2.1	1.9	1.2	0.6	2.8
United Arab Emirates	151	84	15	8	8.6	3.9	47	-4.8x	-0.9x	6.6	4.4	2.3	2.1	3.9
United Kingdom	161	23	10	6	4.2	3.2	40	2	2.5	2.3	1.8	1.8	1.2	0.1
United States	151	26	12	8	3.9	2.5	33	2	2.1	2.2	2.0	2.1	0.6	-0.2
Uruguay	138	56	23	12	4.4	4.1	48	1	1.2	2.9	2.5	2.1	0.7	1.0
Uzbekistan	69	-	74	43	-	3.4	42	-	0.7	6.5	4.2	2.6	2.2	3.1
Vanuatu	79	155	62	36	4.6	3.4	42	-0.5x	-0.3	6.3	4.9	3.9	1.2	1.5
Venezuela (Bolivarian Republic of)	110	62	33	21	3.2	2.8	36	-2	-0.6	5.4	3.4	2.6	2.2	1.8
Viet Nam	122	87	53	17	2.5	7.1	68	-	6	7.0	3.7	2.2	3.2	3.2
Yemen	41	303	139	100	3.9	2.1	28	-	1.5	8.6	8.1	5.6	0.3	2.3
Zambia	13	181	180	182	0.0	-0.1	-1	-2	0	7.4	6.5	5.3	0.7	1.2
Zimbabwe	39	135	76	105	2.9	-2.0	-38	0	-2.4	7.4	5.2	3.3	1.8	2.9

SUMMARY INDICATORS

		1970	1990	2006	1970-1990	1990-2006		1970-1990	1990-2006	1970	1990	2006	1970-1990	1990-2006
Sub-Saharan Africa		243	187	160	1.3	1.0	14	-	1.1	6.8	6.3	5.3	0.4	1.1
Eastern and Southern Africa		220	165	131	1.4	1.4	21	-	1.2	6.8	6.0	5.0	0.6	1.1
West and Central Africa		264	208	186	1.2	0.7	11	-	1	6.8	6.6	5.6	0.1	1.1
Middle East and North Africa		195	79	46	4.5	3.4	42	0	2.2	6.8	5.0	3.1	1.5	3.1
South Asia		199	123	83	2.4	2.5	33	2	3.9	5.7	4.3	3.0	1.4	2.2
East Asia and Pacific		121	55	29	3.9	4.0	47	6	6.7	5.6	2.5	1.9	4.1	1.7
Latin America and Caribbean		123	55	27	4.0	4.4	51	1	1.4	5.3	3.2	2.4	2.5	1.8
CEE/CIS		91	53	27	2.7	4.2	49	-	1.1	2.8	2.3	1.7	0.9	2.1
Industrialized countries[§]		27	10	6	5.0	3.2	40	2	1.9	2.3	1.7	1.7	1.3	0.2
Developing countries[§]		164	103	79	2.3	1.7	23	3	4.1	5.8	3.6	2.8	2.3	1.6
Least developed countries[§]		244	180	142	1.5	1.5	21	-	2.3	6.7	5.8	4.7	0.7	1.3
World		145	93	72	2.2	1.6	23	2	2.3	4.7	3.2	2.6	1.9	1.4

§ Also includes territories within each country category or regional group. Countries and territories in each country category or regional group are listed on page 148.

DEFINITIONS OF THE INDICATORS

Under-five mortality rate – Probability of dying between birth and exactly five years of age, expressed per 1,000 live births.

Reduction since 1990 (%) – Percentage reduction in the under-five mortality rate (U5MR) from 1990 to 2006. The United Nations Millennium Declaration in 2000 established a goal of a two-thirds (67 per cent) reduction in U5MR from 1990 to 2015. This indicator provides a current assessment of progress towards this goal.

GDP per capita – Gross domestic product (GDP) is the sum of value added by all resident producers plus any product taxes (less subsidies) not included in the valuation of output. GDP per capita is gross domestic product divided by midyear population. Growth is calculated from constant price GDP data in local currency.

Total fertility rate – Number of children who would be born per woman if she lived to the end of her childbearing years and bore children at each age in accordance with prevailing age-specific fertility rates.

MAIN DATA SOURCES

Under-five mortality rate – UNICEF, United Nations Population Division and United Nations Statistics Division.

GDP per capita – World Bank.

Fertility – United Nations Population Division.

NOTES
- Data not available.
- x Data refer to years or periods other than those specified in the column heading, differ from the standard definition or refer to only part of a country. Such data are not included in the calculation of regional and global averages.
- e A negative value indicates an increase in the under-five mortality rate since 1990.

Acronyms

ACSD	Accelerated Child Survival and Development	**IMNCI**	Integrated Management of Neonatal and Childhood Illnesses
ACT	artemisinin-based combination therapy	**ITN**	insecticide-treated mosquito net
AIDS	acquired immune deficiency syndrome	**MDG**	Millennium Development Goal
AIS	AIDS Indicator Surveys	**MTEF**	medium–term expenditure framework
AARR	average annual rate of reduction	**ODA**	official development assistance
BCG	anti-tuberculosis vaccine (bacille Calmette-Guérin)	**OECD**	Organisation for Economic Co-operation and Development
BSS	Behavioural Surveillance Surveys	**PAB**	protection at birth
C-IMCI	Community Integrated Management of Childhood Illness	**PMTCT**	prevention of mother-to-child transmission (of HIV)
DAC	Development Assistance Committee (OECD)	**PMNCH**	Partnership for Maternal, Newborn & Child Health
DALY	disability-adjusted life year	**PRSP**	Poverty Reduction Strategy Paper
DOTS	Directly Observed Treatment, Short-Course	**SSHE**	school sanitation and hygiene education
FFF	food supplementation, family spacing, female education	**SWAp**	sector-wide approach
		SWS	safe water system
FGM/C	female genital mutilation/cutting	**TB**	tuberculosis
GDP	gross domestic product	**TT**	tetanus toxoid vaccine
GFATM	Global Fund to Fight AIDS, Tuberculosis and Malaria	**U5MR**	under-five mortality rate
		UIS	UNESCO Institute for Statistics
GNI	gross national income	**UNAIDS**	Joint United Nations Programme on HIV/AIDS
GNP	gross national product		
GOBI	growth monitoring, oral rehydration, breastfeeding, immunization	**UNESCO**	United Nations Educational, Scientific and Cultural Organization
HepB	hepatitis B vaccine	**UNFPA**	United Nations Population Fund
Hib	Haemophilus influenzae type b	**UNICEF**	United Nations Children's Fund
HIV	human immunodeficiency virus	**USAID**	United States Agency for International Development
HMN	Health Metrics Network		
IMCI	Integrated Management of Childhood Illness	**WHO**	World Health Organization